# DK COMPLETE
# SAILING
# MANUAL

# DK COMPLETE SAILING MANUAL

## STEVE SLEIGHT

EDITORIAL CONSULTANT TRUMAN MORRIS

DK Publishing, Inc.

www.dk.com

## A DK PUBLISHING BOOK

### WWW.DK.COM

**Senior Editor** Mary Lindsay
**Senior Art Editor** Sarah Hall
**US Editor** Alrica Goldstein
**DTP Designer** Robert Campbell
**Production Controllers** Michelle Thomas,
Silvia La Greca Bertacchi
**Picture Research** Anna Grapes

**Managing Editor** Stephanie Jackson, Jonathan Metcalf
**Managing Art Editor** Nigel Duffield

Produced for Dorling Kindersley by

13 SOUTHGATE STREET WINCHESTER HAMPSHIRE SO23 9DZ

**Project Editor** Jo Weeks
**Project Art Editor** Sharon Moore
**Editor** Nicola Hodgson
**Designer** Helen Bracey

First American Edition, 1999
DK Publishing, Inc.
95 Madison Avenue, New York, New York 10016

DK Publishing offers special discounts for bulk purchases for sales promotions
or premiums. Specific, large-quantity needs can be met with special editions,
including personalized covers, excerpts of existing guides, and corporate imprints.
For more information, contact Special Markets Dept./DK Publishing, Inc./
95 Madison Ave./New York, NY 10016/Fax: 800-600-9098.

Library of Congress Cataloging-in-Publication Data
Sleight, Steve.
DK complete sailing manual / Steve Sleight. -- 1st American ed.
p. cm. Includes index.
ISBN 0-7894-4606-5 (alk. paper)
1. Sailing Handbooks, manuals, etc. I. DK Publishing, Inc. II. Title. III. Title:
Complete sailing manual. IV. Title: Dorling Kindersley complete sailing manual.
GV811.S546 1999
797.1'24--dc21                99-28974 CIP

Reproduced in Singapore by Colourscan
Printed and bound in Italy by Lego

---

## KEY

The following symbols appear throughout the book.

| **WIND DIRECTION** | **TIDE DIRECTION** | **BOAT DIRECTION** |

# CONTENTS

# FOREWORD

Although I won the Olympic Gold Medal for sailing in 1984, I wasn't always an expert. Like anyone else, I started out as a beginner – and a dreamer. Even before my first sail, I had an old lifeboat rigged with sails in the backyard. I played on it for hours, racing or taking voyages to the corners of the globe. My imagination was primarily fueled by books. The text and photos of the many sailing books around our house provided the images that stimulated my young brain to action.

I started sailing on my parents' Alberg 35 at age ten, and have been sailing continuously for the last 30 years. By age 13 I was sailing on my own, taking the bus or riding my bike to the marina. I had quite a comprehensive knowledge of sailing, despite my very limited experience! I think this allowed me to dive right into the sport without fear, but with enough sense to stay out of real trouble.

As I move along in my sailing experience, I continue to read voraciously about all aspects of the sport; from technical racing pieces to chronicles of long-distance cruising. These writings have continued to stimulate my thought processes, providing ideas for new projects and insights into sailing better and faster. Through them, I can think about sailing without actually being on the water, which helps me both technically and emotionally. I learn new things, and also escape to the watery world where I am the most comfortable.

I'm a sailing dabbler, which is why I enjoy this book. Although I have a reputation as a short-course dinghy specialist, I love cruising and ocean racing just as much. If you're like me, you'll appreciate this comprehensive book for its great introduction to all aspects of sailing, which enables you to decide for yourself what area of sailing to pursue first. Extensive illustrations provide the images to help you visualize sailing – and actively ignite your imagination.

Knowledge is freedom. Take the ideas presented here and go forth with respect for the sea, but without fear. Do some dreaming and then play around on some boats. Let sailing take you to new places; you may be surprised where you end up!

Bon Voyage,

JONATHAN MCKEE

# JOY OF SAILING

"THERE IS NOTHING – absolutely nothing –
half so much worth doing as simply messing
about in boats." With those words in
*The Wind in the Willows*, Kenneth Grahame
summed up the lure of sailing. This book is
a practical guide to a wonderful sport, and I
hope it also reflects the joy of being on the
water. It is dedicated to Tanya, my daughter.

*Dolphins leaping in a sunlit bow wave capture the
perfect joy of sailing. For many, sailing is more
than a sport or recreation – it is a way of life.*

# INTRODUCTION

For those who catch the sailing bug, there is rarely any cure. Sailing is far more than a very competitive sport; it is enjoyed by millions who sail for relaxation and – for the truly hooked – it quickly becomes a way of life. It was not always that way, of course. The idea of sailing for sport or recreation would have seemed preposterous to the seafarers who manned the sailing ships that explored and charted the planet, and who helped to develop nations through world trade and conquest. For them, sailing was a fact of life – and a hard life at best – but it was the only way to cross the oceans that cover two-thirds of the earth's surface.

△ ROYAL YACHT
*The Royal Yacht* Mary *firing a gun salute. The* Mary *was presented to King Charles II in 1660 and introduced the concept of yachting as sport in England.*

## FROM TRADE TO RECREATION

Trade, exploration, and conquest were the driving forces that made the world's great seafaring nations prosperous and powerful, and which helped to develop their empires. Key to their expansion was the domination of the sea and the ability of their naval designers, builders, and sailors to produce and handle the huge variety of sailing ships on which their power depended.

### SAILING AND TRADE
For thousands of years, the world depended exclusively on sail power for long-distance travel across water. Whether on great rivers, such as the Nile or the Amazon, or on seas and oceans, such as the Mediterranean, Atlantic, or Pacific, sail power was the only alternative to muscle power applied to oars and paddles. In every part of the world, local populations devised their own solutions to the challenge of harnessing the wind and building boats capable of carrying

people and cargo long distances. These local solutions created unique craft, some of which still survive. Viking longboats traveled thousands of miles under oars and their simple square sails. The square-sail rig became common in most European countries, although it was really only suitable for sailing on downwind courses.

Arabian dhows developed their characteristic huge lateen (triangular) sails as an efficient sailing solution. A dhow could sail upwind well and was fast compared to square-rigged ships. Its disadvantage – the large crew that was needed to handle it – was not a problem in an area where cheap and compliant labor was plentiful.

The Chinese solution to sail power was the Chinese lugsail, commonly referred to as a junk rig, with its short mast and woven sails supported by long bamboo battens. They were quite efficient, simple to handle, easy to repair, and required a small crew.

CLIPPER SHIPS ▷
*The* Cutty Sark *was perhaps the most famous clipper ship of all. The clippers raced across oceans to be the first to Western markets.*

△ THE *AMERICA*

*The schooner* America *visited England in 1851 and raced the leading British yachts on a course from Cowes around the Isle of Wight.* America *won the prize of the Hundred Guinea Cup, which was renamed the America's Cup and is now the oldest trophy in international sport.*

In the Pacific Ocean, the Polynesian islanders developed the proa – their unique multihulled craft – using hollowed-out tree trunks for the main canoe, with a stabilizing outrigger to help keep it upright. Paddles and a lateen-type sail were used for power. These fragile craft made many long ocean passages, with the navigator using only the natural signs from the sky, wind, and sea as his guides to making a distant landfall.

Wood was the natural choice of building material for ships of all types and sizes, but, if wood was lacking, human ingenuity still allowed boats to be built – often using woven reeds. It was not until the development of iron and steel, which allowed builders to produce cheaper and stronger hulls, that wood began to be replaced as the main boat-building material.

Designs for warships, merchant ships, and fishing vessels all evolved to suit their function, resulting in many types of boats, each with special strengths and advantages. The famous Thames barges, for instance, evolved as the best design solution for carrying cargo in the shallow waters of the Thames Estuary and on the East Coast. They were sailed by a crew of two, usually a man and a boy.

Hundreds, if not thousands, of boat designs evolved, each with its own specific advantages to suit local needs. Perhaps the design pinnacle of cargo-carrying sailing ships was the magnificent clipper ships of the 19th century, so-called because they clipped short the time required for a given passage. Designed and built for speed, they raced across oceans to be first to market and capture the best prices for their precious cargoes of wool and tea.

## EARLY DAYS OF YACHTING

The terms "yacht" and "yachting" are derived from the Dutch word *jaghen*, which means to pursue or chase. By the end of the 16th century, the word *jaght* was in use to denote any light and swift ship used for trade, war, or enjoyment.

It is appropriate that the idea of sailing for pleasure originated in the Netherlands, because the country was the world's leading maritime power in the 16th and 17th centuries. Its large maritime fleet supported the most prosperous economy in Europe, and its trade links extended to Africa, India, and the Far East.

The earliest yachts were used occasionally for pleasure, but mostly they served for transportation and communication, being very practical in the Netherlands' sheltered waters.

While in exile in the Netherlands, the English king, Charles II, learned of the Dutch habit for using small yachts for transport. On his return to England in 1660, Charles received the gift of a 52ft (15.8m) Dutch yacht called the *Mary*, which naturally stimulated English shipbuilders to attempt to improve on the design.

## THE FIRST RACES

By 1661, two yachts had been built by the Pett brothers: the *Catherine* for King Charles, and the *Anne* for the King's brother, the Duke of York. These yachts staged the first recorded race between two pleasure vessels when the King beat his brother on a course from Greenwich to Gravesend and back along the Thames.

The world's first yacht club, The Water Club of Cork, was formed in Ireland around 1720. Records for the club disappear in the late 18th century, but it was reestablished as The Cork Yacht Club in 1828, and it became The Royal Cork Yacht Club in 1830.

In 1815, a group of English gentlemen formed The Yacht Club, which became The Royal Yacht Club in 1820 when the Prince Regent, who was already a member, became King George IV. The club acquired its clubhouse in Cowes in 1824 and, in 1833, it changed its name by royal request to the Royal Yacht Squadron. Its first official race took place on August 10 1826, with fireworks on Cowes Parade on the following night. Apart from during the two World Wars, an annual Cowes Week regatta with fireworks has taken place in early August ever since.

By 1830, there were three royal clubs: The Royal Yacht Squadron, The Royal Cork Yacht Club, and The Royal Thames Yacht Club. The seeds of organized yachting were sown and were to flourish quickly at home and abroad. The first yacht club outside the British Empire was founded in Sweden in 1830. In 1844, the New York Yacht Club became the first club of its kind when it was inaugurated by nine yachtsmen who met aboard James Cox Stevens' schooner *Gimcrack*.

▽ J-CLASS YACHTS
*Two British J-class yachts,* Velsheda *and* Endeavour. *J-class yachts raced for the America's Cup in the 1930s, when they were the pinnacle of yacht design.*

# MODERN SAILING

The early part of the 20th century was perhaps a golden era for gentlemen's yachting. The huge J-class yachts, however, represented the final chapter in a style of racing that had become prohibitively expensive, and sailing as we know it today originated shortly after the Second World War.

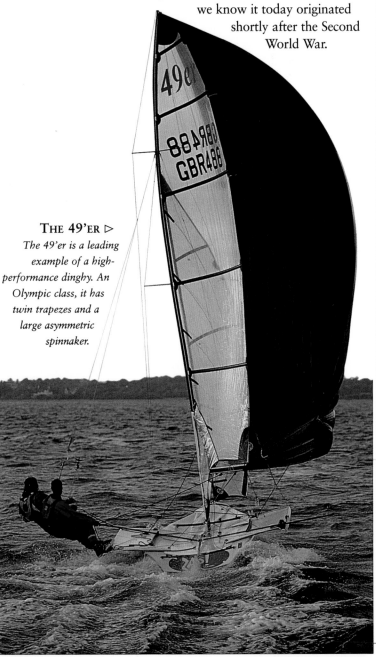

THE 49'ER ▷
*The 49'er is a leading example of a high-performance dinghy. An Olympic class, it has twin trapezes and a large asymmetric spinnaker.*

## SAILING DINGHIES

The development of plywood was quickly seized upon by boat designers as an ideal building material for the production of strong, lightweight sailing dinghies, many of which were suitable for home construction. Increasing leisure time and disposable income provided the desire and the means for many people to indulge in sport and recreation, and a new type of sailing developed that was more accessible than ever before.

Dinghy sailing developed rapidly during and after the 1960s as dozens of new, cheap and exciting dinghy designs appeared on the market. Home boat-building became popular because of the new, easy-to-use materials, and many hundreds of small boat-building companies were formed to meet the demands of the developing sport.

Millions of people worldwide discovered the pleasures to be had from sailing dinghies, and, while many preferred to cruise in local waters – or even to travel further in larger sailing dinghies – even more chose to race. Dinghy racing provided a relatively cheap and accessible entry to competitive sailing, with events available for all levels of ability. From standard club racing, through class open meetings, to National, World, and Olympic championships, dinghy racing could be enjoyed at any level to suit the experience and aspirations of the competitors.

Fiberglass appeared as a convenient and flexible boat-building material in the late 1960s, and, more recently, other high-performance materials

have led to the development of lighter boats and more powerful rigs. These scientific developments have created another revolution in performance by facilitating the design of enormously fast boats, such as the 49'er, that are exciting and challenging to sail.

## CRUISING

While racing offers many attractions and rewards for the competitively inclined, the joy of sailing is no better illustrated than in the pleasures to be had from cruising under sail.

To be at sea aboard a cruising boat, out of sight of land, and solely responsible for your own destiny is regarded by devotees as the epitome of pleasure, while the joy of a safe landfall on a new coastline is the ultimate in satisfaction.

Offshore cruising aboard small sailing boats dates back to the mid-19th century, a time when the large racing yachts of the day were sailed almost exclusively by professional crews. To them, the idea of cruising offshore in a small yacht bordered on madness, yet a few individuals, most notably British sailor Richard Tyrrell McMullen, pioneered yacht cruising and inspired thousands of others through their example. McMullen sailed thousands of miles around the British Isles from 1850. He died at the helm of his yacht in the English Channel in 1891.

Other pioneers include London barrister John Macgregor, who cruised in a small sailing canoe and, of course, American Joshua Slocum, who, in 1898, aboard the 36ft (10.1m) *Spray*, became the first person to complete a single-handed circumnavigation of the globe.

Many influential cruising sailors followed over the next few decades, but few popularized ocean cruising more than the English couple, Eric and Susan Hiscock, who completed three circumnavigations between 1952 and 1976 in a series of yachts, all named *Wanderer*. Today, more and more people are discovering the joys of cruising, whether on coastal or offshore passages, or ocean voyages.

## CRUISER RACING

The heyday of cruiser racing was the 1970s, when yacht racing became extremely popular. Since then, problems with handicapping rules, escalating costs, and increasing professionalism have reduced the numbers participating, although the standard of racing has risen considerably among the grand-prix fleets. At club level, cruiser racing is still accessible and great fun, and the latest types of day-racing sportsboats have brought increasing numbers back to keel-boat racing.

△ **CRUISING PLEASURES**
*Cruising yachts give their crews the unique ability to explore the loneliest parts of the planet. Here, the specially built* Pelagic *explores Antarctica.*

# SAILING FOR EVERYONE

The popular perception of yachting is that it is a sport that is exclusive, very expensive, and accessible only to the rich or well connected. Alternatively, it is assumed that it takes place aboard super yachts with professional crews doing the work while the owner and his guests sip cocktails in the sunshine on the after deck.

The reality (for most of us) is that sailing sometimes involves getting wet and cold, occasionally scares the hell out of you, and usually costs more than we will admit to our nearest and dearest. Why do we do it? Because more than most other activities, it offers a reward that, if it could be bottled, would be worth a fortune. Satisfaction at learning new skills (and you never stop learning aboard boats), and being responsible for ourselves in a potentially hostile environment are just part of the reward.

The sea attracts many of us to its ever-changing face, its echo of a less-developed past, and its direct connection to our planet's pulse. For those of us lucky or determined enough to sail, we can experience these things first-hand, in a way that a landsman will never know or even begin to understand.

It does not matter how or what you sail. If you are at home on the sea, and in tune with it, you will be happy in any boat – although you will no doubt soon begin to dream about acquiring your ideal boat.

The best thing about sailing is that it offers you these rewards whatever your age, gender, status, color, religion, or physical ability. There are no restrictions to experiencing the joys of sailing for yourself. Of course, at some levels the sport can be exclusive, expensive, and even cliquey, but you can avoid all these things by choosing carefully the type of sailing you do, the people you sail with, and the clubs you join. The sea is a great leveler. It is no respecter of status, and teaches humility, caution, and self-reliance.

## YOUNG AND OLD

There is no doubt that it is best to start sailing young – not because it is difficult to learn to sail at a later stage, but because you waste less time missing out on the joys of sailing.

Children learn to sail easily, as long as they choose to do it and are not pushed into it by their parents. If your children show an interest in sailing, encourage their desire as much as possible, because nothing develops confidence, independence, and self-reliance as effectively as sailing. Sailing has the advantage of being an extremely healthy sport,

▽ ALL AGES
*Age is no barrier to sailing – if you have the desire to sail, and the right boat, the joy of sailing is available to everyone.*

developing physical fitness, and it is sufficiently complex to introduce applied science as the novice learns something of the theory of sailing and finds out how it works in practice.

It is no surprise that sailing is often used in adventure-training schemes to help underprivileged or antisocial young people learn about themselves and appropriate ways to relate to others. Sailing aboard larger boats as part of a crew builds teamwork skills and teaches the importance of being able to rely on others and contribute to a team.

Children as young as five can learn to sail in an appropriate small boat, but if you did not have the opportunity to start young, do not despair. Sailing is almost unique among sports in that it can be enjoyed, even in competitive racing, at virtually any age. Even if you are aged 80 years or more, you can still sail – all that is needed is the desire. There really are no obstructions if you want to sail.

## SAILING FOR THE DISABLED

The proof that there are no obstacles to sailing is amply demonstrated by the increasing opportunities available to disabled people who wish to sail. Many marinas and sailing clubs now provide appropriate facilities for the disabled, including wheelchair access to docks.

Unlike many other sports, sailing offers opportunities for people with all types of disabilities. Individuals with physical, visual, hearing, or learning impairments can all participate in sailing aboard a wide variety of boats, including tall ships, multihulls, sailing dinghies, and keelboats, many of which have been specially adapted.

Q801

Abacus

Organizations exist in many parts of the world, providing opportunities for beginners as well as promoting international events such as the Paralympics and the Blind Sailing World Championships, which provide competitive sailing to the highest level. Disabled crews have competed very successfully against professional racing crews in prestigious events, such as the Whitbread Round the World Race, or the BT Challenge, and many disabled sailors race smaller boats or cruise offshore – in fact, they can enjoy the whole range of sailing experiences.

Nothing better demonstrates that sailing is accessible, and offers the same level of challenges, rewards, and satisfaction to all, than the incredible achievement of blind yachtsman Geoffrey Hilton-Barber who, in 1998, became the first blind sailor to sail across an ocean single-handedly – sailing the Indian Ocean from Durban, South Africa, to Fremantle, Western Australia. His achievement is a lesson to all of us who dream of the joys of sailing – don't wait, just do it.

△ **BLIND PASSION**
*Geoffrey Hilton-Barber achieved the seemingly impossible when, in 1998, he became the first blind yachtsman to sail single-handedly across an ocean.*

# FIRST ESSENTIALS

·····································

THERE ARE A NUMBER of basic principles and

terms that are common to all types of sailing –

from the smallest sailing dinghies to ocean-

going yachts. If you are new to the sport, it

will help if you acquaint yourself with these

essentials so that you have a thorough

understanding of the fundamentals of good

sailing before you head out for the first time.

·····································

*Sailing is a great sport for all the family.
Here, a cruiser moored to a buoy acts as
a base for children in their dinghies.*

# SAFETY AFLOAT

*Water is a potentially hostile environment, so safety is an important consideration whenever you sail. Sailing is not a particularly dangerous sport as long as a few sensible guidelines are followed, including wearing suitable clothing and using appropriate buoyancy gear. You should aim to develop a healthy respect for the water and only sail within the limits of your experience. This will minimize any risks and help to ensure that your sailing is not marred by accidents.*

## CHOOSING CLOTHING

There is a huge variety of modern clothing and safety gear now available to cater to all types of sailing, from windsurfing to offshore cruising. Do not be tempted to rush out and buy a whole new wardrobe of expensive gear as soon as you decide to try sailing. Get some experience in a boat first. This will help you to decide what sort of sailing attracts you most and, from this, you can choose the sort of gear that will be most appropriate for your needs. What you wear when sailing will also depend on the weather and the air and water temperatures. Some boats are wetter than others but, whatever boat you are sailing, there is always a chance that you will get wet, if only from spray, so choose your clothing accordingly.

## STAYING WARM

The key to comfort on the water is to stay warm. As a general rule, it is wise to wear one more layer than you think you will need. Do not go sailing in only a swimsuit. It is never as hot on the water as you think unless there is no wind and baking sunshine, in which case you risk severe sunburn.

For your first few sailing trips you can make do with comfortable pants and jumpers; avoid jeans and cotton tops as these become cold when wet. Wool is the best natural material, but most effective of all is clothing made from synthetic pile, which is very light and warm. This fabric wicks water away from the skin and dries extremely quickly.

Heat loss is one of the biggest dangers that you face when sailing. Prolonged exposure to cold will quickly lead to exhaustion, and the speed with which this occurs always surprises the inexperienced. If immersed in water at 62°F (17°C), even a fit person, clothed normally and not exerting himself, will lose consciousness in two to three hours. If the water is colder or rough, survival time will be considerably reduced. Even aboard the boat, energy levels quickly deteriorate if you allow yourself to get wet and cold.

◁ **WEARING THE RIGHT GEAR**
*When offshore cruising, a waterproof jacket with a pair of chest-high pants is ideal gear. Jacket and pants can be worn separately or together as conditions dictate.*

## CONTROLLING HEAT

Wear several thin layers rather than one thick one. Layers increase insulation by trapping air; heat control is simply a matter of removing or adding a layer.

## KEEPING DRY

To stay warm while sailing, you usually need to keep dry by wearing a waterproof layer over your warm clothing. Multi-purpose windbreakers and lightweight waterproof pants will see you through your first few sails, but eventually you will want to buy sailing clothing more suited to your specific requirements.

The alternative to keeping warm by staying dry is to wear a close-fitting neoprene wetsuit, which is designed to trap a thin layer of water between the material and the skin. The water is quickly warmed to near body temperature by your body heat. Sailors in high-performance dinghies commonly wear wetsuits, but if you are dinghy sailing for recreation rather than racing, then you may choose to wear waterproof gear. A wetsuit is not appropriate aboard a larger boat where you can more easily stay dry, so choose waterproof pants and jacket.

## AVOIDING SUNBURN

Protection from the sun is important when sailing because reflection from the water, even in overcast weather, quickly produces sunburn. Remember to apply a sunscreen of at least factor 15 to all exposed skin before you go onboard, and re-apply it at intervals.

Sunglasses that filter out the sun's ultraviolet rays are essential to protect your eyes while sailing, and it is often worth wearing a hat to keep direct sunlight off your head. Use a suitable retainer, such as a length of cord, to keep your hat and sunglasses secure.

## SAILING ACCESSORIES

When sailing, it is important to consider protection for your head, hands, and feet. You will probably be able to make do with what you already own until you gain some experience, then you can buy extra gear as necessary to suit your needs.

### HEADGEAR

One-third of body heat is lost through the head, so a warm hat or balaclava will make a significant contribution to your comfort on colder days. On sunny days, a hat will help to prevent sunburn and sunstroke. Tie long hair back or secure it under a hat. This prevents it blowing about and getting in your eyes or being caught in the rigging – which can be painful.

### GLOVES

Wear gloves to protect your hands and keep them warm. Specialized sailing gloves – which have non-slip, reinforced palms and fingers to help your grip – will resist wear from ropes. Open-fingered sailing gloves, which allow you to deal with more intricate tasks, are also available. Fleece-lined mittens can be used on cruisers when sailing in cold weather, but they are too restrictive for use in a dinghy.

### FOOTWEAR

Correct footwear will protect your feet and provide the grip you need to stay upright and with the boat. Shoes and boots for sailing should have flat, non-slip soles without a heel. Do not sail in bare feet as you will risk injury from deck gear.

### SAILING KNIFE

A stainless-steel sailing knife with retractable blade and shackle key can be attached to a length of line and tied to your waist. Keep the blade sharp for cutting rope and use the key to fasten and undo shackles.

## PERSONAL BUOYANCY

Personal buoyancy is essential for anyone using a small boat, whether a rowboat or a sailing dinghy, or even windsurfing. Do not go afloat unless you are wearing either a buoyancy aid or a lifejacket, and always make sure that it is properly fastened.

### TYPES OF PERSONAL BUOYANCY

A buoyancy aid is designed to provide some support when you are in the water with the minimum amount of physical discomfort. A lifejacket is more cumbersome to wear, but it provides total support. It is designed to turn an unconscious person face upward to facilitate breathing.

### BUOYANCY AIDS

Buoyancy aids (*p.54*) use closed-cell foam in a vest-type jacket that is very comfortable to wear, which makes them the usual choice for racing-dinghy sailors or inland sailors. They are often worn over a wetsuit (which also provides a degree of buoyancy).

### LIFEJACKETS

Ocean sailors may choose the added security of a lifejacket (*p.164*). They are available in a variety of styles to suit all shapes and sizes, but you must ensure that you buy a size that is suitable to your body weight. Some lifejackets use closed-cell foam to provide all the buoyancy but most use manual or automatic gas inflation and are worn deflated until required.

# PARTS OF A BOAT

*K*nowing and understanding the names used for the different parts of a boat are important first steps in learning to sail. These names, along with the terms used to describe the various maneuvers, are part of the language of sailing, which has developed over centuries to define all aspects of seamanship. All sailing boats have a number of parts in common, and while it is not necessary to memorize the contents of the nautical dictionary, it will help if you are familiar with the basic terms.

### THE HULL AND FOILS

The hull is the body of the boat, which provides the buoyancy to float itself, equipment, and crew. In most sailing dinghies, and in many larger boats, the hull is commonly constructed out of fiberglass, but sailing dinghies may also be built of wood or molded plastic. Cruiser hulls can also be made of aluminum, steel, or ferrocement.

To reduce sideways drift (leeway), the hull of a sailing boat has a foil underneath called a keel. Dinghies usually have a movable keel called a centerboard or a daggerboard. Larger boats have keels that are usually permanently fixed under the boat and which, unlike movable keels, provide stability through their weight.

A centerboard is adjusted by pivoting it within its case. It is brought up out of the way when launching or recovering a dinghy, and it is rarely removed from its case. A daggerboard moves vertically. It is lifted out of its case when the boat is not in use, and it is often stored in a protective bag.

### THE RUDDER

A rudder is used to steer the boat. In a dinghy, it is controlled with the tiller, which usually has an extension that allows the helmsman to sit on the side of the boat. Dinghy rudders can either have a lifting or a fixed blade. A lifting blade is useful as it can be raised when sailing to and from the shore. A fixed blade is common in racing dinghies as it is lighter and potentially stronger, but it makes the boat harder to sail in shallow water. In larger yachts, the rudder is often controlled by a wheel mounted on a pedestal in the cockpit.

### THE RIG AND FITTINGS

The rig (*p.24*) – comprising a mast, boom, and sail or sails – harnesses the wind and converts its force into drive to push the boat forward. Details of rigs depend on whether the boat is a dinghy or a larger cruiser, and will also vary between individual models.

In most boats, the mast is supported by a system of wires called the standing rigging. However, single-handed dinghies often have a free-standing mast without any of the standing rigging found on other boats.

Sails are hoisted and controlled by ropes collectively known as the running rigging. Pulleys (blocks) and pulley systems (tackles) help to adjust and control the running rigging, while cleats are used to secure ropes. Control systems range from very simple on basic sailing dinghies to highly complex on racing dinghies and cruiser-racers, on which the crew can adjust sail shape and mast bend to maximize performance.

### A DINGHY HULL

Most dinghy hulls have a pointed bow, but some smaller ones have a square bow known as a pram bow, which increases forward buoyancy. Many have a foredeck covering the bow area, and sidedecks along the sides. A thwart provides a seat across the boat and side benches often run under the sidedecks. A case for the centerboard or daggerboard runs fore and aft in the middle of the boat, with a slot that allows the board to project through the bottom of the hull.

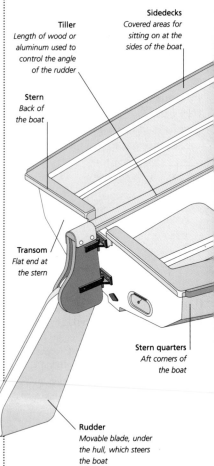

**Tiller**
*Length of wood or aluminum used to control the angle of the rudder*

**Sidedecks**
*Covered areas for sitting on at the sides of the boat*

**Stern**
*Back of the boat*

**Transom**
*Flat end at the stern*

**Stern quarters**
*Aft corners of the boat*

**Rudder**
*Movable blade, under the hull, which steers the boat*

## BUOYANCY TANKS ▷

*All sailing boats have some form of added buoyancy so that they float if capsized or swamped. The buoyancy is often provided by sealed compartments in the hull.*

Port tank

Central tank

Starboard tank

**SEALED TANKS IN A DINGHY**

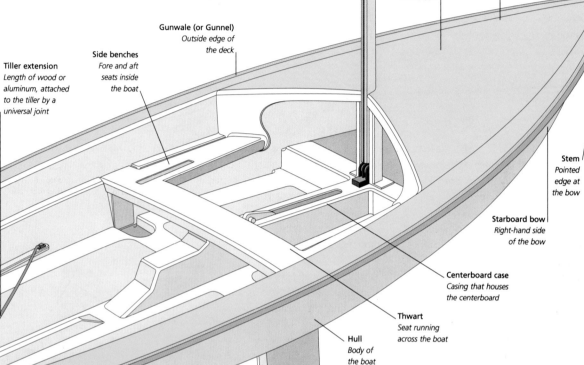

**Port bow**
*Left-hand side of the bow*

**Bow**
*Front of the boat*

**Foredeck**
*Covered area at the bow*

**Gunwale (or Gunnel)**
*Outside edge of the deck*

**Tiller extension**
*Length of wood or aluminum, attached to the tiller by a universal joint*

**Side benches**
*Fore and aft seats inside the boat*

**Stem**
*Pointed edge at the bow*

**Starboard bow**
*Right-hand side of the bow*

**Centerboard case**
*Casing that houses the centerboard*

**Thwart**
*Seat running across the boat*

**Hull**
*Body of the boat*

**Centerboard**
*Foil that can be pivoted into its case*

## A CRUISER HULL

A cruiser hull is designed and built to sail offshore and be capable of coping with bad weather.

### HULL FEATURES

A cruiser has larger and heavier gear than a dinghy, and it usually has a fixed, weighted keel to increase stability. A cabin provides accommodation for the crew, and an inboard engine is normally fitted to provide motoring ability.

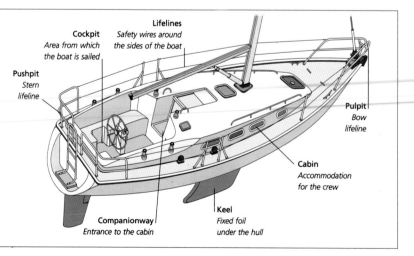

**Lifelines**
*Safety wires around the sides of the boat*

**Cockpit**
*Area from which the boat is sailed*

**Pushpit**
*Stern lifeline*

**Pulpit**
*Bow lifeline*

**Cabin**
*Accommodation for the crew*

**Companionway**
*Entrance to the cabin*

**Keel**
*Fixed foil under the hull*

# THE RIG

Many sailing dinghies are rigged as a Bermudan sloop with a mainsail and a jib, both of which are triangular in shape. The jib, which is set on the forestay, adds drive and makes the mainsail more efficient than it would be alone. In addition, many dinghies carry a spinnaker for increased speed when sailing downwind. Standing rigging includes all the wires and ropes that support the mast and boom, while running rigging is used to hoist and control the sails.

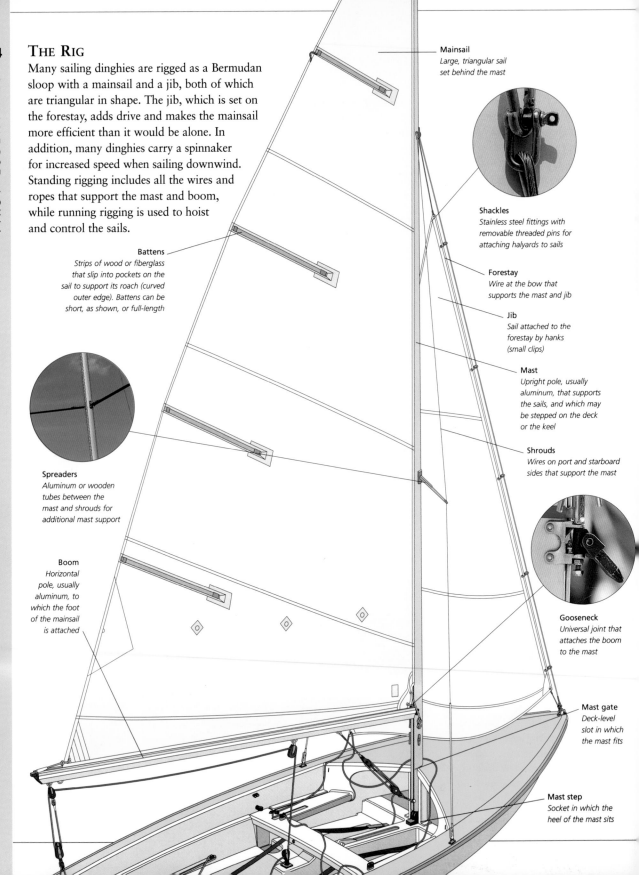

**Mainsail**
*Large, triangular sail set behind the mast*

**Shackles**
*Stainless steel fittings with removable threaded pins for attaching halyards to sails*

**Forestay**
*Wire at the bow that supports the mast and jib*

**Jib**
*Sail attached to the forestay by hanks (small clips)*

**Mast**
*Upright pole, usually aluminum, that supports the sails, and which may be stepped on the deck or the keel*

**Shrouds**
*Wires on port and starboard sides that support the mast*

**Gooseneck**
*Universal joint that attaches the boom to the mast*

**Mast gate**
*Deck-level slot in which the mast fits*

**Mast step**
*Socket in which the heel of the mast sits*

**Battens**
*Strips of wood or fiberglass that slip into pockets on the sail to support its roach (curved outer edge). Battens can be short, as shown, or full-length*

**Spreaders**
*Aluminum or wooden tubes between the mast and shrouds for additional mast support*

**Boom**
*Horizontal pole, usually aluminum, to which the foot of the mainsail is attached*

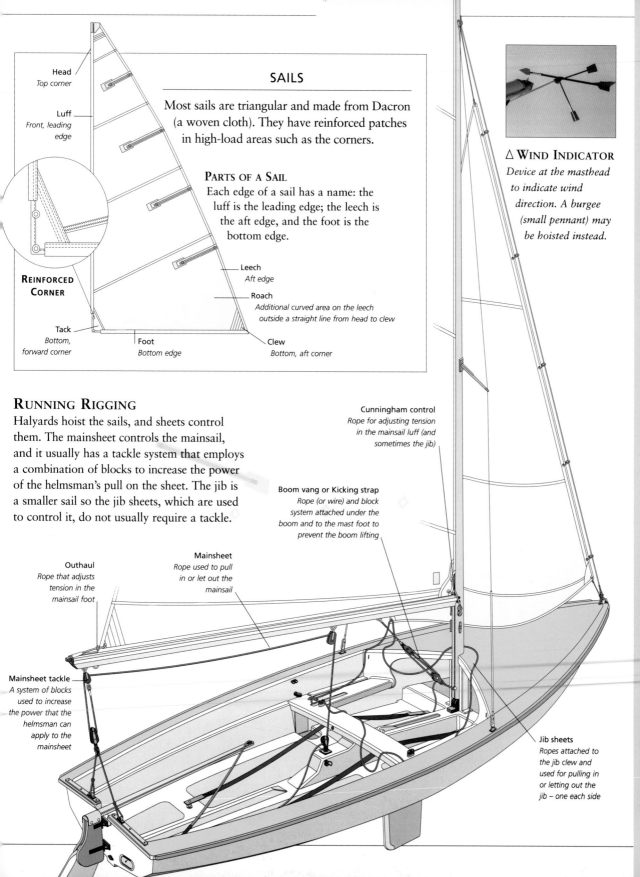

## SAILS

Most sails are triangular and made from Dacron (a woven cloth). They have reinforced patches in high-load areas such as the corners.

### PARTS OF A SAIL

Each edge of a sail has a name: the luff is the leading edge; the leech is the aft edge, and the foot is the bottom edge.

**Head**
*Top corner*

**Luff**
*Front, leading edge*

**REINFORCED CORNER**

**Tack**
*Bottom, forward corner*

**Foot**
*Bottom edge*

**Leech**
*Aft edge*

**Roach**
*Additional curved area on the leech outside a straight line from head to clew*

**Clew**
*Bottom, aft corner*

△ **WIND INDICATOR**
*Device at the masthead to indicate wind direction. A burgee (small pennant) may be hoisted instead.*

## RUNNING RIGGING

Halyards hoist the sails, and sheets control them. The mainsheet controls the mainsail, and it usually has a tackle system that employs a combination of blocks to increase the power of the helmsman's pull on the sheet. The jib is a smaller sail so the jib sheets, which are used to control it, do not usually require a tackle.

**Cunningham control**
*Rope for adjusting tension in the mainsail luff (and sometimes the jib)*

**Boom vang or Kicking strap**
*Rope (or wire) and block system attached under the boom and to the mast foot to prevent the boom lifting*

**Outhaul**
*Rope that adjusts tension in the mainsail foot*

**Mainsheet**
*Rope used to pull in or let out the mainsail*

**Mainsheet tackle**
*A system of blocks used to increase the power that the helmsman can apply to the mainsheet*

**Jib sheets**
*Ropes attached to the jib clew and used for pulling in or letting out the jib – one each side*

# SMALL-BOAT FITTINGS

Various fittings are attached to the boat to help the crew control the rig and sails. Fairleads, which may be fixed, or mounted on a track for adjustment, are used to guide ropes. Cleats, which are employed to secure the ropes, are usually provided so that the crew is not obliged to hold sheets continuously. Other important fixtures and fittings include the toe rails, which keep the crew from slipping; the painter, the rope used to moor the boat; and block-and-tackle systems that help to control the running rigging. Sailing dinghies and small daysailers usually have simple fittings but more complex equipment will be found on high-performance boats.

**Jib fairlead**
*Smooth eye or rotating pulley for altering the direction of the jib sheet. The sheet is led through the fairlead to a cleat and may be fixed, or mounted on a track for adjustment*

**Horn cleat**
*A traditional horn cleat may be used to secure halyards. The rope is wrapped around the two horns and friction holds it fast*

**Fairlead track**

**Block**
*Blocks are used to alter the direction of a rope. Here, the block is designed to lead the spinnaker sheet to a cleat*

**Weep holes**
*Flaps that open to drain water from the cockpit after a capsize or swamping. They are closed for normal sailing and when stationary*

**Toe rails**
*Retaining straps for the feet of both helmsman and crew to avoid slipping*

**Cleat**

**Mainsheet block**
*The block that directs the mainsheet to the helmsman's hand. It may have a cleat attached so that the helmsman can secure the sheet*

**Cam cleat**
*Used for making fast a rope. The rope is held between the two cams and released by pulling and lifting it out of the cleat. Cam cleats may be used for sheets and control lines*

**Bow fitting**
*Fitting to which the forestay, jib, and painter (mooring rope) are attached*

**Shroud adjusters**
*Metal plates that secure the shrouds to the hull and allow adjustment to rake the mast backward or forward*

## RELATIVE TERMS

On shore, we usually describe the position of things in relation to ourselves – "left," "right," "in front," or "behind." On the water, they are described in relation to the boat or the wind.

### THE BOAT
The terms "port" and "starboard" are used to relate to the boat. Facing the bow, the port side is to the left and the starboard side is to the right.

### THE WIND
Windward and leeward relate to the wind. The windward side of the boat is the side toward the wind; the leeward side is the side away from the wind.

**AHEAD**
**(IN FRONT OF THE BOAT)**

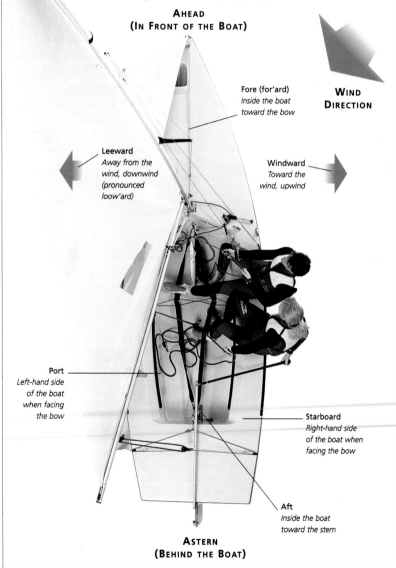

**WIND DIRECTION**

**Fore (for'ard)**
*Inside the boat toward the bow*

**Leeward**
*Away from the wind, downwind (pronounced loow'ard)*

**Windward**
*Toward the wind, upwind*

**Port**
*Left-hand side of the boat when facing the bow*

**Starboard**
*Right-hand side of the boat when facing the bow*

**Aft**
*Inside the boat toward the stern*

**ASTERN**
**(BEHIND THE BOAT)**

# ESSENTIAL EQUIPMENT

*As well as any removable rigging, there are several other items that should be aboard when you set sail. In particular, there must be some means of propelling the boat if you cannot sail. There must also be adequate buoyancy to keep the boat afloat in the event of a capsize, and bailing equipment to remove any shipped water. An anchor and warp (anchor line) are also important if you sail on the sea. All equipment must be stowed safely so that it stays in place if the boat heels or capsizes.*

## PADDLES OR OARS

You must always carry at least one paddle so that you can move the boat in a calm. A pair of oars is worth considering if you have the space. They will propel the boat much more efficiently than a paddle. If you do use oars, you will need a pair of rowlocks mounted in sockets on the gunwales. Some oars are jointed in the middle to make stowage easier.

## BUOYANCY

Buoyancy must be sufficient but not excessive, and it must be distributed so that the boat floats level when capsized. Buoyancy is usually provided either by tanks that are permanently built in to the structure, as is the case with most modern boats, or by removable buoyant materials, such as inflatable airbags, which are securely attached to the hull.

## BAILERS

All boats can get water in them even if they do not capsize, and it is important to be able to remove it easily. Apart from making you wetter than necessary, water that is allowed to build up in the bottom of the boat will slop from side to side and make the boat heel more.

Bailing may be done automatically through retractable self-bailers, which are lowered when the boat is moving. The flow of water under the hull and past the bailer sucks the water out from inside the boat. Most have a non-return valve to prevent water from entering the boat when it slows down, but it is best to raise them if you stop, and, to avoid damage, you should remember to retract them when taking the boat out of the water. Some racing dinghies have open transoms that allow any water in the boat to flow straight out through the stern.

## ANCHOR AND WARP

An anchor can be an important piece of equipment, particularly for sailing at sea without safety cover. In the event of an accident, a foul tide, calm weather, or even if you are simply in need of a rest, an anchor allows you to stop the boat in shallow water without drifting on the tide.

A small, folding anchor can be a good compromise because it takes up little space, but for serious anchoring – perhaps when cruising in a larger vessel – a small CQR, Danforth, or Bruce anchor should be used. These are burying anchors that dig into the seabed and provide more security than a folding anchor. You will also need a warp, which can be used if your boat needs to be towed. Make sure that the anchor and warp are stowed securely.

---

### HOW TO BAIL

Automatic self-bailers fitted in the bottom can be opened to let the water out when you are sailing quickly. Some boats have a pair of weepholes at the stern, which allow water to go out but not get in. Alternatively, you can bail by hand using a scoop.

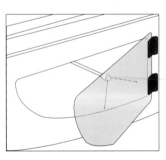

△ **WEEPHOLE**
*Hinged flaps in the transom get rid of water after a capsize or swamping. They stay shut when the boat is stationary or sailing slowly.*

SCOOP BAILER

△ **BAILING BY HAND**
*Always bail over the leeward side of the boat or else the water may be blown back on board (or into your face). A bucket is best for removing a large amount of water after a capsize; a scoop bailer is useful for smaller quantities. Get rid of the last few drops with a sponge.*

# STOWING GEAR

There is very little room for extra items in a dinghy, so store everything neatly and carefully. Use the area under the foredeck for things that you want to keep dry, such as spare clothes, which are best put in waterproof bags beforehand. Place heavy items, including the anchor, near the middle of the boat, so that they do not affect fore and aft trim. Any space under the sidedecks is ideal for storing oars or paddles.

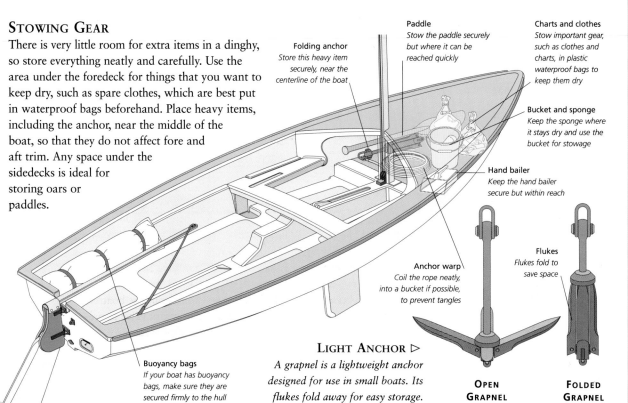

**Paddle**
*Stow the paddle securely but where it can be reached quickly*

**Folding anchor**
*Store this heavy item securely, near the centerline of the boat*

**Charts and clothes**
*Stow important gear, such as clothes and charts, in plastic waterproof bags to keep them dry*

**Bucket and sponge**
*Keep the sponge where it stays dry and use the bucket for stowage*

**Hand bailer**
*Keep the hand bailer secure but within reach*

**Anchor warp**
*Coil the rope neatly, into a bucket if possible, to prevent tangles*

**Flukes**
*Flukes fold to save space*

**Buoyancy bags**
*If your boat has buoyancy bags, make sure they are secured firmly to the hull*

### LIGHT ANCHOR ▷
*A grapnel is a lightweight anchor designed for use in small boats. Its flukes fold away for easy storage.*

**OPEN GRAPNEL**

**FOLDED GRAPNEL**

---

## EFFICIENT BOAT BUOYANCY

The ideal amount of buoyancy will allow the boat to float level on its side when capsized, with the centerboard within reach. The boat will have relatively little water in it when righted.

### CHECKING BUILT-IN TANKS
Most built-in tanks have removable bungs that should be taken out when the boat is not being used, to allow trapped water to drain away. Any inspection hatches should also be removed when the boat is not afloat.

### CHECKING BUOYANCY BAGS
Check buoyancy bags to ensure that there are no leaks and that the fastenings are tight. There should be at least three straps on each bag. When the boat is capsized or full of water, the fastenings take an enormous load. It is vital that they do not break, as the boat could then sink or be impossible to right.

### △ TOO LITTLE
*With too little buoyancy, the boat sits low in the water. It is difficult to right when capsized because the hull floats low. It comes up with a lot of water.*

### △ CORRECT
*With the correct buoyancy in the hull, the boat floats level when capsized, and is relatively easy to right. The boat comes up with little water when righted.*

### △ TOO MUCH
*With too much buoyancy, the boat sits high in the water and is more likely to capsize. It is prone to turning upside down during a capsize recovery.*

**TOO LITTLE BUOYANCY**

**CORRECT BUOYANCY**

**TOO MUCH BUOYANCY**

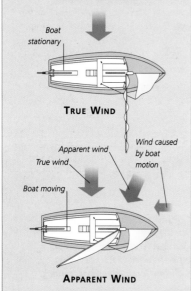

*Boat stationary*

**TRUE WIND**

*Apparent wind*

*True wind*

*Wind caused by boat motion*

*Boat moving*

**APPARENT WIND**

### △ WIND EFFECTS
*When a boat is stationary, you feel true wind. When the boat moves, it creates its own wind which combines with the true wind to form the apparent wind.*

# HOW BOATS SAIL

*Before you begin sailing, it helps to have some understanding of how sails work and interact to produce forward drive. By studying some of the theory before going afloat, you will spend less time learning by trial and error on the water.*

## DRIVING FORCE

Sailing boats derive their power from the wind flowing across the curved surfaces of the sails. This is very similar to the way an airplane wing produces lift to keep the plane in the air. A sail, like an airplane wing, works at its best at one small angle to the wind. Therefore, efficient sailing requires constant sail adjustment (trimming) to keep it at the correct angle. If a sail is let out too far, it will simply flap like a flag and produce no forward drive. If it is pulled in too much, the airflow over it will break down and the sail will stall – like an airplane that tries to fly too slowly.

## SIDEWAYS FORCE

Not all of the force produced by the sail pushes the boat forward. The total force produced by the sail has a sideways element that attempts to push the boat sideways. The strength

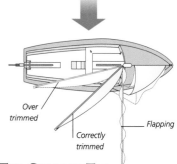

*Over trimmed*

*Correctly trimmed*

*Flapping*

### △ THE CORRECT TRIM
*To find the correct trim for a sail, let it out until it begins to flap at the luff, then pull it in until the shaking just stops.*

of the sideways force depends on the point of sailing. It is at its greatest when the boat is close-hauled, and it is least significant when running. If the sail is pulled in too far and stalls, the driving force drops and the sideways force increases.

On upwind courses, the boat always slips sideways slightly. A keel or centerboard is used to resist the sideways force, but it is never completely eliminated. The difference between the course steered and the course actually sailed is called leeway.

## HEELING FORCE

Because the total force generated by the sail acts some distance above the waterline, the sideways force tries to heel the boat. The sideways resistance provided by the centerboard increases the heeling effect which is counter-balanced by the crew's weight or by the weight of a keel in a cruiser.

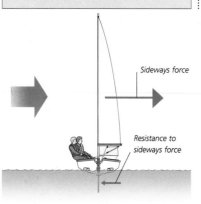

*Sideways force*

*Resistance to sideways force*

### △ SIDEWAYS FORCE
*Part of the force generated by the sails pushes the boat sideways. It is resisted by the centerboard or keel.*

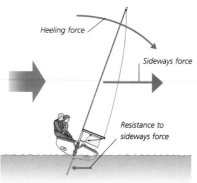

*Heeling force*

*Sideways force*

*Resistance to sideways force*

### △ HEELING FORCE
*The vertical separation between the sideways force and the resistance from the keel causes a heeling force.*

# THE DYNAMICS OF SAILING

Boat sails work in a similar way to the wings of an airplane; their shape produces a force from the passage of the wind. In an airplane, the engine pushes the horizontal wing through the air to create lift; in a boat, the wind across the vertical sail is converted into a force that produces forward drive.

### AIRFLOW

A properly trimmed sail with wind moving across it deflects the airflow, which splits at the leading edge of the sail. The airflow moving across the convex (leeward) surface has to travel further than that moving across the concave (windward) side and speeds up accordingly. When the airflow moves faster, its pressure drops and so the pressure on the convex side of a wing is lower than the pressure on the concave side. The difference in pressure sucks the sail to leeward and creates a force at right angles to the sail at all points on its surface. The sum of these forces drives the boat forward.

### FORWARD DRIVE

All the forces acting on a sail's surface can be thought of as one force acting at a single point, which is known as the center of effort. This force can be split into two: the driving force and sideways force. The driving force depends considerably on a sail's curved shape (camber). When a sail is trimmed correctly, drive is maximized and sideways force minimized.

### DRIVE WITH TWO SAILS

When a jib is added in front of a mainsail, it creates its own drive in the same way as a single sail, but it will also increase the efficiency of the mainsail. As the air flows through the slot between jib and mainsail it is compressed between them and so accelerates. This further reduces the pressure on the leeward side of the mainsail, increasing its drive. To work properly, the jib and mainsail must be trimmed to match each other and to produce a smooth slot between them.

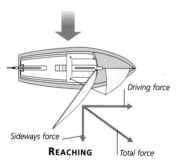

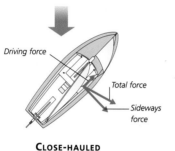

**REACHING**

**CLOSE-HAULED**

Driving force
Sideways force
Total force

Driving force
Total force
Sideways force

### ◁ DRIVE AND SIDEWAYS FORCE
*The relative strength of the driving and sideways forces depends on the point of sailing and the angle of the sail to the boat. When close-hauled, drive is less than when reaching, but the sideways force is greater.*

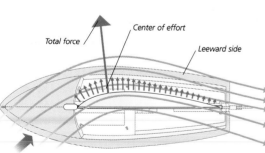

Total force
Center of effort
Leeward side

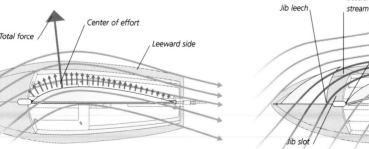

Jib leech
Compressed and accelerated air stream
Mainsail luff
Jib slot

### △ AIRFLOW AND ONE SAIL
*As the wind flows across a sail, it moves faster on the leeward side, creating low pressure, and slower on the windward side, which creates a high-pressure area. This effectively sucks the sail to leeward and produces forces acting at right angles to the sail's surface at each point on the sail. The sum of these forces acts at what is known as the sail's center of effort.*

### △ AIRFLOW AND TWO SAILS
*When two sails are used, their interaction is critical to performance. Although the jib is much smaller than the mainsail, it is potentially a more efficient sail because it does not have a mast in front of it to disturb the airflow. If the jib is trimmed so that the slot between the jib leech and the mainsail luff is parallel all the way up, the air flowing through is compressed and will accelerate. This further decreases the pressure on the leeward side of the mainsail and so increases drive.*

# THE MAIN CONTROLS

*Rudder, centerboard, sails, and crew weight are the main controls in a sailing dinghy. They need constant adjustment to keep the boat sailing efficiently, to steer, and to alter course. Knowing how to combine these controls to manage the movement of the boat is a crucial aspect of learning how to sail that should be practiced regularly until it becomes instinctive. When sailing with a crew, the helmsman is responsible for the mainsail and the rudder while the crew takes care of the centerboard and the jib.*

## USING THE RUDDER

The rudder is moved using the tiller (and tiller extension if fitted), which the helmsman usually holds in the hand nearest the stern. The rudder is effective only if it has water flowing past it. Consequently, you can only steer with it when the boat is moving.

The quicker you are sailing, the more effective it becomes due to the speed of the water moving across it. When the boat is moving forward, the bow will turn in the opposite direction to the way in which the tiller is pushed. (When it is moving backward, the action of the rudder is reversed.)

## TURNING USING THE RUDDER

The rudder is the main control used to alter course. Practice using the tiller to turn the rudder, and familiarize yourself with its effects by sitting on the side of the boat opposite the sails and watching the direction in which the bow turns as you make adjustments.

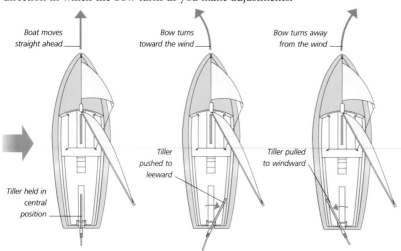

*Boat moves straight ahead*

*Tiller held in central position*

△ **STRAIGHT COURSE**
*The tiller is kept in the middle of the boat to sail on a course that is straight ahead.*

*Bow turns toward the wind*

*Tiller pushed to leeward*

△ **LUFFING UP**
*The tiller is pushed away to luff up (turn toward the wind).*

*Bow turns away from the wind*

*Tiller pulled to windward*

△ **BEARING AWAY**
*The tiller is pulled up to bear away (turn away from the wind).*

## USING THE CENTERBOARD

The effect of the centerboard (or daggerboard) is altered by moving the blade to different depths in the water. It is lowered when the boat is turned toward the wind and raised when the boat is turned away from the wind.

The centerboard has a significant effect on the performance of the boat. It should be raised when you are sailing away from the wind, otherwise it will make the boat slower and more difficult to control. It must be lowered when turning into the wind, otherwise the boat will simply slip sideways as there is nothing to counteract the sideways force of the wind (*p.30*).

## USING THE SAILS

A sail works best at a particular angle to the wind, so it must be trimmed (adjusted) as you alter course and checked regularly while sailing to ensure the setting is correct. To find the optimum angle, ease the sail out until it starts to shake at the luff (*p.25*), then pull it in again just far enough to stop it shaking. Pull the sail in tight only when you are sailing close to the wind (*p.35*).

## USING THE CREW'S WEIGHT

A sailing dinghy moves fastest when it is upright in the water, and when the heeling force (*p.30*) is balanced by the weight of the helmsman and crew. Their placement, fore and aft, determines the boat's trim (how it sits in the water). The helmsman sits on the windward side, opposite the sails, so that he has a clear view of the sails and the course. The crew moves his weight according to the point of sail and wind strength. By moving his weight distribution, the crew can heel the boat to help it alter course.

## TURNING USING THE SAILS

To learn about the turning effects of the sails, let either sail out while keeping the other filled correctly and the boat upright. Allow the tiller to move freely in your hand and the boat will turn.

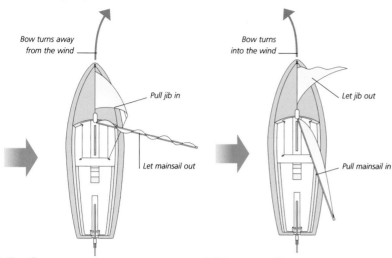

Bow turns away from the wind

Pull jib in

Let mainsail out

Bow turns into the wind

Let jib out

Pull mainsail in

### △ JIB ONLY
*The mainsail is allowed to flap and the jib is pulled in. Sailing with the jib alone makes the boat turn away from the wind.*

### △ MAINSAIL ONLY
*The jib is allowed to flap and the mainsail is pulled in. Sailing with just the mainsail makes the boat turn toward the wind.*

## TURNING USING THE CREW'S WEIGHT

Experiment by moving around the boat to see how it changes direction when it is balanced differently. When sailing with both a helmsman and crew, it becomes the responsibility of the crew to make any major adjustments to the boat balance.

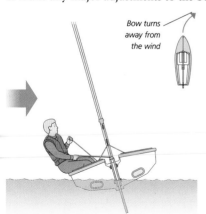

Bow turns away from the wind

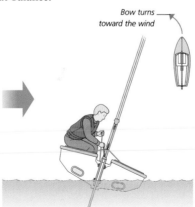

Bow turns toward the wind

### △ HEELING TOWARD
*The helmsman uses his weight to heel the boat to windward so that the boat turns to leeward (away from the wind).*

### △ HEELING AWAY
*The helmsman uses his weight to heel the boat to leeward so that the boat turns to windward (toward the wind).*

## TACKING AND JIBING

The two most important maneuvers in sailing, tacking and jibing, involve using the main controls together to make a significant course change.

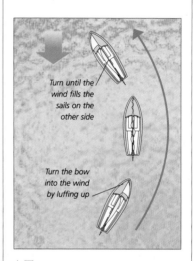

Turn until the wind fills the sails on the other side

Turn the bow into the wind by luffing up

### △ TACKING
*During tacking (pp.78–81) the bow of the boat is moved through the wind using the rudder, sails, and crew weight.*

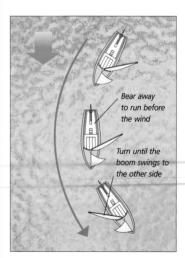

Bear away to run before the wind

Turn until the boom swings to the other side

### △ JIBING
*Jibing (pp.82–85) involves turning the stern of the boat through the wind using the rudder, sails, and crew weight.*

# POINTS OF SAILING

*T*he direction in which a boat is being sailed is often described in relation to its angle to the wind. Collectively, these angles are known as the "points of sailing." When you change from one point of sailing to another, the sails, the centerboard, and the position of the crew all need to be adjusted to suit the new angle of the boat in relation to the wind.

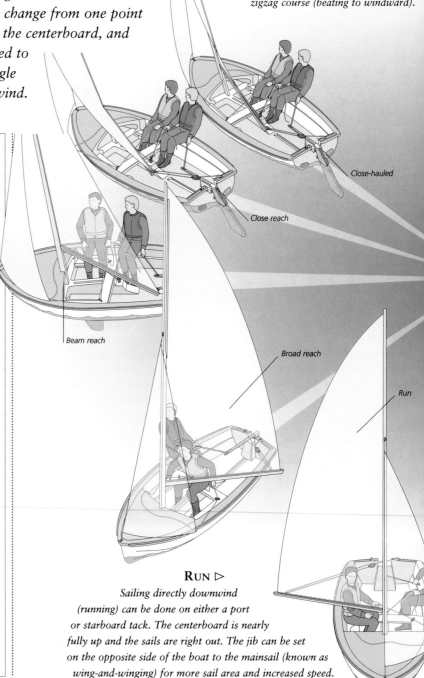

**NO-SAIL ZONE ▽**
*Boats cannot sail directly into the wind. The closest that most can achieve is an angle of 45° either side of the direction of the true wind. Progress toward the wind is made by sailing a zigzag course (beating to windward).*

*Close-hauled*

*Close reach*

*Beam reach*

*Broad reach*

*Run*

**RUN ▷**
*Sailing directly downwind (running) can be done on either a port or starboard tack. The centerboard is nearly fully up and the sails are right out. The jib can be set on the opposite side of the boat to the mainsail (known as wing-and-winging) for more sail area and increased speed.*

## SAILING COURSES

Various terms and phrases are used to clarify the direction and type of sailing course that you are on and to describe exactly what the boat is doing in relation to the wind.

### LUFFING AND BEARING AWAY
If you turn the boat toward the wind you are luffing, if you turn away from it you are bearing away.

### UPWIND AND OFFWIND
All courses that are closer to the wind (heading more directly into it) than a beam reach are called upwind courses. Those further away from the wind than a beam reach are known as offwind, or downwind, courses.

### PORT AND STARBOARD TACK
The boom's position is used to describe which tack you are on. If it is over the port side of the boat you are on a starboard tack. If it is over the starboard side you are on port tack. Even on a dead run with the wind directly astern you are still on one tack or the other, depending on which side your boom is on.

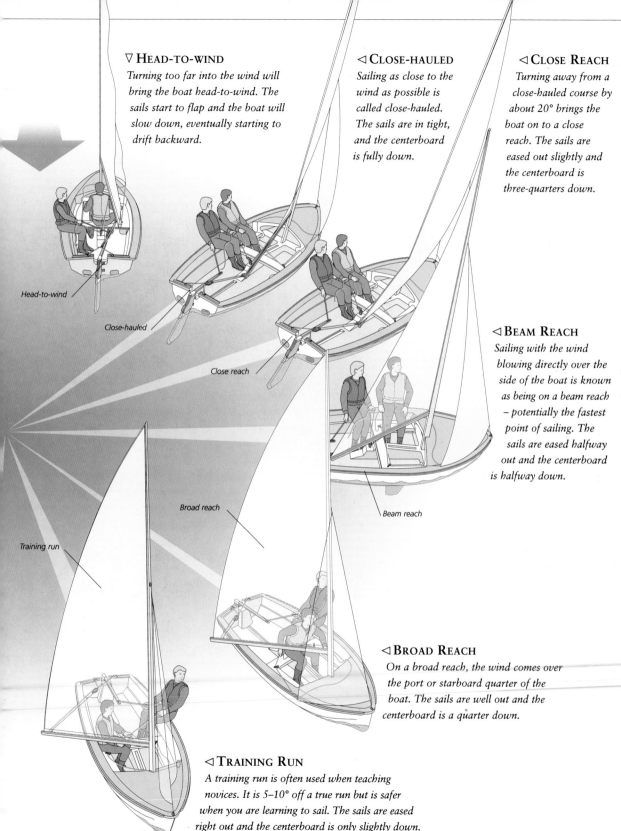

## ▽ HEAD-TO-WIND

*Turning too far into the wind will bring the boat head-to-wind. The sails start to flap and the boat will slow down, eventually starting to drift backward.*

Head-to-wind

## ◁ CLOSE-HAULED

*Sailing as close to the wind as possible is called close-hauled. The sails are in tight, and the centerboard is fully down.*

Close-hauled

## ◁ CLOSE REACH

*Turning away from a close-hauled course by about 20° brings the boat on to a close reach. The sails are eased out slightly and the centerboard is three-quarters down.*

Close reach

## ◁ BEAM REACH

*Sailing with the wind blowing directly over the side of the boat is known as being on a beam reach – potentially the fastest point of sailing. The sails are eased halfway out and the centerboard is halfway down.*

Beam reach

Broad reach

Training run

## ◁ BROAD REACH

*On a broad reach, the wind comes over the port or starboard quarter of the boat. The sails are well out and the centerboard is a quarter down.*

## ◁ TRAINING RUN

*A training run is often used when teaching novices. It is 5–10° off a true run but is safer when you are learning to sail. The sails are eased right out and the centerboard is only slightly down.*

## TYPES OF ROPE

Rope can be made from many different fibers and in a number of ways. The material and the type of construction determine how the finished rope behaves in terms of stretch, strength, durability, and flexibility.

◁ **THREE-STRAND OR LAID ROPE**
*Yarns are twisted into strands that are then twisted in the other direction, making a strong, flexible rope.*

◁ **BRAIDED ROPE**
*A core of braided strands is encased in a sheath. The core provides strength and the sheath protects against abrasion.*

◁ **POLYPROPYLENE**
*Polypropylene is used to make low-cost, general-purpose, three-strand ropes that are light and will float.*

◁ **POLYESTER**
*Polyester rope can be braided or three-strand. It is strong, with low stretch, and does not float.*

◁ **NYLON**
*Nylon rope is strong and elastic. It does not float and loses strength when wet.*

◁ **HMP AND ARAMID**
*Aramid and high-modulus polyethylene fiber ropes are very strong and light. They also have a very low stretch under load.*

# ROPES AND KNOTS

U*sed to secure the boat and to hoist, trim, and adjust the sails, ropes are an essential feature of all sailboats. To sail safely and efficiently you need to understand how to handle rope and how to keep it tidy when not in use. Learning a little about the different properties of the various ropes available will enable you to select the most suitable rope for any particular task. It is also vital to know how to tie the small selection of knots that are the most useful for sailing purposes.*

## HANDLING ROPES

Modern sailing ropes are constructed using synthetic materials, which are lighter and stronger than natural fibers. Modern ropes are immune to rot caused by dampness and they are available in a range of colors for easy identification. There are two main types of rope: three-strand rope, in which three sets (strands) of already twisted yarns are twisted together; and braided rope, in which the yarns and strands are plaited together.

### CHOOSING ROPE

It is important to choose the right rope for a particular job. Polypropylene rope makes a cheap mooring line, and, because it floats, it is ideal for safety lines. Polyester rope is strong with low stretch, so it is suitable for mooring lines, sheets, and halyards. Nylon rope is excellent at absorbing shock loads, so it is often used for mooring or anchoring. Aramid and HMP ropes are expensive but they are

---

### CLEATING ROPE ON MOORING CLEATS

The horn cleat is a common fixture on most sailboats. Rope is secured on it by a series of figure eight turns over its two horns. When the rope has been made fast, any surplus should be coiled and hung on the cleat to keep it tidy and out of the way during sailing.

**①** Bring the rope's working end to the back of the cleat, then make a full turn around the base of the cleat.

**②** Take the rope across the top of the cleat, pass behind the upper horn, and then bring it back across the front to form a figure eight.

**③** Add several figure eight turns to ensure that the rope is secure. Finish off with another full turn around the base of the cleat.

## HOW TO COIL A THREE-STRAND ROPE

To prevent kinks, three-strand rope is coiled in the same direction in which the strands are twisted, usually clockwise. As the loops are made, the rope must also be twisted slightly in the same direction so that the coils lie flat.

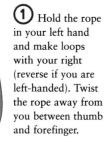

**1** Hold the rope in your left hand and make loops with your right (reverse if you are left-handed). Twist the rope away from you between thumb and forefinger.

**2** Finish coiling the rope leaving a long working end. Wrap this several times around the whole coil to bind the individual loops together.

**3** Make a loop with the remainder of the working end and push this through the top of the coil, above the bound part.

**4** Bring the loop forward over the top of the coil and down to the bound part, then pull the working end to secure it.

---

excellent for halyards as they stretch very little. However, their yarns can be susceptible to breakage if the rope is bent around tight curves.

## COILING ROPE

On boats, all ropes must be coiled and secured so that they are out of the way but easy to use when necessary. Three-strand rope is coiled in equal-sized loops (*above*), whereas braided rope is best coiled in figure eights to balance the left and right twists of the plaited strands.

## CLEATING ROPE

A cleat is used to secure a rope and prevent it slipping. Cleats may be of the cam, clam, or horn variety (*p.26*). A rope is cleated in a cam cleat by pulling it down and through the cam

jaws, which hold it in place. In order to cleat a rope in a clam cleat, simply pull it down into the V-shaped holding groove. To secure a rope to a horn cleat, it must be wrapped around the cleat in a series of turns (*left*).

## KNOTTING ROPE

Many thousands of knots have been developed over the centuries, each with its own name and practical or decorative use. You need to know only a few knots when you start sailing. In fact, the reef knot, the sheet bend, the figure eight, the bowline, the round turn and two half hitches, and the clove hitch (*pp.38–39*) will take care of most of your needs throughout your sailing career. Spend some time practicing tying them so that your technique becomes fluent.

---

## ROPE AND KNOT TERMS

There are several terms that are used to identify the various parts of the rope during knot tying. These help to clarify knotting instructions by distinguishing between the two ends of a rope as well as describing the different shapes that are made while the knots are being tied.

*Working end*

*Standing part*

#### △ THE PARTS OF A ROPE
*The part of the rope you are using to tie a knot is called the working end. The rest of the rope (that part that remains unaffected) is called the standing part.*

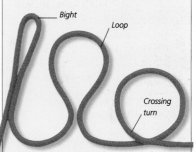

*Bight*   *Loop*

*Crossing turn*

#### △ BIGHTS, LOOPS, AND CROSSING TURNS
*A bight is made by folding the rope back on itself; a loop is made by forming a circle without crossing the rope; and a crossing turn is made by crossing one part of the rope over or under another.*

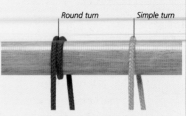

*Round turn*   *Simple turn*

#### △ SIMPLE AND ROUND TURNS
*A simple turn involves passing the rope around one side of an object, whereas a round turn takes the rope one-and-a-half times around the object.*

# SIX BASIC KNOTS

## REEF KNOT

*Used for tying the ends of rope of equal diameter, the reef knot is named after its most common use: tying the ends of a sail's reef lines when putting in a reef (p.62). It is easy to tie it properly, just remember the rule: left over right, then right over left.*

**1** With the rope under the object, cross the two ends of the rope with the left working end over the right working end.

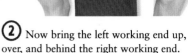

**2** Now bring the left working end up, over, and behind the right working end.

**3** Bring both working ends up and tuck the now right working end over the left working end and through the middle.

**4** Tighten the knot by pulling on both the working ends, producing the distinctive square-shaped reef knot.

## SHEET BEND

*A sheet bend is one of the best ways of joining two ropes together. If they are of different diameter, make the loop in the thicker rope. For more security, tie a double sheet bend by taking an additional turn around the loop (repeat steps 2 and 3).*

**1** Make a loop in the blue rope then pass the working end of the white rope through the loop from below.

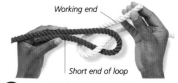

**2** Pass the working end of the white rope around and under the short end of the loop in the blue rope.

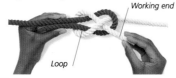

**3** Bring the working end of the white rope over the long end of the loop, back to the top, and then under itself.

**4** Finally, tighten the sheet bend by pulling on the loop and the standing part of the white rope.

## FIGURE-EIGHT

*A figure-eight is a stopper knot that is used in sailing to prevent a rope end running out through a block or fairlead. It is simple to tie, does not jam, and is easily undone.*

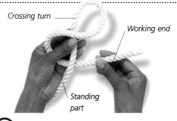

**1** Make a crossing turn, bringing the working end of the rope over and then under the standing part.

**2** Bring the working end up to the top of the knot and then pass it through the center of the crossing turn. Pull tight.

## BOWLINE

*If you learn only one knot before you go sailing make it this one. The bowline (pronounced bow-lynn) is used to make a loop in the end of a rope or to tie to a ring or post. The bowline cannot be untied under load.*

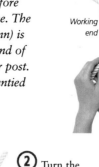

Standing part

Working end

Rotate this hand

**①** With the working end of the rope held in the palm of the hand over the standing part, rotate the hand so the working end is pushed under the standing part as the palm turns face upward.

Working end     Standing part

**②** Turn the hand and the working end so that a crossing turn is created around the hand and the working end.

Standing part

**③** Finally, pass the working end behind the standing part and then down through the crossing turn. Tighten the knot by pulling on the standing part and the doubled working end.

Working end

---

## ROUND TURN AND TWO HALF-HITCHES

*This knot is very useful for tying a rope to a post, rail, or ring. It is easily untied, even when under load, so it is good for moorings.*

Standing part          Working end

◁ **①** Form a round turn by bringing the working end of the rope up through the ring (or around a post or rail), from bottom to top, twice.

▷ **②** Take the working end over the standing part. Pass it below the standing part then bring it to the top again and tuck it under itself, making a half-hitch.

Working end

Standing part

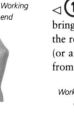

◁ **③** Pass the working end below the standing part again, then bring it to the top and tuck it under itself again, making the second half-hitch. Pull both ends to tighten.

Working end

Standing part

## CLOVE HITCH

*The clove hitch is used for short-term mooring to a ring or post, or for hitching fenders to a rail. Make it more secure with a long working end.*

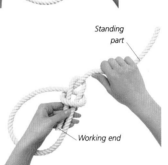

Working end

◁ **①** Make a turn around the post, bringing the working end up over the standing part.

Standing part

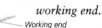

▷ **②** Use the working end to make a second turn in the same direction, taking it behind the post and bringing it around to the front again.

Working end

Standing part

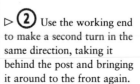

Standing part          Working end

◁ **③** Tuck the working end under the second turn. Pull on the working end and the standing part to tighten the knot.

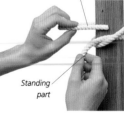

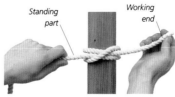

# OARS AND PADDLES

*The way in which you handle a dinghy under oars is one of the best indications of your seamanship skills. Rowing a dinghy that has been specifically designed for the purpose is a very satisfying exercise: good rowboats are easy to row and move straight and smoothly under oars. Larger dinghies can also be moved with one oar, using the impressive art of sculling. However, sailing dinghies are rarely designed for rowing or sculling, and paddling may be the only viable option.*

## ROWING

The easiest craft to row are long, relatively narrow dinghies, which are stable in the water. The worst are inflatables, which are flat bottomed and badly affected by wind. You will need the longest oars that can be used with the boat and a pair of oarlocks or crutches, which slot into plates on the gunwales and act as pivot points for the oars. Remove oarlocks when alongside a boat or dock, or else they may cause damage.

There are some basic points to bear in mind when rowing. To come alongside another boat or a dock, you must turn parallel to it and then detach the inboard oar so that it does not get trapped or broken. As soon as the boat is secured, detach the other oar. If you are rowing in choppy water, the blades may get caught by the waves as you swing them forward. To reduce this problem, feather them (turn them so that they are parallel to the water's surface) as you complete the stroke.

## SCULLING

Sculling involves moving the boat by using a single oar over the transom. The sculling oar is retained in an oarlock, or in a sculling notch cut into the transom. If rowing is an art, then sculling is sublime. Little is more striking than watching an experienced boatman sculling a dinghy with casual aplomb. Sculling is best learned in a heavy dinghy when there is no wind or waves. It is one of those skills that seem to be impossible at first, but that simply require some dedicated practice before you are rewarded with a great sense of achievement.

## PADDLING

With many dinghies, the most convenient alternative to sailing is paddling. Paddles take up less room than oars and do not need oarlocks. Paddling requires relatively little skill, but bear the following points in mind for increased efficiency: keep your arms straight as you pull on the paddle, lean well forward to put the paddle into the water, and use your torso rather than just your arms to provide the power for each stroke.

## HOW TO ROW

*Sit on the thwart in the middle of the boat facing the stern. If you have one passenger, he should sit in the stern. If you have several passengers, position them to keep the dinghy level.*

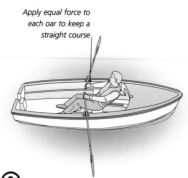

Lean forward, keeping your arms straight and your hands low

Apply equal force to each oar to keep a straight course

**1** Place your hands a shoulder-width apart and lean forward. Then, dip the oars into the water so that the blades are at right angles to the surface.

**2** Lean back, pulling on the oars and keeping your arms straight. As you lean fully back, bend your arms in to your chest to complete the stroke.

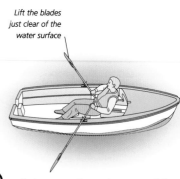

Lift the blades just clear of the water surface

**3** Push down gently on the oars to lift the blades clear of the water, then lean aft, swinging the oars forward clear of the water, and repeat steps 1 and 2.

## HOW TO SCULL

*To scull, stand upright in the dinghy facing aft, with your legs apart so that you are balanced. The basic sculling stroke is a figure eight made from side to side across the stern. Place passengers in the middle of the boat.*

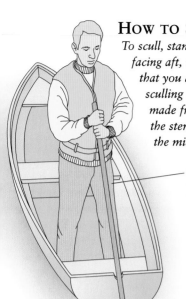

**Sculler**
*Stand at the stern, legs apart*

① Hold the oar with both hands, thumbs underneath, at shoulder level. Make sure the blade is vertical and fully immersed; the oar should be balanced, its weight taken by the sculling notch or oarlock.

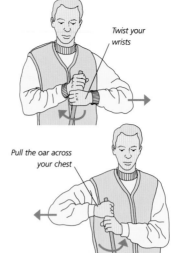

*Twist your wrists*

*Pull the oar across your chest*

② Twist the oar so that the blade is slanted to one side then move your hands sideways – in the opposite direction to the way the oar blade is slanted.

③ At the end of the stroke, roll your wrists to twist the blade in the opposite direction and move your hands toward the other side.

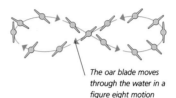

*The oar blade moves through the water in a figure eight motion*

④ Repeat steps 2 and 3 to keep the boat moving forward. The motion of the blade through the water should be smooth and steady throughout the stroke.

## HOW TO PADDLE

If you are alone, you can paddle facing forward, with the sails down and rudder stowed or held against your knee (*below*). Alternatively, paddle stern first, kneeling at the transom, and make drawing strokes that pull the boat backward. With two people, either both can paddle, or else one person can steer using the rudder while the other paddles – the paddler sits forward, on the opposite side to the helmsman.

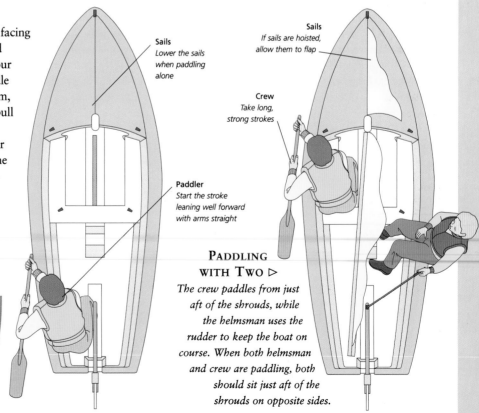

**Sails**
*Lower the sails when paddling alone*

**Sails**
*If sails are hoisted, allow them to flap*

**Crew**
*Take long, strong strokes*

**Paddler**
*Start the stroke leaning well forward with arms straight*

**PADDLING ALONE ▷**
*Sit well aft. Move the paddle through the water, turning the blade away from the side of the boat at the end of the stroke. This helps prevent the boat turning away from the paddle – an effect that can also be reduced by lowering the centerboard or daggerboard.*

**PADDLING WITH TWO ▷**
*The crew paddles from just aft of the shrouds, while the helmsman uses the rudder to keep the boat on course. When both helmsman and crew are paddling, both should sit just aft of the shrouds on opposite sides.*

# MOVING SMALL BOATS

*The majority of small boats are kept on shore between sailing trips as they are not stable enough to be left on moorings and would be vulnerable to damage if left afloat. They are easily transported between venues on a car trailer or roof rack. However, the boat is most vulnerable to damage when it is on land so it is important to know how to move it safely. Learning a few basic lifting and moving techniques will also protect you from personal accidents and injuries.*

### ROAD TRAILERS

The road trailer should be designed for the boat, with plenty of chocks and rollers to provide adequate support. Over-run brakes, which cut in when the car brakes, should be fitted to the trailer if it has to carry a heavy dinghy or keelboat. Always ensure that the boat is securely attached before driving off. Tie the mast and any other removable equipment to the boat or the trailer.

Some road trailers have an integral launching cart that rides on top of the trailer when the boat is transported on the road. The boat sits on the cart, which is loaded and unloaded by lifting the cart handles and wheeling it onto or off the trailer from the back.

### ROOF RACKS

Smaller and lighter dinghies are usually transported on a roof rack, which should be sturdy and securely attached to the vehicle. Pad the rack and ropes to prevent damage to the boat. It is usually best to carry the boat inverted on the rack with the bow facing forward. Tie it securely to the rack, or strong points on the car, using rope or straps. Lash the mast and boom to the roof rack, alongside the boat, and stow all other removable equipment in the car.

### ROLLERS

Solid or inflatable rollers are a good alternative to carts or trailers for short trips across beaches or up to boat parks. They are particularly useful for moving heavy boats across sand or shingle. At least three rollers

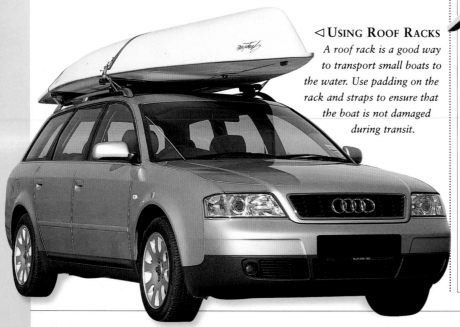

◁ **USING ROOF RACKS**
*A roof rack is a good way to transport small boats to the water. Use padding on the rack and straps to ensure that the boat is not damaged during transit.*

---

### LIFTING A BOAT

Dinghies can be heavy and awkward to lift – several pairs of willing hands make much lighter work of it. Some dinghies have lifting handles, but with most you will have to grasp the inside or outside edges of the sidedecks.

*Place the boat at an angle to the car*

**1** First turn the boat over. Make sure that the bow is facing forward before leaning the boat gently against the back of the car.

*Then slide the boat on from the back*

**2** Slide or lift the boat onto the rack either from the side or from behind the car, depending on which is easiest with your vehicle.

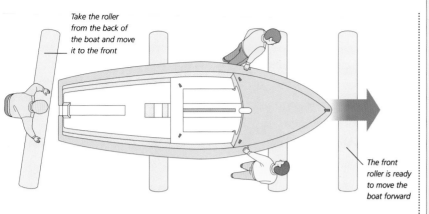

*Take the roller from the back of the boat and move it to the front*

*The front roller is ready to move the boat forward*

### △ USING ROLLERS

*At least three people and three rollers are needed to roll a boat smoothly. Place each in turn under the bow of the boat then roll the boat forward, removing each roller as it appears at the stern.*

are required. They are placed under the bow and the boat is pushed over them. Each roller is retrieved as it reappears behind the stern, and it is then brought around in front of the bow to continue the movement until the destination is reached.

### LAUNCHING TRAILERS

A launching trailer is the usual means of moving a dinghy from the boat park to the water, and it is often used to store dinghies on the shore. Before

moving a boat (or storing it) on its trailer ensure that it is sitting correctly on the chocks and that it is tied securely with its painter to the trailer handle. The ease with which your trailer moves depends on the type of wheels. Small solid wheels work well only on hard surfaces. If you need to launch across a beach, choose larger wheels, preferably with inflatable tires.

To launch the boat, push the trailer into the water until the boat floats off. Make sure that someone keeps hold of the painter. Take the trailer above the high-water mark, out of the way of others. Reverse this procedure to bring the boat ashore, tying the boat to the trailer handle and making sure that it is on its chocks before pulling it out of the water.

### ◁ INTEGRAL TRAILER

*Designed to transport a small Laser dinghy, this road trailer has an integral launching trailer. The launching trailer has been built with a lightweight metal frame for ease of handling. This model has solid rubber wheels.*

## AVOIDING DAMAGE

A boat is most likely to be damaged when it is being transported on land, or when it is being launched or recovered from the water. Most damage can be avoided by following a few simple rules.

### WHILE LAUNCHING
When you are launching the boat using a trailer, always push the trailer into the water until you can float the boat off. Never drag the boat off the trailer as this will scratch the hull. Similarly, when recovering, float the boat onto the trailer rather than dragging it on.

### WHILE ON LAND
Avoid stepping into a dinghy while it is on shore or on its launching trailer. Without the support of the water underneath it, the bottom of the boat may be deformed or broken by your weight.

### WHILE CARRYING
You will need at least four people to carry an average dinghy. Most of the weight is concentrated in the front part of the boat, so, if you need to carry it over any distance, make sure you distribute the lifting power accordingly.

### WHILE MOVING
Always look up before you move boats to check that your tall aluminum or carbon fiber mast is not about to become entangled with a high-voltage cable. People have been electrocuted when moving their boats, so be aware of your surroundings.

### WHILE NOT IN USE
Whenever you leave the boat for any length of time, clean and dry the sails and all other equipment and stow everything neatly, then cover the boat to protect it from the elements (*pp.104–105*).

# STAYING CLEAR OF OTHERS

*Every type of craft on the water, from the smallest dinghy to the biggest supertanker, is governed by the International Regulations for Preventing Collisions at Sea, often referred to as the "Col Regs" or "the rules of the road." Additional rules, the US Yacht Racing rules, govern boats when racing, but the Col Regs always take precedence. The full rules are complex and cover every eventuality, but when you start sailing you need to know only the basic rules covered here.*

## KEEPING CLEAR

Keep a careful watch around and try to anticipate the actions of others. Remember to look astern regularly – novices are often startled by unseen overtaking boats. When it is your responsibility to keep clear, it is important that you do so in plenty of time. Make a large alteration to your course so that your intentions are obvious to the other vessel, and pass astern rather than ahead of it. When you are underway, keep a safe distance from boats at anchor or on a mooring. Always give boats fishing or trawling a wide berth to avoid the possibility of becoming entangled in nets or lines.

When one vessel is in the process of overtaking another, the overtaking boat must keep clear until completely passed, even if it is a sailing boat that is overtaking a powered vessel.

## NEGOTIATING CHANNELS

When proceeding along a channel or fairway, all boats should stay close to the starboard side of the channel in whichever direction they are going. Avoid crossing busy channels or shipping lanes. If you must do so, always cross as nearly as possible at a right-angle to the traffic flow. Do not pass close in front of vessels that are moving along the channel and make sure that you complete the crossing as quickly as possible.

## GIVING WAY

In general terms, a power vessel gives way to a sailing vessel. However, in practice, this is not always the case. For example, the rule does not apply to large ships in confined waters, which are usually restricted in their ability to maneuver. Fishing boats are

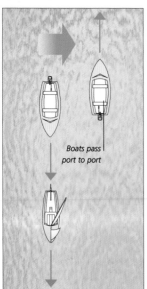

△ **CHANNEL RULES**
*All vessels, whether under sail or power, must stay close to the starboard side of channels so that they pass port to port.*

Boats pass port to port

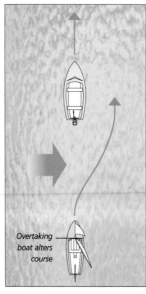

△ **OVERTAKING RULE**
*An overtaking vessel must keep clear of the one being passed even if it is a sailing boat that is overtaking a power boat.*

Overtaking boat alters course

### STARBOARD-TACK RULE

A sailing boat that is on starboard tack (with the boom to port) has the right of way over a boat on port tack. A boat on port tack (with the boom to starboard) must give way to a starboard-tack boat. When you first start sailing it is sometimes difficult to remember which tack you are on. Solve this problem by marking the boom as shown below.

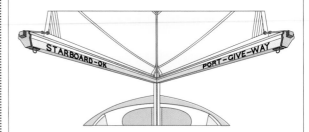

△ **MARKING YOUR BOOM**
*Mark your boom "Starboard – OK" on the starboard side and "Port – Give Way" on the port side. This will serve as a reminder to which tack you are on and the give-way rule that applies.*

# AVOIDING COLLISIONS

Whenever two boats – whether under sail or power – meet in a potential collision situation, there is a rule that specifies which one has right of way. The boat with right of way, known as the "stand-on" vessel, must maintain its course, while the other boat, known as the "give-way" vessel, is obliged to keep clear.

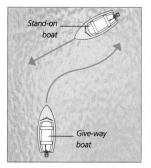

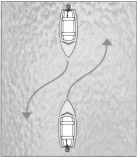

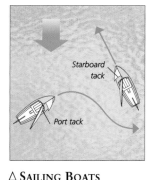

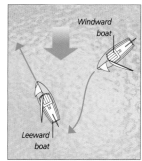

△ **POWER BOATS CROSSING**
*The boat on the other vessel's starboard side has right of way, so the give-way boat alters course to pass behind it.*

△ **POWER BOATS HEAD-ON**
*When power boats meet head on both must give way – by steering to starboard so as to pass port to port.*

△ **SAILING BOATS ON OPPOSITE TACKS**
*The boat on the port tack alters its course to pass behind the boat on the starboard tack.*

△ **SAILING BOATS ON THE SAME TACK**
*The windward boat must keep clear and steers to pass behind the leeward boat.*

also a special case and you must keep clear of them. Large ships may have a blind spot under their bows, where a dinghy will be hidden. In such circumstances, it is the responsibility of the small boat sailor to get out of the way as quickly as possible.

In a narrow channel, such as on the approach to a marina, even a small yacht under power may not have enough room to alter course, so dinghies should keep clear. In fact, unless the power vessel is about the same size as your boat, it is always best to stay out of its way. Remember, too, that a dinghy under oars is classed as a power-driven vessel and must keep clear of sailing boats.

**IN A CHANNEL ▷**
*In some sailing areas dinghies and yachts share the same waters as large vessels. If crossing a channel, pass behind ships and give them as wide a berth as possible.*

# WEATHER BASICS

*The most important factor to take into consideration when you go sailing is the weather, especially the strength and direction of the wind. Once you are on the water, the complexity of the weather – how quickly it can change, and how variable the wind direction and strength can be – may surprise you if you are not used to sailing. You need to be able to recognize onshore and offshore winds because they determine the ease or difficulty of leaving and returning to shore, as well as conditions further out.*

### WEATHER FORECASTS

Always check the weather forecast before you sail. Although forecasts are available from many different sources, not all will give specific information on wind conditions, so it is advisable to use a sailing forecast that covers your area in as much detail as possible. In ports or harbors, the offices of the harbormaster often display the local forecast. Sailing clubs may also provide forecasts. At clubs, you can also seek information and advice from more experienced sailors with extensive local knowledge. Always bear in mind your sailing capabilities and the limitations of your experience. If in doubt, stay ashore.

### WIND DIRECTION

It is always more pleasant to sail in warm sunshine than cold drizzle, but neither temperature nor rain are critical to sailing. The wind, on the other hand, is vital, and you should constantly be aware of its direction and strength. Check it before you go afloat, and continue to monitor it once you have set sail.

### WIND INDICATORS

As you gain experience, you will find that you automatically register wind direction by the feel of it on your face. Until this becomes second nature, however, you must try to estimate the wind direction and force by studying all available signs. Look at the wind indicator at the top of your mast, if fitted, or those on other boats, and study the movement of flags ashore. Smoke from chimneys will blow in the direction of the wind, and the angle of the smoke will give an indication of its strength. Moored boats will often point into the wind, but remember to take into account any tides or currents.

Bear in mind that the wind shifts very frequently even if the weather is apparently stable, and it can be bent from its true direction by trees, tall buildings, or hills. A river valley will often affect the wind, causing it to blow up or down the river.

### OFFSHORE WIND

When you are planning a sailing trip, do not underestimate the strength of a wind that is offshore (blowing from

◁ **STRONG WINDS**
*Wind strength can increase quickly and dramatically, and its force can easily cause damage such as torn sails. Be prepared for conditions to change when you are afloat.*

# WIND STRENGTH

Learn to recognize when it is safe to set sail by studying the Beaufort Scale, which indicates the strength of the wind and describes its visual effects. For initial outings, a force three is the ideal wind strength. Seven to ten knots will fill the sails but will be gentle enough to allow you to keep control of your vessel. Anything less than a force three will cause the boat to move slowly and lack responsiveness; anything more and beginners should be wary about going out. A force six is a dinghy-sailor's gale; only experienced crews should sail in winds that can reach 27 knots.

| FORCE | DESCRIPTION | EFFECTS ON SEA | SIGNS ON LAND | WIND SPEED |
|---|---|---|---|---|
| 0 | Calm | Mirror-smooth water. Dinghies tend to drift rather than sail. | Smoke rises vertically and flags hang limp. | Less than 1 knot |
| 1 | Light Air | Ripples on water. Sufficient wind to maintain motion. | Smoke drifts slightly, indicating wind direction. | 1–3 knots |
| 2 | Light Breeze | Small wavelets with smooth crests. Sufficient wind to sail steadily but upright. Wind can be felt on the face. | Light flags and wind vanes respond with small movements. Leaves rustle. | 4–6 knots |
| 3 | Gentle Breeze | Large wavelets with crests starting to break. Ideal conditions for learning to sail a dinghy. | Light flags extend outward, and leaves and small twigs are set in motion. | 7–10 knots |
| 4 | Moderate Breeze | Small waves with fairly frequent white horses. The crew will be working hard. Boats plane easily. Beginners should head for shore. | Small branches move on trees, and dust and paper are lifted off the ground by the breeze. | 11–15 knots |
| 5 | Fresh Breeze | Moderate waves with frequent white horses. Ideal conditions if experienced; otherwise, capsizes are common. | Small trees sway visibly and the tops of all trees are in motion. | 16–21 knots |
| 6 | Strong Breeze | Large waves start to form and spray is likely. This is a dinghy-sailor's gale. Only experienced crews with good safety cover should race. | Large trees sway and the wind whistles in telephone wires. It becomes difficult to use an umbrella. | 22–27 knots |

the land across the shore and out over the water). Offshore winds can be quite misleading as there is likely to be a calm patch close to the shore, but beyond this the wind will be stronger and the waves much larger. If you set sail in an offshore wind and then discover that the weather conditions are more severe further out, you may experience difficulties returning home.

## ONSHORE WIND
When the wind is onshore (blowing from the water toward the shore), you will feel its full force and waves may break on the shoreline. Onshore winds bring different sailing challenges. Attempting to launch the boat and leave the shore through breaking waves can be difficult with the wind against you. However, away from the beach the waves should calm down. You will also find that it is easier to return home in an onshore wind.

# INLAND OR SEA?

Whether you sail on inland waters or on the ocean depends on the type of sailing you want to do, as well as on where you live. Learning to sail is usually easier and safer on inland waters, but once you have some experience you will probably want to be more adventurous and try ocean sailing. Wherever you learn to sail, it is important for both your safety and your enjoyment that you have an understanding of tides and how they affect sailing at sea and on inland waterways.

## INLAND WATERS

Inland waters vary from small lakes and reservoirs, which are often made from flooded gravel pits, to more significant stretches of water, such as large lakes and wide rivers. If the stretch of water is new to you, remember to find out in advance whether you need permission to sail there. Look out for bylaw notices on the banks and shorelines.

All types of inland waters have their own characteristics and potential hazards, so ask for advice at a local sailing club before you go afloat. If you plan to sail without safety cover on a large stretch of inland water make sure that someone on the shore knows your plans before you set sail. Look for bridges and overhead power lines that may be lower than the mast, and check for notices that indicate weirs or locks.

The rules of the road (pp.43–44) apply wherever you are sailing. In constricted waters, such as a narrow river or small lake, you may find that the sailing conditions are congested, which will test your maneuvering skills. When you are sailing on a river, be aware that you are likely to have to contend with a current as the water flows downstream towards the sea. On some rivers these can get very strong, especially if there has been heavy rain upstream. Some rivers, especially large ones, also have a tidal flow that may reach some way inland from the sea.

## TIDES

Tides are vertical movements of the water due to the gravitational attraction of celestial bodies (primarily the moon) on the earth's surface.

Gravitational pull is strongest on the water surface closest to the moon

C   B   A

MOON

EARTH

◁ GRAVITATIONAL PULL
The gravitational pull of the moon (strengthened or weakened by that of the sun) attracts the water on the near side (A), the earth itself (B), and the water on the far side (C) by decreasing amounts. This pull causes two bulges, on opposite sides of the planet. We experience these bulges as tides.

The horizontal movement of water produced by the tides is called a tidal stream. This flows along coasts and up and down estuaries and rivers. When the tide is rising, the stream is said to be flooding; when it is falling, the stream is said to be ebbing. Flood tides run up rivers and estuaries while ebb tides run back toward the sea. The speed of the tidal stream is affected by the difference in the height of the water surface between low tide and high tide. It runs much faster during spring tides than during neaps, and is at its strongest during the third and fourth hours of the flood or ebb.

## SEA SAILING

If you are planning to sail at sea, make sure that you are conversant with all the relevant tidal information. Details about the times of high and low water can be found in a local tide table, and a tidal atlas for your area will show the direction of the stream for each hour of the tidal cycle.

Remember that when a tidal stream flows through deep channels or around headlands it is at its strongest. If it is constricted in any way, such as by a headland, an uneven bottom, or rapidly shoaling water, then you can expect tidal races, eddies, and overfalls. Stay away from these in a small boat, especially if the wind is strong or is blowing against the stream. It will be apparent when the wind blows in opposition to a tidal stream, as it will kick up waves that are bigger and steeper than you would otherwise expect. When the tide turns to run with the wind, these waves will quickly die down again.

When you are sailing in tidal waters, always make sure that someone ashore knows your plans, and store an anchor aboard so that you have the option of anchoring in shallow water if the wind drops or if you get into difficulties.

# THE CAUSES OF TIDES

Tides are caused by the moon's gravitational pull (and to a lesser extent that of the sun) on the surface of the water. The combined influence of these two celestial bodies determines tidal ranges.

## TIDAL RANGES

The gravitational pull of the moon and the sun produces two high tides and two low tides in most places every day. The difference in height between a low tide and the next high tide is called the tidal range.

## SPRING AND NEAP TIDES

The juxtaposition of the sun and moon affects the height of the tides at different times of the month. At the times of a full and new moon, when the sun, earth, and moon are in line, the gravitational pull is largest. This causes spring tides, with the largest range between high and low tides. When the moon is in its first and last quarters, the sun, earth, and moon are at right angles to each other and cause neap tides, with the smallest range between high and low water. The strength of tidal streams depends on the range, so expect strong streams at springs and weaker ones at neaps.

### SPRING TIDES ▷

*During spring tides, which are associated with the new moon and the full moon, there is a significantly larger difference between the water's height at low tide and high tide.*

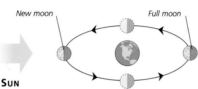

*New moon*      *Full moon*

**SUN**

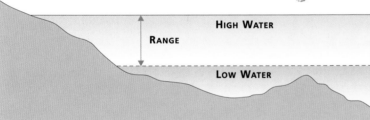

HIGH WATER

RANGE

LOW WATER

### NEAP TIDES ▷

*During neap tides, which are associated with the first quarter of the moon and the last quarter, the height of the water's surface changes least between low and high tide.*

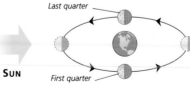

*Last quarter*

**SUN**    *First quarter*

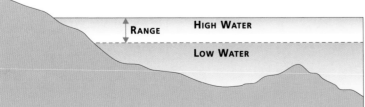

RANGE    HIGH WATER

LOW WATER

# TIDE INDICATORS

When you are sailing in tidal waters it is important to know when the tide turns. When the tidal stream runs in your favor it is easy to make progress over the ground, but if it runs against you, progress may be slow or impossible until the tide turns.

## CHECKING THE DIRECTION

One of the easiest ways of checking the direction of the tidal stream is to look at boats at anchor or on a mooring. They will usually point into the stream, unless they have a shallow draft (like dinghies or motor boats), in which case they are more likely to lie head-to-wind, especially if the wind is strong. Look at deep-keeled cruisers for an accurate indication of the tidal stream. The tide also flows around buoys and posts, or any other fixed object in the water, and reveals its direction and strength by the wake that streams downtide of the object.

△ BUOY

*Buoys are very useful indicators of the direction of a tidal stream as they often lean away from the direction of the stream, especially if it is strong. A tidal stream also produces a wake or bow wave as the water sweeps past the buoy.*

# SAILING DINGHIES

..............................................................

DINGHIES OFFER THE BEST introduction to sailing
because they are so responsive to wind and
waves and to your actions on the tiller and
sheets. General-purpose sailing dinghies are
ideal for learning the basics about rigging and
launching, experiencing the different roles of the
helmsman and crew, and becoming proficient
in all the important sailing maneuvers.

..............................................................

*Even simple dinghies, such as this single-hander,
can offer exciting and rewarding sailing. They are
relatively cheap to buy, and easy to rig and sail.*

# CHOOSING A DINGHY

*There are literally hundreds of different types of dinghies on the market. They are available in a huge variety of designs for a wide range of sailing activities, from relaxed day-cruising to highly competitive racing. Most modern dinghies are built with strong, lightweight materials, and many offer tremendous performance potential while requiring little maintenance. You are bound to find at least one that will suit your level of skill, experience, and sailing ambitions, as well as your finances.*

### FIRST STEPS

General-purpose boats are usually the most appropriate type of dinghy when you are first learning to sail. These boats are relatively stable, so any mistakes are easier to rectify without mishap than they would be in a sensitive high-performance dinghy. Most sailing clubs and schools use general-purpose dinghies for teaching because they often have enough space for an instructor and two students.

### EXPANDING YOUR HORIZONS

Once you have progressed and are sailing confidently, you will probably consider buying your own boat. As the choice is so vast, it is best to draw up a detailed short list of your specific requirements. For a start, think about where you are going to do most of your sailing and what type of sailing you want to do. High-performance racing boats (*pp.110–111*) are fun and exciting to sail, but they are not suitable for family outings or for use with oars or an outboard motor. If you want to race, make sure you choose a boat that is popular where you are going to do your sailing, and check that there is a good fleet in which to start racing.

Do not pick a high-performance boat until you have the experience to handle it. Many general-purpose

sailing dinghies have racing fleets and are a good option to start racing. If you are unsure as to whether you are ready to race your own boat, consider crewing for someone else in order to gain experience and develop skills.

If you want to day sail or cruise, choose a strong and stable boat that is specifically designed for this type of sailing – a boat with plenty of space for additional people and equipment.

### JOINING A CLUB

You will need to join a club in order to race. In fact, it is well worth joining one anyway, before buying your own boat, because this will enable you to meet more experienced sailors who will usually have sailed in a range of dinghies. Crewing for club members in as wide a range of boats as possible is a very good way of adding to your sailing experience at low cost.

### BUYING A SAILING DINGHY

List the boats that seem suitable and arrange to have trial sails to assess their merits. If the manufacturer cannot organize this, contact the class association who will be able to help you arrange a sail with an existing owner. If you are buying secondhand, ask an experienced owner to check the boat and advise you on its condition.

---

## HULL SHAPE

The shape of the hull seen from behind is a good indication of the purpose for which the dinghy is designed. A flat, shallow, usually rounded hull shape, indicates that the dinghy is intended for high-performance sailing and racing. Deeper and heavier hulls are more often used for general-purpose boats that are ideal for beginners.

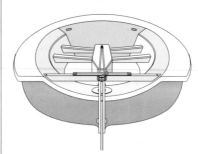

△ **ROUND-BILGE HULL**
*If the hull is shallow, usually with a round bilge (curved shape), it is probably meant for racing. The shallower the hull the more likely it is to be designed for speed.*

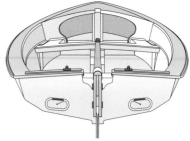

△ **DOUBLE-CHINE HULL**
*If the hull is deep, the boat is likely to have been designed as a general-purpose dinghy. Also, general-purpose hulls often have one or two chines (angled, flat panels).*

# TYPES OF BOATS

There is a wide range of sailing dinghies that are suitable for beginners and recreational sailing, as well as a varied selection for single-handed sailing or specifically for children and young adults. Although not necessarily designed for racing, there is no reason why a general-purpose boat cannot be raced; indeed, many of the popular classes have good racing fleets. Small day sailing keelboats are not classed as dinghies as they have weighted keels. However, they offer dinghy-like sailing with much less risk of capsize.

## GENERAL-PURPOSE DINGHIES

**WAYFARER**

The Wayfarer is a classic general-purpose dinghy. Although it is heavier than most dinghies when handled ashore, it is large and stable enough to be kept afloat on a mooring. There is competitive class racing, and some Wayfarers have cruised across oceans.

**ENTERPRISE**

The popular Enterprise, with its distinctive blue sails, is smaller and lighter than the Wayfarer. It is still large enough for day-sailing with the family, however, and it is easier to handle ashore. The Enterprise is an international class, and it is very popular for racing.

**MIRROR**

The Mirror is a two-handed boat that can also be sailed single-handed, rowed, or used with an outboard motor. It is suitable for older children and adults. It has red sails and its rig includes a spinnaker. The Mirror is an international class.

## SMALL KEELBOATS

**FLYING FIFTEEN**

The Flying Fifteen is a small, open keelboat intended for day sailing and racing. It has a weighted keel so that it is not reliant on crew weight to keep it upright, yet it is light enough to plane. It has a mainsail, jib, and spinnaker, and is a popular, international class.

## BOATS FOR CHILDREN

**OPTIMIST**

The Optimist, often known as the "Oppie", is a favourite for children. A small, light single-hander with a simple rig, it is ideal for starting to sail and developing talents on the race course. It is raced very competitively all over the world and is an international class.

**BLUE JAY**

The Blue Jay is designed to be sailed by two children. It is rigged with a mainsail, jib, and spinnaker. It is an international class that has strong racing fleets. The Blue Jay is an excellent youth-training boat that has introduced many sailors to the pleasures of racing.

**TOPPER**

The Topper is an extremely popular, international single-hander, which is particularly suitable for children. It is generally used as a fun boat, but it can also be raced in highly competitive fleets. The Topper is built from molded plastic, and it is virtually indestructible.

## BOATS FOR YOUNG ADULTS

**420**

The 420 is an international class that is ideal both for beginners and for more experienced young sailors starting to race. It is recognized as the leading youth race-training dinghy. The 420 provides a good introduction to the use of a trapeze and a spinnaker.

# PROTECTIVE DINGHY GEAR

*When you sail in dinghies, you are very exposed to the elements, so it is important for your comfort to wear clothing that keeps you warm. Although the choice of what to wear is very wide, there are only two basic approaches. One is to wear a drysuit or foul weather gear over warm clothing, the other is to wear a wetsuit. It is inevitable that you will sometimes find yourself in the water, so it is also vital that you have a buoyancy aid to help keep you afloat if you capsize.*

## STARTING OFF

If you learn to sail at a sailing club or school, you will probably be provided with a buoyancy aid and foul weather gear. Casual or sports clothing will suffice underneath, and you can wear boatshoes on your feet. Once you start to sail your own boat, you will want to invest in some specialized clothing.

## DRYSUITS

A drysuit has latex seals at the neck, wrist, and feet to keep all water away from the body. They are generally made as one-piece suits, but two-piece versions are available. To control body temperature when wearing a drysuit, you need to take care when choosing the clothing you wear underneath. Shorts and a T-shirt often suffice in warm weather, but you will need thin, thermal clothing in colder conditions.

## FOUL WEATHER GEAR

If you choose foul weather gear, you have to decide between a one-piece suit and a separate jacket and pants. A one-piece suit is usually preferred for dinghy racing as it has fewer water entry points, but separates allow you to wear the jacket or pants alone when required and so may be more useful if you are sailing for recreation. Foul weather gear is usually made with an outer layer of nylon for extra strength, and an inner, waterproof layer that is bonded to the nylon. The waterproof layer might be PVC, which is fairly cheap, or a breathable fabric like Gore-Tex, which will be considerably more expensive. However, breathable fabrics do offer far superior performance, allowing water vapor and perspiration to escape rather than accumulate and eventually soak your clothing.

## WETSUITS

When you are likely to be soaked, a wetsuit offers you a means of staying warm without worrying about how to stay dry. Wetsuits are made from neoprene and are tailored to be very close fitting. When you get wet, a thin layer of water is trapped between your skin and the neoprene. This is quickly warmed up by your body heat to insulate you from the cold.

Different weights of neoprene are used for summer and winter sailing. Choose a weight that is most suited to the climate that you sail in.

## BUOYANCY AIDS

Buoyancy aids – as opposed to lifejackets – are the usual choice for dinghy sailors, especially for racing and inland sailing. They are available in a variety of designs to suit all shapes and sizes.

### CHOOSING A BUOYANCY AID

Ensure that the buoyancy aid that you choose is of a type that is approved by your national standards authority. Also, make sure that the size of the buoyancy aid is suitable for your body weight. A range of styles is available to suit all types of dinghy sailing and small-boat activity, with special sizes available for children (and even for pets). Try the buoyancy aid on before you commit to buying; check that it fits comfortably over your wetsuit, foul weather gear, or drysuit. Choose a bright color that will be clearly visible from a distance.

◁ **SLEEVELESS STYLE**

**Closed-cell foam**
*Provides a minimum of 50 Newtons (5kg/11lb) buoyancy*

**Waist belt**
*Always fasten and tighten the waist belt for security*

**VEST STYLE** ▷

**SAILING GEAR**

Once you have decided to purchase your own set of sailing clothing, it is advisable to buy good-quality items that fit you properly. Do not forget accessories, such as gloves, hats, and boots. They are just as important as the clothing because they protect your extremities from injury and the cold.

Peaked cap
*A peak shields your face from the sun*

△ **HAT**
*A hat keeps the sun off, and, in colder conditions, reduces heat loss.*

Joints
*Flexible joints allow easier movement*

Latex collar
*A soft latex collar forms a close seal to keep the water out*

Cuffs
*Latex cuffs stop water getting in*

△ **GLOVES**
*The best sailing gloves have reinforced palms and fingers for gripping rope securely – even when wet – and protecting the hands.*

△ **WETSUIT**
*A wetsuit with full sleeves and legs provides the maximum protection. Choose a good quality, well-fitting suit to ensure that you stay warm throughout your sail.*

Non-slip sole
*A razor-cut tread improves grip on wet surfaces*

Ankles
*Velcro and fabric tabs reduce damage to the latex seals*

Enclosed feet
*Latex socks totally seal the drysuit around the feet*

**DINGHY BOOTS** ▷
*Boots made from neoprene and with molded soles are ideal for sailing because they keep your feet warm and dry, and provide good grip.*

Reinforced instep
*This stops the dinghy toe rails from rubbing*

△ **DRYSUIT**
*An all-in-one drysuit has close-fitting latex cuffs, collar, and feet, which are designed to form a waterproof seal, thus keeping the wearer dry.*

# RIGGING THE BOAT

*Before going afloat you must rig the boat, which involves fully preparing it for sailing. This is usually done in the park before moving the dinghy to water. If it is stored in the launch area or kept afloat on a mooring, the mast is usually left in place. However, if you have transported the boat to the sailing area, you will need to step the mast and attach and adjust the standing rigging before the sails can be hoisted. Once the mast and rigging are in place, the boom is placed in the boat. The sails are then rigged, and all the running rigging (sheets, halyards, and control lines) are attached and checked to ensure that they are led correctly. Finally, you should collect any other gear you need to take on the water and stow it securely.*

## UNSTAYED MASTS

Boats that have unstayed masts (*pp.130–31*) are usually stored without their mast, particularly if the mainsail is attached to the mast via a sleeve (the sleeve slides down the mast and the sail can be removed or attached only when the mast is unstepped).

Unstayed masts are often made in two sections that are slotted together. The sail is fitted to the mast, which is then lifted vertically and lowered into the mast step. There is normally a locking arrangement fitted in the step, which is used to secure the mast in place. Alternatively, a rope downhaul or cunningham line is used to secure the sail and mast to the boat.

## STAYED MASTS

Stayed masts can be stepped either on deck or on the keel. In either case, a mast step is attached to the boat to accept the mast's heel fitting. With keel-stepped masts, the fore-and-aft position of the step can sometimes be adjusted to allow alterations to the mast position and rake (lean). In both cases, the mast is supported by wires, called standing rigging, which are attached to the mast at the hounds and to the boat at the chainplates. The shrouds brace the mast to port and starboard. They run through the ends of the spreaders, which are attached to the mast at about mid-height. Shroud tension is adjusted with a rigging link or bottlescrew. The forestay, which runs from the hounds to the bow-fitting, prevents the mast from falling backward. It is usually adjusted with a rigging link.

## STEPPING THE MAST

Before you attempt to step the mast, make sure that it will not hit any overhead obstructions such as power cables when you lift it into place. It is quite often possible to step the mast on small boats on your own, but the job is much easier, and much safer, with two people. Although most dinghy masts are light in weight, their length and windage (resistance to the wind) can make them unwieldy to lift in and out of the boat. It helps to have the boat on its trailer in a bow-down position so that the mast will lean forward against the support of the shrouds when it is placed in its step. Make sure that the tails of all halyards and other rope ends are tied out of the way so that they cannot be trapped under the mast heel. When you are lifting the mast, keep it as close to vertical as possible and position your hands quite wide apart on it to give better leverage.

## RAKING THE MAST

Once you have stepped the mast, you may need to adjust the shrouds and forestay to get the correct rake of the mast. Most boats sail best with their masts raked aft slightly (typically with the mast head about 2in (6cm) aft of the gooseneck), but the mast must always be upright in a sideways direction. In general-purpose boats the amount of rake is not too critical; however, if you progress to racing dinghies, you will need to set precisely the correct measurement for top-performance sailing.

◁ **STEPPING AN UNSTAYED MAST**
*With the sail sleeved over the mast from the top, the mast is lifted into a vertical position and lowered into the mast step. Place your hands some distance apart on the mast to give more leverage.*

# STEPPING A STAYED MAST

## KEEL STEPPING

*Boats with keel-stepped masts are usually quite easy to step because the mast heel can be positioned into its step before it is pulled into the upright position. Once the mast is in the mast gate, it is held quite securely.*

**Mast Step**
*Locate the heel in the mast step*

**Forestay**
*Pull on the forestay until the mast is upright*

**KEEL FITTING**

**Forestay**
*Fasten the forestay to the bow-fitting*

**Shrouds**
*Attach the shrouds to the chainplates*

**①** Lay the mast and rigging on the boat, with the mast heel resting on the mast step and with the front side of the mast uppermost. Attach the two shrouds to the chainplates on the sidedecks.

**②** As one person lifts the mast and positions the heel into the mast step, the other pulls on the forestay. The person supporting the mast guides it into the mast gate.

**③** Attach the forestay and close the deck-level mast gate. Check the mast rake. Make sure that the halyards are not twisted around the rigging, and ensure that they are led correctly to their respective cleats.

## DECK STEPPING

*Deck-stepped masts do not have the additional support of a mast gate. They must be lifted vertically before being fitted into the mast step, and have less support until all the rigging is secured.*

**MAST STEP**

**Mast**
*Slot the mast into the recessed fitting in the foredeck*

**③** Allow the mast to lean forward, held by the shrouds, and attach the forestay to the bow-fitting. Next, adjust the shrouds and forestay to get the desired rake. Finally, ensure that the halyards are not twisted and that they are led correctly to their respective cleats.

**Mast**
*Lay the mast alongside the boat*

**Mast**
*Lean the mast forward to attach the forestay*

**①** Lay the mast on the ground next to the boat with the aft side uppermost and the top toward the bow.

**②** Attach the shrouds to the chainplates and stand the mast alongside the boat then lift it vertically until it can be stepped.

# RIGGING THE JIB

Rigging the jib is a one-man job that is usually carried out by the crew, who is responsible for handling the sail. It is always good practice to check the sail for damage as you unfold it and while you are attaching it to the boat. In particular, check the corners and seams for worn or frayed stitching.

## JIB FITTINGS

Some jibs are built with a wire sewn into the luff to take the high loads that are imposed on this edge of the sail. Others have a rope or high-strength tape sewn into the luff. If a luff wire is kinked it is weakened, and broken strands can tear the sail.

The jib is rigged by attaching the tack to the bow-fitting using a shackle or lashing. The luff is then attached to the forestay, usually with a series of plastic, brass, or stainless-steel clips, known as hanks. Start hanking on the luff from the tack, working toward the head, and make sure that the luff is not twisted between the hanks. The halyard may be attached to the head now, or attached immediately before you launch the boat.

The jib is trimmed (pulled in and out) using two jib sheets – one on each side of the boat – that pass through fairleads on the sidedecks and then to cleats. The jib sheets are attached to the jib clew, usually with a bowline.

## TEMPORARY STOW

If you are not sailing immediately, then the rigged jib can be gathered into a bundle on the foredeck and tied with a jib sheet to prevent it from blowing around. Alternatively, you can hoist the jib, then furl it on the forestay by wrapping it repeatedly around the stay (secure it with a jib sheet tied around the roll and stay).

## ATTACHING THE JIB

*Remove the sail from its bag, and lay it on the foredeck. Check that you have two jib sheets. A wire-luffed jib will have been stowed by coiling the luff in circles to prevent the wire kinking. Uncoil it carefully, and make sure that there are no twists in the sail by running your hand along the luff from tack to head. If the wind is strong, make sure that the sail does not blow off the boat. Avoid dragging the sail along the ground and try to keep it clean while you are handling it.*

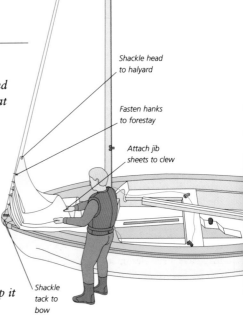

Shackle head to halyard

Fasten hanks to forestay

Attach jib sheets to clew

Shackle tack to bow

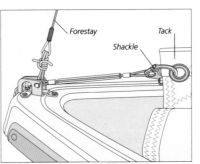

Forestay

Tack

Shackle

**1** Attach the tack of the jib to the bow-fitting on the dinghy, just behind the point where the forestay is fastened. This is usually done with a shackle or lashing.

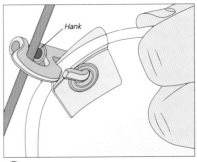

Hank

**2** Starting at the tack and working your way up the luff, attach each hank to the forestay in turn, making sure that the luff is not twisted between the hanks.

Jib sheet

**3** Fasten the jib sheets to the clew using a bowline (p.39) or a loop (as here). Lead the other end of the sheet outside the shrouds and through the jib fairlead, and tie a figure eight knot (p.39) in the end.

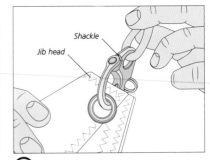

Shackle

Jib head

**4** Check aloft to ensure that the halyard is not tangled, then attach it to the head of the jib with a bowline or a shackle. If you are not ready to hoist the jib, make sure that it cannot blow around.

# COMMON MAINSHEET SYSTEMS

The mainsheet is used to adjust the position of the boom and to help control the shape of the mainsail. When the mainsail is full of wind, there can be quite a heavy load on the mainsheet, so it is run through a system of blocks, called a mainsheet tackle, to make it easier for the helmsman to hold and adjust.

## MAINSHEET SYSTEMS

There are two main types of mainsheet system: center and aft. On the former system, the end of the sheet leads to the helmsman's hand from a block forward of the helmsman. In aft-mainsheet systems, the sheet is led from aft of the helmsman. Either type may have a traveler on a track, which can be used to position the mainsheet athwartships. Center mainsheets are common on racing boats as they offer more control of the sail. Boats with aft-mainsheet systems have more room in the cockpit, which makes them the most popular design for general-purpose sailing dinghies.

## RIGGING MAINSHEETS

Mainsheet systems are usually left in place when the boat is not being sailed. When rigging, check that the fittings are secure and that the sheet runs correctly and smoothly through the various blocks in the tackle. Also, ensure that the mainsheet has a figure eight knot in the end to prevent it from running out through the blocks.

## CENTER-MAINSHEET SYSTEMS

In most center-mainsheet systems, the top block of the mainsheet tackle is attached to the middle of the boom. This means it has less leverage and more load than an aft mainsheet, so more blocks are needed in the tackle. The lower block may be attached to an athwartships-track, which runs across the middle of the boat, or it can be fitted on the floor, on a raised hoop, or on the centerboard case. There is usually a cleat attached to the lower mainsheet block so that the sheet can be jammed securely when the helmsman chooses. If an athwartships track is fitted, the mainsheet tackle's lower block is attached to a traveler that runs on the track. The position of the traveler is usually controlled by lines led to the sidedeck within reach of the helmsman.

## AFT-MAINSHEET SYSTEMS

In an aft-mainsheet system, the top block of the tackle is normally attached to a swivel plate at the end of the boom. The bottom block is often attached to a traveler that runs on a track across the transom. Other, simpler designs may be found: sometimes the lower mainsheet block is attached to a rope bridle attached to the transom corners. If a traveler is used, it may have control lines to adjust its position on the track. Aft-mainsheet systems do not usually have a jamming block for the sheet, but they may have a ratchet block to reduce the load that the helmsman has to hold. Because the mainsheet leads from aft of the helmsman, he must face aft when tacking.

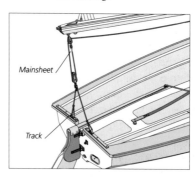

Mainsheet

Track

△ **ALTERNATIVE ARRANGEMENT**
*Mainsheet arrangements often vary considerably. Here, an aft-mainsheet block is attached to a bridle on two short tracks.*

△ **CENTER MAINSHEET**
*In this Laser II, the mainsheet tackle is attached near the end of the boom. The lower block is on an adjustable rope-bridle system. The end of the sheet leads to the helmsman's hand via blocks.*

△ **AFT MAINSHEET**
*In this conventional aft-mainsheet arrangement, the lower block is attached to a traveler running on a track mounted on the transom. The traveler position may be adjusted using control lines.*

# RIGGING THE MAINSAIL

If you are sailing a boat with an unstayed mast (p.56) and a sleeved sail, you must fit the mainsail onto the mast before it is stepped. In most boats, however, the sails are attached only after the mast has been stepped and the standing rigging adjusted. A mainsail is attached to the mast along its luff and to the boom at its foot. There are two main methods that are employed to attach the mainsail to the boom. In the majority of boats, the mainsail is fitted by sliding its foot into a groove in the boom. In this case, the sail will have a bolt rope sewn in a hem at the foot. Less often, the mainsail is loose-footed, which means that it is attached to the boom only at the tack and clew (p.25).

## MAINSAIL FITTINGS

Most dinghy mainsails have three or more battens, which can be fitted either before or after the sail is attached to the boom. Battens act as stiffeners, holding out the roach (the curved shape of the leech). Without them, all the sail that is outside a direct line between head and clew would curl over and be ineffective. The battens may differ in flexibility, depending on which batten pocket they are made for, and the inner end of the batten may be more flexible than the outer end to allow for the curve in the sail. If this is the case, the battens will be marked to indicate which pocket they belong in and which end should be inserted first.

## BOOM FITTINGS

The boom is attached to the mast via a gooseneck and a boom vang. The gooseneck locates it and allows it to pivot from side to side, while the boom vang prevents it from lifting.

## ATTACHING THE SAIL TO THE BOOM

*Take the mainsail out of its bag and unroll it inside the boat, with the luff nearest to the mast. Check that you have the requisite number of battens and that they are all in place (below). Once you have fitted the mainsail to it, put the boom inside the boat until you are ready to hoist the sail. Do not put the boom onto the gooseneck until after the sail is hoisted. The boom is likely to slide off if fitted earlier.*

Bolt rope

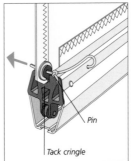

Tack cringle

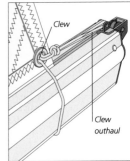

Clew

Pin

Clew outhaul

**①** Holding the clew, slide the bolt rope into the groove at the forward (mast) end of the boom. Make sure that none of the sail cloth gets caught in the groove with the bolt rope.

**②** Pull the clew until all the foot of the sail is in the groove. Fix the tack to the forward end of the boom (usually by sliding a pin through the tack cringle and the boom).

**③** Pull the foot of the sail so that it is taut, and keep the sail tensioned by fastening the clew outhaul (usually a line attached to the clew and tied to the end of the boom).

## BATTENS

Battens are made of wood, fiberglass, or plastic. They slot into pockets sewn into the sail and are either tied into the pocket or slipped under a flap sewn into its outer end. Battens are often made for specific pockets, so make sure that they are inserted the right way around and in the correct pocket.

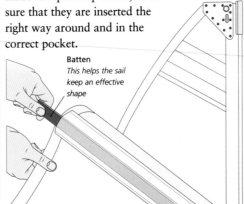

Batten
*This helps the sail keep an effective shape*

**TAPERED FIBERGLASS BATTEN**

**WOODEN BATTEN WITH TIE-INS**

**PLASTIC BATTEN**

◁ **FITTING A BATTEN**
*Check to see if one end of the batten is more flexible and insert this end first. Slide the batten into the pocket and secure it by slipping the outer end under the flap or by tying it in place.*

# ATTACHING THE SAIL TO THE MAST

*The mainsail is not hoisted until you are ready to launch or are already afloat. The sail can be prepared for hoisting, however, by inserting the headboard into the mast groove and pulling it up a couple inches. Cleat the halyard and loosely flake the sail on top of the boom inside the boat, and secure it with the end of the mainsheet.*

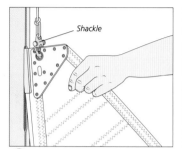

Shackle

**①** Check that the luff is not twisted, and that the halyard is not caught around anything aloft. Then, attach the halyard to the head of the sail with a shackle or bowline.

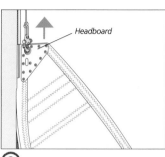

Headboard

**②** Slot the headboard into the mast groove and hoist the mainsail a couple inches using the mainsail halyard. Cleat the halyard loosely, and flake the sail over the boom.

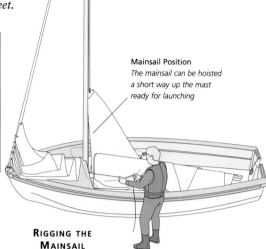

**Mainsail Position**
*The mainsail can be hoisted a short way up the mast ready for launching*

**RIGGING THE MAINSAIL**

## THE GOOSENECK

The gooseneck is a hinged fitting that attaches the boom to the mast, just below where the mast groove opens out for the mainsail luff rope. It can pivot to left and right and up and down, and allows the boom to move freely in these directions. When fully inserted in the boom, the gooseneck prevents the boom from rotating.

**SLIDING GOOSENECK**

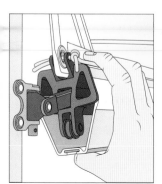

**FIXED GOOSENECK**

◁ **FITTING THE BOOM**
*The gooseneck is often fixed in one position, although some can be slid up or down to adjust the boom's height. Its square-shanked pin is inserted into the matching socket on the end of the boom.*

## THE BOOM VANG

The boom vang, or kicking strap, is an adjustable tackle of rope (or wire) and blocks that prevents the boom from rising under the pressure of wind in the mainsail. It is attached to the boom a ways back from the gooseneck, and to the mast just above the heel, making an angle of about 45° between mast and boom.

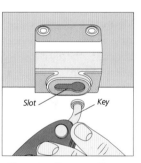

Slot          Key

**KEYHOLE SLOT ON BOOM**

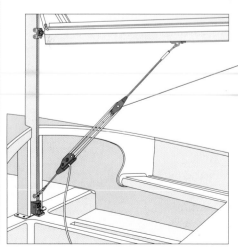

**Boom Vang**
*The vang runs between the base of the mast and the boom*

◁ **FITTING THE BOOM VANG**
*The top of the boom vang is attached to the boom by a key and slot. The bottom is attached near the base of the mast using a shackle.*

# REEFING A DINGHY

*I*f the wind increases beyond Force 3, many sailing dinghies start to become harder to handle. Reducing the sail area, known as reefing, makes the dinghy more stable and easier to control in stronger winds. There are three main methods of reefing a mainsail: traditional slab reefing; rolling the sail around the boom; and rolling the sail around the mast. The method you use will depend on the design of your boat. A jib can be changed for a smaller one or rolled around the forestay.

**SAILING WITH A REEFED SAIL**

## METHODS OF REEFING

Slab reefing involves taking a portion out of the mainsail, and dinghies designed for this method will have one or two rows of reef points (thin ropes stitched to the sail) or cringles (reinforced eyes in the sail) for lacing a reefing line. Dinghies with unstayed masts can be reefed by rolling the sail around the mast, although this is not easy to do afloat. Dinghies with aft-mainsheet systems are most commonly reefed by rolling the sail around the boom – a method that cannot be used when the mainsheet is attached in the middle of the boom.

## WHEN TO REEF

Racing dinghies are hardly ever reefed, and races are frequently postponed in strong winds. When sailing for recreation, however, reefing allows you to sail under control in strong winds and reduces the risk of capsize. You can reef while you are afloat if your boat has slab or boom roller reefing, but it is much easier to reef ashore before you set sail. A single-handed dinghy with a sleeved sail should be reefed before sailing.

When reefing a dinghy that has a mainsail and a jib, you should change to a smaller jib if possible when you reef the main in order to keep the sail plan balanced.

## TRADITIONAL SLAB REEFING

*The traditional method of reefing is to take a "slab" (portion) out of the mainsail. This is done by partially lowering the sail and then tying down a luff cringle and a leech cringle, leaving a fold of sail parallel to the foot, along the boom. The fold may be left hanging or it can be tied up using reef points. An alternative method is to lace a reefing line through a row of cringles running horizontally across the sail, and secured to the boom at either end.*

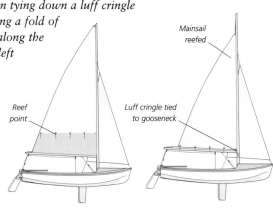

Mainsail reefed

Reef point

Luff cringle tied to gooseneck

**UNREEFED SAIL**

**SAIL WITH ONE REEF TAKEN IN**

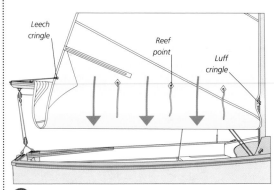

Leech cringle

Reef point

Luff cringle

**①** Undo the mainsail halyard and lower the mainsail until the appropriate luff and leech cringles are level with the boom, removing a batten if necessary. Re-cleat the halyard, then tie the luff cringle to the boom near the gooseneck and the leech cringle to the aft end of the boom.

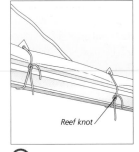

Reef knot

**②** Secure the loose fold of spare sail by tying reef knots (p.38) at the reef points sewn into the sail. If there are cringles on the sail, thread a lacing line through them and secure.

# ROLLING THE SAIL AROUND THE BOOM

*The most common method of reefing dinghies with aft-mainsheet systems (p.59) is rolling the mainsail around the boom. It requires two people: one at the gooseneck and one at the aft end of the boom. A tuck is put in the leech to stop the boom from drooping after reefing. The rolled sail covers the boom-vang fitting so a replacement fitting must be rigged using a sail bag, a length of rope, or a webbing strap. This improvised fitting is tucked into the sail as it is rolled around the boom. The vang is tied to it and tightened once the sail is reefed.*

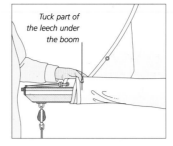

Tuck part of the leech under the boom

**①** Slacken the halyard. Take the boom off the gooseneck and make a 6in (15cm) tuck in the leech. Pull the tuck tightly aft and wrap it under the aft end of the boom. Holding the tuck in place, rotate the boom, pulling the sail taut at both leech and luff as you go.

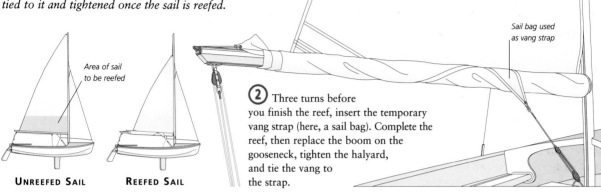

Sail bag used as vang strap

**②** Three turns before you finish the reef, insert the temporary vang strap (here, a sail bag). Complete the reef, then replace the boom on the gooseneck, tighten the halyard, and tie the vang to the strap.

Area of sail to be reefed

**UNREEFED SAIL**     **REEFED SAIL**

# ROLLING THE SAIL AROUND THE MAST

*A mainsail rigged on an unstayed mast (p.56) is reefed by rolling the sail around the mast. Boats with unstayed masts usually have a loose-footed mainsail, which is attached to the aft end of the boom by the clew outhaul. The outhaul must be released before the sail can be reefed. With the sail free to flap like a flag, it can be passed around the mast a number of times or the mast can be rotated to roll it up. Once sufficient sail has been rolled around the mast, the clew outhaul is re-attached and the clew pulled out to tighten the foot. The clew outhaul should be fastened around the boom as well as to the end to hold the clew close against the boom.*

Roll the mainsail around the mast

**①** Release the clew outhaul and remove the boom from the mast. Wrap the sail around the mast or rotate the mast to roll the sail up. In the latter case, release the mast lock or the downhaul (depending on which system the boat employs) to allow the mast to rotate, resecuring the mast when the sail has been reefed.

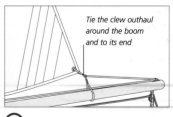

Tie the clew outhaul around the boom and to its end

**②** Fit the boom back onto the mast and re-fasten the clew outhaul, making sure that you tie it around the boom as well as to the boom end. Tighten the boom vang.

Clew

Area of sail to be reefed

**UNREEFED SAIL**     **REEFED SAIL**

# HELMSMAN AND CREW

*In a two-man dinghy, both crew members have distinct roles that must be carried out if the boat is to sail safely and efficiently. The helmsman is in overall charge of the dinghy. He is also responsible for steering the boat and trimming the mainsail. The crew follows the helmsman's instructions and is responsible for trimming the jib and adjusting the centerboard. Both crew members must be prepared to move their weight to keep the boat balanced and correctly trimmed, although the main balancing work is the responsibility of the crew.*

## THE HELMSMAN'S ROLE

The windward sidedeck is the best position for the helmsman. He should sit far enough forward to be clear of the end of the tiller, while holding the tiller extension in his aft hand and the mainsheet in his forward hand. This position allows him the clearest view of the water all around the boat, as well as affording a clear view of the sails. It is the most comfortable place from which to control the rudder and trim the mainsail. To perform his role as chief decision-maker, the helmsman must have a good knowledge of the rules of the road (*pp.44–45*) so that he knows when to keep clear of other boats and when he has right of way. His instructions to the crew must be clear; they must be loud enough to be heard over the noise of wind and water. They must also be given early enough for the crew to be able to respond in good time. Although he

△ **POSITION OF THE CREW**
*When sailing in good conditions, both members of the crew usually sit side by side on the windward sidedeck, with the crew being prepared to move as necessary to keep the boat balanced.*

is in charge of the boat, the helmsman should encourage input from his crew, and must be prepared to listen to information and advice.

## THE CREW'S ROLE

The crew sits just forward of the helmsman but must be ready to move in and out of the boat to keep it upright while allowing the helmsman to stay on the windward sidedeck. He must learn to anticipate changes in the direction or strength of the wind; and should be ready to counteract their effects by altering his position quickly.

When sitting out, both the helmsman and crew tuck their feet under toe rails to allow them to lean

◁ **BALANCING THE BOAT**
*The helmsman is sitting where he has a good view of the sails while the crew is sitting out hard to balance the boat.*

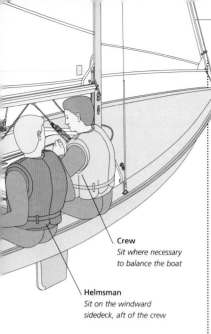

Crew
*Sit where necessary to balance the boat*

Helmsman
*Sit on the windward sidedeck, aft of the crew*

## UNDERSTANDING HEEL AND TRIM

One of the most important factors contributing to fast, efficient, and easy sailing is the correct sideways balance, and fore-and-aft trim of the boat. Much of the effort expended by the helmsman and crew during sailing goes into maintaining the ideal trim.

### CORRECTING HEEL

When sailing in light winds, upwind or on a reach, the helmsman sits to windward and the crew corrects heel by sitting to leeward. If the wind increases, the crew moves first into the middle of the boat, then to sitting beside the helmsman. When sailing downwind, the heeling force is almost zero, so the crew sits in the middle of the boat or opposite the helmsman.

### CORRECTING TRIM

In moderate winds, the boat should be level fore and aft when the helmsman and crew sit side by side – the crew sitting just behind the windward shroud. By sitting close together, they reduce wind resistance and also keep their weight centered, which allows the bow and stern to lift easily to waves. If their weight is too far forward, the bow is depressed and steering can become difficult. If their weight is too far back, the stern is depressed, which makes the boat slow down and difficult to sail upwind.

When sailing upwind in very light winds, the helmsman moves forward to just behind the shroud, and the crew sits in the middle or to leeward. This lifts the aft sections of the boat and reduces drag. When sailing downwind in strong winds, the helmsman and crew move aft to lift the bow, but not so far as to make the stern drag.

out without overbalancing. The toe rails should be adjusted so that both can sit out comfortably.

The crew should trim the jib to match any changes in wind direction or the boat's course. He should raise and lower the centerboard (or daggerboard) to suit the point of sailing. He, too, should keep a good look out all around the boat, especially to leeward where it can be difficult for the helmsman to see. He must warn the helmsman about any potential collision situations in good time. An experienced crew will also discuss sail trim with the helmsman.

## COORDINATION

It is important that the helmsman and crew learn to coordinate their movements. When the boat heels, the crew should move first to adjust the balance – the helmsman moves only if there is a large change in trim. When a course change is required, good crews move together smoothly to assist the turn and to maintain balance and speed. This teamwork becomes increasingly important when sailing in high-performance dinghies and when racing.

◁ CORRECTING TRIM
*The boat is being sailed fast with the helmsman and crew sitting slightly aft of their normal positions. This action causes the bow to lift and helps the boat to plane or surf on waves when sailing fast downwind.*

◁ CORRECTING HEEL
*The crew moves his weight to balance the boat and allow the helmsman to sit on the windward sidedeck from where he can see the sails and course. Here, the dinghy is on a run in light air so the crew sits to leeward, under the boom, to balance the boat. From here, he can see the jib trim and hazards to leeward.*

# TURNING FORCES

A dinghy's performance is determined by the efficient interaction of the main controls – hull balance and trim, sails, rudder, and centerboard. When used correctly, these make the boat easy to steer and sail efficiently. However, the hull, sails, and centerboard can produce powerful turning forces, which, in extreme cases, may overcome the effects of the rudder. You need to learn how to keep all these forces in balance, otherwise the boat will slow down and become more difficult to sail.

## BALANCE AND TRIM

Although the sensation of speed may be greater when your dinghy is heeled well over, sailing this way is actually slower than sailing with the boat upright. A dinghy hull is designed to be at its most efficient when it sits on its natural waterline, level sideways (balance) and fore and aft (trim). When it is balanced and trimmed in this way, the boat will sail fast and will tend to move in a straight line.

Balance is achieved by the crew moving their weight in and out of the boat to port and/or starboard in order to counteract the heeling force of the sails. When the boat is upright, the shape of its underwater section is symmetrical and it will move in a straight line. However, if the boat is allowed to heel, the shape changes and it will try to turn.

The fore-and-aft trim of the boat is just as important as its sideways balance. The amount of the hull in the water – its waterline shape – can be altered by the crew moving forward or aft and this shape will have an effect on the way the boat handles. If the crew moves forward in the boat this will depress the bow while lifting the stern. This can be useful to reduce hull drag in very light winds but it is slow in other conditions and the boat will tend to turn toward the wind.

If the crew move their weight aft, the stern will be depressed and the bow raised. This is often done when sailing downwind in strong winds or when planing (p.110) to prevent the bow from digging into the water. In other situations, however, it will slow the boat down and tend to make it turn away from the wind.

## THE SAILS

The sails are trimmed to create the force that drives a dinghy forward, but they can also be used to help change direction. Most dinghies have two sails – a mainsail behind the mast and a jib forward of it. When both are trimmed correctly (and the hull is upright and the centerboard in the correct position), the boat will be well balanced and will require little use of the rudder to keep it on course.

Most of the time you will trim the sails to work efficiently together and eliminate their turning effects. When you want to change course, however, the sails can be a very useful aid in making the maneuver as smooth and efficient as possible. By using the sails to help turn the boat you will reduce the amount you need to use the rudder (p.69). The helmsman and crew must coordinate their actions in trimming the mainsail and jib in order to achieve the desired turning effect.

## THE CENTERBOARD

A centerboard or daggerboard is used to resist sideways force (pp.30–31). It also acts as the pivot point around which the boat turns.

Most dinghies are fitted with a centerboard that pivots inside a case. When it is raised and retracted into its case, its tip moves back and upward. This decreases the area of centerboard under the boat and also alters its position along the fore-and-aft line. This fore-and-aft movement has an effect on the steering. When it is in its correct position, the turning forces of the jib and mainsail are balanced around the pivot point. If the centerboard is raised, the boat will turn away from the wind as the pivot point moves aft. Conversely, if the centerboard is lowered further, the pivot point moves forward and the boat will tend to turn into the wind.

Daggerboards move vertically inside their case. When a daggerboard is raised, the area under the boat is reduced but its position along the fore-and-aft line remains the same and has no turning effect.

## THE RUDDER

The rudder is the primary control for changing direction. However, it is important to remember that whenever the rudder is moved off-center by more than four degrees it acts as a brake as well as a turning control. The further the rudder is turned, the greater the braking effect. Rudders work most efficiently when the boat is moving quickly. The braking effect is, likewise, most dramatic at speed, when careful handling is required. At slow speeds, the rudder's effect is reduced because the water moves past it more slowly, and it has no effect when the boat is stopped. Remember that the effect of the rudder is reversed when the boat moves backward.

## BOAT TRIM

The natural tendency of most beginners is to sit too far aft in the boat. In normal conditions the helmsman should sit forward of the end of the tiller so that he can move it freely without it hitting his body. The crew should sit just forward of the helmsman, which in most dinghies will mean he sits just aft of the shrouds. Helmsman and crew should sit close together to keep their weight centered in the boat and to reduce the wind resistance of their bodies. In light winds they should move forward to lift the stern and reduce hull drag, especially when sailing on a windward course. In strong winds, and especially when sailing downwind, they should move aft to lift the bow.

### △ HULL LEVEL
*The crew trim the boat so that it sits in the water on its natural waterline. This is the fastest trim in most conditions.*

### △ BOW DOWN
*By moving forward, the crew depress the bow and lift the stern. The boat will tend to turn toward the wind.*

### △ BOW UP
*By moving aft, the crew depress the stern and raise the bow. The boat tends to turn away from the wind.*

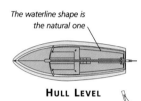

*The waterline shape is the natural one*

**HULL LEVEL**

*The waterline shape moves forward*

**BOW DEPRESSED**

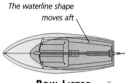

*The waterline shape moves aft*

**BOW LIFTED**

## BOAT BALANCE

When the hull is level in the water, sideways as well as fore and aft, it has a symmetrical waterline shape and will tend to sail in a straight line. However, if the boat heels to windward or to leeward, the shape of the waterline becomes asymmetrical, which makes the boat try to turn.

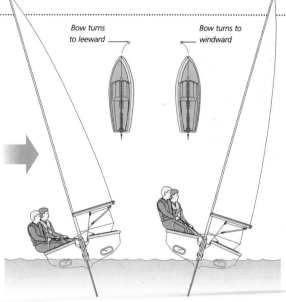

*Bow turns to leeward*

*Bow turns to windward*

### △ HEELING
*As the boat heels, the underwater shape changes and the rudder and centerboard become off-center in the underwater area, this makes the boat try to turn in the direction opposite to the heel.*

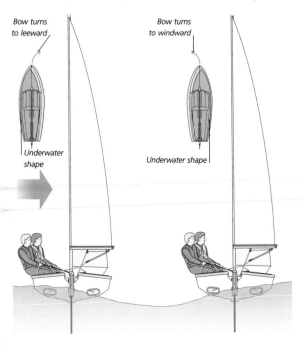

*Bow turns to leeward*

*Bow turns to windward*

*Underwater shape*

*Underwater shape*

### ◁ WAVES ON THE BEAM
*The turning effect also occurs when a wave passes under the hull from the side. First, the windward side is more immersed and the boat tries to turn away from the wind; then, the leeward side is more immersed and the boat tries to turn toward the wind.*

## USING THE SAILS

Both the mainsail and the jib can be used separately to create a force that will turn the boat. Because the jib is smaller than the mainsail, its turning effect is not quite as large as the mainsail, but it will still be significant. The jib used alone acts in front of the centerboard's pivot point, so pulls the bow away from the wind. The mainsail used alone acts behind the pivot point, so pulls the stern away from the wind and the bow toward it. The turning effect of each depends on the other sail being let out.

### ▽ TURNING EFFECT OF THE MAINSAIL

*If the mainsail is pulled in while the jib is allowed to flap, the boat will move forward and turn to windward. The more quickly you pull in the mainsail, the faster the boat turns. You will also produce this effect by sheeting in the mainsail too much when the jib is not sheeted in enough.*

**Jib**
The jib is allowed to flap freely so that it has no turning effect on the boat

**Mainsail**
The mainsail is sheeted in to turn the boat into the wind; in this case, it will turn to port

**Jib**
The jib is sheeted in to turn the boat away from the wind; in this case, to starboard

**Crew**
Sheet in the jib

### ◁ TURNING EFFECT OF THE JIB

*If the jib is pulled in while the mainsail is allowed to flap, the boat will move forward and will turn away from the wind. You can also produce this effect if you sheet in the jib too much when the mainsail is not sheeted in enough.*

**Mainsail**
The mainsail is allowed to flap freely so that it has no turning effect on the boat

---

## SAIL SETTING USING TELL-TALES

Tell-tales are light strips of wool or nylon, sewn or glued about 6–9in (15–23cm) in from the luff on both sides of the sails. They indicate whether the air stream at the sail surface is smooth or turbulent.

### HOW TELL-TALES WORK

If the sail is trimmed correctly, the tell-tales on both sides will fly parallel. If those to windward fly higher, pull in the sheet; if those to leeward fly higher, let out the sheet.

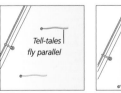

Tell-tales fly parallel

**CORRECT TRIM**

Windward tell-tale higher

**UNDER-TRIMMING**

Leeward tell-tale higher

**OVER-TRIMMING**

## Using the Centerboard

The centerboard or daggerboard provides most of the resistance to sideways movement, so it is vital that the centerboard or daggerboard is used properly, especially if you are sailing close-hauled (when it should be fully down). Beginners often forget to lower the board when sailing away from land, or when turning onto a close-hauled course. If you try to sail close to the wind with the board up, the boat will move as fast sideways as it does forward, resulting in a crab-like course and making it difficult for the helmsman to steer a course.

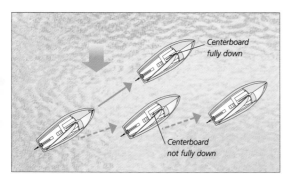

**Centerboard fully down**

**Centerboard not fully down**

◁ **CENTERBOARD**
*If the centerboard is not lowered sufficiently, the sideways force will not be resisted and the boat will slide sideways. This leeward motion is most apparent when sailing upwind, when full centerboard is needed.*

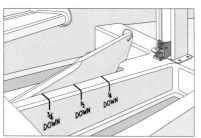

¾ DOWN   ⅓ DOWN   ¼ DOWN

◁ **CENTERBOARD MARKING**
*Marking the centerboard case, quarter down, half down, etc, is a good way to indicate how much of the centerboard is protruding below the hull at any given time. Position the leading edge against the marks. If your dinghy has a daggerboard, mark the daggerboard itself, not its case.*

## Using the Rudder

Sitting in the helmsman's position on the windward side of the boat, push the tiller away to turn the boat toward the wind. As the boat turns, the sails should be trimmed for the new course. If the turn continues, the boat will reach head-to-wind and stop. To turn away from the wind, pull the tiller toward you. As the boat turns further downwind, the sails must be let out to keep them set correctly.

Keep your actions smooth. When the rudder turns, it acts as a brake as well as a turning device, so avoid jerking it backward and forward.

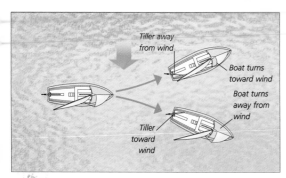

**Tiller away from wind**

**Boat turns toward wind**

**Boat turns away from wind**

**Tiller toward wind**

◁ **STEERING**
*Sit to windward opposite the sails when steering. Gently push or pull the tiller to move the rudder and turn the boat. When moving forward, the bow always turns in the direction opposite to the way you move the tiller.*

## USING ALL THE TURNING CONTROLS

To understand fully how all the turning forces work in practice, you can try the following exercises when you go afloat. Start by sailing the boat onto a beam reach, then make sure that both sails are only partly full of wind, the centerboard is half down, and the rudder is centered. Now try running through these two sequences.

### TURN TOWARD THE WIND
• Firstly, the helmsman gently pushes the tiller away from him.
• The crew lowers the centerboard.
• Next, the helmsman pulls in the mainsheet to trim the mainsail, and the crew lets out the jib.
• At the same time, heel the boat slightly away from the wind.

### TURN AWAY FROM THE WIND
• The helmsman gently pulls the tiller toward him.
• The crew raises the centerboard.
• The crew pulls in the jib and the helmsman lets out the mainsail.
• At the same time, heel the boat slightly toward the wind.

△ **UNDER CONTROL**
*Here, the crew are sailing fast downwind under full control by keeping the boat correctly trimmed and balanced, and using sail trim to help steer the boat as it surfs down a wave front. The boat is well balanced so it is easy to steer.*

# GOING AFLOAT

*T*he first time you set sail, whether it is alone or with an instructor, you will begin to appreciate the challenges, rewards, and responsibilities of sailing. When you are learning with an instructor you need concentrate only on acquiring new skills, leaving the safety aspects to him. If you sail off alone, however, you are in sole charge of your destiny. This is one of the greatest attractions of sailing, but you must be aware of the risks and take sensible precautions if you are to enjoy the experience.

### BEFORE LAUNCHING

Whenever you decide to go sailing, choose a suitable location and only go afloat when the weather and water conditions are appropriate to your level of expertise. When you arrive at your chosen sailing area, be prepared to ask local sailors for their advice before you go on the water as they will have experience of the prevailing conditions. Make sure that they are aware of your level of experience.

Many people start learning to sail on inland waters as they are generally more sheltered than the sea and there are no tides to complicate matters. Help is usually close at hand, too,

should you find yourself in difficulties. However, there is no reason why you should not learn how to sail on the sea, provided that you are prepared to take the recommended safety precautions.

### ASSESSING THE WIND

For your first trip alone, pick a day when the wind is Force 3 or less. Check the weather forecast, paying most attention to the local area sailing forecast. Do not be afraid to cancel your trip if you are not sure that the conditions will be right.

When you arrive at the sailing area, take a careful look at all the wind indicators to help you build a

picture of the conditions. Make a note of flags, both on the shore and on moored boats, check the direction of any smoke from chimneys, consider the behavior of trees moving in the wind, and look at waves on the water (*pp.46–47*). It is also very important that you know whether the wind is onshore or offshore as it can make a great difference to your trip.

### ONSHORE WINDS

If the wind is onshore, it will feel stronger. If it is moderate or strong, it will cause waves to break on the beach. An onshore wind makes it harder to launch and sail off because it will blow you back onto the shore. On the other hand, it is easy to return to the shore in an onshore wind, and you will not be in danger of being blown away from your base.

### OFFSHORE WINDS

If the wind is offshore, it can be very difficult to judge its true strength while you are on land. As you sail further from the shore, its strength is likely to increase and may be more than you are happy with. In an offshore wind it is easy to launch and sail away as there are no waves on the beach and you will be blown clear of the shore. Getting back, on the other hand, could be difficult and there is a danger of being blown away from your base and unable to return.

If you are sailing on the sea, avoid going afloat in offshore winds on your first few trips. On inland waters, make sure that another boat is nearby or that a safety boat will be available if you need a tow back to base.

### ◁ NO WIND

*If there is no wind, wait until it rises, especially if a tidal stream is present as shown here by the moored boats.*

◁ **ONSHORE WIND**
*Even a Force 3 blowing onshore will cause waves to break on the lee shore. If the water is shallow a long way out, the waves will break first some distance from the beach; if the shoreline is steep, the waves will break on the shore.*

**OFFSHORE WIND** ▷
*A Force 3 wind causes quite different conditions when blowing offshore than it does blowing onshore. Close to land, the sea is sheltered and there will be no waves. Further out, the conditions may be much rougher than they appear from the beach.*

## CHECKING THE TIDE

If you are sailing on a river or the sea, you may have to deal with tidal conditions (pp.48–49). Obtain a copy of the local tide tables and check it for the times of high and low waters. Again, experienced local sailors will be able to give you advice.

Before you go on the water, make sure that you know the state of the tide. Find out the direction of the tidal stream and at what time it will turn. Plan your trip so that you can sail back to your base with the tide when you are ready to return.

## AVOIDING COLLISIONS

Before you go afloat, remind yourself of the procedures for the prevention of collisions on the water (pp.44–45). It is your responsibility as skipper of your own boat to be familiar with the rules of the road.

When you are learning to sail, avoid busy shipping channels. Keep to the shallower water at their edges where you will not meet larger boats. If you do have to cross a channel, remember to do so at right angles so you get across as quickly as possible.

If you think you are in a potential collision situation and you are not sure of the rules that apply, then it is safest to assume that you have to keep clear. Make a large alteration of course to pass behind the other boat so that your intentions are obvious to the other skipper.

Remember to check regularly all around the boat. Beginners often forget to look astern and are startled when another vessel suddenly appears. The area behind the jib and mainsail can be hidden from helmsman and crew when they are sitting out to windward. Check this area regularly, asking your crew to move to leeward briefly for a clearer view if necessary.

### TIDAL TIPS

Verify information given in tide tables by observing the shoreline: a wet shoreline means that the tide is going out, a dry one signals that it is coming in.

## FINAL PREPARATIONS

Before you go afloat there are several checks that you should run through to ensure that you have a safe, enjoyable sail and an easy return. Do not be tempted to ignore these, even if you are in a hurry – your safety may depend on them.

### CONDITIONS CHECK

Before you decide to sail, ask yourself about the conditions.
• Is the wind strength suitable for your level of experience?
• Is the wind onshore or offshore?
• Is the wind strength forecast to increase or decrease?
• Do you know the state of the tide, and will you be able to return without having to fight the current?
• Are there other sailors nearby who can help you if necessary?

### TELL SOMEONE YOUR PLANS

Once you have decided that it is safe to sail, you need to make sure a responsible person knows your plans – where you expect to sail and when you plan to return. When you do get back from your sail, remember to tell them you are back safely or they may notify the rescue services unnecessarily.

### EQUIPMENT CHECK

When you are at the shoreline and ready to sail, check that you are fully prepared to go afloat.
• Is your clothing adequate?
• Are all the crew wearing personal buoyancy – fastened correctly?
• Is all the sailing gear rigged properly and in good condition?
• Are all the bungs and hatches in position?
• Are the oars or paddles on board and tied securely?
• Are the anchor and warp aboard and tied in securely?
• Is all personal equipment stowed neatly in waterproof containers and tied in securely?

# LAUNCHING THE BOAT

*A well-planned routine for preparing and launching your dinghy will ensure that you rig it properly, and that all the necessary equipment is on board and in good working order. A launching trailer is the usual means of moving a boat to the water, and how you launch from there depends on whether it is a beach or slipway launch, or a dock launch. Whichever it is, work out a system with your sailing partner to build on the teamwork that will make you good sailors on the water.*

## USING A LAUNCH TRAILER

Most damage is done to sailing dinghies while on the shore, so it is important to move the dinghy and launch it in a way that prevents the hull from coming into contact with the ground (pp.42–43); a launching trailer is ideal for this. Sailing dinghies are quite heavy and awkward to lift, so if it has been transported on a roof rack or road trailer, find a few people who are willing to help lift it onto its trailer to make the job easier.

Position the boat so that there is not too much weight on the front of the trailer when you lift it by the handle, and tie the painter around the trailer handle to prevent the boat from sliding off. To secure the painter, use a round turn and two half-hitches (p.39). If the trailer has a T-shaped handle, you can secure the rope with figure eight turns.

## PREPARING THE BOAT

Step the mast if necessary (pp.56–57), and check that all the bungs are in position. Collect all the equipment, incuding the sails, rudder, paddles, and any other important removable gear, before you move the boat close to the launching point.

Sails are usually rigged (and lifting rudders fitted) before launching but, in some circumstances, such as launching from a dock, you may wish to rig them after launching. A lifting rudder can be fitted before launching from a slipway, but a fixed blade must be left until you are afloat and in water deep enough to take it. Make sure that if you put it in the boat, it is under the boom and mainsail, otherwise it may be thrown about when the sail is hoisted. The centerboard should be up when you launch; if you have a daggerboard, lay it in the bottom of the boat until you go afloat. In most situations, hoist the jib before you go afloat unless its flapping will be a nuisance while launching. If the boat can be kept head-to-wind when launching from a slipway, you can also hoist the mainsail; otherwise, it is hoisted when you are afloat.

## READY TO GO

Do a final check around the boat to ensure that you have everything you need. Wheel the boat to the water, and launch, following the instructions for a beach, slipway, or dock (p.73).

## FITTING THE RUDDER

*Both fixed and lifting rudders are secured to the boat by means of fittings on their stock. Fit a lifting rudder before launching from a beach or slipway. Fit a fixed rudder after launching, ensuring the water is sufficiently deep first.*

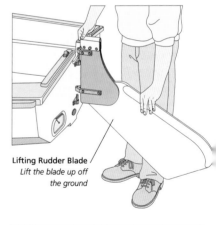

**Lifting Rudder Blade**
*Lift the blade up off the ground*

**①** Slide the fittings on the stock onto their counterpart fixings on the boat's transom. Make sure that the blade is held up so it cannot scrape on the ground.

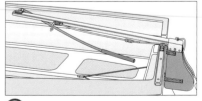

**②** If the tiller is removable, slide it into the rudder head and make sure it is a tight fit.

**③** Secure the tiller – usually with a pin that passes through the rudder head and the tiller.

**④** If you fit the rudder and tiller before hoisting the mainsail, make sure that the sail and boom do not catch the tiller when you raise the sail. Ensure that the extension does not catch under the sidedeck.

## HOISTING THE JIB

The helmsman hoists the jib by pulling on the jib halyard until the forestay goes loose as the jib luff takes the full weight of the mast.

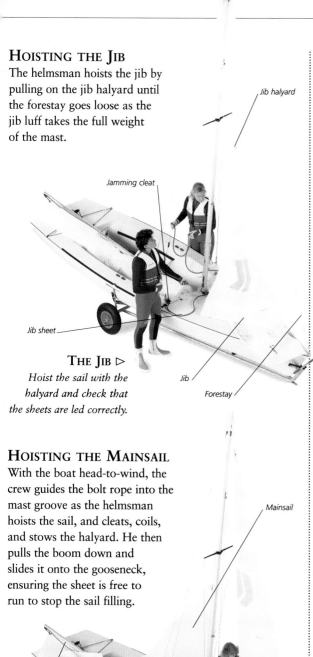

Jib halyard

Jamming cleat

Jib sheet

### THE JIB ▷
*Hoist the sail with the halyard and check that the sheets are led correctly.*

Jib

Forestay

## HOISTING THE MAINSAIL

With the boat head-to-wind, the crew guides the bolt rope into the mast groove as the helmsman hoists the sail, and cleats, coils, and stows the halyard. He then pulls the boom down and slides it onto the gooseneck, ensuring the sheet is free to run to stop the sail filling.

Mainsail

Boom

### THE MAINSAIL ▷
*Pull the halyard until the head of the mainsail reaches the masthead.*

Gooseneck

## BEACH OR SLIPWAY LAUNCH

*To launch from a beach or slipway, you and your sailing partner should use the trailer to wheel the boat into the water. Wheel it deep enough for the boat to float clear of the trailer. As soon as the boat floats free, it will come under the influence of the wind and waves so hold it firmly. For beach launches, you will need balloon tires on the trailer to cope with the soft surface. Be careful on slipways as they are often covered in slime and can be very slippery.*

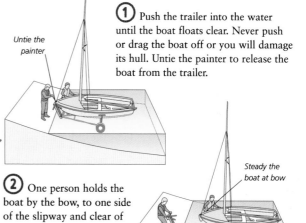

**①** Push the trailer into the water until the boat floats clear. Never push or drag the boat off or you will damage its hull. Untie the painter to release the boat from the trailer.

Untie the painter

Steady the boat at bow

**②** One person holds the boat by the bow, to one side of the slipway and clear of other users. The other takes the trailer to above high-water level and parks it clear of the slipway.

## DOCK LAUNCH

*If you have to launch over the side of a dock, it is best to do it before hoisting the sails. Dock launches need at least two people, one on either side of the boat.*

Lift the stern over the water

**①** With one person holding the painter, lift the boat until its stern is over the water. Lower the stern into the water, then gently push the boat back until the bow can be lowered over the side.

**②** Lead the boat to the end of the dock and turn it head-to-wind. Secure the painter fast on the dock before hoisting the sails and fitting the rudder.

Turn the boat head-to-wind

# BASIC TECHNIQUES

*In order to become proficient at handling a boat, you need to practice using the main controls (pp.32–33). You must learn how the boat reacts to the wind on all points of sailing, and you must be able to change course smoothly and efficiently. You will also want to know how to stop the boat. When you start sailing, you will not yet have the skills needed to leave and return to the shore under sail, so on your first few trips afloat, row or paddle away from shore, then hoist the sails once you are in clear water.*

## FIRST SKILLS

As soon as you launch a sailing dinghy, the wind will begin to move it. There are three basic ways to stop it from moving in the water, each of which involves making the wind work in your favor. The most controlled method, but also the most complicated, is heaving-to. Two further simple techniques for stopping a boat are the lying-to method and the head-to-wind method, both of which work by emptying the sails of wind so that they flap and lose forward drive. Lying-to is the more stable option as the boat will simply drift until you pull in the sails. In a head-to-wind position, the wind will push the boat backward due to the wind resistance of the flapping sails, and the bow will start to turn in one direction or the other (depending on the position of the rudder) until the sails fill and the boat starts to sail. This method is used mainly when you need to stop alongside a mooring or dock or other boat.

When you are confident with these two ways of stopping, you can try the more controlled heaving-to (*p.88*).

### NO-SAIL ZONE

The head-to-wind method of stopping exploits the fact that there is an area of about 45° on either side of the wind direction into which it is impossible to point the boat and keep sailing. This area is known as the no-sail zone. When the boat is

### USING THE WIND TO STOP AND START

To lie-to, turn the boat onto a close reach (*p.35*) and let both sails out fully. It is not possible to lie-to when the boat is pointing further offwind because, as you let out the mainsail, the boom hits the shrouds and the sail refills with wind. To sail away from the lying-to position, sheet in both sails and the boat will move forward.

To stop head-to-wind, turn the sailing dinghy until the bow points into the wind. This makes the sails shake along the centerline of the boat and it will come to a stop. To sail away from a head-to wind position, decide which way you want the bow to move and pull the jib across to the opposite side. This is known as backing the jib and will push the bow in the desired direction. When the boat has turned, trim both sails and sail off.

### LYING-TO METHOD ▷
*Turn the boat using the tiller until the wind is blowing from a point just forward of abeam. Let both sails out fully so that they flap. The boat will stop and drift gently until you pull in the sails.*

### HEAD-TO-WIND METHOD ▷
*Turn the boat using the tiller until the bow is pointing directly into the wind. The sails will flap and the boat will come to a stop before starting to move backward and gradually turning away from the wind.*

close-hauled, you are sailing along the edge of the no-sail zone. If you try to point closer to the wind, turning into the no-sail zone, the sails will shake, the boat will slow down and stop.

To get to a point upwind within the no-sail zone it is necessary to sail a series of zigzags, first on one tack then on the other, making progress to windward with each tack. This process is called beating to windward *(p.80)*.

## STARTING TO SAIL

When you first start sailing, it is easiest to get accustomed to using the main controls while sailing on a beam reach. This is the fastest and easiest point of sailing. It ensures good responsiveness while not demanding very accurate steering, sail trimming, centerboard positioning, or crew balance.

## BOAT SPEED

The speed at which you can sail is dependent on a number of factors, including the strength of the wind, the point of sailing you are on *(pp.34–35)*, the type of boat you are sailing, and how well you are sailing it. Tidal streams and waves will also affect speed *(pp.48–49)*.

**SPEED VERSUS POINT OF SAIL** ▷
*Potential boat speed on specific points of sailing and in a particular wind strength are shown using a polar diagram. The concentric circles represent potential boat speed. The further away from the central circle you are, the faster the boat is sailing. The precise shape of the performance curve depends on the design of the boat. The diagram shows the performance curve of a typical general-purpose dinghy. It reaches its maximum speed on a beam reach and moves slowest when sailed on a run.*

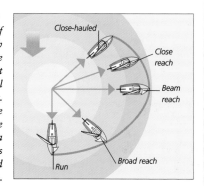

Close-hauled

Close reach

Beam reach

Broad reach

Run

## THE FIVE ESSENTIALS

There are five essential elements to sailing efficiently: sail trim, centerboard position, boat balance, boat trim, and the course made good. Whenever one changes, you should quickly review the other four and correct them if necessary. Remember to check the five essentials every time you make a course alteration.

### SAIL TRIM
To check trim, ease the sails out until they shake along their luffs, then pull them in until the shaking just stops. Make it easier to check trim by fitting tell-tales, which show the wind flow across the sails *(p.68)*.

### CENTERBOARD POSITION
The centerboard is used to counteract sideways force *(p.87)*, which is greatest when you sail close-hauled. So, the closer you sail toward the wind, the more you must lower the centerboard, and the further you turn away from the wind, the more you must raise the centerboard, until it is almost fully up on a run. Always keep it down at least a small amount to provide a pivot point around which the boat can turn.

### BOAT BALANCE
The heeling force increases as you sail closer to the wind, so the helmsman and crew must both sit out in most winds to keep the boat upright. If the wind strength changes, or the course alters, the crew should move first to balance the boat.

### BOAT TRIM
Always check that the boat is trimmed correctly in a fore and aft direction. In light winds, trim the boat slightly down by the bow; in strong winds, move back slightly. Check that the wake is not very disturbed, which indicates that you are sitting too far aft. Helmsman and crew should sit close together to keep their weight concentrated in the middle of the boat. This allows the bow and stern to lift easily with the waves.

### COURSE MADE GOOD
Always remember to keep an eye on your course. Your objective is to sail the fastest route to your destination. This is not necessarily the straight-line course. If your objective is to windward, for example, you will have to sail a zigzag course to reach it. This means that you must decide when to tack and you will also have to allow for leeway. Even when you are sailing on a reach, the sideways force will cause a small amount of leeway, and your actual course through the water will be slightly to leeward of the course you are steering. Allow for this by steering upwind of your objective by a small amount. Be aware, too, of any tidal stream that may push you off course.

# CHANGING COURSE

Learning to change course introduces you to all the different points of sailing (pp.34–35). It enables you to understand a little about how a boat works, and to experience the changing effects of the wind from different angles before you go on to learn how to tack and jibe. The best way to go through a complete change of course – from sailing toward the wind (an upwind course) to sailing away from it (a downwind course) – is to start on a beam reach with the boat sailing directly across the wind.

## STARTING TO LUFF UP

Turning the boat towards the wind is known as luffing up. Whenever you want to turn onto a more upwind course you have to luff up.

To luff up, the helmsman pushes the tiller gently away from him and sheets in the mainsail. The crew sheets in the jib and lowers the centerboard. As the boat turns toward the wind, the apparent wind (p.30) will increase in strength and the heeling force (p.30) also increases, so the crew will need to sit out even further to keep the boat level.

## STARTING TO BEAR AWAY

Turning away from the wind is called bearing away. Whenever you want to turn onto a more downwind course you have to bear away.

To bear away, the helmsman pulls the tiller gently toward him and lets the mainsail out. The crew lets out the jib and raises the centerboard. As the boat turns further away from the wind, the apparent wind decreases in strength and the heeling force reduces so the crew must move inboard to keep the boat level or to prevent it heeling to windward.

## LUFFING UP: TURNING TOWARD THE WIND

*Luffing up requires coordinated action with the tiller, centerboard, sail trim, and boat balance. The crew should lower the centerboard before the turn, and then concentrate on keeping the boat level and sheeting the jib in as the helmsman turns the boat and sheets in the mainsail.*

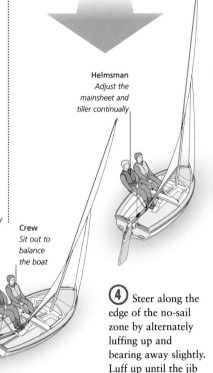

**Helmsman**
*Adjust the mainsheet and tiller continually*

④ Steer along the edge of the no-sail zone by alternately luffing up and bearing away slightly. Luff up until the jib luff starts shaking, and then bear away slightly until the shaking just stops.

**Crew**
*Sit out to balance the boat*

③ Luff up to very nearly close-hauled, sheeting both sails in tightly. Lower the centerboard fully and sit out even further.

**Helmsman**
*Sheet in the mainsail until it is still at the luff*

② Luff up to a close reach by pulling in the sails and pushing the tiller away from you. Lower the centerboard until it is three quarters down, and sit out more to counterbalance the increased heeling force in the sails.

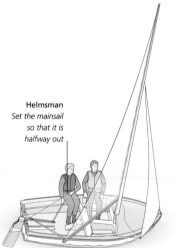

**Helmsman**
*Set the mainsail so that it is halfway out*

① Sail on a beam reach with the sails set correctly (p.35), the tiller centered, the boat upright, and the centerboard halfway down.

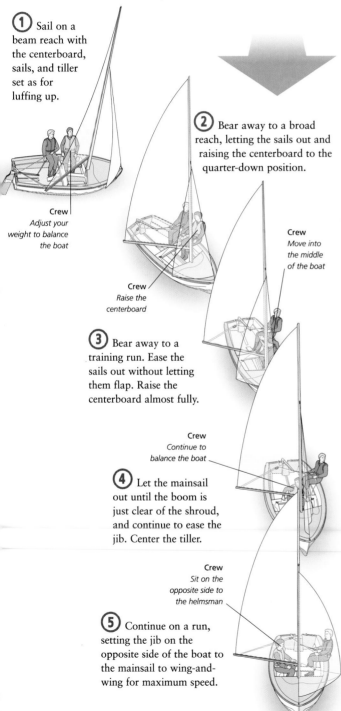

# BEARING AWAY: TURNING AWAY FROM THE WIND

*Make sure the boat is upright before the maneuver, because any heel to leeward will make it difficult to bear away. Let the sails out as the boat turns, and raise the centerboard.*

**(1)** Sail on a beam reach with the centerboard, sails, and tiller set as for luffing up.

**Crew**
*Adjust your weight to balance the boat*

**(2)** Bear away to a broad reach, letting the sails out and raising the centerboard to the quarter-down position.

**Crew**
*Move into the middle of the boat*

**Crew**
*Raise the centerboard*

**(3)** Bear away to a training run. Ease the sails out without letting them flap. Raise the centerboard almost fully.

**Crew**
*Continue to balance the boat*

**(4)** Let the mainsail out until the boom is just clear of the shroud, and continue to ease the jib. Center the tiller.

**Crew**
*Sit on the opposite side to the helmsman*

**(5)** Continue on a run, setting the jib on the opposite side of the boat to the mainsail to wing-and-wing for maximum speed.

## TECHNIQUES FOR SHEETING THE MAINSAIL IN AND OUT

The technique for sheeting the mainsail in and out varies according to your mainsheet system. Both methods require the helmsman to make adjustments while keeping the tiller still to avoid altering course unintentionally. To ease the sheet, let it slide out through your hand.

### CENTER MAINSHEET

*Use sheet hand to pull in mainsheet*

*Grasp the sheet near the block and pull*

**(1)** Pull in the mainsheet using your sheet hand. Holding the tiller extension in your tiller hand as if it were a dart, swing the extension across your body and down to grasp the sheet.

**(2)** With sheet and tiller extension in your tiller hand, swing the extension aft. With your sheet hand, grasp the sheet at a point near to the block and pull as far as you can. Repeat as necessary.

### AFT MAINSHEET

*Pull in the mainsheet as far as possible*

*Secure sheet under the tiller thumb*

**(1)** Keep your tiller hand steady on the tiller extension. With your sheet hand, pull in the mainsheet as far as possible, bringing the sheet across your body from the stern.

**(2)** Trap the sheet under the thumb of your tiller hand. Let go of it with your sheet hand, and then reach across your body to grasp the sheet and pull it again. Repeat these steps as necessary.

# TACKING

*O*ne of the key sailing maneuvers, tacking is used to change direction by turning the bow of the boat through the eye of the wind. It requires good coordination between helmsman and crew. A tack can be performed from any upwind course but is most often employed to change from one close-hauled course to the other. When tacking an aft-mainsheet boat, the helmsman faces aft; if a center-mainsheet is fitted, he must face forward. The movements of the crew remain the same.

**7** Helmsman and crew trim the sails to suit the new course and balance the boat accordingly.

## TACKING ROLES

The helmsman decides when to tack. He and the crew must turn the boat, trim the sails, and move their weight across the boat while keeping it as upright as possible. The helmsman ensures that the new course is clear and that the crew is ready. During the tack, the helmsman must change hands on the mainsheet and the tiller while moving across the boat, manipulating both controls at the same time. After the tack, he must check sail trim, boat balance, and the new course.

The crew is responsible for releasing the jib sheet, picking up the new jib sheet, and moving across the boat to sheet in the jib on the new side as the boat completes the turn. The crew must be alert to the instructions given by the helmsman, and he must confirm that the turning area is clear before committing to the turn.

## THE TACKING MANEUVER

Tacking is actually a prolonged luffing-up maneuver in which the boat turns sufficiently for the sail to fill on the opposite course. The maneuver begins with luffing up (*p.76*). The tack itself occurs when the bow of the boat passes through the eye of the wind, and the maneuver is complete when you are sailing on the new course.

## TACKING A CENTER-MAINSHEET BOAT

*This sequence shows a boat with a center-mainsheet being tacked from a reach to a reach. The boat must be sailing fast before the tack, and you must steer it firmly through the turn, or else it may fail to complete the tack, stopping head-to-wind – a position known as being "in irons" (p.81).*

**1** Sail on a beam reach, trim the sails, and put the centerboard half-down. The helmsman checks that the course is clear of obstructions then calls "ready about" to warn the crew.

**Helmsman**
*Check the course before starting to tack*

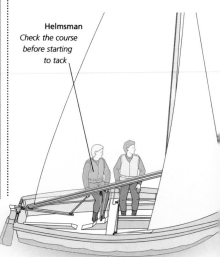

---

### TACKING FROM A REACH TO A REACH

When you are learning to tack, you will start by sailing on a beam reach with the wind on one side of the boat, and will then tack onto the opposite beam reach with the wind on the other side.

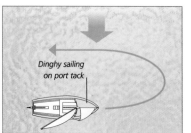

*Dinghy sailing on port tack*

◁ **A BEAM-REACH TACK**
*Tacking from a beam reach to the opposite beam reach involves a turn of 180°. Turning through such a large angle gives the helmsman and crew more time to cross the boat before the sails fill on the new side. It does, however, require the boat to be sailing fast before the tack so that it has sufficient momentum to complete the turn.*

**Helmsman**
*Release the tiller from the old tiller hand and grasp the mainsheet. Bring the tiller extension in front of you using the new tiller hand*

**Helmsman**
*Sitting on the new deck, steer onto the new course with the tiller behind you. Bring your sheet hand (still holding the mainsheet) back to grasp the tiller extension*

*Boat on starboard tack – boom on the port side*

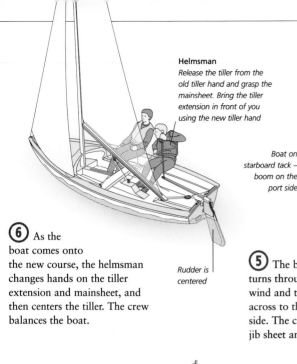

**6** As the boat comes onto the new course, the helmsman changes hands on the tiller extension and mainsheet, and then centers the tiller. The crew balances the boat.

*Rudder is centered*

**5** The bow turns through the wind and the jib blows across to the new leeward side. The crew pulls in the new jib sheet and balances the boat.

*Boat turns through the wind*

**4** As the boat turns head-to-wind, the helmsman keeps the tiller pushed over and crosses the boat facing forward. The crew moves to the middle of the boat and prepares to pull in the new jib sheet.

**3** The helmsman calls "hard-a-lee" and pushes the tiller to leeward to start the turn. As the jib flaps, the crew lets out the old jib sheet and picks up the new jib sheet.

**Helmsman**
*As the boom swings into the center of the boat, move into the middle, ducking under it. Lead with your rear foot*

**2** The crew checks the area and, if all is clear and he is ready, replies "ready." He then uncleats the jib sheet but does not let it out.

**Helmsman**
*If the mainsheet is cleated, uncleat it*

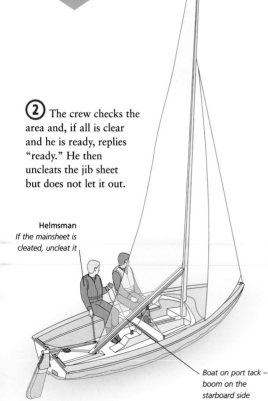

*Boat on port tack – boom on the starboard side*

**Helmsman**
*Start the tack by pushing the tiller extension away, moving it about 30° from the centerline*

## SAILING TO WINDWARD

Once you have learned how to tack, you can experiment with sailing to windward. Although you can sail close-hauled along the edge of the no-sail zone (*p.34*), if you turn closer to the wind, into the no-sail zone, the luffs of the sails will start to flutter and the boat will eventually stop. Pull the tiller gently toward you to turn away from the wind and resume sailing efficiently. Do not bear away too far, however, otherwise you will give up valuable distance. To reach a point upwind, within the no-sail zone, you will need to follow a zigzag course – a process that is known as beating to windward.

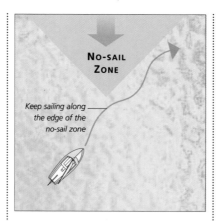

△ **EDGE OF THE NO-SAIL ZONE**
To sail as close to the wind as possible, sheet in both sails tight and luff up gently until the luff of the jib starts shaking. Bear away slightly to stop the sail shaking then repeat to sail along the edge of the zone.

**BEATING TO WINDWARD ▷**
*To sail upwind or get to a point that is within the no-sail zone you have to tack and sail a zigzag course. Here, the boat starts on port tack then tacks onto starboard tack, making progress to windward with each turn. The helmsman can choose to make a series of short tacks or a smaller number of longer ones depending on the distance to his objective.*

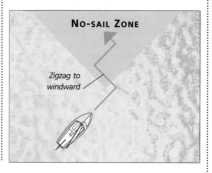

## TACKING FROM CLOSE-HAULED

Tacking is most often used to turn from one close-hauled course to the other as part of the process of beating to windward. The boat turns through only ninety degrees, so the tack is relatively quick.

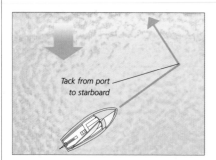

◁ **A CLOSE-HAULED TACK**
*Tacking from close-hauled to close-hauled involves a turn of only 90° and will happen much more quickly than when tacking from a reach to a reach. You should avoid turning too far after the tack, otherwise you will end up further off the wind than the intended close-hauled course and will sail a longer distance.*

## TACKING AN AFT-MAINSHEET BOAT

*This sequence shows an aft-mainsheet boat tacking from close-hauled on port tack to close-hauled on starboard tack. Because it is an aft mainsheet, the helmsman must cross the boat facing aft and change hands on the tiller extension and mainsheet before the tack. The crew crosses the boat facing forward as usual. The boat turns through only 90°, so the maneuver happens very quickly, compared to tacking from a beam reach to a beam reach (p.78). The crew and helmsman must cross the boat swiftly before the sails fill.*

① The helmsman prepares to tack by checking that the course is clear. If it is, he calls "ready about." The crew makes sure that the centerboard is fully down, checks for obstructions, and replies "ready." He uncleats the jib sheet, but does not let it out.

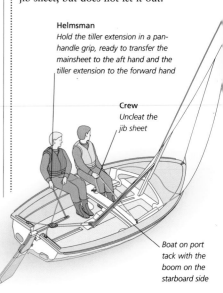

**Helmsman**
*Hold the tiller extension in a pan-handle grip, ready to transfer the mainsheet to the aft hand and the tiller extension to the forward hand*

**Crew**
*Uncleat the jib sheet*

*Boat on port tack with the boom on the starboard side*

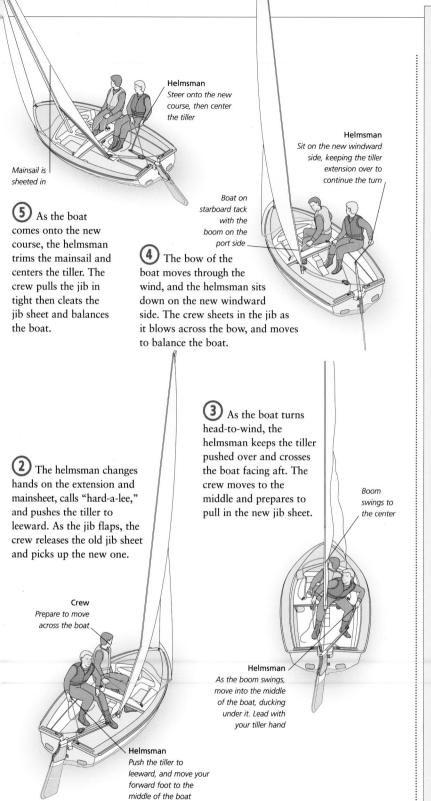

*Mainsail is sheeted in*

**Helmsman**
*Steer onto the new course, then center the tiller*

**Helmsman**
*Sit on the new windward side, keeping the tiller extension over to continue the turn*

**(5)** As the boat comes onto the new course, the helmsman trims the mainsail and centers the tiller. The crew pulls the jib in tight then cleats the jib sheet and balances the boat.

*Boat on starboard tack with the boom on the port side*

**(4)** The bow of the boat moves through the wind, and the helmsman sits down on the new windward side. The crew sheets in the jib as it blows across the bow, and moves to balance the boat.

**(3)** As the boat turns head-to-wind, the helmsman keeps the tiller pushed over and crosses the boat facing aft. The crew moves to the middle and prepares to pull in the new jib sheet.

*Boom swings to the center*

**(2)** The helmsman changes hands on the extension and mainsheet, calls "hard-a-lee," and pushes the tiller to leeward. As the jib flaps, the crew releases the old jib sheet and picks up the new one.

**Crew**
*Prepare to move across the boat*

**Helmsman**
*As the boom swings, move into the middle of the boat, ducking under it. Lead with your tiller hand*

**Helmsman**
*Push the tiller to leeward, and move your forward foot to the middle of the boat*

# A FAILED TACK

When a boat fails to tack, it may end up "in irons." There are several reasons why a tack fails: the boat is sailing too slowly, the helmsman is steering badly, or the crew has pulled in the new jib sheet too early, making it fill on the wrong side.

### ESCAPING FROM "IN IRONS"

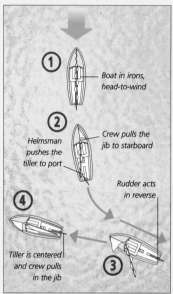

*Boat in irons, head-to-wind*

**Helmsman pushes the tiller to port**

*Crew pulls the jib to starboard*

*Rudder acts in reverse*

*Tiller is centered and crew pulls in the jib*

**(1)** To escape from being in irons, the helmsman must push the tiller toward the side of the boat in the direction he wants the bow to go. Here, the tiller is pushed to port.

**(2)** At the same time, the crew must pull the jib to the opposite side of the boat so that it fills with wind – a technique known as "backing the jib."

**(3)** The boat will move backward and the rudder acts in reverse. The backed jib will help to push the bow in the desired direction.

**(4)** As soon as the boat is pointing the right way, the helmsman centers the tiller and the crew sheets in the jib on the correct side. The boat is now ready to continue its course.

# JIBING

*Like tacking, jibing involves turning the boat to change tack and bring the wind to the other side. In jibing, however, it is the stern, rather than the bow, that turns through the wind. When you jibe, the mainsail stays full of wind throughout the maneuver, and its swing across the boat can be sudden and violent. This is very unlike tacking, where the sails lose drive and flap harmlessly until the turn is complete. Unless the boat is correctly balanced throughout, you may lose control or capsize.*

## JIBING ROLES

The helmsman decides when to jibe. He is responsible for ensuring that the new course is clear, and for making sure that the crew is ready. During the jibe, the helmsman must change hands on the mainsheet and tiller, while keeping control of both. He must also move across the boat during the turn. After the jibe, he has to steer onto the new course and check the sail trim and boat balance.

The crew is responsible for releasing the old jib sheet, picking up the new jib sheet, and moving across the boat to sheet in the jib on the new side as the boat completes the jibe. He must concentrate on balancing the boat throughout the jibe.

## PREPARING TO JIBE

Jibing begins with bearing away until the jib hangs limply behind the mainsail, indicating that you are on a dead run (*p.34*). You then luff up very slightly so that the jib just fills on the same side as the mainsail. This is a training run, which, when you are learning how to jibe, is the correct starting point for the maneuver.

---

## JIBING FROM A TRAINING RUN

When you are learning, you will start by sailing on a training run with the wind behind you at an angle of about 5–10° off a true run. After the jibe, you will probably be sailing on a broad reach.

Move the tiller to windward as boat jibes

◁ **TRAINING-RUN JIBE**
*Learning to jibe by starting from a training run gives you more time to prepare for the maneuver and to adjust your weight to balance the boat. The boat will turn through quite a wide arc and, if you are not quick enough to straighten the tiller as the boom swings across, may turn onto a broad reach on the new tack. The helmsman should watch the mainsail leech carefully for signs that it is about to jibe. He should be in the middle of the boat as the boom comes across, with the tiller centered.*

---

**4** As the boom reaches the centerline, the helmsman centers the tiller and moves his weight to the new windward side. The crew moves to keep the boat upright and trims the jib.

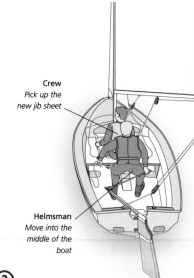

*Boom may swing across very suddenly*

**Helmsman**
*Center the tiller as the boom reaches the centerline*

**Crew**
*Pick up the new jib sheet*

**Helmsman**
*Move into the middle of the boat*

**3** The helmsman calls "helms-a-lee" and bears away further. He moves into the middle of the boat, ducking under the boom. The crew grasps the new jib sheet and balances the boat.

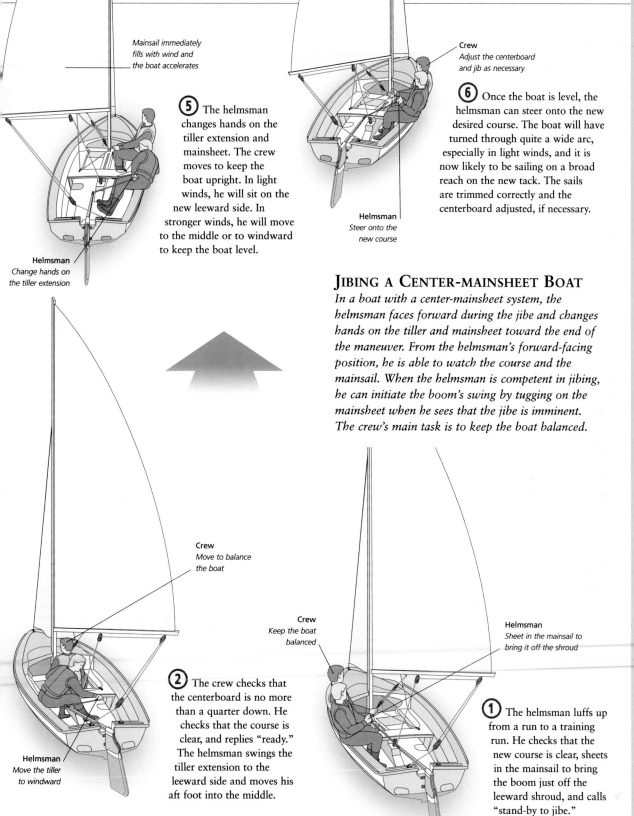

**5** The helmsman changes hands on the tiller extension and mainsheet. The crew moves to keep the boat upright. In light winds, he will sit on the new leeward side. In stronger winds, he will move to the middle or to windward to keep the boat level.

*Mainsail immediately fills with wind and the boat accelerates*

**Helmsman**
*Change hands on the tiller extension*

**Crew**
*Adjust the centerboard and jib as necessary*

**6** Once the boat is level, the helmsman can steer onto the new desired course. The boat will have turned through quite a wide arc, especially in light winds, and it is now likely to be sailing on a broad reach on the new tack. The sails are trimmed correctly and the centerboard adjusted, if necessary.

**Helmsman**
*Steer onto the new course*

## JIBING A CENTER-MAINSHEET BOAT

*In a boat with a center-mainsheet system, the helmsman faces forward during the jibe and changes hands on the tiller and mainsheet toward the end of the maneuver. From the helmsman's forward-facing position, he is able to watch the course and the mainsail. When the helmsman is competent in jibing, he can initiate the boom's swing by tugging on the mainsheet when he sees that the jibe is imminent. The crew's main task is to keep the boat balanced.*

**Crew**
*Move to balance the boat*

**Crew**
*Keep the boat balanced*

**Helmsman**
*Sheet in the mainsail to bring it off the shroud*

**2** The crew checks that the centerboard is no more than a quarter down. He checks that the course is clear, and replies "ready." The helmsman swings the tiller extension to the leeward side and moves his aft foot into the middle.

**Helmsman**
*Move the tiller to windward*

**1** The helmsman luffs up from a run to a training run. He checks that the new course is clear, sheets in the mainsail to bring the boom just off the leeward shroud, and calls "stand-by to jibe."

## JIBING SAFELY

Make sure that the boat is upright before the jibe. If it heels to leeward, it will be harder to jibe as the boat will try to luff up and turn in the wrong direction.

The centerboard must be no more than a quarter down when you jibe. If it is any lower, the boat will try to luff as the boom swings across and, as a result, may trip over the centerboard and cause the boat to capsize. If your sailing dinghy has a daggerboard, make sure that it will not catch on the boom or boom vang as the mainsail swings across, or you will capsize.

Jibing in strong winds can be hazardous and can be avoided by luffing up to a reach, then tacking around before bearing away to the desired course. If you choose to jibe in strong winds, do so when the boat is sailing as fast as possible. Because the boat is sailing away from the true wind, the apparent wind is reduced by the speed of the boat's movement. This reduces the forces on the sail and makes jibing easier. Pick a time when the boat is surfing down the front of a wave and jibe when the boat is at its maximum speed.

## JIBING TIPS

Once you are committed to jibing, do not hesitate or change your mind. Turn the boat smoothly and be prepared to move fast as the boom comes across.

You can obtain advance warning of when the boat is about to jibe by watching the leech of the mainsail, about one-third up from the boom. When the jibe is imminent, the leech folds back to windward, showing the wind is getting behind the sail.

As the boat jibes and the boom swings across the centerline, it is very important that both the helmsman and the crew are in the middle of the boat, and that the tiller is centered.

It is often necessary to turn the boat through quite a wide arc before the boom starts to move across the boat, particularly in light winds. You can get around this by giving a sharp tug on the mainsheet when you see the jib blow across the bow. This will start the boom moving across the boat earlier than it would do otherwise.

## ACCIDENTAL JIBES

If you continue to bear away from a broad reach to a run, sailing further and further away from the wind, the boat will eventually jibe on its own as the wind swings across the stern. As this is an uncontrolled jibe, it can result in you taking an unexpected swim. Ensure that you do not jibe accidentally by continually checking the wind direction whenever you are sailing downwind. An early warning sign of an unplanned jibe is when the jib tries to blow across to the windward side of the boat. This means that you are on a dead run, so if you bear away any more, then the boat will jibe.

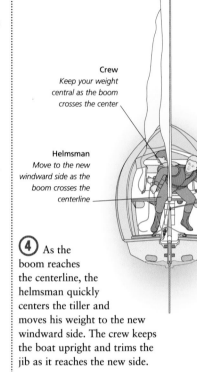

**Crew**
*Keep your weight central as the boom crosses the center*

**Helmsman**
*Move to the new windward side as the boom crosses the centerline*

**④** As the boom reaches the centerline, the helmsman quickly centers the tiller and moves his weight to the new windward side. The crew keeps the boat upright and trims the jib as it reaches the new side.

---

## JIBING FROM A DEAD RUN

Although you will usually learn to jibe by starting on a training run and ending on a broad reach, it is possible to jibe while sailing on a dead run with no course alteration at all, or only a minor one.

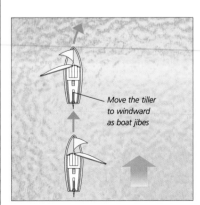

*Move the tiller to windward as boat jibes*

◁ **A DEAD-RUN JIBE**
*To jibe on a dead run with minimal course alteration, it is necessary for the crew or helmsman to pull the mainsail across to the new leeward side, rather than using the wind to move it by turning the boat during the jibe. Sail on a dead run with the helmsman in the middle of the boat and the crew balancing it as necessary. When the helmsman calls "helms-a-lee," the crew grasps the boom vang and swings the boom across. In a center-mainsheet boat, the helmsman can grasp the mainsheet tackle and use it to swing the boom over instead.*

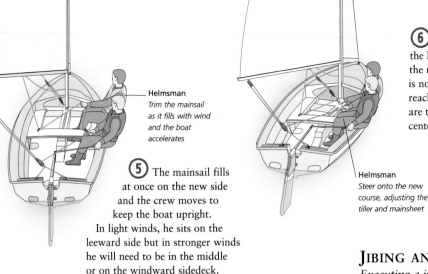

**Helmsman**
*Trim the mainsail
as it fills with wind
and the boat
accelerates*

**⑤** The mainsail fills
at once on the new side
and the crew moves to
keep the boat upright.
In light winds, he sits on the
leeward side but in stronger winds
he will need to be in the middle
or on the windward sidedeck.

**⑥** Once the boat is level,
the helmsman can steer onto
the new desired course. The boat
is now likely to be on a broad
reach on the new tack. The sails
are trimmed correctly and the
centerboard adjusted if necessary.

**Helmsman**
*Steer onto the new
course, adjusting the
tiller and mainsheet*

## JIBING AN AFT-MAINSHEET BOAT

*Executing a jibe in a boat with an aft mainsheet
differs from jibing one with a center-mainsheet
in that the helmsman changes hands on the
mainsheet and tiller before the jibe, and he
faces aft during the jibe. This means that he
cannot see what is in front of the boat during
the maneuver, so it is important that the jibe is
completed as quickly as possible. The crew, as in
all maneuvers, crosses the boat facing forward.*

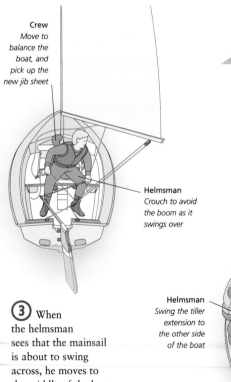

**Crew**
*Move to
balance the
boat, and
pick up the
new jib sheet*

**Helmsman**
*Crouch to avoid
the boom as it
swings over*

**③** When
the helmsman
sees that the mainsail
is about to swing
across, he moves to
the middle of the boat,
pivoting on the balls
of his feet to face aft.

**②** The
helmsman calls
"helms-a-lee,"
changes hands on the
tiller and mainsheet, and
puts his front foot into the
center. He swings the extension to
leeward and the tiller to windward.

**Helmsman**
*Swing the tiller
extension to
the other side
of the boat*

**①** The helmsman luffs up to a
training run, checks the new course,
sheets in to bring the boom clear of
the shroud, and calls "stand-by to
jibe." The crew checks the course
and centerboard and calls "ready."

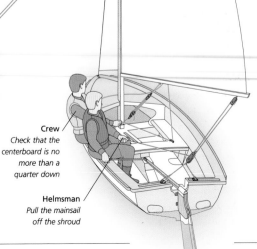

**Crew**
*Check that the
centerboard is no
more than a
quarter down*

**Helmsman**
*Pull the mainsail
off the shroud*

# SAILING A COURSE

One of the best ways to develop your skills is to sail a course that requires you to tack and jibe, and encompasses all the points of sailing (pp.34–35). How you arrange your course depends on your sailing area. A small island would be ideal to sail around. Alternatively, you could use a few buoys as your turning points, or else simply sail an imaginary circuit to bring you back to your starting point. Whatever course you set, try to sail out of the way of other boats on your first few attempts.

## SAILING UPWIND

Start by sailing on the upwind courses (beam reach, close reach, and close-hauled). On these courses you can slow down and stop, if necessary, simply by letting out the sails until they shake.

### BEAM REACH

Steer onto a beam reach with the centerboard half down. Trim the sails and move your weight to keep the boat upright. If it heels significantly even though you are sitting out fully, consider reefing (p.62). Experiment with moving the tiller until you are happy with the way it alters the boat's course. Watch its effect by looking at how the bow moves in relation to the horizon. Keep checking the trim of the sails. In moderate winds, this will be the fastest point of sailing (pp.34–35).

### CLOSE REACH

When you have got the feel of the boat sailing on a beam reach, you can luff up to a close-reaching course.

### SAILING AROUND A COURSE ▷
Choose an area clear of other boats, ideally with something to sail around – either a small island or a series of small buoys to form turning points on your course.

Lower the centerboard to the three-quarters-down position and sheet in the sails to keep them full. You will need to sit out harder to counter the increased heeling force. In light winds, this will be the fastest point of sailing.

### CLOSE-HAULED

Sailing close-hauled is difficult to get right and requires plenty of practice. Lower the centerboard fully and luff up to a close-hauled course. Ask the crew to pull the jib in tight and cleat

### STEERING A COURSE ▷
You will need to luff up, bear away, tack, and jibe to complete this course. It is advisable to try to pick light to medium winds for your first few outings. Sailing in strong winds is obviously tricky, but very light winds can also be difficult to sail in – the boat will be slow to react and will require skillful sailing to keep it moving.

**START**

Beam reach
A beam reach is a good course for beginners to start on

Tack

the sheet. Next, sheet the mainsail in tight and steer the boat by watching the luff of the jib. Your aim is to sail along the edge of the no-sail zone, making as much distance to windward as possible. Gently ease the tiller away from you, luffing up slowly, and watch for the moment when the jib

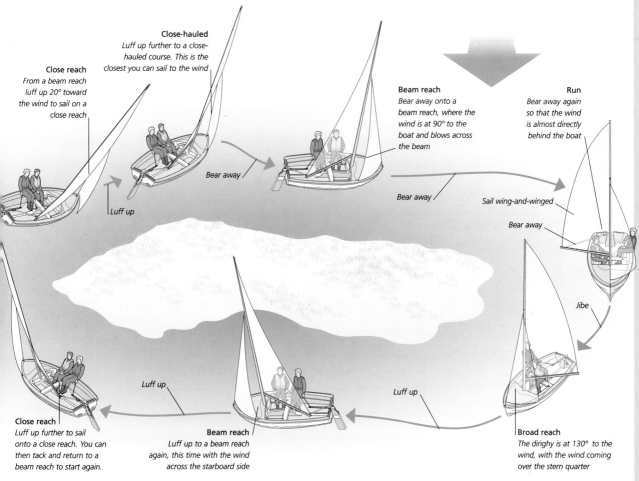

**Close reach**
*From a beam reach luff up 20° toward the wind to sail on a close reach*

**Close-hauled**
*Luff up further to a close-hauled course. This is the closest you can sail to the wind*

**Beam reach**
*Bear away onto a beam reach, where the wind is at 90° to the boat and blows across the beam*

**Run**
*Bear away again so that the wind is almost directly behind the boat*

*Luff up*

*Bear away*

*Bear away*

*Sail wing-and-winged*

*Bear away*

*Jibe*

*Luff up*

*Luff up*

*Luff up*

**Close reach**
*Luff up further to sail onto a close reach. You can then tack and return to a beam reach to start again.*

**Beam reach**
*Luff up to a beam reach again, this time with the wind across the starboard side*

**Broad reach**
*The dinghy is at 130° to the wind, with the wind coming over the stern quarter*

luff shakes. At that point, pull the tiller toward you very slightly to bear away until the luff stops shaking. To maintain a close-hauled course, you must constantly repeat this gentle luffing up and bearing away, which demands concentration when you are learning. If you lose concentration you will find that you are sailing either too close or too far off the wind. The former is obvious as the jib will shake and the boat will slow down; the latter is more difficult to spot.

If you find that the boat heels too far in gusts of wind, even though you are sitting out, reduce the heeling force by easing the mainsheet slightly to bring the boat upright again. When the gust passes, pull the sheet in again or the boat will heel to windward.

## UNDERSTANDING LEEWAY

As you sail on upwind courses, you will notice that your boat slips sideways to some extent. Called leeway, this sideways drift is at its most obvious when you are sailing a close-hauled course.

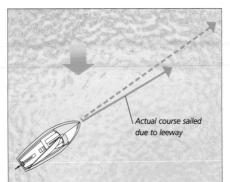

*Actual course sailed due to leeway*

◁ **COUNTERACTING THE SIDEWAYS FORCE**
*The centerboard minimizes leeway and is most effective when the boat is moving quickly. Consequently, the effect of leeway is most noticeable when you are sailing slowly. When sailing close-hauled, do not try to steer further to windward to counteract leeway as the boat will simply slow down and leeway will increase. Instead, be prepared to put in a tack to reach your objective.*

# SAILING DOWNWIND

After the upwind courses, you will notice a big difference as you sail onto the downwind courses (broad reach, training run, and dead run). The difference is especially obvious in moderate to strong winds. The wind strength will seem to decrease due to the effects of apparent wind (p.30). You will not have to sit out so hard to balance the boat; and you will not be pushing into the waves but sailing with them. Any spray that was flying upwind will disappear and the environment will seem warmer.

## BROAD REACH

From a beam reach, bear away to sail on a broad reach. Ease out both sails until they set correctly, watching the luffs or tell-tales to see when the optimum trim is achieved. Raise the centerboard so that it is a quarter-down and move inboard to keep the boat level (shift your weight back slightly to lift the bow if it seems to be burrowing into the waves). In strong winds, a broad reach is likely to be the fastest point of sailing.

## TRAINING RUN

From the broad reach, bear away to a training run so that the wind comes over one stern quarter, and ease the sails out as far as possible. Remember that you cannot ease the mainsail fully because the boom will hit the leeward shroud. Keep it just clear of the shroud to prevent chafe. If the boom seems to be rising too high at the outer end and the boat is rolling, tighten the boom vang to hold it down.

Unlike the mainsail, the jib is not limited in how much it can be let out. It should be set using the tell-tales (p.68) or by watching for a shaking luff. If the jib collapses behind the mainsail, you have turned the boat too far from the wind, so luff up slightly until the jib fills again.

To sail efficiently on a training run, you need to raise the centerboard until little more than the tip protrudes below the dinghy. If the boat rolls and feels unstable, put a bit more of the centerboard down

to help stabilize it. Depending on the strength of the wind, the crew should sit in the middle of the boat or to leeward to balance the weight of the helmsman. To have a good view of the sails and the course, the helmsman should remain seated on the windward sidedeck.

## DEAD RUN

Sailing on a dead run is the trickiest point of sailing for the helmsman and crew. With the sails eased out fully and the wind blowing from straight behind the boat there is no heeling force to balance against and the boat will tend to roll from side to side. The maximum speed is obtained by pulling the centerboard almost fully up, but this will increase the tendency to roll. If rolling becomes a problem, lower the centerboard to the quarter-down position.

The helmsman should sit on the windward side, but the crew will usually have to move right across to leeward to balance the helmsman's weight. The crew must be ready to move quickly but smoothly if the boat rolls either way. The helmsman must concentrate carefully on his course to avoid an accidental jibe.

## WING-AND-WINGING

Once you have gained confidence on a run, you can try wing-and-winging by setting the jib on the opposite side of the mainsail. This will increase your speed and will also help to balance the pull of the mainsail and make the boat easier to steer on a straight course. To wing-and-wing, bear away to a dead run so that the wind is coming directly over the transom. This makes the jib collapse as it is now in the wind shadow of the mainsail. Pull it across the foredeck using the other jib sheet until it fills with wind and sets on the opposite side of the boat.

---

## HEAVING-TO

Heaving-to, or the hove-to position, is more effective than lying-to (p.74) if you need to halt for anything longer than a few moments. It is a good position if you need to reef or if you want to rest.

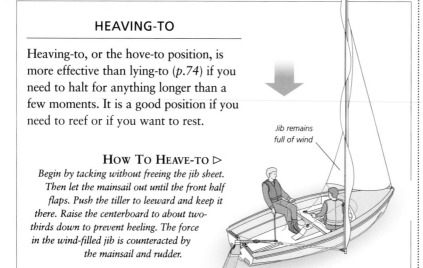

*Jib remains full of wind*

### HOW TO HEAVE-TO ▷
*Begin by tacking without freeing the jib sheet. Then let the mainsail out until the front half flaps. Push the tiller to leeward and keep it there. Raise the centerboard to about two-thirds down to prevent heeling. The force in the wind-filled jib is counteracted by the mainsail and rudder.*

## WHISKER POLES

Some boats that are not designed to have spinnakers (*pp.122–23*) have a short pole, known as a whisker pole, that is used to boom out the jib when it is wing-and-winged. The whisker pole is clipped to a ring on the front of the mast and usually has a point on the other end that is pushed into the cringle at the jib clew. Tension is maintained on the jib sheet to prevent it from slipping out.

The whisker pole can be a very useful accessory if you have some distance to sail on a dead run. It keeps the jib wing-and-winged even if the helmsman luffs slightly to a training run. Without the help of the whisker pole, it is much harder for the crew to keep the jib set in this way. Make sure that you remove and stow the whisker pole safely before you jibe or luff up.

### ▽ USING A WHISKER POLE

*This Sharpie is a traditional dinghy class that does not use a spinnaker. Instead, a long whisker pole helps boost speed downwind and reduce rolling by poling out the jib on the windward side.*

## SAILING IN TIDES

When you sail in tidal waters, it is important to allow for a tidal stream, which will make your boat drift in relation to the seabed. It will influence how you steer to follow your course.

### TIDAL EFFECTS

To get a better idea of how the tide affects your boat, imagine you are walking on a moving floor. If you walk in the same direction that the floor is moving in you will travel faster than you would if the floor was static. If you turn around and walk in the opposite direction to that in which the floor is moving, it is harder to make forward progress and will take you longer. Walk across the floor and its movement will take you sideways, away from your destination. These effects are identical to what happens to your boat when you sail in tidal waters.

### TIDAL DIRECTION

If you are going to sail in tidal waters, make sure that you know the direction of the tidal stream before you go on the water. Also, find out whether the direction is due to change while you are sailing.

### COPING WITH TIDES

When you find yourself in a tidal stream, the following few tips will help you to keep out of trouble.
• Remember that the strongest tidal stream is usually found in the deepest water, while the the weakest streams occur in shallow water.
• If the tide is going with you, maneuver into the strongest stream to maximize the benefit.
• If the tide is against you, get out of the strongest stream by heading for shallow water, but be careful not to run aground.
• If you have to sail across the current, head upstream of a straight-line course to allow for the tide sweeping you sideways.

# From and to the Shore

*Setting off for your sailing trip and returning from it afterwards are usually the trickiest parts of the day. The shoreline is a solid obstacle that is a potential hazard to you and your boat if you do not know how to deal with it. Docks and slipways require certain skills if you are to leave them and return to them without problems. You also need to know how to cope with onshore and offshore winds and changing tidal conditions, as well as obstacles, such as other boats.*

## Weather Shore

The main factor that will determine the ease or difficulty of leaving and returning to the shore is the wind direction in relation to the shoreline.

If the wind is blowing off the land, the shore is called a weather shore and the wind is called an offshore wind. In this situation, it is easy to leave the shore as not only do you have the wind blowing you off the shore, but the water will be flat, with no waves breaking close to the land. To return to the shore, beat to windward (*p.80*). To stop the boat, simply turn head-to-wind when you reach shallow water.

## Lee Shore

When the wind blows onto the land, the shore is called a lee shore and the wind is referred to as an onshore wind. Leaving a lee shore can be difficult, especially in strong winds from a beach with breaking waves. Once launched, beat to windward to get away from the shore. To return, simply sail downwind. Landing on a lee shore can be difficult however – especially in breaking waves – and should be avoided if possible.

## ▽ Launching from a Slipway

*A slipway is an easier launching point than a beach. Once the dinghy is afloat, park the trailer, and sail or paddle off.*

## Along the Shore

If the wind is blowing along the shoreline, you have an easy launching situation as you can simply sail from and to the shore on a beam reach.

## Leaving a Beach

Most dinghies can be launched from a beach, but this is not normally as easy as launching from a slipway or dock. To move the boat across soft sand, you will need several people to carry it or a trailer with large tires. A stone or shingle beach is also difficult to negotiate, and you may damage the hull on the stones. Some beaches, usually sandy ones, have a shallow slope into the water, which remains shallow for a long way out, making it difficult to fit the rudder and use the centerboard or daggerboard. Stony or shingle beaches often have a steeper slope where the water depth quickly increases. However, beaches with steep slopes are more prone to large, breaking waves in an onshore wind, which make launching more difficult.

## Leaving a Slipway

Using a proper slipway is easy, but be sure to examine the type of shoreline that lies to either side of it. You may discover that the slipway is just a ramp between two sections of sea wall, which will present a significant hazard when returning to shore – or even as you are leaving – should you make a mistake. Beware of slipways that end suddenly with a steep drop into deep water. If you are launching at low tide you may find yourself unexpectedly falling off the end.

Aptly named, slipways are often covered in algae and other slimy weeds, so take care not to lose your footing. Always hold on to the boat's painter so that the dinghy does not sail off without you should you slip, and be wary of losing control of the trailer.

## Leaving a Dock

A dock is usually the easiest point to launch from, especially if there is a slipway alongside to get the boat into and out of the water. Once your boat is in the water, you can move it to a berth alongside the dock and take your time leaving. When you return, you can lower and stow the sails at leisure before taking the boat out of the water. If the dock protrudes into deep water, consider any tidal stream effects (*right*).

## Leaving a Weather Shore

Before you decide to leave from a weather shore, check the forecast. Because the wind is blowing off the land, it will be extremely difficult to judge how strong it is further away from the shore and beyond the sheltering effects of the land. There will not be any significant waves close to the shore but as you sail further out you may get a nasty surprise as the wind increases and the waves grow in size. You sail away from a weather shore on a broad reach or run, but to return you will need to beat to windward. This may be difficult if conditions further out are worse than you anticipated. Be prudent when sailing from a weather shore, and sail only when certain that the conditions offshore are within your capabilities.

## Leaving a Lee Shore

You will probably be fully exposed to the prevailing conditions on a lee shore. In fact, the wind and waves may seem to be more daunting when you are on the beach than they actually are when you sail further out. This is especially likely if the shore is steep, in which case waves will break onto it even in moderate winds. In this case, the hardest part of the sail is getting off the beach and sailing through the surf line to calmer water.

## LAUNCHING IN TIDES

The presence of a current or tidal stream in the launching area may complicate leaving and returning maneuvers. In some circumstances, its direction and strength will determine the way in which you should leave or approach the shore.

### Shallow Water

When sailing off a beach, you do not usually have to worry about the effect of a tidal stream along the shoreline because you are launching into shallow water where the stream, if any, will be minimal. Be aware, however, of the direction and strength of the stream offshore and plan your course accordingly.

### Deep Water

In deep water, the tidal stream will affect how you sail away and return. Except when the tide is weak in relation to the wind, you should always treat it as the most significant force. If in doubt, sail away from the dock or slipway pointing into the tide and using just the jib if the wind is behind the beam. When you are returning, plan ahead and aim to turn into the tide to stop when you reach the dock or slipway. If this means that the wind will be behind the beam on your approach, lower the mainsail and sail in under the jib.

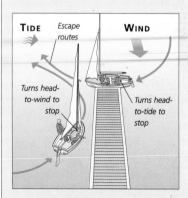

**WIND AND TIDE AT A DOCK**

# WEATHER SHORE

## LEAVING A BEACH

*When you leave a weather shore from a beach,
begin with the usual launching procedure,
preparing the boat and moving it to the
edge of the water (pp.72–73). Turn the
dinghy so that it is head-to-wind and
hoist the sails (pp.58–61). Launch the
boat carefully, then, while one of you
holds the boat by the painter, the
other parks the trailer up the beach
and out of the way. You are now
ready to get on board and sail away.*

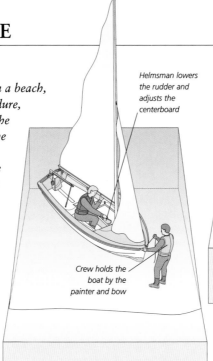

Helmsman lowers
the rudder and
adjusts the
centerboard

Crew holds the
boat by the
painter and bow

**(1)** The crew holds the boat by the
bow while the helmsman gets aboard,
checks that all gear is stowed, and fits
the rudder. The helmsman lowers the
rudder blade (if it is the lifting type) and
puts the centerboard about a quarter
down if the water is deep enough.

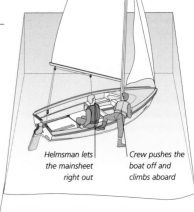

Helmsman lets
the mainsheet
right out

Crew pushes the
boat off and
climbs aboard

**(2)** The crew turns the boat until he is
by the windward shroud, pushes off, and
climbs aboard. He then pulls in the jib to
turn the boat further from the wind. The
helmsman trims the mainsail and steers
onto their chosen course.

## LEAVING A DOCK

Launch the boat down a slipway, if
available, or over the edge of the dock
if necessary (p.73). Move the boat to
the part of the dock from which it will
be easiest to leave – usually at an end
on the leeward side. The helmsman
gets aboard and fits the rudder and
tiller. He hoists the jib, then the
mainsail, and lowers the centerboard
about half way. Before the crew can
untie the boat and get aboard, he and
the helmsman must plan their course
to open water.

   Check to see if there is any tidal
stream affecting the boat. If the tidal
stream is significant, plan to leave
pointing into the stream. Remember
to look around before you sail off to
ensure that there are no other boats or
obstructions in your path. Make sure
that your crew understands the planned
maneuver before you cast off.

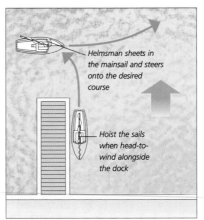

Helmsman sheets in
the mainsail and steers
onto the desired
course

Hoist the sails
when head-to-
wind alongside
the dock

### △ CLEAR WATER ASTERN

*The crew unties the painter and steps
aboard, pushing the boat backward. The
helmsman pushes the tiller in the direction
he wants the bow to move (here, to port)
while the crew backs the jib. The boat
moves backward and turns. Finally, the
crew sheets the jib in on the leeward side
of the dinghy to sail away.*

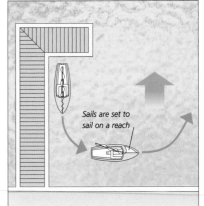

Sails are set to
sail on a reach

### △ OBSTRUCTION ASTERN

*The crew pushes the boat forward and
away from the dock. He gets aboard and
then backs the jib, while the helmsman
turns the boat away from the wind. As
soon as the boat has turned, the crew sets
the jib on the leeward side to sail away on
a broad reach. The helmsman lets the
mainsheet run out to help bear away.*

## ARRIVING AT A BEACH

When you return to a weather shore, you will need to tack in toward the beach or slipway. The way you approach will depend on whether the water close to the shore is shallow or deep. If you are going to sail into shallow water, the crew must be prepared to raise the centerboard just enough to clear the bottom and the helmsman must be ready to lift the rudder blade if necessary. After you have raised the rudder blade, make only very gentle movements with the tiller because when the blade is in the raised position it is very vulnerable to breakage. Remember, too, that once the centerboard is raised, the boat will make more leeway, so do not expect to be able to sail efficiently on a close-hauled course.

Plan your course into the beach, and discuss the plan of approach with your crew so that he understands what is required. Check that there are no other boats or obstructions in the way. If you are approaching a slipway, wait until it is clear of other users. When you reach the shore, the crew should step out on the windward side and hold the boat by the bow.

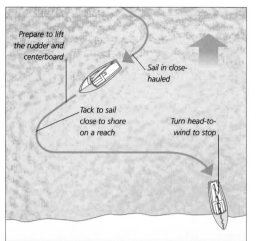

Prepare to lift the rudder and centerboard

Sail in close-hauled

Tack to sail close to shore on a reach

Turn head-to-wind to stop

### SHALLOW WATER ▷

*Tack in to the shore, aiming for your chosen landing spot. As the water gets shallower, the crew raises the centerboard and the helmsman lifts the rudder. Make the final approach on a close reach. At the landing point, turn head-to-wind. The crew gets out and holds the boat, while the helmsman lowers the sails, removes the rudder, and raises the centerboard fully.*

### ◁ DEEP WATER

*Where the water is deep at the shoreline, tack in close, then sail parallel to the land until you reach your chosen landing point. The helmsman turns the boat head-to-wind to stop. The crew gets out just behind the shroud, taking care to avoid stepping into deep water, and holds the boat while the helmsman lowers the sails, removes the rudder, and raises the centerboard fully.*

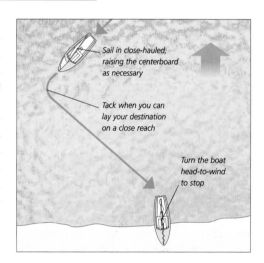

Sail in close-hauled, raising the centerboard as necessary

Tack when you can lay your destination on a close reach

Turn the boat head-to-wind to stop

## ARRIVING AT A DOCK

Approach the dock by sailing on a close reach. As you near the dock, ease out the sails to slow down, then turn head-to-wind to stop alongside. Docks usually have plenty of depth of water beneath them so you do not need to raise the centerboard or the rudder until you are safely alongside.

If there is a tidal stream present consider its effects on your boat and, if it is strong, plan to turn into the tide to stop. Always plan an escape route in case you arrive at the dock going too fast to stop. Once alongside, the crew gets out to secure the boat.

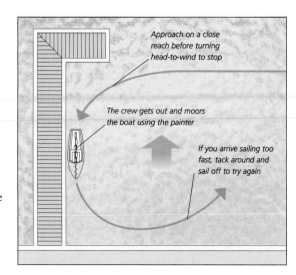

Approach on a close reach before turning head-to-wind to stop

The crew gets out and moors the boat using the painter

If you arrive sailing too fast, tack around and sail off to try again

### ◁ STOPPING AT A DOCK

*As you reach the dock, turn head-to-wind so that the boat comes to a stop alongside. The crew secures the dinghy while the helmsman deals with the sails and other equipment. It is important that you do not approach the dock sailing too quickly.*

# LEE SHORE

Leaving a lee shore is complicated because you are obliged to sail close-hauled or on a close reach, which is difficult, especially if you cannot lower the centerboard fully due to shallow water. If the wind is directly onshore, you have no choice but to start on a close reach until you can lower the centerboard fully and head up to a close-hauled course.

Fortunately, the wind often blows onto the shore at an angle, giving a larger angle between the shore and one edge of the no-sail zone. Choose the tack that allows you to sail in the larger angle. Curved shores usually produce the same effect by providing a greater angle to sail in on one tack.

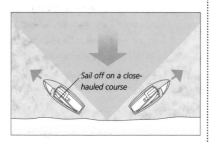

*Sail off on a close-hauled course*

**WIND DIRECTLY ONSHORE**

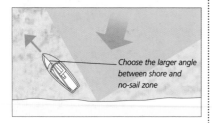

*Choose the larger angle between shore and no-sail zone*

**WIND AT AN OBLIQUE ANGLE**

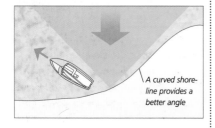

*A curved shore-line provides a better angle*

**WIND ON A CURVED SHORELINE**

## LEAVING FROM A BEACH

When leaving from a beach in deep water, turn the boat head-to-wind and hoist both sails ashore. When you are ready to launch put the boat half in the water and wait for a suitable wave to lift the boat, then push off and sail away. In shallow water, hoist the jib before launching the boat, then hoist the mainsail. Lower the rudder and centerboard as soon as possible but be careful not to let them hit the bottom or they could break or stop the boat.

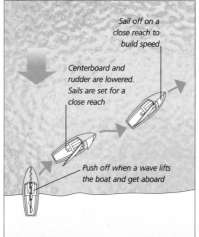

*Sail off on a close reach to build speed*

*Centerboard and rudder are lowered. Sails are set for a close reach*

*Push off when a wave lifts the boat and get aboard*

## LEAVING FROM A DOCK

Launch the boat and turn it head-to-wind. If the wind is at an angle, put the boat on the leeward side of the dock. The helmsman steps aboard and hoists the sails, fits the rudder, and lowers the centerboard. He tells the crew how he wants to leave.

**SAILING AWAY ▷**

*The crew pushes the bow away from the dock and steps aboard. The helmsman sheets in the mainsail and the crew sheets in the jib to sail away on a close reach.*

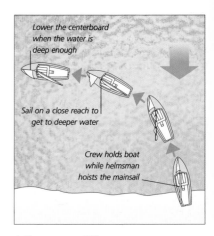

*Lower the centerboard when the water is deep enough*

*Sail on a close reach to get to deeper water*

*Crew holds boat while helmsman hoists the mainsail*

**△ SHALLOW WATER**

*The crew holds the boat by the bow and walks the boat out until the depth is about 3ft (1m). The helmsman climbs aboard and hoists the mainsail.*

**◁ DEEP WATER**

*Lift the boat so that its front half is in the water. Decide on your leaving direction, then both stand by the side that will be to windward. Watch the waves as they approach. When one floats the boat, push it into deep water and climb aboard. Sheet in both sails, and lower the centerboard and rudder blade as soon as possible. Sail fast on a close reach to get through the waves and clear of the beach. Luff up to sail over each wave crest, then bear away.*

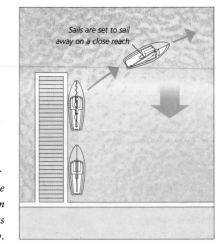

*Sails are set to sail away on a close reach*

# ARRIVING AT A BEACH

With the wind behind you, it is easy to approach a lee shore, but you must be careful with your stopping techniques. Arriving at a lee shore in strong winds is dangerous because the waves are likely to be steep and breaking, especially if the shore slopes sharply into deep water. Always keep to the windward side of the boat when jumping out, otherwise breaking waves or a strong gust of wind could push the boat on top of you, causing injury. Get the boat ashore quickly. In areas where a dinghy club sails from a steep beach, a shore team will often be present to help crews land and lift boats out of the water quickly.

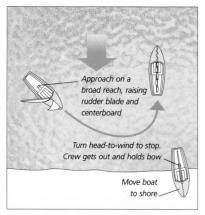

Approach on a broad reach, raising rudder blade and centerboard

Turn head-to-wind to stop. Crew gets out and holds bow

Move boat to shore

## △ A SHALLOW WATER APPROACH

*In shallow water, approach on a broad reach under full sail. When the water is about 3ft (1m) deep, turn into the wind to stop. The crew steps out on the windward side to hold the the bow while the helmsman lowers the sails, and removes the rudder.*

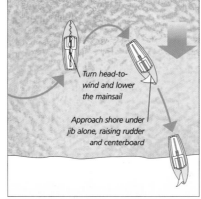

Turn head-to-wind and lower the mainsail

Approach shore under jib alone, raising rudder and centerboard

## △ THE SAFE APPROACH

*Some way offshore, turn head-to-wind and lower the mainsail. Approach the shore under jib alone on a run or broad reach. Close to the shore, let the jib flap and drift in. Helmsman and crew jump out when the water is shallow enough.*

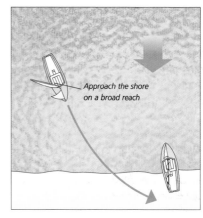

Approach the shore on a broad reach

## △ A FAST APPROACH

*To land in large waves, approach fast on a broad reach and raise the rudder blade at the last moment. Just before the boat hits the beach, both crew jump out on the windward side, run the boat up the beach, and turn it head-to-wind to lower the sails.*

# ARRIVING AT A DOCK

You often have a choice when approaching a dock on a lee shore. You can decide to lower the mainsail and approach under just the jib or, provided there is a dock at right angles to the shore, you can come in with both sails set. If in doubt, it is safest to lower the mainsail and come in under jib alone.

If the dock is in tidal waters, consider whether the tidal stream will affect your approach. If it is strong, plan to turn into it to stop. If possible, plan an escape route in case the boat is moving too fast to stop in the final approach, although this can be difficult when approaching a lee shore. Drop the sails and paddle in if it will be difficult to retain control under sail.

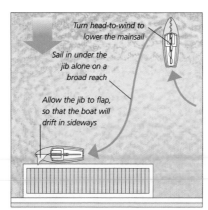

Turn head-to-wind to lower the mainsail

Sail in under the jib alone on a broad reach

Allow the jib to flap, so that the boat will drift in sideways

## △ PARALLEL TO THE SHORE

*Where there is nowhere to moor head-to-wind, sail upwind of your destination and lower the mainsail before approaching under the jib alone. Let the jib flap in the last stages so that you drift in slowly. Once alongside, the crew secures the boat.*

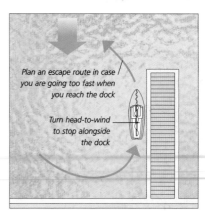

Plan an escape route in case you are going too fast when you reach the dock

Turn head-to-wind to stop alongside the dock

## △ RIGHT ANGLES TO THE SHORE

*Sail on a broad reach close to the shore, then turn head-to-wind to stop alongside. This requires good judgement, so plan an escape route; then you can go around and try again if necessary. If in doubt, lower the mainsail and come in under the jib alone.*

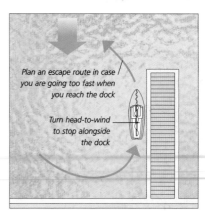

# MOORING AND ANCHORING

*Some larger general-purpose dinghies are kept permanently afloat on moorings, which are often laid in rows called trots. Design varies, but most moorings have heavy concrete sinkers or anchors to secure them to the seabed. Some mooring buoys have a light pick-up buoy, while others have a ring on top to which you secure the boat directly. Anchoring is an art that is rarely used in dinghies nowadays, and still more rarely in high-performance racing boats. Nevertheless, it can be useful in emergencies, for a brief stop, or when dinghy cruising.*

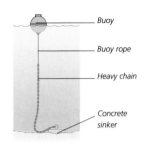

Buoy
Buoy rope
Heavy chain
Concrete sinker

**A MOORING**

### NON-TIDAL WATERS

If you are moored or anchored in non-tidal waters, the boat will always lie head-to-wind, making it simple to sail off with both sails set.

To sail away from the mooring, hoist the sails, lower the centerboard, and fit the rudder and tiller. The dinghy is turned to the desired direction for leaving by backing the jib. Once the backed jib has pushed the bow around, the helmsman can sheet in the mainsail and the crew can then sheet the jib on the leeward side.

If it is important to turn sharply as soon as the mooring is dropped, the crew can help the turn by pulling the buoy aft, down the windward side. The further aft it is released, the more the boat will turn downwind.

### TIDAL WATERS

In tidal waters, the direction and relative strength of the wind and tide will determine how you leave a mooring. If the boat is lying head-to-wind, you can leave in the same way that you would in non-tidal waters. However, if the wind is not clearly well ahead of the beam, it will be impossible to hoist the mainsail without it filling immediately and attempting to sail the boat around the mooring. In this case, you must leave under the jib alone.

### PREPARING TO LEAVE A MOORING

Prepare to leave a mooring by "singling up" the mooring line: run the working end of the painter through the eye on the mooring buoy, bring it back aboard, and make it fast. Undo the permanent mooring line, and release it. The dinghy can now be released simply by freeing the working end of the painter and pulling it back through the mooring eye.

**LEAVING WITH BOTH SAILS ▷**

*If the dinghy is head-to-wind, leave with both sails hoisted. The helmsman picks the direction to leave. The crew backs the jib on the other side of the boat and slips the mooring. If it is important to turn sharply away from the mooring, the crew passes the buoy along the windward side to the helmsman who then releases it at the stern.*

Dinghy is head-to-tide

Turn head-to-wind to hoist mainsail

Leave under jib alone

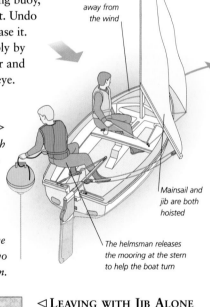

Bow turns away from the wind

Mainsail and jib are both hoisted

The helmsman releases the mooring at the stern to help the boat turn

**◁ LEAVING WITH JIB ALONE**

*If the wind is not ahead of the beam, you must leave the mooring under the jib alone. Prepare both sails for hoisting, fit the rudder and tiller, and single up the mooring. Hoist the jib but let it flap, and lower the centerboard. The helmsman chooses the course to sail away and the crew slips the mooring and sheets in the jib. When you are clear of all obstructions, luff up so that you are head-to-wind, and then hoist the mainsail.*

## PICKING UP A MOORING

Before you commit to an approach to a mooring, look at other boats already on the moorings, especially those that are similar to your own, to see if they are head-to-wind or being influenced by the tide. Assume that your boat will take up a similar position, and decide where the wind will be. If it will be well ahead of the beam, you can approach under both the mainsail and jib. However, if it is further aft, you should approach under the jib alone.

Taking into account the proximity of other boats or obstacles, plan your approach to the mooring. If there is a tidal stream, make sure that you will pass other boats on their down-tide side to avoid being swept onto them.

At the mooring, pick up the buoy on the windward side, ahead of the shroud. Fasten the painter to the buoy and lower the sails. Then make fast securely with the mooring rope.

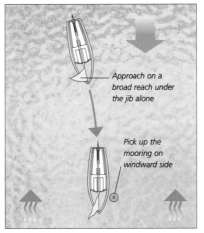

Approach on a broad reach under the jib alone

Pick up the mooring on windward side

### APPROACHING UPWIND ▷

*If the boat will face the wind when it is moored, approach the buoy on a close reach, easing out the sails to slow down, and then luff up so that you are head-to-wind at the mooring. If the wind and tide are together but the wind is light, it may be better to approach on a beam reach to avoid getting swept down-tide.*

### ◁ APPROACHING DOWNWIND

*If the wind and tide are opposed or at an angle to each other so that the boat will not lie head-to-wind when it is moored, you should approach under the jib alone. Lower the mainsail while you are still in clear water, and then approach downwind under the jib, aiming to arrive at the mooring pointing into the tide. Control your speed by using the jib sheet, and let the jib flap to slow down at the mooring.*

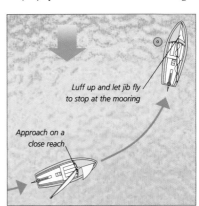

Luff up and let jib fly to stop at the mooring

Approach on a close reach

## ANCHORING A DINGHY

*You will need an anchor warp that is 3–5 times longer than the depth of water. Tie the warp to the mast and coil the bulk of it into a bucket. Take the other end out through the bow fairlead and back in around and behind the windward shroud. Tie it to the anchor.*

**①** *Sail up to your anchorage site and stop exactly as you would at a mooring.*

**②** *Lower the anchor over the windward side. Quickly lower the jib.*

**③** *Lower the mainsail, paying out the anchor warp as the boat drifts back. Raise the centerboard.*

**④** *Now check that the anchor is holding by using a shore transit (pp.244–45), and then stow the sails.*

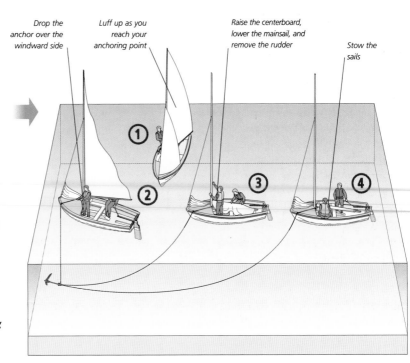

Drop the anchor over the windward side

Luff up as you reach your anchoring point

Raise the centerboard, lower the mainsail, and remove the rudder

Stow the sails

# CAPSIZE RECOVERY

The stability of a dinghy depends entirely on crew weight, which means that a capsize is always possible. It is a common mishap, so practice recovering your dinghy from a capsize until you are fully competent in the procedure. If you fail to right a capsized boat, climb onto the hull, tie yourself on with the end of a sheet, and wait for rescue. Never try to swim to shore. A capsized boat is far easier to spot than a swimmer's head, and the shore is usually further away than it looks.

## LEEWARD CAPSIZE

The most common type of capsize is when the boat tips over to leeward. This typically happens when the wind overpowers the righting effect of the crew's weight and the boat heels so far that water floods in over the leeward gunwale. A typical leeward capsize occurs when the boat jibes and the crew are not quick enough to move their weight to the new windward side, or if the helmsman allows the boat to continue turning. Once a capsize becomes inevitable, the helmsman and crew should slip into the water between the boom and the hull. If they try to avoid getting wet, they will probably invert the boat.

## WINDWARD CAPSIZE

Less commonly, the boat may capsize to windward. This usually occurs when a dinghy is sailing on a run and it rolls heavily toward the wind. As it rolls, the part of the hull that is in the water becomes unbalanced (p.67) and makes the boat turn further away from the wind. The boat continues to roll and then tips over, towards the crew. This sort of capsize is usually considerably quicker and more violent than a leeward capsize and the crew may not have time to react. A typical occurrence is just before a jibe in strong winds. As the boat capsizes on top of them, the crew will usually fall backward into the water.

### CAPSIZED DINGHY ▷

*The crew stays at the stern while the helmsman swims to the centerboard using the mainsheet as a safety line. Once the helmsman has reached the centerboard safely, the crew moves into the boat.*

# DINGHY CAPSIZE

The standard way for righting a capsized two-man dinghy uses the scoop method, so named because the crew is scooped aboard as the helmsman pulls the boat upright. The crew's weight in the boat helps to prevent it capsizing again once it is righted. While the boat is capsized, both helmsman and crew must avoid putting weight on the boat which could make it invert. During a capsize recovery, the helmsman and crew will be out of sight of each other for most of the time. They must keep talking to one another so that both know what is happening. Once the boat is righted, bail out the water before sailing off. A high-performance boat (pp.108–137), with a trapeze system and a spinnaker, may require the system to be modified, but the same principles apply.

## RIGHTING A CAPSIZED DINGHY

*The scoop method relies on the helmsman standing on the centerboard to pull the boat upright. If the centerboard is not fully down, the helmsman can pull it down from under the boat or the crew can push it down from inside. To avoid breaking the centerboard, the helmsman should stand on the part nearest the hull. While waiting to be scooped up, the crew should check that the mainsheet is free so the mainsail can flap loosely when the boat is righted.*

Crew pushes
centerboard
right down

**①** The crew pushes the centerboard down fully, then joins the helmsman at the stern. The helmsman checks that the rudder is still in place. If it has floated off, he secures it with any available line.

Helmsman swims to
the centerboard

**②** The crew passes the end of the mainsheet over the top of the rudder to the helmsman. Using this as a safety line, the helmsman swims around the bottom of the boat to the centerboard.

## CAPSIZE TIPS

Always try to right the boat with the mast coming up against the wind to avoid another capsize. If you capsized to windward, wait until the boat swings around with the mast downwind. Keep calm when you capsize. Even if you are under the sail or hull, you can usually escape fairly easily.

### △ UNDER A SAIL
*To escape from under a sail, raise your hand above your head to lift it clear of the water and create an air pocket. Paddle out, keeping your hand up.*

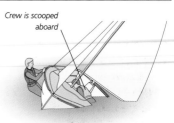

### △ UNDER THE HULL
*To escape from under the hull, move to the outer edge, grasp the gunwale, take a deep breath in the air pocket and pull yourself under the sidedeck.*

*Helmsman catches the end of the jib sheet*

*Helmsman climbs on the centerboard*

*Crew is scooped aboard*

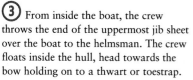

**③** From inside the boat, the crew throws the end of the uppermost jib sheet over the boat to the helmsman. The crew floats inside the hull, head towards the bow holding on to a thwart or toestrap.

**④** Using the jib sheet to help him, the helmsman climbs onto the centerboard, positioning his feet close to the hull. He then leans back with straight arms and legs, pulling steadily on the jib sheet.

**⑤** The boat comes upright, scooping up the crew. The helmsman scrambles aboard by the windward shroud as the boat rights itself, or the crew helps him aboard, moving slowly to avoid another capsize.

## RIGHTING A SINGLE-HANDED DINGHY

Many single-handers float quite high when capsized, so the daggerboard can be difficult to climb onto. Wrap your arms over it and hang your weight on it to make the boat come slowly upright. Alternatively, push the bow deeply into the water, which may make the boat rotate into its upright position.

**(1)** In a leeward capsize, you may be able to avoid getting wet. As soon as capsize appears inevitable, let go of the mainsheet and tiller and climb up over the top gunwale to reach the centerboard.

**(2)** Step over the sidedeck and onto the daggerboard. Turn around to stand on the daggerboard and hold the gunwale. Pull the boat upright, climbing back in as it is righted.

# TOTAL INVERSION

Many modern dinghies are prone to quickly turn completely upside down when they capsize. This is because they usually have a lot of built-in buoyancy distributed along the bottom and sides of the hull. This means that they float high on their sides and easily tip (or are blown over) to the inverted position. In this position their decks often form a seal with the water. This makes it even more difficult to bring them upright, because the water seal has to be broken first.

Dinghies differ in how they are best righted from an inversion. Some can be pulled upright by both crew standing on a gunwale or kneeling on the hull. With others, it is easier if one crew member pushes down on a corner of the transom to break the seal while the other crew member pulls the boat upright. You should get to know the best way to right your own boat.

Inversion also brings the risk of the mast hitting the bottom. Be careful not to put any weight on the boat if the mast is touching the bottom, as it may break. Lie in the water with your feet against the hull while pulling on the jib sheet to avoid damage or ask a safety boat for help in towing the boat into a normal capsized position.

**INVERTED DINGHY ▷**
*Get to know the best way to right your dinghy from the inverted position. Here, the crew depresses the stern quarter to break the seal between decks and water, while the helmsman pulls the boat onto its side.*

## RIGHTING AN INVERTED DINGHY

*The technique for righting an inverted boat is to bring it up to the normal capsized position, lying on its side, before proceeding with the scoop method of recovery (pp.98–99). Try to make sure that the mast comes up against the wind to make the recovery easier and prevent the boat from immediately capsizing again. Sometimes the centerboard will retract when the boat turns upside down. In this case you will have to stand on the lip of the gunwale instead of the centerboard and pull on the sheet.*

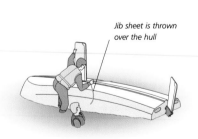

Jib sheet is thrown over the hull

**(1)** One person finds the jib sheet on the leeward side and throws it across the hull, near the centerboard. The helmsman grasps the end of the sheet on the other side and climbs onto the gunwale.

Helmsman and crew stand on the gunwale

**(2)** If possible, the helmsman pulls the centerboard fully down. The crew climbs up beside the helmsman. Both stand on the gunwale, or kneel on the hull, and lean back against the jib sheet.

## MAST IN THE MUD

If you capsize in shallow water, there is a possibility of the mast catching on the bottom. The mast may get stuck if it hits soft mud, and you will have problems pulling it upright using only your body weight. In this case, you may have to ask for a tow. Ensure that the helmsman of the tow boat knows what he is doing, or you may damage the mast.

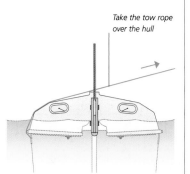

*Take the tow rope over the hull*

**POSITIONING THE TOW ROPE**

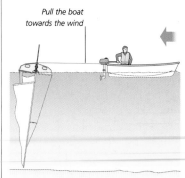

*Pull the boat towards the wind*

### △ HOW TO TOW UPRIGHT
*Take the tow line over the hull and tie it to a chainplate. If possible, attach the line to a leeward chainplate and prepare to pull the boat up against the wind. Motor very slowly at right angles to the boat until it rotates to lie on its side.*

*Helmsman and crew keep the pressure on the jib sheet to right the boat*

*Helmsman climbs onto the centerboard to begin the scoop recovery procedure*

**3** Once the weight of the helmsman and crew has broken the water seal around the hull, the boat will start to come up slowly. They keep pulling steadily until the boat lies on its side.

**4** The boat is now on its side. The crew holds onto the jib sheet to keep the boat steady as the helmsman climbs onto the centerboard. The crew then moves inside the boat to start a scoop recovery.

# MAN OVERBOARD

*It is fairly rare for someone to fall overboard from a dinghy. However, when it does happen, whoever is left in the boat needs to know how to sail it alone and how to turn around to recover the person overboard quickly and efficiently. The most common reason for falling into the water is a toerail breaking or coming undone. To avoid accidents, check yours each time you go on the water, and practice your recovery techniques until you are confident that you could act safely in an emergency.*

## THE RECOVERY PROCEDURE

When someone falls overboard, it is vital that you keep him in sight at all times and get back to him, under full control, as quickly as possible. If you are the crew and your helmsman has fallen overboard, you must immediately let the jib sheet go and move aft to take control of the tiller and mainsheet. The procedure used for recovering a man overboard has the added advantage of teaching you how to sail slowly, under full control, and how to stop exactly where you want to.

## THE DEPARTURE

The safest method of recovery is to put the boat on a beam reach and sail away from the person in the water. This gives you room to maneuver back to pick him up. Do not jibe to get back more quickly as it is too easy to capsize the dinghy, which will cause even more problems.

When you have some sea room between you and the man overboard, tack around and sail back toward him on the opposite beam reach.

## THE APPROACH

From a beam reach, bear away onto a broad reach before luffing up onto a close reach for the final approach. This point of sailing is the only one on which you have complete control of your speed as you make the approach.

## MAN-OVERBOARD RECOVERY

*Release the jib sheet so that the jib flaps (leave it loose for the entire recovery), and steer the boat onto a beam reach. Position the centerboard about three-quarters down. Keep an eye on the person.*

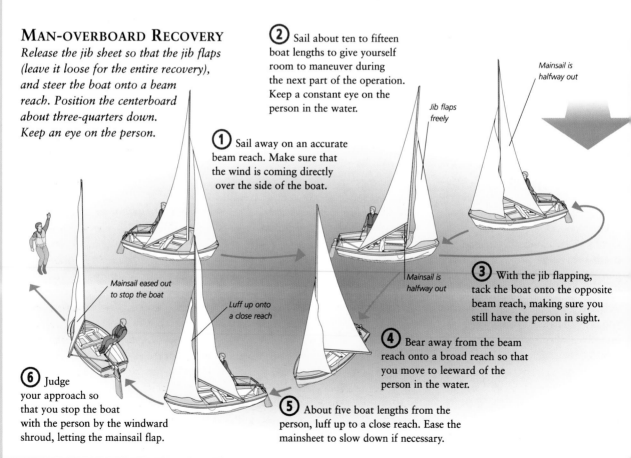

**②** Sail about ten to fifteen boat lengths to give yourself room to maneuver during the next part of the operation. Keep a constant eye on the person in the water.

*Mainsail is halfway out*

*Jib flaps freely*

**①** Sail away on an accurate beam reach. Make sure that the wind is coming directly over the side of the boat.

*Mainsail is halfway out*

**③** With the jib flapping, tack the boat onto the opposite beam reach, making sure you still have the person in sight.

**④** Bear away from the beam reach onto a broad reach so that you move to leeward of the person in the water.

*Mainsail eased out to stop the boat*

*Luff up onto a close reach*

**⑥** Judge your approach so that you stop the boat with the person by the windward shroud, letting the mainsail flap.

**⑤** About five boat lengths from the person, luff up to a close reach. Ease the mainsheet to slow down if necessary.

As you approach the person in the water, make sure that you can stop with him on the windward side of the boat. If you try to pick him up on the leeward side, there is a real danger that the boat will drift on top of him or that you will capsize as you try to get him aboard.

## COMING ALONGSIDE
Once you are alongside the man overboard, tell him to grasp the gunwale at the windward shroud. In this position you can leave the boat to lie quietly with the sails flapping as you bring him aboard. If you try to bring him in too far aft, the bow will probably blow downwind and the boat will start sailing.

When he has a firm hold of the gunwale, give the tiller a flick to windward before letting go of it and moving forward to help him aboard.

## △ RETRIEVING CREW
*Once you have returned to the person in the water, stop the boat with him at the windward shrouds. Move forward and grasp him under the armpits. Lean back to drag him into the boat.*

This flick helps to prevent the boat turning head-to-wind or even tacking around him in the water.

## THE RESCUE
Move to the windward shroud and grasp the person under the armpits. Lean toward him to push the side of the boat toward the water and then lean back and pull. You should now be able to drag his upper half into the boat. From there he can be rolled into the boat. If you have trouble getting him aboard, tie a bowline (*p.39*) in the end of the jib sheet and drop the loop

over the side for him to use as a step. If he is unconscious or too heavy to lift into the boat, tie him alongside and sail slowly for shore.

Once you have the sailor back aboard, check carefully for any injuries or signs of exposure or hypothermia (*pp.308–09*). If the person is wearing a wetsuit or drysuit, he should be no worse for the experience; otherwise, he will be wet and may be suffering from the cold. In this case, lay the person in the boat to warm up, and get to shore as quickly as possible. Seek medical help if necessary.

# STOWING AFTER SAILING

*O*nce you are back ashore, you will probably want to head straight for a hot shower. Before you do, however, it is a good idea to spend a few minutes making sure that the boat is clean and tidy. Make a quick inspection for any damage, and then stow the sails and other removable gear. Lastly, make sure the boat is well secured. A few minutes spent now will prevent damage and stop deterioration, and will ensure that the boat is ready to sail the next time you want to take it out.

## WASHING THE DINGHY

Wash the boat down thoroughly with fresh water as soon as you bring it ashore. Pay particular attention to the blocks, as any traces of dirt or salt left on them will damage the bearings. Make sure you rinse the centerboard casing. Next, wash all the equipment, including the sails and rudder.

## DE-RIGGING

De-rig the boat by going through the rigging order in reverse. First, take out the bungs in the buoyancy tanks or transom and allow any water to drain away, and open any hatches fitted to the tanks to enable air to circulate. If you have a padded rudder-stowage bag, put the rudder into it as soon as you have washed it. Never lay it down on hard surfaces or where it might be stepped on. Be particularly careful with the blade as it is easily damaged. If the centerboard is removed between trips, it is also best stored in a padded bag. A daggerboard is always removed between trips and this, too, should have its own protective bag.

## STOWING THE SAILS

If possible, allow the sails to dry before stowing them in the sailbag. Sails made of modern sailcloth will not be damaged if they are put away wet, but they should still be dried at the earliest opportunity to avoid mildew growth.

Remove the mainsail from the boom and unhank the jib from the forestay. Undo any shackles used to attach the sails to the halyards and re-attach them to the fittings so that they cannot be lost. Remove the jib sheets and coil them up neatly. Stow them in the sailbag or tie them in the boat. If your jib has a wire luff, coil this up, making the jib into a smooth tube, to avoid kinking the wire. Once the sail is rolled up, it can be loosely folded so that it fits into the sailbag.

Fold mainsails carefully to ensure that they are not creased too much and are easy to unfold next time. It is easier for two people to fold them.

## FOLDING THE MAINSAIL

*Because the mainsail is large, it is easier to fold if it is laid out on a clean patch of ground, such as on grass or a concrete or wooden surface. If the ground is dirty, lay the sail over the boat to fold it.*

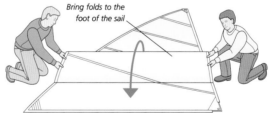

Bring folds to the foot of the sail

**1** Take the battens out of their pockets. Lay the sail flat. Make a quick check for damage. With one person at the luff and the other at the leech, start folding near the foot. Make the initial fold parallel to the foot and about 3ft (1m) in.

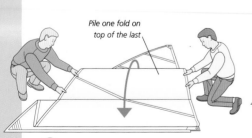

Pile one fold on top of the last

**2** Continue taking folds of about the same size as the first, bringing them down to the foot each time.

Smooth out the folded sail

**3** When the whole mainsail is folded in a series of pleats, parallel to the foot, make sure that it is free of creases.

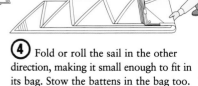

Make several folds

**4** Fold or roll the sail in the other direction, making it small enough to fit in its bag. Stow the battens in the bag too.

## CHECKING FOR WEAR

To keep the boat in top condition, be prepared to spend a few minutes after each sail checking it over. Inspect each piece of gear for wear or damage. If you find any problems, deal with them immediately if possible. Otherwise, make a note to remind yourself of what needs to be done, and note the tools or materials for the repair. Always deal with repairs as soon as possible; otherwise, it is inevitable that the damaged item will fail at the most inopportune moment.

## STORING THE DINGHY

After you have removed and stowed the gear and sails, you will need to put your boat somewhere so that it is safe until the next time you go sailing.

Many sailing clubs have parks in which you can leave your sailing dinghy, and this is certainly more convenient than trailing the boat to and from the sailing area each time you use it. Very small boats can be stored in racks, which save space and provide good protection and support. More usually, boats are stored on their launching trailers.

If you are storing your boat on a trailer, the stern should rest on a soft support, such as a car tire, and the front of the trailer should also be supported so that the dinghy cannot tip forward and damage its hull. This will also allow any rainwater that gets into the hull to drain out through the transom or bung holes.

### HOSING DOWN

As soon as you bring the boat ashore, hose it down with fresh water. Wash all the equipment, including the sails and rudder.

## △ FITTING THE COVER

*Put removable items into the dinghy hull, making sure that they are secure, then fit the cover over the top. Secure it under the hull at the bow and the sidedecks.*

Tie the boat securely to the trailer with the painter, then fit the cover. All boats should have a cover that fits well, and that can be fastened tightly to provide complete protection from the elements. Even glassfiber boats can be damaged by sunlight, so a good cover is a sound investment. It will also discourage the theft of any equipment that you leave in the boat.

Tie the cover firmly under the hull, and make sure that it cannot come loose in high winds. Then tie the boat down to securing points set into the ground, or to heavy concrete blocks, which will prevent it being blown over.

# ADVANCED DINGHY SAILING

ONCE THE BASIC SKILLS OF DINGHY SAILING HAVE

been mastered, they can be refined, and

new ones acquired, by moving up to a high-

performance two-man or single-handed sailing

dinghy. Ability can also be tested and improved

on the racecourse, where the thrust of

competition will highlight any errors.

*The three-man 18ft Skiff is perhaps the ultimate
dinghy. It requires excellent individual skills and
supreme coordination to control its huge rig.*

# HIGH-PERFORMANCE DINGHIES

*If you have learned to sail in a general-purpose dinghy, you will notice a tremendous difference when you first try sailing in a high-performance boat. High-performance dinghies are more sensitive to changes in wind strength, accelerate faster, and require quicker reactions from helmsman and crew than general-purpose dinghies. They make more demands on your abilities and are more difficult to sail well, but they will teach you about the finer points of boat handling more quickly.*

## DESIGN ADVANCES

Until recently, there were a few classic International and Olympic classes that were regarded as being the ultimate in high-performance boats. However, since then, lighter and stronger materials have been developed along with advanced boat designs, and there are now dinghies that are capable of much higher speeds that test even the best crews to the limit of their abilities. Along with these extreme dinghies has come crash-and-burn-type, short-course racing, which offers plenty of thrills and spills.

## MAKING A CHOICE

If you learned in a general-purpose dinghy and want to progress to sailing faster boats, the next step is to sail in a moderately high-performance class that uses a spinnaker (*pp.122–29*) and a trapeze (*pp.116–17*) for the crew. Crew for someone else before buying a boat. If you want to sail as fast as possible – and spend a lot of time capsizing – you may like to consider the latest lightweight dinghies.

## RACING

The most sensible and convenient approach to racing is to pick a class that is raced where you want to sail. Most popular classes have good club-level racing and many give world-class competition. You will also need to decide between speed and tactics. Very high-performance dinghies are great for sheer speed but not ideal for close, tactical racing because of the difficulty in handling their power.

---

## SPEED COMPARISONS

A polar diagram is used to show the potential speed of a boat for a particular wind strength. For every wind strength, each design of boat will have a unique polar curve. Large racing yachts use polar curves to predict the speed they should attain on any point of sailing, and to trim and tune the boat accordingly.

### FACTORS AFFECTING SPEED

Speed is determined by the strength of the wind, the amount of sail area, and the weight of the boat, complete with its crew. In short, the more sail area you have and the less your boat weighs, the faster you will go. High-performance boats are always much lighter than general-purpose boats. They have larger, more complex rigs, and much shallower hulls. They typically have little natural stability and rely solely on the weight of the crew to keep them upright when they are being sailed. Their sole purpose is fast sailing, and they are used only for racing or thrill-seeking sailing.

### POINTS OF SAILING

A general-purpose dinghy will be slower on all points of sailing than a high-performance one. Both will perform better on some points of sailing than others, and reaching courses are faster for both than close-hauled or running courses.

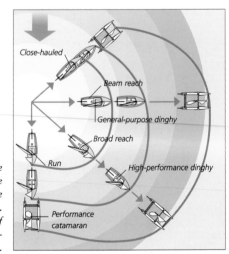

### POLAR DIAGRAM ▷

*This polar diagram compares the potential speeds of a general-purpose dinghy, a typical high-performance dinghy, and a performance catamaran. The catamaran is fastest on all points of sailing, with the greatest gains on beam-reaching and broad-reaching courses.*

Close-hauled

Beam reach

General-purpose dinghy

Broad reach

Run

High-performance dinghy

Performance catamaran

# TYPES OF HIGH-PERFORMANCE SAILING DINGHIES

High-performance dinghies typically have shallow, light hulls with large rigs. They often have at least one trapeze, but the fastest boats have both helmsman and crew on trapezes. The latest dinghies have large asymmetric spinnakers to increase speed downwind. Sportsboats are small, ballasted yachts with many of the characteristics of high-performance dinghies. They are used as fast, day-racing boats and have up to six crew. They are light and have large rigs, often with an asymmetric spinnaker.

## DINGHIES

**INTERNATIONAL 14**

The International 14 is one of the oldest racing classes, and has been developed over the years to keep ahead of the opposition. It now has twin trapezes and is a very demanding boat to sail. There are excellent racing fleets offering the best international racing.

**OLYMPIC 470**

The Olympic 470 is a good boat for those who want to start high-performance sailing. It has a spinnaker and one trapeze. The Olympic 470 provides fine, close racing with separate fleets for male and female sailors. The 470 is especially suitable for light crews.

**OLYMPIC 49'ER**

The Olympic 49'er is one of the new generation of lightweight high-performance boats with huge rigs and twin trapezes. Like other dinghies that were inspired by the classic 18ft Skiff, it uses a large asymmetrical spinnaker set on the end of a long retractable bowsprit.

**INTERNATIONAL 505**

The International 505 is a classic high-performance boat with a large spinnaker and a trapeze for the crew. Racing in the class is of very high quality, with large fleets and good tactical maneuvering. The 505 is more suitable than the 470 for heavier sailors.

**LASER 5000**

The Laser 4000 and Laser 5000 are part of the Laser stable of dinghies. They afford different levels of high-performance sailing to suit the skills of the sailor. The Laser 5000 is the top of the range and offers good racing fleets and exciting high-speed sailing.

**18FT SKIFF**

The 18ft Skiff is the classic high-performance dinghy that originated in Sydney Harbor. It has been developed over the decades to the state-of-the-art boat it is today. Now sailed by three-man crews, the Skiff is the pinnacle of high-performance dinghies.

## SPORTSBOATS

**MELGES 24**

The Melges 24 was one of the first sportsboats to be developed. It is now internationally popular, with highly competitive fleet racing in many parts of the world. It offers exciting sailing, and its large asymmetric spinnaker gives high speeds downwind.

**HUNTER 707**

The Hunter 707 is a lightweight sportsboat designed for exciting day racing. It is cheaper than the Melges 24 but has comparable performance, even though it uses a conventional spinnaker and pole rather than a more modern asymmetric spinnaker.

# IMPROVING YOUR TECHNIQUE

*Once you have mastered the basic sailing techniques, you will be able to rig and launch your boat, handle it on all points of sailing, and return safely to your starting point. When you feel that these basic techniques are second nature, it is time to consider progressing to a faster and more responsive dinghy. There are several techniques that you will need to learn. These include understanding how and when a boat planes, how to refine sail trimming (including how to control twist) for better performance, how to balance the helm, how to sail close-hauled, and how to maintain the speed of your boat while changing course. Developing these skills is challenging but rewarding.*

## PLANING

Planing is the term used to describe the motion of a boat when it skims across the water like a speedboat. A dinghy will plane when it is traveling fast enough to create lift under the hull, raising the boat onto its own bow wave. The shape of the hull is an important factor in planing. Boats that plane well have broad, flat sections in the aft half of the hull. It is on these that the boat rides when it is planing.

Most dinghies, even heavier general-purpose ones, will plane if there is sufficient wind and the crew understand planing techniques, but light boats with a large sail area will plane readily in quite light winds.

Although slower boats may only plane on a beam or broad reach in strong winds, performance dinghies are capable of planing to windward; they will also plane on a run if there is sufficient wind.

## PLANING TIPS

There are several techniques that you can use to encourage your boat to plane. The first is known as pumping. If the boat cannot quite rise onto the plane, wait for a gust of wind, then rapidly trim both sails in, then out again. This produces just a little more power, which should help the boat to move onto a plane.

Another way of helping the boat to plane is to use a wave to help you accelerate. Sailing downwind in waves, wait until the stern lifts on a wave, then bear away to surf down its front. As the boat accelerates, luff up slightly and sheet in the sails. It is

## HOW TO PLANE

*Start on a beam reach in a wind of at least Force 3. Be ready to move your weight aft to help lift the bow onto the plane. Speed will increase quickly as you plane and the apparent wind will shift forward, so be ready to sheet in both sails. Extra speed will make the rudder more efficient; small movements of the tiller will be enough to keep the boat on course. The boat will slow down quickly if it slips off the plane. Ease the sheets as the apparent wind shifts aft, and move your weight forward again.*

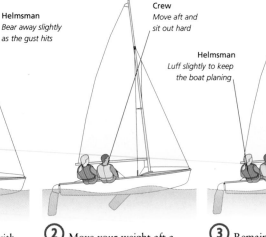

**Helmsman**
*Bear away slightly as the gust hits*

**Crew**
*Move aft and sit out hard*

**Helmsman**
*Luff slightly to keep the boat planing*

**①** Sail on a beam reach with the centerboard no more than half down. Wait for a gust of wind and, as it hits, bear away slightly and ease both sheets a little. Keep the boat upright.

**②** Move your weight aft a little as you feel the boat accelerate. The bow will lift as it begins to plane. If the boat heels when you are sitting out hard, raise the centerboard a little.

**③** Remain planing as long as possible by luffing slightly to keep the apparent wind forward. This may enable you to continue planing until the next gust arrives.

important to keep the boat upright throughout this maneuver. The speed gained from surfing down the wave may create enough wind pressure to keep you on the plane as the apparent wind shifts forwards. If the boat begins to plane, the apparent wind will stay forward, and you will need to set the sails correctly to maintain planing.

## SAIL SETTING

One of the hardest things to get used to when you start sailing is having to adjust sail trim. However, as you develop your skills, trimming the sails to suit even small changes in wind direction becomes almost automatic.

When you sail fast dinghies, you will find that they are very responsive to changes in wind strength and will accelerate or slow down very quickly. As they alter their speed, the apparent wind (p.30) will shift forward (accelerating) or backward (slowing down), and sail trim must be adjusted each time this happens. The apparent wind will also shift aft when a gust hits the boat, so be ready to ease the sails as you see a gust approaching, sheeting them in again as it eases.

## CONTROLLING TWIST

As well as setting the sails at the correct angle to the wind using luff tell-tales (p.68), you also need to adjust the leech tension in each sail to control the amount of twist (the difference between the angle of the sail at the foot and the head). Adjusting twist is important for boat speed. In most conditions, twist is adjusted to maximize power, but in strong winds it is used to reduce heeling. Excessive heeling makes the dinghy slower and harder to steer.

Leech tell-tales (p.112) are a useful indicator of whether your sails have the right amount of twist. The amount needed depends on the conditions and the cut of the sail. In general, you should have some twist in very light conditions, less twist in light-to-moderate winds, and more twist again in strong winds.

Mainsail twist is controlled by tension in the mainsheet or vang. The more tension there is in either, the less twist there is. Jib twist is controlled by the fore-and-aft position of the fairleads and jib-sheet tension. Move jib fairleads forward to reduce twist and aft to increase it.

### TWIST ▷

*These boats are racing in a fairly strong wind with their crews fully extended on the trapeze. Their sails are set with quite a lot of twist to reduce the heeling force.*

### ▽ PLANING

*This lightweight sportsboat is planing well under an asymmetric spinnaker. The crew is well aft, and to windward, to keep the boat level and help the bow lift.*

## USING TELL-TALES

The easiest way to check that you have trimmed the sails correctly and have the right twist and leech tension is to attach tell-tales (*p.68*).

### MAINSAIL TELL-TALES
Attach tell-tales to the mainsail leech, near each batten pocket. When the sail is correctly set, all the tell-tales will stream aft, with the one near the top batten just about to fold behind the sail.

### JIB TELL-TALES
Twist in the jib can be checked by using the luff tell-tales. When the top, middle and lower windward tell-tales all stream aft together, the sail is set with the correct amount of twist. If the top tell-tale lifts before the middle and lower ones, the sail has too much twist, and the fairlead should be moved forward. If the bottom or middle tell-tales lift before the top one, move the lead aft.

Leech tell-tales
*Tell-tales are attached near the batten pockets*

△ **READING LEECH TELL-TALES**
*When all the tell-tales stream aft with the top one about to break and fold behind the leech, the sail is set correctly. If the top tell-tale stays folded behind the leech, ease the mainsheet or vang to increase twist and keep the tell-tale just flying.*

### BALANCING THE HELM
When a boat is sailing upright, trimmed correctly fore and aft, and the sails are accurately set, there should be little or no tendency for it to turn. If you let go of the tiller, the boat will continue on a straight course. This condition is referred to as a balanced helm. If the boat turns to windward when you let go of the tiller, it has weather helm. If it turns to leeward, it has lee helm.

In practice, it is easier to sail a boat that has a small amount of weather helm as this gives some feel to the steering, and if the tiller is dropped by accident the boat will turn into the wind and stop. Lee helm is to be avoided because it makes the boat difficult to sail; if the tiller is dropped it will not automatically turn into the wind and stop.

You can alter the balance of the helm while sailing by adjusting the centerboard. Lift the centerboard slightly to reduce weather helm and lower it to eliminate lee helm. When you tune your boat (*pp.138–41*), you can adjust the rake of the mast to produce the desired helm balance.

### SAILING AT SPEED
Assuming that the dinghy is tuned correctly, the achievement of optimum speed depends on the skills of the helmsman and crew. Concentration and constant attention to sail trim, boat balance, and course steered are

---

### MAINTAINING BALANCE AND TRIM

To get maximum performance, it is essential that the dinghy is sailed upright and level fore and aft. Sitting out will help to maintain balance, and sitting together in a central position will keep the boat level fore and aft. By sitting together, the helmsman and crew also reduce wind resistance and so increase their possible speed.

**BALANCE** ▷
*Sit out or trapeze (pp.116–17) to keep the boat upright. If it still heels, ease the mainsheet to spill some wind. Weight distribution and mainsail trim require constant attention to maintain balance.*

◁ **TRIM**
*Keep the boat level fore and aft by sitting close together. In strong winds move aft slightly to allow the bow to lift; in light winds move forward to keep the transom clear of the water and reduce drag.*

essential if you want to get the best performance from your boat. If you are sailing in a high-performance boat after learning in a general-purpose dinghy, it will take time and practice to get used to the faster reactions that are required to sail it efficiently.

Take care to avoid violent changes of course, especially when sailing offwind, because it will be hard to keep the boat balanced through sharp turns. Remember that the rudder is much more efficient when you are traveling at speed, so much smaller tiller movements are needed than when you are sailing slowly.

## SAILING CLOSE-HAULED
Sailing close-hauled is usually the biggest challenge for the novice. The helmsman must keep the boat sailing as close to the wind as possible without letting speed drop by sailing too close (known as pinching). He must also avoid erring in the other direction and losing ground to windward by sailing too far off the wind. Practice sailing close-hauled using the tell-tales on the jib luff (*p.68*) to follow the best course. Both windward and leeward tell-tales

△ **CHANGING DIRECTION**
*Bearing away around a racing mark, the helmsman eases the mainsail before the turn while the crew prepares to come in but heels the boat to windward.*

should be kept streaming aft. The windward set can be allowed to rise occasionally, but the leeward ones should never lift as this indicates that the boat is sailing too far off the wind.

## CHANGING DIRECTION
One sign of a skilled sailor is the ability to change course without slowing the boat unnecessarily. A good helmsman and crew will always prefer to use sail trim and boat balance to turn the boat (*pp.66–69*) and reduce the need to use the rudder. This is because each time the rudder is turned off the centerline it causes drag and slows the boat. Using heel and sail trim is especially important when bearing away as the rudder may prove ineffective, especially in strong winds, if the boat heels to leeward, or if the mainsail is not eased before the turn. Heel the boat to windward and ease the mainsail to bear away successfully.

## COPING WITH WIND SHIFTS
Spotting and using wind shifts are essential skills, particularly if you want to race. A header is when the wind moves forward; a freer is when it moves aft. On windward courses, wind shifts can either shorten the distance sailed or add considerably to it.

### EXPLOITING WIND SHIFTS
If you have to tack upwind, you will sail the quickest course if you tack when you are headed. If the wind shifts back, it will head you again on the other tack. You can then tack again and make more ground to windward. Remember that a wind shift that is a header on port tack is a freer on starboard tack.

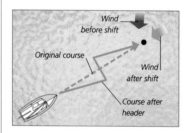

**HEADER**
*A header will force you to bear away from your course in order to keep the sails full. You will then have to tack to reach your destination.*

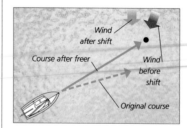

**FREER**
*When the wind moves aft, it is a freer. To prevent your boat sailing too far off course in a freer, you should luff up as soon as the wind shifts.*

# SAILING EXERCISES

*Confident boat handling is a sure sign of a good sailor. It can be developed only through practice on the water, preferably in a range of dinghies as this will show how different characteristics influence handling. The best way to learn the finer points of controlling a dinghy is to experiment with a few boat-handling exercises. The first time you attempt the exercises described here, choose a gentle Force 2–3 wind and sail to a clear stretch of water, free from obstructions or other boats.*

## SAILING WITH ONE SAIL

If you have a two-man dinghy with the standard arrangement of mainsail and jib, you will usually use both sails when sailing. The rig is designed for both sails to work together and to balance their forces around the centerboard. However, when a two-sail dinghy is sailed under a single sail its handling characteristics change considerably, and it may be difficult to complete some maneuvers.

Try sailing on all the points of sailing (*pp.34–35*), first under mainsail alone and then only with the jib. This exercise teaches you about sail balance and how your boat reacts under a single sail. You will also find out how your boat handles at slow speeds, which will be useful when you are sailing to and from the shore or when you are in competition and maneuvering at the start of a race.

## MAINSAIL ALONE

Start by lowering the jib and sailing under mainsail alone. Without the jib in front of it, the mainsail is less efficient (*p.31*) and the boat will sail more slowly, especially on upwind courses. The dinghy's sail plan is designed to balance around its pivot point (at the centerboard); removing the jib moves the center of effort aft, giving the boat weather helm (*p.112*).

It therefore tries to turn into the wind. The helmsman should counteract the weather helm by adjusting the tiller.

The boat will sail reasonably well on a beam reach, but with more weather helm than normal. If you have a centerboard, you can reduce excess weather helm by raising it more than usual to move the pivot point aft. If your boat has a daggerboard, this option is not available to you.

As you turn toward the wind to a close-reaching course, the lack of a jib will impede performance even more. By the time you reach close-hauled, the boat will feel quite sluggish. When you tack, the boat will turn into the wind easily, but it will be slow to bear away on the new tack. Ease the mainsheet after the tack to bear away to a close reach. This will increase speed before you attempt to sail close-hauled on the new tack. The lack of the jib will not be so apparent on downwind courses, because it is the size of the mainsail that contributes most to speed. On a run, the jib is often blanketed behind the mainsail.

## JIB ALONE

Once you have mastered sailing under mainsail alone, try the exercise under jib alone. Without the mainsail, the boat will suffer from lee helm on a beam reach or upwind courses. It will

be considerably slower than usual on all points of sailing. Sailing downwind is easy but slow, but sailing on upwind courses is likely to be difficult. Some dinghies will sail to windward under jib alone but, without the balancing effect of the mainsail, there will be a considerable amount of lee helm. Sail with the centerboard further down than usual to counter this.

Tacking under the jib is difficult or impossible in some boats or weather conditions. Experiment to see how your boat behaves.

## SAILING BACKWARD

Having the skill and confidence to sail backward can be useful when leaving a dock, slipway, or mooring, or when you are maneuvering at the start of a race. Remember that the action of the rudder is reversed when the boat is moving astern, so the bow will move in the same direction in which you move the tiller.

To sail backward, stop the boat head-to-wind (*p.74*). First have the crew push the boom right out to one side and hold it there. Let the jib flap so that it does not interfere with the maneuver. The boat will start moving backward, and you will be able to steer it quite easily with small movements of the tiller. Keep the crew weight well forward to stop the transom dragging, which will make the boat turn.

The rudder is now leading the boat as it moves backward, so its effects are exaggerated. Try not to move the tiller far from the centerline, or the boat may swing quickly to lie at an angle to the wind.

To sail forward again, push the tiller in the direction you want the bow to move. Wait until the boat turns, then center the tiller, sheet in the sails, and sail off.

## SAILING WITHOUT A CENTERBOARD

Although centerboards rarely break, it is useful to try sailing without one so that you can see just how much they influence the way a dinghy behaves. Stop the boat on a close reach and raise the centerboard completely. Now sail off on a beam reach and watch the way in which the boat slides sideways, making considerable leeway *(p.69)* as it sails forward. Tacking is difficult or impossible without a centerboard to pivot around. On upwind courses it is hard to make headway because the dinghy will crab sideways as fast as it goes forward. Experiment with heeling the boat to leeward slightly and moving the crew's weight forward. If you sail a dinghy with a very shallow hull, it could be impossible to make any progress upwind. Even on a beam reach you will make considerable leeway. It is only when you are on downwind courses, when the centerboard would usually be slightly down, that the boat will sail normally.

## SAILING WITHOUT A RUDDER

Another good exercise is to sail around a triangular course without the rudder. This teaches you the importance of sail trim, centerboard position, and boat balance and trim. Without the rudder, the effects of the other controls become more obvious. It is usually best to try this in light winds with only one person in the boat. This gives you total control over all turning forces and avoids confusion between the helmsman and the crew.

A triangular course will seem impossible at first as you will tend to sail in circles, but with practice you should be able to achieve it in moderate conditions. Once you are proficient at sailing on your own without a rudder, practice the exercise with your crew so that you learn to coordinate your movements.

## PRACTICING WITHOUT A RUDDER

*Take the rudder off the boat. Keep the centerboard half down to start with and use the jib and mainsail, together with boat heel, to turn the boat.*

**②** To bear away, pull in the jib, let out the mainsail, and heel the boat to windward.

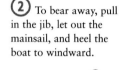

**Helmsman**
*Ease out the mainsheet so that the mainsail flaps*

**①** To luff up, let out the jib, sheet in the mainsail, and allow the boat to heel to leeward.

**③** To sail a straight course, keep the boat upright using crew weight, and balance the mainsail and jib.

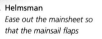

**Jib**
*Ease out the jib sheet so that the jib flaps*

# USING TRAPEZES

*Sailing dinghies rely on the weight of their crew to keep them upright when they are being sailed. In many general-purpose dinghies, this is achieved by the helmsman and crew sitting out as far as possible with their feet under toe rails. However, high-performance dinghies usually have a much larger sail area than general-purpose dinghies and in most conditions sitting out is simply not sufficient to balance the power of the sails. Trapeze systems are used in these boats to increase the righting power.*

## SWINGING OUT AND IN

*Practice getting out onto the trapeze and back into the boat until your movements are smooth and confident. Then practice while tacking until you can swing in, unhook, move across the boat while trimming the jib, and swing out on the trapeze on the new windward side.*

**1** Hook the trapeze to the harness and sit out, allowing the trapeze wire to take your weight. Hold the handle lightly in your front hand for control and security.

*Hold the jib sheet in your aft hand*

**2** Put your front foot on the gunwale and push yourself out, keeping your body at right angles to the boat. Bring your aft foot up so that you are standing on the gunwale.

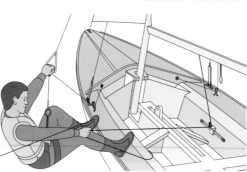

*Place your front foot on the gunwale*

**3** Lean back at full stretch with your feet about a shoulder-width apart. To come in, reverse the procedure. Take your aft foot off the gunwale first.

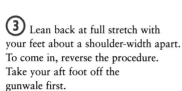

*Stretch out supported by the trapeze*

## TRAPEZE SYSTEMS

A trapeze system consists of a trapeze harness attached to a trapeze wire suspended from the hounds. It enables sailors to hang out over the side of the boat. Formerly, the standard arrangement was a single trapeze for the crew only. This is still used in dinghies such as the 505 and the 470. With the appearance of ever larger rigs, however, twin trapezes have become common. The Olympic 49'er and International 14 are examples of twin-trapeze boats.

Good communication between helmsman and crew is vital in a trapeze boat. The helmsman must give the crew plenty of warning of a tack or jibe to allow him time to come in off the trapeze. The helmsman must also be ready to ease the mainsheet to keep the boat upright as the crew swings in.

## SINGLE TRAPEZE

On a single trapeze, wires run from just above the hounds, one on each side of the mast, to suspend the crew outside the gunwale. The end of the wire comes down just aft of the shrouds. The wire has a handle and a two-position ring for attachment to the trapeze harness. The trapeze ring often has an adjustment system to allow control of the height at which the trapeze is held. A length of stretchy shock cord connects the two trapeze wires and runs around the front of the mast. It keeps the leeward wire taut when the crew is on the windward trapeze.

## MULTIPLE TRAPEZES

Some high-performance boats are fitted with multiple trapeze systems to enable both the helmsman and crew to trapeze. The 18ft Skiff sails with three crew on trapezes, and the unique Ultra 30 class has nine crew, all on trapezes. Sailing a boat with multiple trapezes requires great skill, coordination, and plenty of practice, as well as good communication.

Boats with multiple trapeze systems often have racks extending out from each gunwale. The crew stands on these when trapezing to move their weight even further outboard. Trapeze wires and rings are the same as on a single trapeze, although the helmsman's trapeze does not usually have a handle as both his hands are full with the

mainsheet and tiller extension. When trapezing, the helmsman uses a very long tiller extension. He passes this aft when tacking and jibing.

## TRAPEZING TECHNIQUES

When you are out on the trapeze, you must move your weight to adjust to changes in boat heel and trim. This will be most effective if you trapeze as low as possible, parallel to the water with the boat upright. When there are big waves, raise your position to keep clear of the water. This will make it easier to move in and out rapidly.

## BALANCE

The trapeze wire leads upward and forward from your body, so it will pull you forward. Resist this tendency by keeping your front leg straight and bending your aft leg to remain balanced. If the boat slows rapidly for any reason, such as plowing into a wave, the force trying to pull you forward will increase very quickly,

so be prepared to swing your weight aft. Many boats have footstraps fitted on the gunwale toward the stern to allow the trapezing crew to secure their aft foot and avoid being pulled forward.

## HEEL AND TRIM

Adjust to changes in heel by stretching outward to help the boat sail through gusts and bending your knees to swing your weight inboard if the wind dies.

Maintain fore-and-aft trim by moving your weight along the gunwale. As the boat bears away, move aft to help the bow lift. This is especially important when planing under a spinnaker (*p.123*).

## ▽ ULTRA 30

*The unique Ultra 30 dinghy has nine crew, all on trapezes. Racks are used to extend the crew far outside the hull to increase righting momentum. When trapezing on racks, keep your body higher than usual.*

---

## HARNESSES

The secret to being relaxed on a trapeze is a comfortable harness. Choose one with a high, broad back to give good support.

### FITTING AND MAINTENANCE
Make sure that the harness fits well over your sailing gear and that it spreads the load of your weight hanging from the trapeze into your back and lower body. The trapeze ring is attached to a hook on a metal plate on the harness. Adjust the harness so that the hook is just below the waist. Check the harness's stitching regularly and wash it in fresh water after each sail.

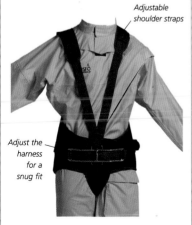

*Adjustable shoulder straps*

*Adjust the harness for a snug fit*

**TRAPEZE HARNESS**

# TACKING AND JIBING

When you tack and jibe in a high-performance dinghy, your balance and boat-handling skills are really put to the test. Your movements must be smooth and quick, and they must be timed carefully. A tack nearly always slows the boat, and a jibe can result in a capsize. However, in light winds, you can try roll tacking and roll jibing to ensure that you maintain speed through the maneuvers – indeed, with a good roll tack or jibe, it is possible to gain speed.

**Helmsman**
*Sheet in the mainsail as the crew swings out*

## TACKING

High-performance boats are very sensitive to weight distribution and turn very quickly. The fastest dinghies are inherently unstable and are not forgiving of mistakes. They have more stability when sailing fast than when moving slowly, such as during a tack. The helmsman and crew must aim to complete each tack, and get the boat sailing fast on the new tack, as quickly as possible.

Good communication between helmsman and crew is vital. In a single-trapeze boat, the helmsman has to pace the turn to suit the speed of the crew. In a twin or multiple-trapeze boat, the helmsman may also be trapezing, and cannot tack very fast as he has to move across onto the new trapeze while handling a long, single tiller extension or twin extensions.

### TACKING WITH A TRAPEZE
*When learning to tack a boat with single or multiple trapezes, the helmsman should start by tacking fairly slowly. Too fast a tack will make it difficult for the crew to get across the boat – and out on the new trapeze – before the sails fill again. This will result in the boat heeling and slowing down considerably.*

**④** The crew then swings out on the trapeze, hooks on, and sheets the jib fully home.

**Helmsman**
*Ease the mainsheet when the boat is head-to-wind and move to the new side*

**③** As the boat passes head-to-wind, the crew sheets the jib partly in on the new side.

**Crew**
*Move into the boat*

**Crew**
*Unhook and prepare to move in*

**①** When the helmsman calls a tack, the crew unhooks while remaining on the trapeze using the handle.

**②** As the helmsman starts the tack, the crew swings into the boat and moves into the middle, keeping the jib sheet taut.

**Crew**
*Adjust weight to balance the boat*

## △ MULTIPLE-TRAPEZE TACK

*In a boat with multiple trapezes, the helmsman has to deal with mainsheet, trapeze, and tiller extension. With a double extension, he releases the old one and picks up the other when he has crossed the boat.*

**④** Once the boat is upright, the crew moves quickly back to the middle or to leeward to balance the helmsman's weight to windward.

**Helmsman**
*Change sides and sit down*

## ROLL TACKING

*In most conditions, a tack causes the boat to slow down. However, in light airs, speed can be maintained (or even increased) by roll tacking. Rolling the boat through a tack in light winds drags the sails through the air, increasing the speed of the airflow, and accelerating the boat.*

**Crew**
*Heel the boat to windward*

**③** When the boat is halfway between head-to-wind and the new close-hauled course, both helmsman and crew move up to the new windward side and pull the boat upright. As they do so, the helmsman sheets in the mainsail to its correct setting.

**①** Just before a roll tack, bear away slightly to increase boat speed, then heel the boat to leeward and steer into the tack.

**Helmsman**
*Steer into tack and heel the boat*

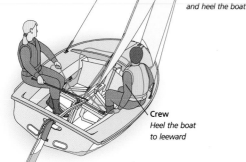

**Crew**
*Heel the boat to leeward*

**②** As the boat comes up into the wind, both helmsman and crew lean out hard on the windward side, rolling the boat towards them. As the boat passes head-to-wind, the crew sheets the jib to the new side and the helmsman eases the mainsheet.

# JIBING

When you jibe a high-performance boat, the keys to completing the maneuver successfully are speed and boat balance before the jibe. You should also take care to check the centerboard position before you jibe. High-performance boats sail downwind under a spinnaker or asymmetric, and you need to learn how to handle these sails during a jibe (*p.82*). Twin or multiple-trapeze boats sail downwind with the crew trapezing, and require even greater skill and agility when jibing than other high-performance boats (*p.108*)

## SPEED AND BALANCE
Speed before the jibe reduces the strength of the apparent wind, which makes it easier to bring the mainsail across to the new leeward side and reduces the wind pressure on the rig. When sailing in waves, you should jibe when the boat is on the face of the wave as this is when it will be sailing at its fastest. Wait until the boat's bow drops down the face of a wave (and the boat accelerates) before turning into the jibe. Never jibe on the back of a wave, when the boat will be slowing down, causing the apparent wind to increase.

Keeping the boat balanced will help you to avoid a windward capsize before the jibe, or a leeward capsize after it. Heeling to windward, as you bear away into the jibe, can result in a rapid wipe-out to windward. Alternatively, if the boat is allowed to heel to leeward, it will be more difficult for the helmsman to turn into the jibe. It will also risk the boom hitting the water after the jibe, which in medium or strong winds will cause the boat to heel further, slow down, and possibly capsize.

## CENTERBOARD POSITION
The risk of capsizing is increased if the centerboard or daggerboard is too far up or down. In most boats, it pays to have the board about one quarter down during the jibe. Any further down and it will be difficult to bear away into the jibe when sailing fast. There is also a risk of the boat "tripping" over the board and broaching (turning rapidly to windward) after the jibe. If the board is too far up, the boat may roll as you bear away into the jibe, making it hard for the helmsman to retain control, and risking a capsize.

## JIBING WITH A TRAPEZE
Single-trapeze boats with a spinnaker often sail downwind on broad-reaching courses, which do not require the crew to be on the trapeze except in strong winds. In this case, the helmsman and crew jibe in the standard way. Twin-, or multiple-trapeze boats, however, usually sail downwind with an asymmetric on a shallower course, with the crew trapezing. In this case, the boat must turn through a broader angle in the jibe and the crew have to move quickly to jibe, and get out on the trapezes on the new side.

◁ **TWIN-TRAPEZE JIBE**
*On a twin-trapeze boat, the helmsman steers onto a run and moves into the boat just before the crew. He swings the long tiller extension aft and around to the new side during the jibe. He then changes hands on the extension and mainsheet, and he hooks onto the new trapeze, ready to move out as he luffs onto the new course.*

## ROLL JIBING

*For boats without a
spinnaker, a roll jibe is a
very effective technique for
maintaining speed in light
winds. When using a
spinnaker or asymmetric, you
can use a small roll to help the
boom over in light winds.
A large roll may make the
spinnaker collapse.*

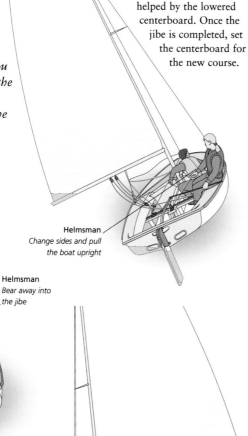

**③** The boat will
accelerate out of the jibe,
helped by the lowered
centerboard. Once the
jibe is completed, set
the centerboard for
the new course.

**Helmsman**
*Change sides and pull
the boat upright*

**Helmsman**
*Bear away into
the jibe*

**② The boat should be**
heeled enough so that the end of
the boom just touches the water
after the jibe. As it does so, pause
until the mainsail fills, then pull the
boat upright using crew weight.

**Crew**
*Prepare to roll
the boat*

**① Before the jibe,**
lower the centerboard fully.
With the boat on a run, the
crew rolls it to windward and
prepares to pull on the vang
to swing the boom across.

**Helmsman**
*Rotate the
tiller extension
to leeward*

## TIPS ON ADVANCED TACKING AND JIBING

Tacking and jibing are always a
good test of skill, and you can
judge a dinghy crew's teamwork
by how they tack and jibe,
especially in very light or very
strong winds. Both these
extremes demand excellent
"feel", good communication,
and quality boat handling.

### COMMUNICATION
Tacking or jibing requires very close
coordination between the helmsman
and crew. A wrong move by either,
or poor synchronization during the
turn, can unbalance and slow the
boat. In light airs, this will stop the
boat, and in strong winds it risks a
capsize. If you race a high-
performance boat, you will quickly
discover that quite small mistakes
mean the difference between
winning a race or being an also-ran.
Improve your performance by good
communication in the boat and by
discussing maneuvers, and your
technique, when on shore.

### PRACTICE
The quickest way to improve your
skills is by spending lots of time
practicing on the water. Leading
Olympic and International crews
spend several hours on the water
nearly every day, honing their skills.
Normal club sailors cannot devote
so much time, but even a few hours
of serious practice will be rewarded
by smoother and faster maneuvers.

### FEEL
The elusive skill you should seek is
called "feel". It tells you how the
boat is about to react and how to
"find the groove" – the fine, ever-
changing edge on which a boat sails
when perfectly balanced; with a
light helm, little heel, and a
willingness to accelerate.

# SPINNAKERS

*L*oved by artists, photographers, and spectators
because of their shape and their bright colors,
spinnakers often cause concern for the crews who
have to trim them. In fact, if a simple routine is
followed, these large, lightweight sails are not
difficult to fly and they add tremendously to the
sail area, providing much-increased power. A
spinnaker brings a performance dinghy alive.

## ANATOMY OF A SPINNAKER

Spinnakers were originally used only
on downwind courses, but modern
sailcloth and new shapes, including
the popular asymmetric design
(*p.124*), allow high-performance boats
to carry spinnakers on a beam reach.

    The spinnaker is attached only at
its three corners, rather than to a spar
or stay along any of its sides, and it
relies on the force of the wind to keep
it in position when hoisted. It requires
skill and practice to hoist, set, and
lower a spinnaker properly.

    Apart from the spinnaker itself,
you will need a spinnaker pole, a
halyard and hoisting system, and
sheets. The sheets lead from each clew,
outside all the rigging, to blocks and
cleats on the sidedecks. The sheet on
the windward side of the boat is
known as the guy. When you jibe, the
old sheet becomes the new guy and
vice versa. Many crews use a
continuous sheet system in which a
single piece of rope is attached at each
end to the clews.

## SPINNAKER DESIGN

Spinnakers are made from lightweight
nylon sailcloth. The way the sail sets is
determined by the way the panels are
cut and sewn together. Downwind
spinnakers are generally cut with a full
shape, a wide mid-section, and a

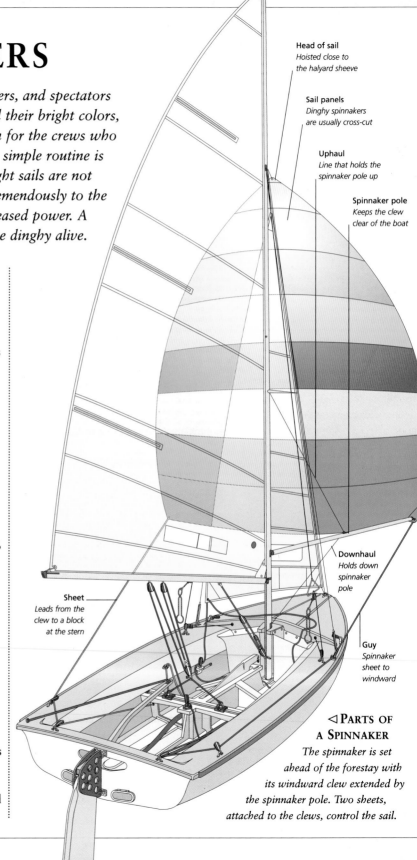

**Head of sail**
*Hoisted close to
the halyard sheeve*

**Sail panels**
*Dinghy spinnakers
are usually cross-cut*

**Uphaul**
*Line that holds the
spinnaker pole up*

**Spinnaker pole**
*Keeps the clew
clear of the boat*

**Downhaul**
*Holds down
spinnaker
pole*

**Sheet**
*Leads from the
clew to a block
at the stern*

**Guy**
*Spinnaker
sheet to
windward*

◁ **PARTS OF
A SPINNAKER**
*The spinnaker is set
ahead of the forestay with
its windward clew extended by
the spinnaker pole. Two sheets,
attached to the clews, control the sail.*

◁ USING A SPINNAKER
*A spinnaker adds considerably to the sail area when sailing off the wind. Here, a 470 sails on a beam reach with a spinnaker set and the crew on the trapeze.*

broad head, whereas those for reaching have a flatter and narrower design. Dinghies usually have one good all-round spinnaker, whereas yachts may have several spinnakers for use in a range of conditions.

## SPINNAKER POLE
The spinnaker pole is used to extend the spinnaker clew away from the boat and allow the sail to set correctly. It is usually made of aluminum but may be carbon fiber. The pole's inner end clips onto a bracket on the front of the mast, and the outer end is clipped onto the spinnaker guy. The pole is held vertically by an uphaul and downhaul with which you can alter its angle and the height of the outer end in order to set the spinnaker correctly for the wind strength. The fittings on the ends of the spinnaker pole have retractable plungers, which are controlled by a light line that runs along the pole from one end-fitting to the other. The pole is set with the end-fitting's openings uppermost. Systems for stowing the spinnaker pole vary. In

some classes the pole is stowed in the boat, whereas in many high-performance boats it is stowed in brackets that are fitted to the boom.

## TURNING BLOCKS
The turning blocks for the sheets are usually placed as far aft as possible on the sidedecks, with a hook, called a reaching hook, just aft of the shrouds on each side. The guy is led under the reaching hook when the boat is sailing on a broad or beam reach. This holds it down and keeps it out of the way of the crew when they are sitting out or trapezing. Sometimes pigging lines are used instead of reaching hooks. A pigging line comprises a small block with a light line attached to it. The block runs along the spinnaker sheet, and the line leads through another block, mounted on the gunwale, just aft of the shroud, and then to a cleat where it can be adjusted. In use, the pigging line on the guy is pulled tight to hold the guy down by the shroud; the pigging line on the sheet is left slack.

## MARKING THE SHEETS
Setting the spinnaker can be made more straightforward by marking the sheets so that you can effectively preset the sail for hoisting and jibing. To mark these preset positions on the sheets, first hoist the spinnaker on land, with the boat stern-to-wind. Set the sail square across the bow of the boat, without the pole fitted, and with neither sheet under a reaching hook, then cleat the sheets. Use a permanent marker pen to mark each sheet at the point where it passes through its cleat. In the future, when you prepare to jibe the spinnaker, simply cleat each sheet at its mark and the sail will be correctly set for the jibe.

To make hoisting easier, especially when hoisting from a windward pouch (*p.126*), put another set of marks on the sheets. Hoist the sail as before, and take each of the spinnaker clews in turn to a point 3ft (1m) ahead of the forestay, pull it tight and cleat it. Mark the sheet at its cleat. Before a hoist, cleat the guy at its mark and the pole will be easier to fit.

## STOWAGE SYSTEMS
Methods of stowing, hoisting, and lowering the spinnaker vary according to the design of the boat. A good system allows you to hoist and lower the spinnaker quickly, with the minimum chance of a foul-up, and stow it neatly without twists, ready for hoisting again. Most modern dinghies are fitted either with a pouch stowage (*pp.126–27*) system on either side of the mast or with a chute system at the bow (*p.125*).

# ASYMMETRICS

Asymmetric spinnakers look like a cross between a large jib and a spinnaker. They are now common on very high-performance dinghies and some sportsboats. An asymmetric spinnaker is set from a long, retractable bowsprit (a spar projecting from the bow) rather than a spinnaker pole, which makes it much easier to handle when hoisting, jibing, and lowering, as the crew does not need to handle a pole. The bowsprit is usually made from carbon fiber for strength and lightness; the sail is made from lightweight, nylon sailcloth.

## HANDLING ASYMMETRICS

An asymmetric spinnaker is usually bigger than a conventional spinnaker and is often flown from a point higher on the mast, with the halyard emerging between the hounds and masthead. These large sails generate considerable power but are easier to handle than a conventional spinnaker because the tack is attached to the end of the bowsprit, and they do not require adjustments to a spinnaker pole. They are controlled by two sheets, both of which are attached to the clew, just like a jib.

## HOISTING AND LOWERING

An asymmetric spinnaker is stowed and launched from a chute or pouches, depending on the specific boat design. The bowsprit is normally retracted when the asymmetric is not being used and so it has to be extended when the sail is hoisted. While the helmsman hoists the sail, the crew pulls a line to launch the bowsprit. In many boats a single-line system extends the bowsprit and pulls the sail's tack to the outer end at the same time. In other boats, separate lines are used and the crew first launches the bowsprit, then pulls the clew to its outer end. The process is reversed to drop the sail.

## SAIL TRIMMING

An asymmetric sail is trimmed using two sheets. The sheets lead to the aft quarters of the boat and may have pigging lines (*p.123*) to move the lead forwards when sailing on a broad reach. An asymmetric is inefficient when running, so sailing downwind is done in a series of jibes and reaches. The crew must avoid over-sheeting the sail and try to keep it trimmed with a slight curl in the luff for top speed.

∇ **FLYING AN ASYMMETRIC**
*This 49'er's crew are sailing under their large asymmetric. Both the sailors are trapezing high for better visibility and control, and the crew has the asymmetric trimmed with a slight curl in the luff.*

# SPINNAKER CHUTES

Many high-performance dinghies use a chute to stow the spinnaker and allow easy hoisting and lowering.

## CHUTE SYSTEMS

Chute systems are built into the boat. They have a bell-shaped mouth set into the foredeck just ahead of, or to one side of, the forestay. A long fabric sock or rigid plastic tube runs under the foredeck from the mouth of the chute. This contains the spinnaker when it is stowed.

Chute systems are useful because the spinnaker cannot become twisted when it is hoisted and lowered. Spinnakers designed to be used with a chute are often given a silicone finish to reduce friction and to shed water quickly, as chutes tend to funnel water over the sail when it is stowed.

## USING A SPINNAKER CHUTE

The spinnaker is hoisted from the chute using the halyard attached to the head of the sail. This halyard, which is operated by the helmsman, runs down inside the mast, then aft along the boat to a jamming cleat situated near the aft end of the centerboard case. The spinnaker is lowered using a downhaul, which is attached to the middle of the sail and runs down through the chute mouth and tube. The halyard and downhaul usually consist of one continuous piece of rope. When the halyard is released and the downhaul is pulled, the sail collapses and is drawn down into the chute ready to be hoisted once again. A chute system allows the spinnaker to be hoisted and lowered relatively easily, even when sailing on a beam reach. However, it is safer in strong winds to bear away to a broad reach or run before hoisting or lowering.

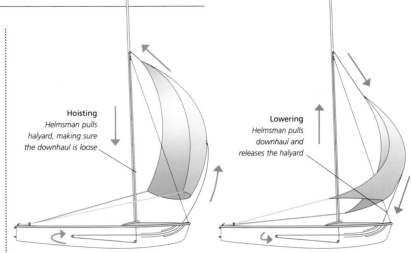

Hoisting
*Helmsman pulls halyard, making sure the downhaul is loose*

Lowering
*Helmsman pulls downhaul and releases the halyard*

## △ HOISTING FROM A CHUTE

*The helmsman hoists the sail by pulling on the halyard, while the crew sets the sheet and guy to their marks and attaches the pole. The helmsman then cleats the halyard and trims the sheet and guy while the crew is dealing with the pole.*

## △ LOWERING INTO A CHUTE

*The crew sheets the foot of the sail tight against the forestay. Uncleating the halyard, the helmsman pulls on the downhaul. As soon as the middle of the sail enters the chute, the crew releases the sheet and guy and removes the pole.*

---

## PACKING THE SPINNAKER IN A CHUTE

It is important that the spinnaker is packed correctly in its chute before the boat goes afloat. It must be packed without twists, or it will be difficult for the crew to set the sail when it is hoisted.

### PACKING PROCEDURE

With the boat on dry land, attach the halyard, sheets, and downhaul to the spinnaker and hoist the sail to ensure that it is not twisted. Pull on the downhaul as you lower the spinnaker so that the sail is drawn into the chute. Keep pulling steadily until all the spinnaker has disappeared completely into the mouth of the chute. Take all the slack out of the halyard and the sheets and cleat them.

STOWING THE SPINNAKER ▷
*When the spinnaker is pulled into the chute using the downhaul, the head and two clews should be the last parts to disappear into the chute. When the helmsman pulls on the halyard to hoist the sail, it will slip smoothly out of the chute without any twists, and will set easily as the wind fills it.*

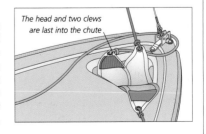

*The head and two clews are last into the chute*

# SPINNAKER POUCHES

Handling spinnaker pouches requires a little more skill than handling chutes. The spinnaker must be stored correctly with no twists to ensure that it can be hoisted easily when it is needed.

## USING POUCHES

With a pouch system, the dinghy is fitted with two light fabric pouches, one either side of the mast. The sail is best stowed in the pouch that will be to leeward when hoisting, as this makes hoisting easier. When the sail is stowed, the halyard is hooked under the reaching hook to keep it neat.

## HOISTING FROM A LEEWARD POUCH

*A spinnaker is easier to hoist from the leeward pouch because the helmsman can hoist it directly out of the pouch without help from the crew. Bear away to a run or broad reach to hoist.*

Spinnaker pole

Guy

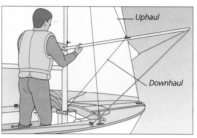

Uphaul

Downhaul

**(2)** The crew attaches the uphaul and downhaul, and clips the inboard end of the spinnaker pole onto the mast bracket, which is positioned above the boom.

**(1)** The crew releases the halyard from the reaching hook and pulls on the guy to draw the windward clew towards the forestay. As the helmsman hoists the sail, the crew clips the pole to the guy.

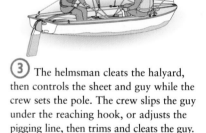

**(3)** The helmsman cleats the halyard, then controls the sheet and guy while the crew sets the pole. The crew slips the guy under the reaching hook, or adjusts the pigging line, then trims and cleats the guy.

## HOISTING FROM A WINDWARD POUCH

*Good coordination and teamwork are needed when hoisting from a windward pouch. Ensure that the sheets are marked correctly (p.123) so that you can cleat the guy in the correct position beforehand. Bear away to a broad reach or run. The crew has to take the bundled spinnaker out of the pouch, and throw it up and forward, while the helmsman rapidly hoists it.*

Crew holds bundled spinnaker

**(1)** The crew frees the halyard and cleats the guy so that the clew will clear the forestay. He removes the spinnaker from the pouch, holding it tightly.

Crew throws bundle up and forward

**(2)** The helmsman hoists rapidly as the crew throws the sail forward. The crew pulls on the sheet to bring the sail around to leeward of the forestay.

Helmsman trims sheet and guy

**(3)** The helmsman controls the sheet and guy while the crew rigs the pole. The crew slips the guy under the reaching hook and cleats it, or pulls on the pigging line.

## LOWERING THE SPINNAKER

You can choose between lowering the spinnaker into either the windward or leeward pouch. The safest and quickest method is to drop the spinnaker into the windward pouch as this keeps the crew's weight on the windward side. Only drop the sail into the leeward pouch if you need it in that pouch for a later leeward hoist. For either method, steer onto a broad reach or run.

## WINDWARD DROP

*For a windward drop the crew must remove and stow the pole before lowering the sail. He then pulls on the guy until the clew is in his hand and pulls the sail down by its luff, stuffing it into the windward pouch. He stows the halyard under the reaching hook.*

◁ **LEEWARD DROP**

*The crew pulls hard on the sheet until he can reach the clew, then releases the guy and pulls the sail under the boom and into the leeward pouch. Once all the sail is in the pouch, and the halyard is hooked under the reaching hook, the crew removes and stows the spinnaker pole.*

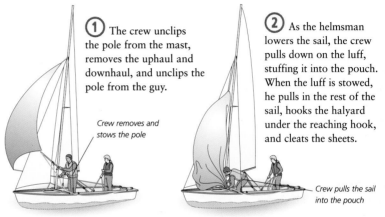

**1** The crew unclips the pole from the mast, removes the uphaul and downhaul, and unclips the pole from the guy.

*Crew removes and stows the pole*

**2** As the helmsman lowers the sail, the crew pulls down on the luff, stuffing it into the pouch. When the luff is stowed, he pulls in the rest of the sail, hooks the halyard under the reaching hook, and cleats the sheets.

*Crew pulls the sail into the pouch*

---

# PACKING THE SPINNAKER IN A POUCH

It is important to ensure that the spinnaker is correctly packed into its pouch so that it can be hoisted quickly and easily. The best way to do this is to hoist the sail while the boat is ashore and then lower it into the pouch in the same way as for a windward drop. This can be done by the crew alone but is easier with two.

**1** Attach the halyard and sheets to the spinnaker and then hoist the sail.

*Hoist the sail by pulling on the halyard*

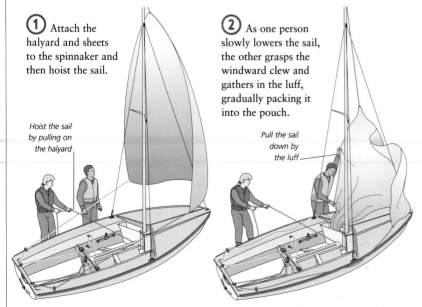

**2** As one person slowly lowers the sail, the other grasps the windward clew and gathers in the luff, gradually packing it into the pouch.

*Pull the sail down by the luff*

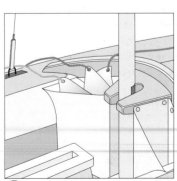

**3** Once the luff is stowed, gather in the rest of the spinnaker so that it ends up in the pouch with the head and both clews on top. Hook the halyard under the reaching hook to keep it out of the way, and take any slack out of the sheets before cleating.

# TRIMMING SPINNAKERS

*Successful spinnaker work demands plenty of practice and good communication between the helmsman and crew. Once set, the spinnaker has an enormous effect on the handling of a boat, and it must be kept under control at all times. This is primarily the crew's job, and it requires great concentration. The crew must learn to trim the spinnaker correctly and should understand how to cope with gusts. Spinnaker jibing requires practice if it is to be completed without an embarrassing mishap.*

## PLAYING THE SHEET

Each spinnaker shape needs trimming in a slightly different way, but there are some general rules to help you get the best out of your boat. The most important thing is to keep the sail symmetrical about its center line; this involves keeping the clews level, at the same height above the water. You must also encourage the spinnaker to fly as far as possible from the mainsail so that air can pass freely between the two sails. When the spinnaker is set correctly, the crew will be able to ease the sheet until the luff starts to curl back on itself about halfway up. A well-designed, stable spinnaker can be sailed with some luff curl without collapsing. The point at which the luff starts to curl is the optimum trim in any particular wind strength and point of sailing. As the boat speed changes, the apparent wind shifts forward or backward, and the sheet must be trimmed continually to keep the spinnaker on the edge of curling.

## HANDLING GUSTS

You must know how to handle gusts, to avoid the power in the spinnaker overcoming rudder control. As a gust hits, the crew eases the spinnaker sheet to curl the luff and allows the boat to accelerate. Failure to do this will make the boat heel and develop considerable weather helm (p.112), making it hard for the helmsman to stay on course or bear away. The apparent wind will shift forward as the boat accelerates and the crew must be ready to sheet in to prevent the spinnaker collapsing. When the boat slows down, the apparent wind will shift aft and the sheet must be eased.

## POLE ANGLE AND HEIGHT

The pole angle and height must be adjusted correctly so that the sail is set at its most efficient position and can be trimmed effectively. The crew adjusts pole angle using the guy, which is cleated once the correct angle has been set. The height of the pole is altered, usually by the crew, using the uphaul and downhaul.

### POLE ANGLE

Set the angle of the pole just greater than a right angle to the apparent wind. This means bringing the pole aft as the boat sails further downwind, and easing it forward as the boat turns on to a reach. Always keep the pole off the forestay or it may bend or break. Remember to adjust the guy after putting it under the reaching hook or tightening the pigging line.

### POLE HEIGHT

When the pole is horizontal it holds the spinnaker as far away as possible from the rest of the rig, but it is even more important to ensure that the clews of the sail are kept level, at the same height above the water. The windward clew (attached at the pole end) is held in place by the pole, but the clew to which the sheet is attached is free to move up and down, depending on the strength of the wind and the boat's course. If the leeward clew is lower than the tack, lower the pole. If it is higher than the tack, raise the pole.

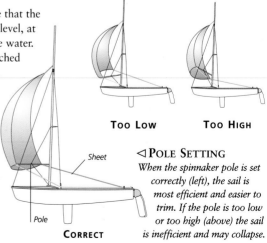

**TOO LOW**   **TOO HIGH**

Sheet

◁ **POLE SETTING**
*When the spinnaker pole is set correctly (left), the sail is most efficient and easier to trim. If the pole is too low or too high (above) the sail is inefficient and may collapse.*

Pole

**CORRECT**

## JIBING THE SPINNAKER

*Successful jibing with a spinnaker set requires a standard routine and plenty of practice. It is vital to keep the boat upright and to complete the jibe quickly to prevent the spinnaker getting out of control. To prepare for the jibe, the helmsman bears away to a run and the crew removes the guy from the reaching hook and sets the sail square across the bow. If the sheets are marked (p.123), they can be set at the jibing position quickly and easily. The boat is now ready to be jibed.*

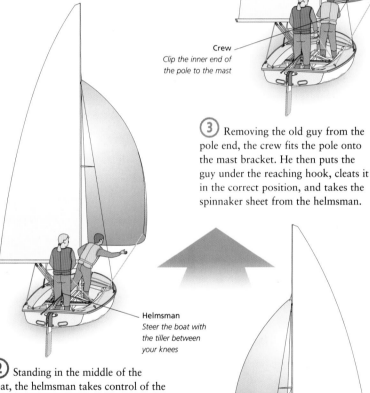

**Crew**
*Clip the inner end of the pole to the mast*

③ Removing the old guy from the pole end, the crew fits the pole onto the mast bracket. He then puts the guy under the reaching hook, cleats it in the correct position, and takes the spinnaker sheet from the helmsman.

**Helmsman**
*Steer the boat with the tiller between your knees*

② Standing in the middle of the boat, the helmsman takes control of the guy and sheet to keep the spinnaker full. The crew removes the pole from the mast, clips it onto the new guy, and pushes it out to the new side.

**Crew**
*Pull on the vang to help the boom over*

① With the boat pointing dead downwind, the mainsail and jib are jibed. The crew helps the boom over by pulling on the vang, and sheets the jib onto the new side.

## USING ASYMMETRICS

Asymmetrics are set at the end of a bowsprit so there is no pole angle or height to worry about. There is also no guy. Instead, the sail is controlled by two sheets, just like a jib. The sail is trimmed like a spinnaker, by easing the sheet to keep the luff on the point of curling.

### JIBING

Jibing is easy with an asymmetric as the sail is jibed just like a jib. As the boat turns through the jibe, the old sheet is eased well out so that the sail blows around the forestay, and is sheeted in on the new side.

### COUNTERING LEE HELM

Asymmetrics tend to generate considerable lee helm because of the long bowsprit. Reduce this by heeling to about 15°. You must also avoid sailing too close to windward of other boats; if a gust hits, the boat will bear away and you will need space to leeward.

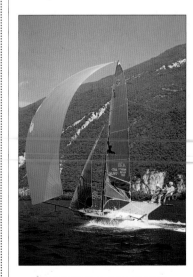

**CORRECTLY SET ASYMMETRIC**

# SINGLE-HANDED SAILING

*The purest form of sailing is when you go on the water alone and are solely responsible for balance, trim, and handling. You learn quickly when you sail single-handed, and you can sail whenever you want to, without having to find a crew. Single-handed boats are usually cheaper than two-man dinghies. They are normally lighter and can often be transported on a roof rack. Another benefit is that they are usually quick to rig, so you can be sailing within minutes of arriving at the venue.*

## RIGGING AND LAUNCHING

Most single-handed sailing dinghies have a mainsail only. This is set on a mast that is stepped much further forward than on a two-sailed dinghy.

The mast is often unstayed (*p.56*) and is flexible so that it can be bent to provide an efficient sail shape and to release excess power in strong winds. Whereas a stayed mast and sail arrangement allows you to hoist the sail before or after launching, as conditions dictate, an unstayed mast with a sleeved mainsail must be rigged before launching and the boat kept close to head-to-wind.

A single-hander is launched in the same way as a two-man dinghy. You usually have to do the job on your own, although it is easier to launch and recover the boat if someone else is available to deal with the trailer.

## SAILING

Single-handed dinghies are usually light and thus sensitive to changes in trim and balance. The helmsman must move his weight in and out, and fore and aft, to keep the boat upright and correctly trimmed. It is important that the sail is set correctly, and you must get used to adjusting its shape using the outhaul, Cunningham control *p.141*), mainsheet, and vang.

## ONE-MAN DINGHY ▷

A typical single-hander has an unstayed mast and a single, sleeved sail that slips over the mast. It is designed to be straightforward to rig, launch, sail, and recover alone.

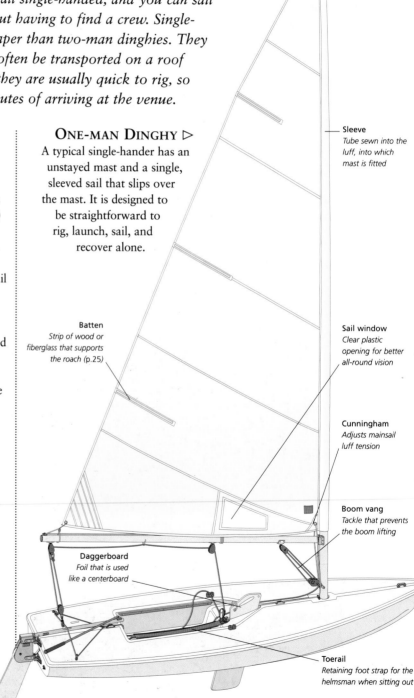

**Webbing strap**
*Fits over top of mast to hold sail*

**Sleeve**
*Tube sewn into the luff, into which mast is fitted*

**Batten**
*Strip of wood or fiberglass that supports the roach (p.25)*

**Sail window**
*Clear plastic opening for better all-round vision*

**Cunningham**
*Adjusts mainsail luff tension*

**Boom vang**
*Tackle that prevents the boom lifting*

**Daggerboard**
*Foil that is used like a centerboard*

**Toerail**
*Retaining foot strap for the helmsman when sitting out*

## RIGGING THE BOAT

*Some single-handed dinghies have stayed masts, and their mainsails are rigged like a two-man dinghy (pp.56–61). However, most have unstayed masts, which are light and easy to rig, although it is helpful if someone can assist you. The mast usually comes in two pieces, which are slotted together before the sail is fitted. Most single-handed dinghies use a daggerboard. Make sure that this and the rudder are in the boat before you launch it.*

Gently slide the sail onto the mast

**①** Assemble the mast by slotting the two pieces together. Unfold the mainsail and find the sleeve in the mainsail luff. Slide the mast into the sleeve.

Slip the mast into the mast step

**②** Step the mast and secure it in place. Attach the boom to the gooseneck and lash the clew of the mainsail to the boom using the outhaul. Fit the boom vang.

Downwind courses reveal the biggest differences between a single-hander and a two-man boat. When there is only one sail, there is an increased weather helm and a constant tendency for the boat to turn to windward. This can be reduced by heeling the boat to windward until the helm is balanced, but skill is required to maintain this position. Single-handers usually plane easily and are fun to sail downwind in waves, as they react instantly to the tiller and accelerate rapidly.

## TACKING

Tacking a single-hander well requires good timing and smooth actions. The helmsman's movements are the same as in a two-man dinghy (pp.78–81). The boom is often very low so you will have to duck even lower under it. Ease the mainsheet as you turn through the wind to make it easier to avoid. Do not move off the windward side too early. Wait until the boom is approaching the centerline with the boat heeled toward you, then cross

**TACKING ▷**
*This skilled solo sailor is tacking. He allows the boat to heel toward him and waits for the boom to reach the centerline.*

quickly and get your weight out over the new windward side as the boat completes the tack. Sit out hard and sheet in as the boat comes upright. Change hands on the mainsheet and tiller extension after the tack.

## JIBING

Raise the daggerboard until it is just clear of the boom and vang. If the vang is tight, ease it to prevent the

boom hitting the water and capsizing the boat. The helmsman's actions through the jibe are the same as they are in a two-man dinghy (pp.82–85). Sailing fast on a very broad reach or a run, turn into the jibe and give a sharp tug on the mainsheet to start the boom swinging across. As it does so, straighten the tiller and get your weight out on the new side. Change hands on the tiller and mainsheet.

# CATAMARANS

*If you want exciting, high-speed sailing, try a catamaran. Catamarans consist of two hulls connected by two beams and a trampoline to allow the crew to move from side to side. Their wide beam makes them more stable than single-hulled dinghies, while their narrow hulls and light weight offer little resistance and make them very fast. Catamarans come in a variety of sizes and shapes to suit all ages, sizes, and skill levels.*

## CATAMARAN RIGS

Most catamarans have a large, fully-battened mainsail, and a much smaller jib that is usually tall and narrow. However, single-handed catamarans are usually sailed without a jib. Some use a loose-footed mainsail, set without a boom, in which case the multi-part mainsheet tackle attaches directly to the clew. The lower end of the mainsheet runs on a full-width traveler on the rear beam. The mast is normally designed to rotate so that it can take up an efficient angle to the wind on all points of sailing. The angle of rotation is controlled by a device called a mast spanner that is adjusted by the crew.

Catamarans have twin rudders, one at the stern of each hull, with their tillers connected by a tiller bar. The long tiller extension is attached to the middle of the tiller bar. Many catamarans are fitted with one or two trapezes, and a number of them use asymmetric spinnakers to increase speed downwind. Most of the sailing techniques already described can be used to sail catamarans, but some aspects are different (*pp.134–37*).

## HULL DESIGN

Hull shapes vary depending on the design of boat. Some catamarans have hulls that are identical and are

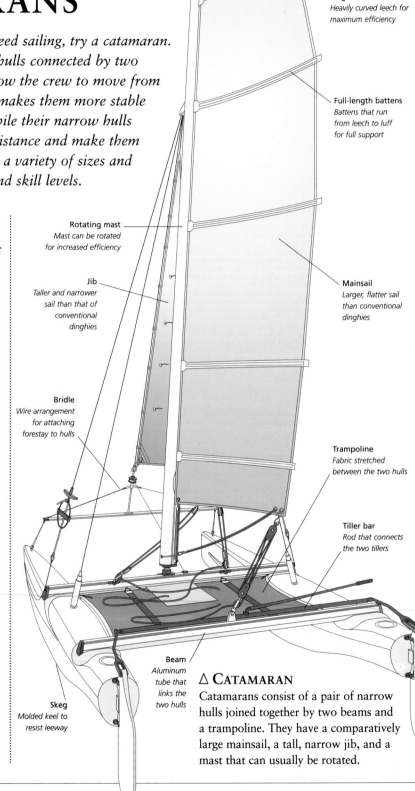

**Large roach**
*Heavily curved leech for maximum efficiency*

**Full-length battens**
*Battens that run from leech to luff for full support*

**Rotating mast**
*Mast can be rotated for increased efficiency*

**Jib**
*Taller and narrower sail than that of conventional dinghies*

**Mainsail**
*Larger, flatter sail than conventional dinghies*

**Bridle**
*Wire arrangement for attaching forestay to hulls*

**Trampoline**
*Fabric stretched between the two hulls*

**Tiller bar**
*Rod that connects the two tillers*

**Beam**
*Aluminum tube that links the two hulls*

**Skeg**
*Molded keel to resist leeway*

## △ CATAMARAN

Catamarans consist of a pair of narrow hulls joined together by two beams and a trampoline. They have a comparatively large mainsail, a tall, narrow jib, and a mast that can usually be rotated.

# TYPES OF CATAMARANS

There are many types of catamarans on the market, so you should be able to find one that is suitable for your particular requirements. If you want to race, choose a boat that has a good fleet near you. Before you make your decision, ask the opinion of expert sailors and have a trial sail in a few different types.

### HOBIE

The Hobie range of catamarans is intended for fast, fun sailing, but there are also good racing fleets in many parts of the world. Hobies have asymmetric hulls without centerboards or daggerboards.

### DART 16

The Dart 16 and its larger brother the Dart 18 are excellent boats for fast sailing and competitive racing, and are extremely popular with catamaran sailors. The Dart uses symmetrical hulls with skegs.

### TORNADO

The International Tornado is the Olympic catamaran class and offers the highest quality racing with an outstanding performance. It uses conventional centerboards in each symmetrical hull.

symmetrical about their centerline. Symmetrical hulls are usually fitted with a centerboard or a daggerboard in each hull to resist leeway. Alternatively, there may be a skeg (a molded-in keel) about two thirds of the way aft on both hulls. The skeg resists leeway without the need for a centerboard or daggerboard. Other catamarans have asymmetrical hulls with a fatter shape on the outboard side of each hull; in which case the two hulls are mirror-images of each other. These do not usually need centerboards or daggerboards.

## ASSEMBLING A CATAMARAN

Catamarans are usually dismantled to be transported. Once at the sailing venue, they have to be reassembled on a flat surface. Grass is best as it will not cause damage; otherwise, protect the hulls with something soft. Lay the hulls side by side, the length of the beams apart. Put one hull on its outer face, and slide the main and rear beams into their sockets. Roll the hull onto its keel, and fit the second hull to the other ends of the beams. Check that the socket-locking mechanisms hold the beams securely. Next, attach the trampoline to the two beams and the inside of the hulls, making sure that it is laced tightly, then tie the toerails between the beams. Step the mast by laying it on the trampoline and fitting it onto the mast step, and attach the shrouds and the forestay bridle. While one person stands on the trampoline to support the mast, the other pulls on the forestay to raise the mast into position. Finallly, fasten the forestay to the bridle, and attach the trapeze wires to the hulls.

## CATAMARANS ON LAND

Catamarans can be unwieldy on land because of their width. However, they are very light so moving them is quite easy, even with only two people.

### MOVING

Most catamarans are moved on a trailer with two wheels and two chocks. The trailer is placed under the hulls at the point of balance and the bows are used as the handle.

### SECURING

If you leave a catamaran with the mast stepped, fasten it securely to the ground to stop it blowing over in strong winds.

# SAILING CATAMARANS

*D*inghy sailors who decide to sail catamarans need to learn a *few new techniques; they will also have to be prepared for the much greater speed potential that is offered by a catamaran. Heading upwind is more difficult in a catamaran than it is in a conventional dinghy and requires a good deal of practice. It is when sailing on downwind courses at speed that catamarans really perform. They are more stable than dinghies and are easier to jibe, but they can still be capsized.*

## WIND AND SPEED

Because catamarans sail so fast, there is a much bigger difference in the direction of true and apparent wind (*p.30*) than in most boats. A wind indicator is usually fitted on the forestay bridle so that the helmsman can constantly check the direction of the apparent wind.

A dinghy sailor must also get used to the high speed of a catamaran, which means that you need to allow more space for maneuvers, especially passing other boats. Be prepared for gusts, too, as the catamaran will accelerate rapidly when they hit.

## SETTING SAIL

The first time you sail a catamaran, you should start on a beam reach, just as you would with a single-hulled dinghy. Put the boat beam-on to the wind and slowly sheet in both sails. The faster acceleration, and the forward shift of the apparent wind mean that the sails have to be sheeted in closer than they would be on a slower-moving dinghy. The load on the sails will also be greater than that in a dinghy. The jib sheet usually has a tackle to make it easier to trim, and the mainsheet on most catamarans requires at least a seven-to-one tackle.

This makes it easier for the helmsman to handle the large loads. Use the mainsheet to control leech tension, and adjust the angle of the sail with the traveler. Set the mainsail twist by using the leech tell-tales as you would in a dinghy (*p.112*). Although the rudders are small, they are efficient at high speeds, when you will need only small movements of the tiller extension to adjust the course. When you tack or jibe, however, the boat slows down and considerable force may be needed to turn the boat.

Daggerboards or centerboards (if fitted) should be lowered about halfway on a reach. The leeward board is usually lowered first and kept at a lower position than the windward board. As you turn onto a close reach, lower the boards further still and sheet in the sails, using the traveler to bring the mainsail closer to the centerline.

## HEELING FOR SPEED

Catamarans sail fastest when the windward hull is kept just skimming the water's surface, giving minimum resistance. However, this slight heel is difficult to maintain and needs a lot of practice. Even in medium winds, the helmsman and crew will have to sit out or trapeze hard to keep the boat balanced. Once the helmsman and crew are fully extended, heel is controlled by the helmsman trimming the mainsail with the traveler and adjusting the course. Luff to maintain heel and bear away to reduce it.

## ◁ CATAMARAN IN STRONG WINDS

*When sailing in strong winds and big waves, the speed of a catamaran means it is possible to take off on the top of a wave.*

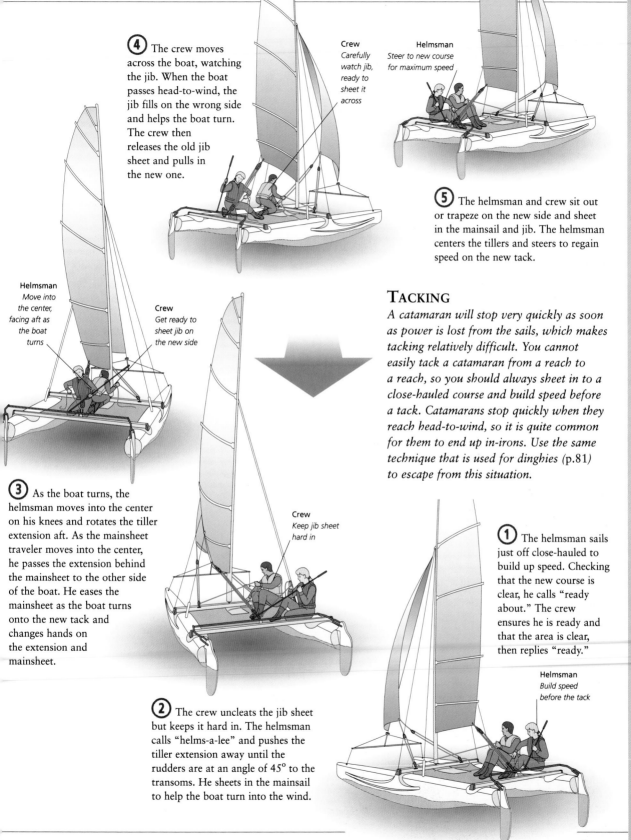

**4** The crew moves across the boat, watching the jib. When the boat passes head-to-wind, the jib fills on the wrong side and helps the boat turn. The crew then releases the old jib sheet and pulls in the new one.

**Crew**
*Carefully watch jib, ready to sheet it across*

**Helmsman**
*Steer to new course for maximum speed*

**5** The helmsman and crew sit out or trapeze on the new side and sheet in the mainsail and jib. The helmsman centers the tillers and steers to regain speed on the new tack.

**Helmsman**
*Move into the center, facing aft as the boat turns*

**Crew**
*Get ready to sheet jib on the new side*

## TACKING

*A catamaran will stop very quickly as soon as power is lost from the sails, which makes tacking relatively difficult. You cannot easily tack a catamaran from a reach to a reach, so you should always sheet in to a close-hauled course and build speed before a tack. Catamarans stop quickly when they reach head-to-wind, so it is quite common for them to end up in-irons. Use the same technique that is used for dinghies (p.81) to escape from this situation.*

**3** As the boat turns, the helmsman moves into the center on his knees and rotates the tiller extension aft. As the mainsheet traveler moves into the center, he passes the extension behind the mainsheet to the other side of the boat. He eases the mainsheet as the boat turns onto the new tack and changes hands on the extension and mainsheet.

**Crew**
*Keep jib sheet hard in*

**1** The helmsman sails just off close-hauled to build up speed. Checking that the new course is clear, he calls "ready about." The crew ensures he is ready and that the area is clear, then replies "ready."

**Helmsman**
*Build speed before the tack*

**2** The crew uncleats the jib sheet but keeps it hard in. The helmsman calls "helms-a-lee" and pushes the tiller extension away until the rudders are at an angle of 45° to the transoms. He sheets in the mainsail to help the boat turn into the wind.

## UPWIND SAILING

When you turn to a close-hauled course, sheet the sails right in and steer using the tell-tales on the jib and the wind indicator. Fully lower both centerboards. Be careful not to pinch (sail too close to the wind) as this makes speed decrease rapidly.

Catamarans are sensitive to fore-and-aft trim, so the helmsman and crew must sit close together, near the middle of the boat, to keep it level. In light winds, move forward to lift the transoms clear of the water – the crew usually lies on the trampoline in the middle of the boat. In stronger winds, move further back to help prevent the bows burying as the boat accelerates.

## DOWNWIND SAILING

In light or moderate winds, fast catamarans can sail faster than the true wind speed, and this speed can be fully exploited downwind. It is more efficient to sail downwind in a series of broad reaches, much as you would tack upwind. Sailing dead downwind is slow, but on a broad reach, the speed of the catamaran pulls the apparent wind forward until it is on the beam, thus increasing its strength. The fastest speed downwind is usually achieved by steering to keep the apparent wind, shown by the wind indicator, blowing at right angles to the boat.

## MODERATE WINDS

Downwind in moderate winds, the helmsman sets the mainsail by letting the traveler right out and uses the mainsheet to adjust the twist in the mainsail. Trim the sail to keep the top leech tell-tale just streaming. The crew eases the jib out as far as possible, keeping all the tell-tales streaming. The helmsman steers to keep the apparent wind at 90° to the boat. The helmsman and crew may have to sit

---

### CATAMARAN COMFORT

Catamarans tend to be wet because they are so fast. Buy good quality foul weather gear or a wetsuit to enjoy the sailing fully.

---

on opposite sides of the boat to keep the weight balanced between the hulls, but the crew moves to windward if the boat starts to heel. If the wind is strong enough, the boat is sailed with the windward hull just touching the water to achieve maximum speed. Where centerboards or daggerboards are fitted, raise them as much as possible; if steering becomes difficult they can be lowered slightly. The helmsman and crew must be prepared to move around the boat to keep it level fore and aft. If the wind drops, move forward to lift the transoms; if it increases, move aft to stop the bows depressing and slowing the boat.

## LIGHT WINDS

Downwind in light winds, both crew and helmsman sit well forward to lift the transoms and depress the bows, and the crew sits on the leeward hull to balance the helmsman on the windward side. To prevent the jib sagging under its own weight, the crew should hold its clew to keep it trimmed, rather than using the sheet.

The helmsman should steer with gentle movements and concentrate on building and maintaining boat speed. In these conditions, it is very easy for the sails to stall, which will make the boat slow dramatically. If this happens, the helmsman must luff until the apparent wind moves forward again and boat speed increases. When the boat is moving fast again, the helmsman can bear away gently to progress further downwind while maintaining speed.

## STRONG WINDS

Catamaran sailing is at its best downwind in strong winds, when the boat reaches its maximum speeds and accelerates rapidly every time a gust hits. The power in the sails depresses the bows, so it is vital that both the helmsman and crew sit out, or trapeze, at the stern of the windward hull. The bows must be prevented from diving under water or you will capsize. The high boat speed increases the apparent wind speed, so the helmsman can steer further downwind while maintaining the apparent wind at right angles to the boat. As gusts hit, the boat will accelerate and the apparent wind will move further ahead, so the helmsman should bear off to retain the constant apparent-wind angle. In lulls, he must head-up to maintain the angle. Be ready to ease the jib in serious gusts to prevent the bows digging in.

---

### CAPSIZE RECOVERY

Catamarans are very stable, but can capsize if the crew makes a mistake. This is especially true in strong winds, when capsizes can be spectacular.

#### RIGHTING A CATAMARAN

You must react quickly in a capsize to prevent inversion; an inverted boat is difficult to right without outside assistance. With most larger catamarans, one crew member should stand on the lower centerboard while pulling on a jib sheet, as when righting a dinghy (pp.98–101). The other crew member should depress the bow or stern of the lower hull to sink it, which will assist righting. Some smaller catamarans can be righted by pushing the stern or bow under water to rotate the boat upright.

**②** Keeping the boat turning, the helmsman swings the tiller extension behind the mainsheet to the new windward side. He changes hands on the mainsheet and tiller, putting his new forward hand on the mainsheet tackle between clew and traveler.

**③** As the sail swings across, the helmsman briefly stops the mainsheet from swinging to leeward so that the mainsail battens flick to their new shape. He then releases the tackle and moves to the windward hull. He steers onto the new course while the crew trims the jib.

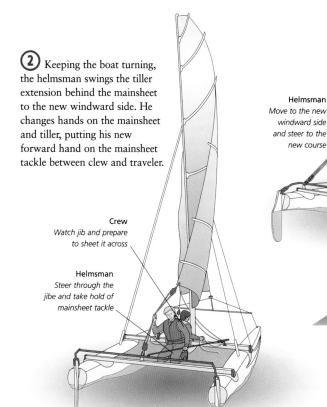

**Crew**
*Watch jib and prepare to sheet it across*

**Helmsman**
*Steer through the jibe and take hold of mainsheet tackle*

**Helmsman**
*Move to the new windward side and steer to the new course*

**Crew**
*Sheet jib across and move to balance the boat*

## JIBING

*A catamaran is easier to jibe than a dinghy because of the stability created by the two hulls, and because its speed reduces the strength of the apparent wind. The catamaran moves quickly, so you must make sure that you have plenty of room for the maneuver and ensure that the boat is under full control before you start the jibe. Jibe with the centerboards or daggerboards fully raised. Catamarans rarely sail dead downwind, so you will jibe through a wide angle, from one broad reach to the other.*

**①** The helmsman bears away from a broad reach to a run and makes sure that the area that the boat will turn into is clear. When ready, he calls "stand by to jibe." The crew also checks the new course. If the crew is ready and the area clear, he replies "ready."

**Helmsman**
*Bear away from a broad reach to a run*

**Crew**
*Pick up new jib sheet and prepare to move across the boat*

# TUNING YOUR BOAT

*In order to get the best from your boat, especially if you want to do well in racing, you have to set it up to suit your combined crew weight and the type of sails you use. Many factors contribute to the way a dinghy performs, and you need to understand each one of them – and how they work together – to tune it effectively for a wide range of conditions. Your aim is to set it up to achieve maximum speed in light, medium, and strong winds, so that you can concentrate on boat handling.*

## HOW TO START

Before tuning your own boat, find out how the fast sailors in your class set up theirs. Many top sailors are happy to help novices learn to tune their boats. Initially, it will be sufficient to aim to set up your boat so that it is exactly the same as the best performer in your class. This will help you achieve a good performance quickly and will prevent you from getting too confused by all the variables that combine to make a fast setup.

Once you are more familiar with tuning techniques, try experimenting with other adjustments. Your class association may be a good source of further information, as many of them publish tuning aids to help people who are new to the subject.

## THE HULL AND FOILS

It is very important that all the underwater parts of the hull, including the centerboard and the rudder, have a perfect finish, free from any blemishes that would disturb the flow of water across their surfaces. Check them regularly and repair any damage immediately, lightly sanding away imperfections. In light winds, when the water is flat and the boat is not sailing at its maximum speed, any small blemishes on underwater surfaces will increase unwanted drag.

While you are working on shore on the underwater surfaces, turn the boat on its side and lower the centerboard fully. Check that it is held rigidly in its case and does not bend when you lean on its tip. If there is any give in it, replace it with a stiffer board – any deflection in the centerboard as it moves through the water will slow the boat. The bottom of the centerboard case should be fitted with rubber or plastic strips, which seal the slot and prevent water turbulence – another source of drag. Check that the rubber strips are in good condition and fit flush with the hull, molding around the board when it is lowered.

If your dinghy has a lifting rudder, check that the blade fits tightly in the stock and that there is no sideways movement that will cause drag and make it harder to steer accurately.

## THE RIG

Most high-performance dinghies have large, powerful rigs with a variety of controls to enable the amount of power delivered by the sails to be adjusted to suit the conditions. Boats that are less focused on performance have fewer controls, but significant changes to the rig can still be made.

The rake (lean) and bend – fore and aft as well as sideways – of the mast is used to alter the shape, and thus the performance of the sails. Full sails deliver maximum power but as the wind increases, the crew's weight, and their ability to keep the boat level, will be overpowered. In strong conditions, the crew need to be able to flatten the sails to reduce power.

## THE MAST

Dinghy masts are usually made from aluminum and are strong and light. They are also designed to be flexible so that they can be bent. Masts come in a variety of cross-section shapes and weights, and each one will bend in a different way. If you have a choice, use a mast of the same type fitted in the top boats in your class. A note of caution – light crews tend to use more flexible rigs than heavier crews, so follow the example of a crew of a similar weight to your own.

## MAST RAKE

It is easier to alter the rake and bend of the mast if it is keel stepped (*p.57*), as the gate at deck level usually has some form of control that can be adjusted. A mast that is stepped on deck can be adjusted only via the spreaders and the shrouds.

Before adjusting your mast's bend, you need to check its rake. This is usually measured between the top of the mast and the top of the transom on the centerline. Again, follow the example of leading sailors in your class and record the measurements for use in the future.

## SAILS AND PRE-BEND

It is vital that the amount of pre-bend in your mast matches the shape your sailmaker has built into the luff of the mainsail. Pick a leading sailmaker for your class, tell him your crew weight, and ask for the fast settings for pre-bend and mast rake, then use these as a starting point for your set up.

# MAST BEND

A key part of setting up the rig for maximum performance is adjusting the pre-bend. This is the amount of bend set in the mast before you start sailing, and it directly influences the mainsail shape. Tuning the mast involves deciding how much you want it to bend and adjusting the controls accordingly.

### DETERMINING PRE-BEND

Many dinghy classes are set up with about 3–4in (75–100mm) of pre-bend. If you have no other figure to go on for your class, this is a reasonable starting point for experimentation.

### SPREADERS AND SHROUDS

The main factors that affect mast bend are the tension in the shrouds and the length and angle of the spreaders.

Typically, spreaders are set up to push the shrouds out and aft of a direct line from the hounds to the chainplates. Tightening the jib halyard tensions the shrouds and causes the spreaders to stiffen the mast sideways and push its middle forward, thus creating pre-bend. Before the mast is stepped, the length or angle of the spreaders can be altered. Some dinghies have adjustable spreaders that allow the angle to be changed afloat.

### KEEL-STEPPED MASTS

If your mast is keel stepped, it will have some form of control to adjust its fore-and-aft position in the mast gate. This might be a strut or a ram, or it may be simple wooden chocks that can be removed or added as required. All these systems are designed to hold the mast back in the gate to stiffen it and limit bend, or to allow it to move forward to increase bend.

### MAST BEND ▷

*The amount of mast bend controls the fullness of the mainsail. Use a straight mast for maximum fullness and power in light to moderate winds. In very light, drifting conditions, increasing pre-bend will flatten the sail and make it easier for the wind to flow around it. As soon as there is a perceptible breeze, however, straighten the mast. In medium to strong winds, when the wind increases to the point where the crew's weight is no longer sufficient to hold the boat upright, the mast should be bent to flatten the sail and reduce power.*

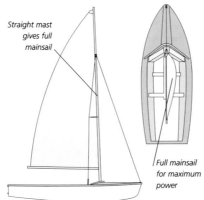

**STRAIGHT MAST**

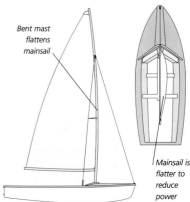

**MAST WITH PRE-BEND**

### SPREADERS ▷

*The length and angle of the spreaders help control mast bend. Long spreaders push the shrouds outward and stiffen the mast sideways. Angling the spreaders aft causes the shrouds to push the middle of the mast forward. This increases mast bend. When the jib halyard is tightened, the shrouds are tensioned and the effect of the spreaders on the mast is increased.*

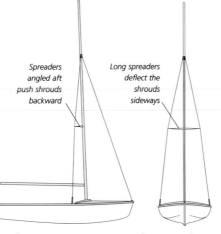

**SPREADER ANGLE**　　**SPREADER LENGTH**

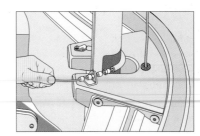

### △ MAST-GATE CONTROL

*A keel-stepped mast usually has a mast-gate control to adjust mast bend. Here, a simple wire with fixed stops is used to restrict or allow mast movement in the gate. This can be used while sailing to adjust the amount of mast bend and control mainsail fullness.*

◁ TUNING FOR SPEED

*This 470 is sailing fast upwind in medium to strong winds. Mast bend, clew outhaul, and the Cunningham are being used to flatten the sail and allow the top of the mainsail to twist, thus reducing power. The jib fairleads have been moved aft to open the slot.*

## THE SAILS

Most high-performance dinghies have a number of controls that can be used while sailing to adjust the shape of the sails and thus to increase or decrease power. These controls are best rigged so that the helmsman or crew can alter them while sitting out or trapezing. Once you have set up your boat on shore, you need to go sailing to continue tuning it. Mark all your controls so that you can record the fast settings in a logbook for easy replication in the future.

## MAINSAIL ADJUSTMENTS

As well as holding down the boom, the boom vang pulls it forward into the gooseneck. If this force is not resisted by chocks or a mast ram it will cause low-down mast bend. This flattens the mainsail in the lower half and increases twist in the upper leech, thereby reducing power in the top of the sail in strong winds.

Moving a center-mainsheet's tackle blocks on the boom to aft of the lower block will also push the boom into the gooseneck when the sheet is tensioned. Like the effect of the vang, this also increases lower mast bend, flattens the sail, and reduces power.

## SAIL CONTROLS

Modern sailcloths are very stable, facilitating sail shapes that perform well in quite a wide range of conditions. As wind strength increases or decreases, however, the crew need to maintain top performance by using the sail controls to adjust the fullness of their sails and to control the position of maximum draft.

| EQUIPMENT | ACTION | RESULT |
|---|---|---|
| Jib halyard | Increasing tension. | Minimizes sagging in jib luff. |
| Jib fairleads | Adjusting fore and aft, and sideways. | Alters shape of jib and adjusts slot between jib and mainsail. |
| Cunningham control | Increasing tension. | Pulls position of maximum camber forward, opens upper leech, increases twist. |
| Boom vang | Adjusting tension. | Helps bend mast low down and controls twist. |
| Mainsheet | Adjusting sheet tension. | Controls boom angle, leech tension, and twist. |
| Clew outhaul | Easing. | Increases fullness in sail, closes lower leech. |

The clew outhaul controls tension in the foot of the mainsail. Loosening it increases the sail's fullness in the lower third of the sail and closes the lower leech. Tightening it flattens the sail and opens the lower leech.

Tensioning the Cunningham control tightens the mainsail luff and brings the point of maximum camber forward. This is useful when strong winds are pushing the camber back from its ideal position, which is usually about 40–45 percent of the way between luff and leech. Applying tension to the Cunningham also opens the upper leech and increases twist.

## Jib Adjustments

Tension in the shrouds is set by the jib halyard. It should be enough to minimize the luff sagging to leeward when close-hauled in medium winds. Many classes use the same tension in light winds, but increase it by 10–20 percent in strong winds.

The position of the jib fairleads and the tension in the jib sheet control the jib's shape and the size of the slot between mainsail and jib. Fairleads should be adjustable fore and aft, and sideways, so that you can alter their position to suit all wind conditions. In general, they are moved forward and inboard to increase power and narrow the slot, and back and out to open the slot and flatten the sail. Make sure that the slot between mainsail and jib leech stays parallel all the way up.

---

### TO INCREASE POWER

- Ease the jib sheet slightly
- Move the jib fairleads forward
- Ease the mainsail outhaul
- Ease the Cunningham control
- Bring the boom closer to the centerline
- Stiffen the mast at deck level using the mast-gate control

---

## MAXIMIZING PERFORMANCE IN ALL CONDITIONS

Start tuning afloat by sailing close-hauled in medium winds of about 7–16 knots, Force 3–4. In these conditions, your boat will be fully powered up, with you sitting out or trapezing as hard as possible to keep the boat level. Use the settings here as a guide, then experiment with the controls one at a time to find the best setup for your boat.

### LIGHT WINDS

In medium winds, the maximum fullness of the sails is used to develop power. In very light winds of 4 knots or less, however, the wind does not have enough energy to bend easily around full sails – if the sails are full, the airflow stalls and the boat slows down dramatically. Therefore, you need to flatten the sails to keep the airflow attached. Remove the mast chocks in the mast gate or ease off the ram to allow the mast to bend forward at deck level and pull the clew outhaul to its maximum extent. Leave the Cunningham and vang slack and adjust the mainsheet to keep the boom close to the centerline with the top leech tell-tale on the point of stalling. Flatten the jib by moving the jib fairleads aft and out, but ease the jib sheet slightly. If the wind strength increases, the mast will try to bend further and creases will appear from the luff of the mainsail. At this point, start restricting mast bend using the chocks or the ram to increase the power in the sail.

### MEDIUM WINDS

In medium winds, aim to achieve maximum power from the rig. Set the jib fairleads in their mid position and sheet the sail so that all the windward tell-tales (p.68) break together. Use the mast-gate chocks or ram to prevent the mast from bending beyond the set amount of pre-bend. Ease the clew outhaul by about 1–2in (2.5–5cm) from its maximum position and leave the Cunningham slack. Sheet the mainsail using the mainsheet and leaving the vang slack. Sheet it hard enough to have the top leech tell-tale (p.112) on the point of stalling. If your mainsheet runs on a traveler, pull it to windward until the boom is nearly on the centerline. The boat should now be fully powered with you and your crew sitting out or trapezing. If the mainsail develops large creases running from the middle of the luff toward the clew, it is an indication that your mast is bending too much and you need to adjust the spreaders or shroud tensions to limit the bend.

### STRONG WINDS

When you sail upwind in strong winds you may need to reduce power to sail fast and stay in control. If you can adjust the rig before sailing, it usually helps to increase the mast rake and the shroud tension. You may also decide to alter the spreader angle to prevent excessive bend.

If the boat becomes overpowered sailing to windward, tension the Cunningham and pull the outhaul tight. The Cunningham pulls the draft in the sail forward and helps flatten it, while the outhaul flattens the lower part of the sail. Use the vang to hold the boom down and increase low-down bend in the mast, and use the mainsheet to trim the sail. You can then ease the vang in the lulls to increase power and tighten it in the gusts to reduce power. Move the jib-sheet fairleads aft and tighten the sheet to flatten the sail, open the slot, and allow the head to twist slightly.

# ROUGH-WEATHER SAILING

*The definition of rough weather is subjective – in conditions that are too difficult for novice sailors, an expert crew will be able to enjoy fast, exciting sailing. The design of the boat influences the way you experience the conditions, as does the wind direction in relation to the shore and tidal stream. Winds of Force 5–6 can be considered as rough weather, but a Force 4 against a strong tide can kick up large waves and make sailing more difficult than a Force 6 in flat water.*

### GAINING EXPERIENCE

As you develop your sailing skills, it is important that you learn to handle your boat in strong winds. It is often best to gain experience while racing, because racing fleets still sail in rough weather and always have safety boats available. When you sail just for fun, however, it will be your decision whether to venture out.

Before you go on the water, check all your gear to ensure that it is in good condition and that nothing is likely to break. Rough weather imposes considerable loads on the boat, sails, and equipment, and it is vital that they are strong enough to handle the stress.

Make sure that your clothing is adequate (*pp.54–55*). Sailing in these conditions can be very tiring and requires concentration, stamina, and endurance. If you find that you are getting tired or cold, return to the shore immediately as your strength will decrease rapidly and you could easily find yourself in trouble.

You will notice that the boat reacts much faster and more violently in rough weather than it does in lighter winds. You will need to react quickly to changes in wind strength and direction. The heeling force will be considerable, and you will need all your strength and agility to keep the boat under control. Depending on your boat and the wind strength, you may find that you plane on nearly all points of sailing. Speed is your ally in these conditions – when the boat is upright and moving fast, it is easier to control and requires smaller tiller movements to keep it on course.

### REACHING

Start by sailing on a reach to get the feel of the conditions. The boat should be planing and the helmsman and crew should move well aft to keep the bow up and the rudder immersed. If the boat heels, ease out both sails to keep the boat upright, allowing them to shake at the luffs if necessary. If the boat is overpowered, move the jib-sheet fairleads back to allow the top of the jib to twist, and ease the vang to twist the mainsail. Watch for gusts, easing the sails and bearing away to keep upright as they pass.

### CLOSE-HAULED

Luff up to a close-hauled course, being careful to sheet in gently as the boat turns so that it stays upright. It is important that heeling is kept to a minimum, and the helmsman must

### ◁ REACHING

*Reaching in strong winds, this Laser sailor eases the vang so that the mainsail twists off and heeling is reduced. This also keeps the boom end clear of waves.*

## TACKING AND JIBING

In rough conditions, your boat is vulnerable at slow speeds, especially when tacking and jibing. The helmsman and crew must work hard to keep the boat balanced through these maneuvers, which must be completed as quickly as possible so that the boat can get back to full speed with minimum delay.

### TACKING
Before tacking, the helmsman must ensure that the boat is moving as fast as possible and should look forward to find a stretch of flat water among the waves. Start the tack when the bow passes through a wave crest so that you are on the new tack and moving again before the next wave hits you. Both helmsman and crew must move across the boat as fast as possible and should get their weight out over the new side before the boat reaches its proper close-hauled course and begins to heel.

### JIBING
Jibing must be completed quickly and smoothly. It should be attempted only when the boat is moving at top speed, never when it is slowing down and the wind pressure is increasing on the sails. Both helmsman and crew must concentrate on getting their weight to the new windward side very quickly to balance the mainsail as it slams across the boat.

### FITNESS
The fitness of helmsman and crew will affect their ability to sail well in strong winds. Rough weather can be physically and mentally exhausting, and will quickly sap strength and stamina. If you want to be able to sail (or race) well in these conditions, make sure that you are fit and try to get as much practice on the water as possible.

constantly trim the mainsheet to achieve this. In the strongest gusts, the mainsail may have to be let out until it backwinds (flaps) across most of its width to spill wind and prevent the boat heeling. Keep the jib sheeted in tight except in the strongest gusts, when it should be eased out slightly until the gust passes.

High-performance dinghies will plane to windward, and the mainsail should be eased as necessary to keep the boat upright. Slower dinghies, which do not plane to windward, can use the no-sail zone as a way of decreasing power. As a gust hits, the helmsman eases the mainsheet a little and steers closer to the wind until the jib luff starts to shake. This reduces the power in the rig, and gains ground to windward. Do not sail too close to the wind, or the boat will slow down and will heel more when you try to bear away to the correct course.

Steer through big waves by luffing up as you climb them, then bearing away as the bow passes through the crest to sail down the other side.

### △ CLOSE-HAULED
*This helmsman and crew are working hard to keep the boat upright and planing to windward. The mainsail is eased slightly to prevent heeling.*

## DOWNWIND COURSES
In strong winds, the boat will plane continuously on a broad reach – and possibly even on a run. Sailing on a run in very strong winds is difficult because there is no heeling force to balance against, and there is always the danger of an unplanned jibe. The boat will sail faster and will be more stable on a broad reach. There will be sufficient heeling force to allow both the helmsman and the crew to sit to windward (well aft to prevent the bow from digging in). When sailing in waves, you must anticipate each wave and bear away down its face as the stern lifts. The boat will accelerate and you should then luff slightly to ride the face of the wave as long as possible, avoiding digging the bow in at the bottom of the trough.

# RACING

*There is no better way to learn to sail a boat well, and to build on your existing skills, than to race against other dinghies that are in the same class. Racing quickly teaches you the intricacies of good boat handling, and you will also learn how to tune your dinghy for a wide range of wind conditions. Join a club that supports the class of boat you are interested in, or, if you already own a boat, but your club does not support its class, consider racing in a mixed, handicap fleet.*

## STARTING TO RACE

Racing is organized through sailing clubs at a local level, and through class associations on a national or international basis. You will need to join your class association, which will arrange for your boat to be measured and certified within the class rules. The association will also be able to provide you with tuning data and can advise you on which clubs provide fleet racing for your type of boat.

At club level, each fleet normally has a class captain who organizes the racing calendar and who is usually an experienced helmsman in the class. He is a good starting point when you are looking for advice on how to get involved in racing. You will nearly always find that other owners are welcoming to newcomers and will be pleased to help you get started.

If you do not own your own boat, you will often find that you can get a crewing position quite easily. Good crews are always in demand, and this is one of the best ways to learn boat handling and racing skills.

## MAKING A CHOICE

If you have ambitions to reach the top in dinghy racing, you should choose one of the recognized International- or Olympic-class boats and be prepared for a long, hard, and expensive route to the top. If, on the other hand, your ambitions do not extend beyond becoming a good club racer or a competitor in a national championship fleet, you will have a wider choice of boats. Narrow down your options by deciding whether you want close, tactical racing or speed, and whether you want to sail with a crew or prefer to sail a single-handed dinghy.

---

### SAILING CLUBS

By far the best way to meet other sailors and develop your skills is to join an active sailing club. These range from those solely dedicated to dinghies to those that embrace both dinghies and larger yachts.

#### CLUBS AND RACING

To improve your dinghy sailing skills, find a local club dedicated to sailing dinghies. The club will probably provide fleet racing for several classes and will also have a handicap fleet in which other less popular dinghies can race. Sailing clubs often have junior or cadet sections that provide training courses and racing for young members. If you have your own boat and want to race against others of the same class, make sure you join a club that has a strong fleet of your class.

◁ **SAILING IN A CLUB**
*Club racing forms the backbone of dinghy sailing and is the starting point for all who wish to race. Once a sailor has become proficient enough to reach the top of a good club fleet, he or she can progress to Class Open Meetings and National Championships.*

◁ **TACTICAL RACING**

*For close, tactical racing pick a class like the Laser – the Olympic single-hander. It has large and very competitive fleets worldwide and is challenging to sail. It is also relatively cheap to buy and run. Whatever your level of skill or ambition, you will always find Laser sailors of your standard to ensure good close racing.*

▽ **ULTIMATE SPEED**

*If speed is what you are after, consider boats like this 18ft Skiff, the Olympic 49'er, the International 14, or the Laser 5000. These are extreme machines with multiple trapezes and huge asymmetric spinnakers. They are quite expensive to buy, and demand skill, coordination, and agility to sail, but offer a great adrenaline rush as ample reward.*

## TACTICS VERSUS SPEED

You do not need to sail the latest high-performance dinghy to enjoy very competitive racing. In fact, many of the largest and most competitive racing fleets are found in classes that were designed many decades ago and which, by modern standards, are quite slow. They may not offer the ultimate in speed, but the racing is often very close and tactically intense.

For speed, look at catamaran designs or the fastest modern mono-hull dinghies with multiple trapezes and large, asymmetric spinnakers. If you prefer not to sail in one of the extreme high-performance dinghies but still want speed, you should consider a catamaran or a sportsboat. Although not strictly dinghies, these will provide exciting sailing – the latter without too much physical exertion.

If you do not want to have to find a crew, consider a single-handed class. When you race a single-hander, you know that the result is entirely dependent on your own skills.

# CRUISER SAILING

..................................................

MANY PEOPLE who learn to sail in dinghies
eventually move on to larger boats, perhaps
because of a desire to sail longer distances or
cruise foreign shores. The basic skills that you
learn in a sailing dinghy are applicable to a
cruiser. However, there are many new skills
that a cruiser sailor needs to master to become
a proficient crew or a competent skipper.

..................................................

*An elegant offshore cruising ketch drops anchor in a
tropical bay. The stuff of which dreams are made, it
can become a reality for the competent cruising sailor.*

# STARTING TO CRUISE

*The best way to start cruising is to sail on a friend's boat or to find a skipper in need of crew. Try a few day sails and at least one overnight or longer passage to help you decide if cruising appeals. If it does, take a course in skippering skills, boat handling, or navigation at a sailing school. If you are used to sailing a dinghy, you will need to learn to handle a larger and heavier boat, and how to function well as part of a team. It is not necessary (or advisable) to buy a boat before you start cruising.*

### WHAT IS A CRUISER?

A cruiser need not be especially big – some, indeed, are little more than large dinghies, although they have a cabin to accommodate the crew. Most have some form of weighted keel, although cruising catamarans do not use keels, but rely on their large beam for stability. All cruisers obey the basic rules of aerodynamics and hydrodynamics that affect all sail boats. There are, however, major differences between various types, in the way they behave under sail and power and in the manner in which their rigs, sails, and equipment are arranged and handled by the crew.

There is a significant difference in handling and performance between a general-purpose dinghy and a high-performance one, but the differences between types of cruisers are even more notable. This is why there is no substitute for on-the-water experience, and why you should try to sail as many different types of cruisers as possible before deciding on the one that will best suit you.

### PASSAGE-MAKING

Skippering a boat on passage requires a wide range of skills. Boat-handling skills are needed to get the boat into and out of harbor and to ensure a fast and comfortable passage. Pilotage and navigation skills take the boat safely and efficiently between ports, and boat-management skills ensure that the boat and its gear are kept in good order. Finally, crew-management skills ensure that yours is a happy ship with a well-rested, well-fed, and highly motivated crew performing at their optimum. The good skipper has all these skills at his or her disposal and, most importantly, understands that their relative importance changes at different times in each passage.

### CRUISING LESSONS

Sailing has up till now avoided excessive bureaucracy, but there is a growing trend toward regulation: some countries require skippers to hold recognized certificates. You should check with your national authority to see which rules apply.

If you aspire toward owning your own cruiser or sailing long passages aboard other people's boats, you can

◁ **SMALL TRADITIONAL CRUISER**
*Gaining experience on a small cruiser is the best way to start. Boats like this small traditional wooden cruiser are less expensive and usually easier to handle and maintain than larger craft.*

(and should) extend your knowledge in a number of ways. Take a sailing course at a school recognized by your national authority, and read as much and as widely as possible on the subject. Once again, and most importantly, it is advisable to get as much sea-time as you can aboard as wide a range of boats as possible in different waters and conditions. Dedicated theory courses at a local night school or college are usually very good, but there is no substitute for hands-on experience, and that can only be obtained by time on a cruiser at sea.

## TEAMWORK

More and more people are now learning to sail in cruisers, rather than starting in dinghies as was the traditional route. This is not ideal as the basic sailing skills are easier, and safer, to learn aboard a small boat. The average size of cruisers is also increasing, and a growing number of people buying their first cruiser choose a boat of about 35ft (11m).

Few of these boats are designed to be sailed single-handed; many need a crew of three or more to sail them efficiently without tiring the crew. Cruiser sailing, therefore, requires more of a team effort than dinghy sailing. It also involves living, eating, and sleeping in close and cramped accommodation with several people for extended periods; the ability to get along with others is crucial. Whereas it is easy to put up with someone's annoying habits when you do not have to see them all the time, trivial things can cause arguments and friction aboard a small boat. A good skipper will be aware of this danger and will attempt to put together a compatible crew, but it is up to each crew member to show tolerance in order to preserve harmony aboard.

## BOAT HANDLING

Handling a cruiser requires greater care than a sailing dinghy because of its larger size and, importantly, its much greater weight. Cruisers also require a range of skills that can only be learned on the job.

### CRUISER SIZE
If you make a mistake coming alongside in a dinghy, a collision can usually be prevented by use of a well-placed foot. Even if a collision occurs, the damage is unlikely to be serious. However, a cruiser's extra weight and momentum makes close-quarter maneuvering far more difficult and mistakes much more expensive.

Another significant difference between a sailing dinghy and a cruiser is the weight of the gear and the load on the sails and sheets. Although it is easy to hold a dinghy's jib sheet in the hands or hoist a sail by hand, a cruiser's sheets and halyards require the use of winches and can impose considerable loads. Learning how to handle ropes and sails under load is an important part of cruiser sailing: correct techniques are essential if personal injury and damage to gear are to be avoided.

### NEW SKILLS
The dinghy sailor, who is used to lightweight gear, has to become accustomed to handling much larger and heavier sails and ropes. The correct, and safe, way to use winches must be learned (p.172), and the sailor new to cruisers must understand the potential danger of more highly loaded gear. New seamanship skills must be acquired to enable the sailor to sail, berth, and moor the yacht safely, and essential navigation skills need to be learned to allow offshore passages to be made in comfort and safety.

## SMALLER CRUISERS
It is not necessary to have a large boat to go on long-distance voyages. Although larger boats are increasingly popular, the average-sized cruiser sailing the world's oceans is still only about 35ft (11m), and many considerably smaller boats have taken their crews around the world. Most long-term voyagers cruise with just two people on board, sometimes with their children or an additional crew member. This means that they are sailing short-handed most of the time, so a smaller boat has advantages in terms of easier boat handling and in the lower cost of ownership. Cruising with a simpler and cheaper boat also means that you can head off sooner than if you were to wait until you could afford your dream boat.

## BUYING A CRUISER
If you do decide to invest in your own cruiser, it is in your own best interests to keep the boat as simple as possible. Keeping the boat simple reduces costs, makes the boat easier to sail, and lessens the likelihood of gear failure ruining a cruise.

Good value for money can often be obtained by purchasing a second-hand cruiser, especially one that has a good inventory of the equipment you want on board. When buying a used boat, however, always have it surveyed to ensure that there are no hidden defects and that the sale price is not excessive. Look for second-hand boats in sailing magazines and by talking to brokers, who will also be able to give you useful advice on finance and surveys.

# CHOOSING A CRUISER

*All cruising boats are a compromise – most commonly between cost, performance, and comfort. You need to be realistic in your ambitions, and your budget, when you set out to choose a cruiser. Even a small cruiser represents a considerable investment, both in purchase price and in maintenance and running costs. Before you buy, decide what sort of cruising or cruiser-racing you want to do, and the areas in which you plan to sail. Get some experience in different boats before you buy.*

## CRUISING

Many people dream of long-term voyaging, but relatively few of us leave our onshore responsibilities and escape to sea full-time. If you are one of the lucky ones who are free to sail away, you have a wide choice of boats that can take you on long voyages for months at a time.

Be realistic about your onshore commitments, however. The reality for most of us is that career and family ties prevent us from achieving more than a few weeks cruising every year, interspersed with weekend cruising or racing. This type of cruising does not require an ocean cruiser equipped with every conceivable luxury.

You must also consider how many people will be on board most of the time. Many cruising boats sail with a crew of only two or three, so you do not need a particularly large boat to enjoy good cruising.

At least when you start cruising, try to keep things as simple as possible: a small boat equipped with only the basic gear will be less expensive to buy and maintain. It will be much cheaper on mooring and insurance costs, and easier to handle, yet it will deliver just as much pleasure as a larger, more complex yacht. The very simplicity of the yacht means that you are likely to spend more time sailing.

## SAILING AREA

The most practical type of cruiser for you will be determined by the area and conditions in which you will do most of your sailing. If you plan to sail in shallow waters, consider the option of a cruiser with bilge keels or a centerboard (p.152), for example. If you plan to undertake long offshore voyages, many standard production cruisers are quite adequate with a little modification. Unless you are very experienced, you would be wise to select a well-built production boat from a reputable builder, rather than having a boat built from scratch.

## RACING

Some people enjoy mixing cruising with club or regatta racing. If you want to race, look at the sorts of boats that are raced at clubs in your sailing area. Some clubs have one-design racing fleets for popular types of cruiser-racers. If your club has such a fleet, consider whether that type of boat would suit your sailing needs.

Remember that you will need to have more crew on board for racing than for cruising, and ensure that the boat is equipped with appropriate safety gear for all the people on board. Racing will add to the costs of equipping and maintaining the boat, especially if you take it seriously.

A good cruiser-racer will often be perfectly suited to most coastal and offshore cruising needs, allowing you to have the pleasure of racing on weekends and the relaxation of some longer cruising passages during vacations. When cruising with the family, use smaller sails than you would if you were racing.

---

### CRUISER TRIALS

Many people dream of sailing away on ocean voyages and save for years to buy their "ideal" boat only to discover that the type of boat is not for them. It is a costly mistake that is easy to avoid.

#### GAINING EXPERIENCE
Before buying your own cruiser, get as much experience as possible of the type of cruising that you hope to do. Sail aboard as many different boats as you can, on both short and long passages. When you decide on your ideal boat, arrange a proper sail in it in order to assess how it handles under power and sail. If you are uncertain, ask an experienced sailor to advise you.

#### CHARTERING BOATS
It is not always necessary to buy your own boat to enjoy cruising. You could try crewing on other people's boats to gain more experience, or chartering a number of different boats to compare their characteristics. Chartering is a cost-effective way of building cruising experience. It also gives you the opportunity to sail in exotic cruising areas away from your home base.

# TYPES OF CRUISERS

The term "cruiser" covers a vast range of boats, from the smallest trailer-sailers to the dedicated long-distance cruiser that is capable of taking its crew safely across oceans. Some are designed to mix cruising and racing. They can offer a level of performance that was unknown a few years ago, even from dedicated racing boats. The range of cruisers includes traditional sailing boats built a century or more ago and still going strong; one-off designs built in wood, fiberglass, steel, aluminum, or even ferro-cement; and a huge number of production boats and family cruisers.

## TRADITIONAL CRUISERS

**TRADITIONAL YAWL**

The term "traditional cruiser" usually means that the yacht is of a heavy-displacement type. It could be gaff or Bermudan rigged, and will have a long keel. An older boat will be wooden, whereas more recent types may be built in fiberglass or steel. Older designs are typically narrower, and often deeper, than modern cruisers.

## TRAILER SAILERS

**26FT (8M) CRUISER**

Trailer-sailers offer the advantage of being small enough to move by road on a dedicated road-trailer. This opens up new cruising areas without the need to sail the boat on long passages to get there. Most trailer-sailers have a lifting centerboard or daggerboard, usually weighted for stability, to allow them to fit on the trailer.

## MODERN PRODUCTION CRUISERS

**35FT (11M) CRUISER**

Most modern production cruisers are built of fiberglass. They have Bermudan-sloop rigs, fin keels, often with skeg-hung rudders. Most are moderate displacement designs, although lighter designs, with a long waterline and short overhangs, are popular. Some are designed for shallow-water sailing, and are fitted with bilge keels or centerboards.

## FAMILY CRUISERS

**33FT (10M) CRUISER**

Many boat-builders design and produce yachts for the family cruising market, because it is the largest cruising market of all. Family cruisers are typically built of fiberglass and are designed for safe sailing with spacious interiors. Many are used only for day-sailing, so dockside comfort is an especially important consideration.

## CRUISER RACERS

**FAST RACER**

A modern cruiser-racer combines fast, efficient cruising with a maneuverability and speed suitable for racing. These designs are usually lighter than a pure cruising yacht. They have efficient Bermudan-sloop rigs, and are likely to have shorter overhangs, larger rigs, and more efficient keels and rudders than other cruisers.

## ONE-OFF CRUISERS

**MODERN CUTTER**

There are many individual designs available to satisfy all cruising tastes. A huge variety of building materials, rigs, and keel and rudder arrangements create many options to suit all requirements. Many people derive enormous pleasure from having a yacht designed and built to their own specifications – some even build their own boats.

# CRUISER DESIGN

With the development of large, production-line boat-builders, many yachts today look very similar. A typical modern cruiser has a Bermudan rig and a fin keel, usually with a free-standing rudder (called a spade rudder) or a rudder that is mounted on a skeg. This configuration originated with racing yachts, and it is highly efficient, especially upwind. For cruising, however, it is not necessary to stick with this conventional approach. Many other rig and keel configurations are available.

△ **JUNK SCHOONER**
*The ubiquitous Bermudan sloop is not the only (or necessarily the best) rig for long-distance cruising. The easily-handled junk rig has many loyal adherents, who enjoy the fact that it is not necessary to go on deck to hoist, trim, reef, or lower the sails.*

## KEELS AND RIGS

Nothing is guaranteed to excite passions as much as a discussion among cruising sailors on the relative merits of keels and rigs. Proponents of traditional design maintain that only a long keel is a suitable choice for an offshore cruiser, and some even argue that this should be combined with a gaff rig for best results. The fact is that traditional keels and rigs were developed to suit the materials their builders had available. New materials and construction techniques offer other design and building methods that traditional builders would surely have used had they been available. Try to sail a variety of boats and make your own judgments about the types of rigs and keels that suit you.

---

## TYPES OF KEELS

Keels have been developed and improved over the years. Most modern yachts are now built with variations on the fin keel, although a number of other keel types are also available. Whatever the arrangement, the keel has two purposes: to resist leeway (*p.87*) and to provide stability. Draft (the depth of the keel) is often an important consideration. Many cruising yachts draw 6.5ft (2m) or less.

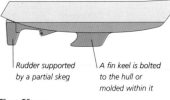

Rudder supported by a partial skeg | A fin keel is bolted to the hull or molded within it

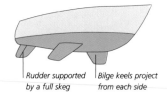

Rudder supported by a full skeg | Bilge keels project from each side

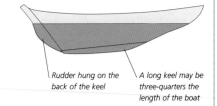

Rudder hung on the back of the keel | A long keel may be three-quarters the length of the boat

### FIN KEEL
*A single ballasted keel is called a fin. It is usually narrow on racers (so there is less drag from surface area), and fairly wide on cruisers. Some fin keels have bulbs or wings at the tip to concentrate the weight as low as possible. The rudder is usually hung on a narrow skeg, although spade rudders are cantilevered on their shafts.*

### BILGE KEELS
*Yachts that are designed to be able to dry out sitting upright have twin keels, known as bilge keels. Bilge keels are slightly less efficient than fin keels, but allow the yacht to be kept afloat in drying harbors and to sail comfortably in shallow waters. These are used mainly in Great Britain as there is currently no manufacturer in the US.*

### LONG KEEL
*The traditional type of keel is fairly long, running for half to three-quarters the length of the vessel. The rudder is hung on the keel's trailing edge. The main reason for having a long keel on traditional wooden vessels was the strength that it gave to the hull. Today, long keels are found only on heavy-displacement cruisers.*

# TYPES OF RIGS

A rig is categorized by its mainsail type and the number of masts and headsails (jibs) carried. Early yachts often had two masts and a gaff rig, as this was the easiest way to handle heavy sails. Improvements in sail materials and rig engineering have made single masts with Bermudan sails today's most popular rig.

## SLOOP

The sloop is the most common and simplest rig. It has one mast, a gaff or a Bermudan mainsail, and a single headsail. A Bermudan sloop can be described as masthead or fractional. A masthead sloop has a larger headsail with the forestay attached at the top of the mast. A fractional sloop has a smaller headsail set on a forestay fixed to the mast some way down from the top. Fractional sloops allow the mast to be bent for sail control. Most dinghies are fractional sloops, but many cruisers are masthead sloops.

## CUTTER

The cutter rig remains quite popular, especially for long-distance cruisers. It has one mast but carries two headsails, each on their own stay. This reduces the size of each headsail and makes them easier to handle. A cutter can have either a gaff or a Bermudan mainsail.

## TWO-MASTED BOATS

Boats with more than one mast are not so common today, but ketch or yawl rigs can be found on older boats more than 35ft (11m) long. In both the ketch and the yawl, a mizzen mast is stepped some way aft of the main mast. The ketch has a larger mizzen mast (stepped further forward) than the yawl. The schooner is another two-masted yacht. Its taller main mast is stepped aft, with a smaller foremast ahead of it.

## UNA RIG

In the una, or cat, rig, the mast is stepped right forward and is usually unstayed. The mainsail is often rigged with a sleeve around the mast. There is no headsail. On larger boats there may be two masts, in a schooner or ketch arrangement.

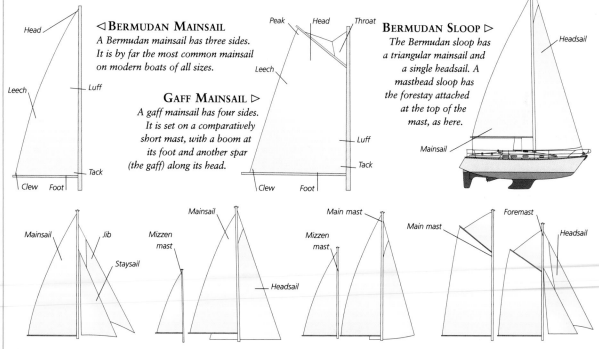

◁ **BERMUDAN MAINSAIL**
*A Bermudan mainsail has three sides. It is by far the most common mainsail on modern boats of all sizes.*

**GAFF MAINSAIL** ▷
*A gaff mainsail has four sides. It is set on a comparatively short mast, with a boom at its foot and another spar (the gaff) along its head.*

**BERMUDAN SLOOP** ▷
*The Bermudan sloop has a triangular mainsail and a single headsail. A masthead sloop has the forestay attached at the top of the mast, as here.*

△ **BERMUDAN CUTTER**
*Cutters have two or more headsails, each set on its own stay. The inner headsail is called the staysail, the outer is the jib.*

△ **BERMUDAN YAWL**
*The yawl rig is characterized by a small mizzen mast stepped aft of the rudder post. It may have any number of headsails.*

△ **BERMUDAN KETCH**
*On a ketch rig, the mizzen is stepped aft of the main mast but ahead of the rudder post. It may have one or more headsails.*

△ **GAFF SCHOONER**
*On a schooner, the main mast is stepped behind the shorter foremast. A gaff schooner has a gaff-rigged mainsail, as shown.*

# RIGGING AND SAILS

Although the Bermudan-sloop rig is the standard rig for large-scale production boat-building, there are a number of variations on this arrangement that are used according to the boat's intended purpose and its level of performance. The number of sails used on a modern sloop rig is relatively limited, but all have a mainsail and one or more headsails. The mast, usually made of aluminum, is supported by an arrangement of wire, called the standing rigging.

## RIGGING

Most modern cruisers are designed with a masthead Bermudan-sloop rig, which is comprised of a mainsail and headsail for efficient sailing upwind and on a beam reach. A spinnaker or gennaker (a cross between a genoa and a spinnaker) provides additional downwind sail area. The mast is supported by standing rigging with the forestay attached at the masthead. The rigging is intended to support the mast and to keep it straight under sail.

Some cruisers are designed with a fractional sloop rig, in which the forestay does not run to the masthead but attaches some way down the mast. A fractional sloop rig is often used on performance-oriented cruisers or cruiser-racers, because it allows for the mast to be bent under sail to help flatten the mainsail in stronger winds. The headsail is also smaller and the mainsail larger on a fractional rig compared to a masthead rig, making it easier for a small crew to handle.

### MASTHEAD RIG

A masthead Bermudan-sloop rig has a genoa for light conditions. The mast is supported by a number of shrouds and stays that hold it straight and upright.

**Masthead instruments**
The masthead houses a range of instruments, usually comprising wind-speed and direction sensors, a VHF radio aerial, and a tricolor navigation light

**Forestay**
The forestay runs from the bow-fitting to the masthead and supports the mast fore and aft together with the backstay

**Cap shrouds**
The main sideways supports for the mast, the two cap shrouds run either side from the chainplate, over the spreader end, to the masthead

**Spreaders**
These widen the angle of the cap shroud to the mast and help to support the mast

**Topping lift**
The topping lift runs from the boom end up to the masthead, then down to deck level where it is adjusted. It supports the boom when the mainsail is lowered but is left slack when the sail is hoisted

**Boom vang**
Used to prevent the boom from rising due to wind pressure in the mainsail, the boom vang can be a rope tackle or an adjustable, rigid strut that also supports the boom

**Boom**
Attached to the mast by the gooseneck fitting, the boom supports the mainsail's foot

**Mainsheet**
This sheet controls the angle of the mainsail

**Lower shrouds**
One or two lower shrouds support the lower mast

**Halyards**
Used to raise and lower sails, halyards are usually led inside the mast and emerge at deck level, where they are led aft to winches for adjustment

**Turn buckles**
Fittings to adjust the tension in shrouds and forestay

**Keel**
The keel resists leeway and provides stability

Rudder

Propeller

# Sails

Every cruiser must have enough sails to keep the boat sailing efficiently in all conditions, including strong winds. The standard cruiser, which is rigged as a Bermudan sloop, has one mainsail that can be reefed to suit the wind strength. It also has either a selection of different-sized headsails to cope with a range of wind strengths, or a roller-furling system on the forestay to reduce the size of the headsail as the wind increases. The Bermudan sloop rig is not as efficient downwind as it is upwind, so many cruisers use a spinnaker or gennaker (sometimes called a cruising chute) to add sail area when sailing downwind in light to moderate winds.

Most mainsails and headsails are made from Dacron, although some large cruisers and cruiser-racers use cloth with aramid fibers for its strength and weight advantages. Spinnakers and gennakers are made from lightweight nylon sailcloth.

## MAINSAIL

The mainsail is the hardest-working sail on a cruising boat. It has to be strongly constructed, but must not be too heavy or it will not set well in light winds. The mainsail will be used from the lightest winds right up to the heaviest conditions, when its size will be reduced by reefing. Most cruising mainsails have three reefs, to allow for a gradual reduction in sail area as the wind increases in strength.

## HEADSAILS

Roller-reefing equipment is convenient, but does not result in a well-setting sail once the headsail has been rolled partly away. For this reason, many people prefer to sail with headsails attached by hanks to the forestay and change between them according to wind strength. Headsails can be categorized further as genoas or jibs. A genoa is a large headsail that overlaps the mast and usually sweeps the deck with its foot. A jib is smaller, does not overlap the mast, and is usually cut with a higher clew and foot. A typical cruiser that does not use a roller-reefing headsail will carry a selection of headsails, usually including a genoa for use in light winds, a working jib for moderate conditions, plus one or more other jibs of smaller sizes to use as the wind increases. Every cruiser should carry a storm jib. This is much smaller than the others, and made to cope with the strongest winds. If the normal headsail is set on a roller furler, the storm jib should have its own, removeable stay.

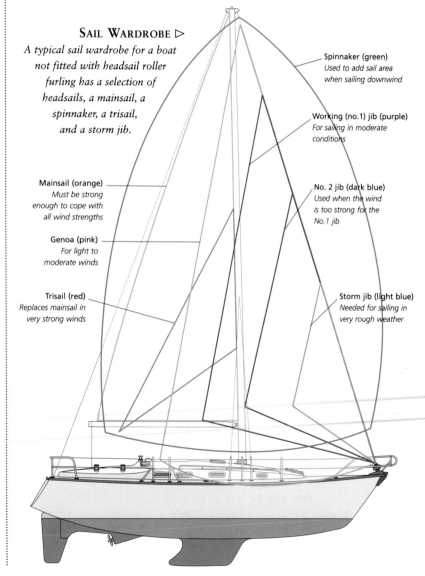

**SAIL WARDROBE ▷**
*A typical sail wardrobe for a boat not fitted with headsail roller furling has a selection of headsails, a mainsail, a spinnaker, a trisail, and a storm jib.*

**Mainsail (orange)**
*Must be strong enough to cope with all wind strengths*

**Genoa (pink)**
*For light to moderate winds*

**Trisail (red)**
*Replaces mainsail in very strong winds*

**Spinnaker (green)**
*Used to add sail area when sailing downwind*

**Working (no.1) jib (purple)**
*For sailing in moderate conditions*

**No. 2 jib (dark blue)**
*Used when the wind is too strong for the No.1 jib*

**Storm jib (light blue)**
*Needed for sailing in very rough weather*

# ABOVE DECK

*The deck and cockpit areas are the parts of a cruiser where the practical business of sailing and boat handling is conducted. Deck layouts vary, but most have fairly similar arrangements. Once you are familiar with one boat, you will find it quite easy to get used to another. There are two main layouts: one has an aft cockpit, and the other has a center cockpit. The aft cockpit layout is the most common, especially in cruisers under about 40ft (12m).*

## DECKS

The foredeck, ahead of the mast, is the foremost part of the boat and the most exposed working area on deck. Aft of the mast, most small and medium-sized boats have a central cabin trunk raised above the level of the side- and foredecks to give some headroom below. In this arrangement, sidedecks run between the cabin trunk and the deck edge. Some larger boats are flush decked, with no cabin trunk, giving wider decks that are easy to work on.

Some sidedecks on smaller boats are quite narrow, and care is needed when moving along them. Tracks for the jib-sheet fairleads usually run fore and aft along both sidedecks. The cap and lower shrouds terminate at chainplates that are fitted either at the deck edge or inboard on the sidedeck. Jackstays should run along the length of both sidedecks: these are lengths of webbing or plastic-covered wire, to which the crew attach their harnesses when working on deck.

## COACH ROOF

The coach roof is the top of the raised cabin trunk in the middle of the boat. The mast is either stepped on the coach roof or passes through it to be stepped on the keel. Halyards and other control lines emerging from the mast are often led aft across the roof to winches at its aft end. Hatches and ventilators are fitted to let light and air into the cabin. A life-raft may also be stowed here. There should be handrails running the length of the roof on either side to provide a secure handhold for crew making their way along the sidedecks. The main hatch is positioned in the aft end of the coach roof, just in front of the cockpit.

## COCKPIT

The cockpit is the main working area of the boat, and the most secure place on deck. The boat is steered from the cockpit by a tiller on smaller boats and a wheel on larger ones. It has become standard for most sail controls to be led to this area. Most importantly, the cockpit footwell should be self-draining, with large drains in the floor quickly shedding any water that finds its way aboard.

The cockpit is separated from the cabin by a raised area called a bridge deck, and by washboards (wooden partitions) that close the companion-way, the entrance to the cabin. Many cruisers have a spray hood fitted over the companionway to protect it and the forward part of the cockpit from spray and to provide shelter for the crew in rough conditions. Weather cloths, known as dodgers, can be laced along the lifelines for added protection.

## CRUISER FITTINGS

A typical modern, fast offshore cruiser is designed to make quick passages that are also safe and comfortable. The boat is sturdily constructed with strong, well-fastened deck gear. It has a deep, comfortable cockpit for crew security, which is sheltered by a large spray hood to offer protection from the elements. There is a stern platform that gives the crew access to the tender.

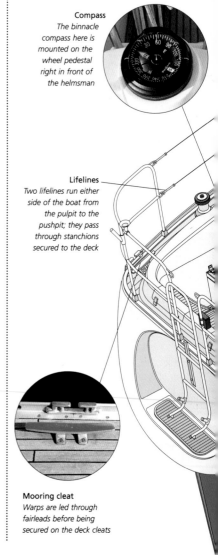

**Compass**
*The binnacle compass here is mounted on the wheel pedestal right in front of the helmsman*

**Lifelines**
*Two lifelines run either side of the boat from the pulpit to the pushpit; they pass through stanchions secured to the deck*

**Mooring cleat**
*Warps are led through fairleads before being secured on the deck cleats*

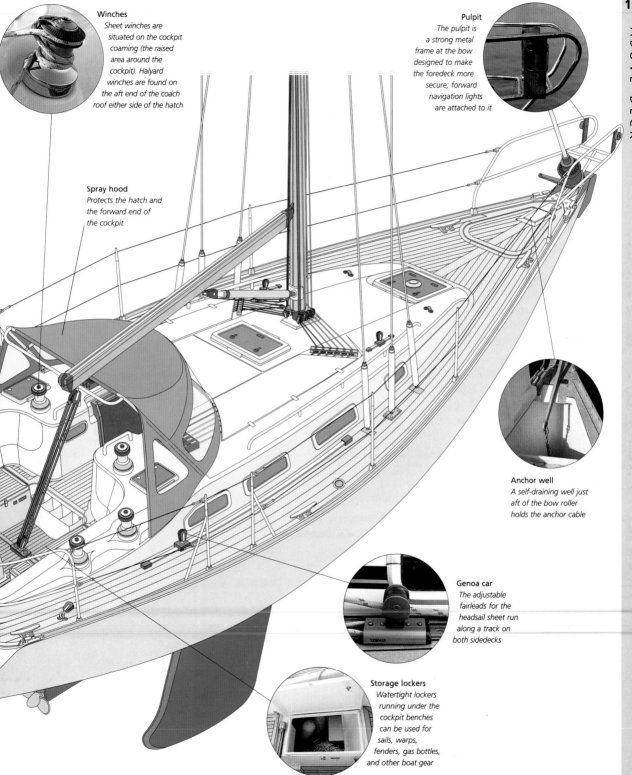

**Winches**
*Sheet winches are situated on the cockpit coaming (the raised area around the cockpit). Halyard winches are found on the aft end of the coach roof either side of the hatch*

**Pulpit**
*The pulpit is a strong metal frame at the bow designed to make the foredeck more secure; forward navigation lights are attached to it*

**Spray hood**
*Protects the hatch and the forward end of the cockpit*

**Anchor well**
*A self-draining well just aft of the bow roller holds the anchor cable*

**Genoa car**
*The adjustable fairleads for the headsail sheet run along a track on both sidedecks*

**Storage lockers**
*Watertight lockers running under the cockpit benches can be used for sails, warps, fenders, gas bottles, and other boat gear*

# DOWN BELOW

*The accommodation in a cruiser is determined by its length, beam, and freeboard (height out of the water). In small cruisers under about 33ft (10m), there is little space for anything more than basic accommodation. In larger cruisers, there is room for more berths, greater privacy, and more luxury. Most interiors are based on an arrangement that has a separate forward cabin, a main saloon, a separate heads (toilet) compartment, a galley, and a chart table.*

## COMFORT IN PORT

When looking at the internal layout of a cruiser, consider the type of sailing you plan to do. The majority of boats spend their time in marinas, so many modern cruisers are designed with interiors that are more suitable for use in port than at sea. If this is the type of sailing you intend to do, then an accommodation layout optimized for use when upright and moored may be appropriate.

## COMFORT AT SEA

Good sea-going interiors provide comfort and security by having lots of handholds, enough secure berths for the off-watch crew, and no sharp corners that can cause injury. The galley should be laid out for safe use when underway, the worktops should have good fiddles (rails) that are effective when the boat is heeled, and the navigation area should allow the navigator to be braced securely while working at the chart table.

The main working areas down below are the galley and the chart table. Both should be designed to provide security for the cook and navigator when the boat is heeled, and should allow easy access to any equipment needed. The galley should have deep single or double sinks to retain water when the boat is heeled

and there should be adequate counter space for preparing meals at sea. The cooker should be hung in gimbals to allow it to swing and remain upright when the boat heels. A restraining bolt should secure the cooker in a fixed position when required.

## SEA-GOING INTERIOR

A typical sea-going interior on a medium-sized offshore cruiser includes a good working area in the galley and at the chart table, a comfortable saloon, and separate heads compartment. There are at least two secure sea-berths.

**Navigation instruments**
*The navigator has navigation instruments, VHF radio, and an electrical panel within easy reach of the chart table*

**Hanging locker**
*Hanging storage space for clothes or gear*

**Heads**
*The heads contains a toilet, basin, and shower*

**Aft cabin**
*The separate aft cabin has a double berth*

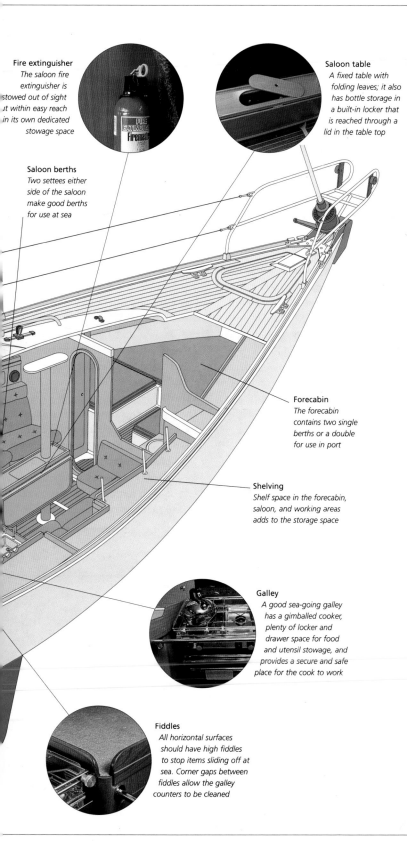

**Fire extinguisher**
*The saloon fire extinguisher is stowed out of sight but within easy reach in its own dedicated stowage space*

**Saloon table**
*A fixed table with folding leaves; it also has bottle storage in a built-in locker that is reached through a lid in the table top*

**Saloon berths**
*Two settees either side of the saloon make good berths for use at sea*

**Forecabin**
*The forecabin contains two single berths or a double for use in port*

**Shelving**
*Shelf space in the forecabin, saloon, and working areas adds to the storage space*

**Galley**
*A good sea-going galley has a gimballed cooker, plenty of locker and drawer space for food and utensil stowage, and provides a secure and safe place for the cook to work*

**Fiddles**
*All horizontal surfaces should have high fiddles to stop items sliding off at sea. Corner gaps between fiddles allow the galley counters to be cleaned*

# STOWAGE

Stowage space is always limited in small boats. It should be arranged so that each crew member has sufficient space for personal gear close to a bunk.

### STOWING THE GEAR
In a well-designed cruiser, there should be a variety of storage areas to cater to the enormous diversity of gear that finds its way aboard a cruising boat. There should be areas, often under bunks, suitable for bulky gear and individual lockers and drawers for smaller items. All lockers should be closed with positive catches, to prevent their doors from bursting open when the boat heels. Dedicated stowage should be provided for items like glasses and crockery, safety gear, and, where possible, foul weather gear and boots. It is useful to prepare a stowage plan and write down where every item is stowed. Otherwise, it can be difficult to find an item in a hurry.

### △ TIDY STORAGE
*There is limited storage space on most cruisers. It is important, therefore, that crew members stow their own gear neatly and ensure that the boat is kept tidy, otherwise it could deteriorate into an unpleasant mess in rough conditions.*

## GALLEY

The galley should be equipped with a small stove, usually fuelled by bottled gas or, sometimes, paraffin. The stove is normally mounted on gimbals so that it remains upright when the boat heels, but it is possible to use a fixed stove fitted with high rails and clamps to keep cooking pans in place while in use. If gimbals are fitted, they should allow the stove to swing freely through as wide an arc as possible, and it should also be possible to lock the stove upright for use in port. Ideally, the stove should be placed where spillages will not land on the cook, but this is not always possible in a small boat. A restraining strap is useful for the cook to lean against when the boat is heeled and a crash bar should be fitted in front of the cooker to prevent the cook being thrown onto the hot stove.

The sink should be deep but narrow for use at sea. Twin sinks are useful if space is available. The fresh-water supply can be delivered by hand or by electric pump. Electric pumps are convenient, but consume more water. If an electric pump is

△ **GALLEY**
*A galley that will be used at sea should have deep sinks situated near the boat's centerline and deep fiddles on the counter tops. A crash bar should be fitted in front of the cooker to protect the cook.*

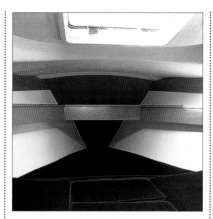

△ **FORECABIN BERTHS**
*Most forecabins on small yachts have a V-shaped berth in the bows that can be used as a double berth. These berths are not comfortable at sea but are used in port.*

fitted, there should be a manual pump as a back-up. Some yachts also have a hot-water supply pumped to the galley and the heads compartment. A sea-water tap in the galley is useful for use when well away from land, when clean sea water can be used for washing up and cooking vegetables.

A small icebox or refrigerator may be fitted, and there must be sufficient stowage for crockery, pans, and supplies within easy reach. Work-surface space is often limited, but there should be enough room to prepare a meal without using the chart table, which the navigator may also need. A fire extinguisher and fire blanket must be easily accessible, as the galley is a likely place for a fire to start. If bottled gas is used, the bottle should be stored in its own self-draining, gas-tight compartment. The supply should be turned off at the bottle when not being used. This can be done by hand or, more conveniently, by fitting a solenoid valve near the bottle, with its control switch in the galley. Make a habit of turning off the gas as soon as you have finished cooking.

## BERTHS

On a cruiser intended for offshore passages, there should be a sea berth available for every off-watch crew member. Berths for use at sea should be arranged so that they are parallel to the fore and aft line of the boat, and not too far toward the bow or stern, where the motion at sea will be worse than near the middle of the boat.

Canvas lee-cloths or solid wooden leeboards should be fitted to all sea berths. These ensure that you cannot roll or be thrown out of the berth in rough conditions. Leecloths are more comfortable to use than solid leeboards and can be easily removed and stowed under the mattress when not in use. Either type should be securely fastened as they can be subjected to considerable loads.

## HEADS

The toilet compartment is often situated between the main saloon and the fore cabin in a small compartment, although some boats have sufficient space for a heads sited near the companionway. The position further aft has the benefit of being situated conveniently for the

△ **HEADS**
*Make sure you understand how to use the marine toilet, as incorrect usage can lead to a blockage. Good ventilation and regular cleaning will keep unpleasant odors to a minimum.*

◁ **SALOON**
*The saloon is the relaxation and
entertainment center of the yacht. It
should be comfortable, well lit and
ventilated, and have secure handholds.*

▽ **LEE-CLOTHS**
*To prevent yourself from falling out of
your bunk when the boat heels, rig up a
canvas lee-cloth or leeboard on the open
side of the bunk to keep you secure.*

cockpit and is in the area where the motion of the boat is felt least, making the heads more comfortable to use.

Most heads contain a marine toilet, a small washbasin, and lockers for personal items. Some also have a shower facility with hot and cold water. The heads can be a convenient spot for oilskin stowage if there is space for a hanging locker.

The seacocks for the inlet and outlet pipes must be easily accessible and should be kept closed when the heads is not in use. This is essential if the toilet bowl is installed on or below the waterline, otherwise flooding could occur.

Make sure that all crew and visitors understand how to operate the heads. Mistakes here can cause much misery, especially for the crew member (usually the skipper) who has to unblock or repair the toilet. Put instructions for use near the toilet.

## CHART TABLE
The chart table should be close to the companionway, so that the navigator can communicate easily with the cockpit crew. It should be a self-contained area out of the way of the main living spaces and the galley. All instruments and radio sets should be situated here, where they can be easily accessed. Most navigators prefer an arrangement that allows them to sit at the chart table, usually facing forward. The chart table should be large enough to hold a chart folded no more than once, and there should be secure stowage for pencils, plotters, and other navigation equipment. Charts are usually stored in the space under a lifting chart-table top, or in a drawer underneath. Space is also needed for reference books, many of which will be quite large. The main electrical switch panel is often mounted in this area.

## SALOON
The saloon is usually situated in the center of the cabin and is the area that is reserved for sitting, eating, and entertaining. It is the largest interior space in the boat and should have plenty of good handholds to make it easy to negotiate at sea when the boat is heeled. Handholds should be placed at various heights to that they can be used when sitting or standing – by children or adults. The corners of all furniture should be rounded so that there are no sharp edges to injure people falling against them.

Good lighting and ventilation help make the interior more pleasant. Natural light is supplied by plenty of ports, windows, and hatches, all of which should be strong and well fastened. Ventilation should be provided by hatches, opening ports, and dedicated ventilators that can be used at sea without letting in water.

# PROTECTION AFLOAT

Having the right clothing and safety equipment is always important when you go afloat, but especially when you are cruising. The dinghy sailor can look forward to a hot shower at the end of a trip, but the cruising sailor may be at sea, sometimes in unpleasant conditions, for hours, days, or even weeks. In these circumstances, the only way to ensure your continuing comfort is to wear the right clothing. It is also essential to have proper safety gear, such as harnesses and life jackets, on board.

## CRUISER CLOTHING

It is always cooler on the water than on the shore and, for those sailing in temperate areas, the key requirement is to stay warm. Cold reduces your ability to think and act efficiently and also increases the risk of seasickness. When sailing in anything other than perfect conditions, it is important to wear the right clothing to maintain a comfortable working temperature.

To stay warm, your clothes should provide sufficient insulation, with a barrier layer to stop the warm layer getting wet and to eliminate wind chill. Silk and wool are the best natural insulators, but modern synthetic fibers are also excellent. They are very light, dry quickly, and wick moisture away from the skin, keeping the wearer dry and warm.

Marine-clothing manufacturers make specialist, multi-layered clothing systems. These consist of a thin, light, underwear layer, over which is worn a thicker, warm layer. Either layer can be worn separately to suit different temperatures. A top, waterproof layer keeps the wearer dry.

The latest designs use foul weather gear made of breathable material. These keep water out and allow perspiration trapped inside to pass through, keeping the wearer dryer than with conventional clothing. These designs are expensive, but many sailors believe them worth buying because they are the lightest, most comfortable, and warmest sailing clothes available.

### HATS AND GLOVES

Use a hat to protect yourself from the sun in hot weather and to reduce heat loss in cold conditions. A thermal balaclava provides warmth when sailing in the coldest weather. Whatever headgear you choose, make sure that it fits comfortably under the hood of your waterproof jacket.

Sailing gloves protect your hands from ropes and keep them warm in cold weather. Gloves are available with non-slip palms to grip ropes, and with cut-off fingers to allow maximum sensitivity for delicate tasks. In very cold weather, gauntlet-style fleece-lined gloves keep the hands warm but must be removed when handling ropes.

### ◁ HANDLING HEAT

*Shorts and T-shirts are the best clothes in hot weather, but take precautions against sunburn and wear sunglasses to protect the eyes; a hat will prevent sunstroke.*

**Suspenders**
*Elastic suspenders keep overalls in place*

**The neck**
*A well-insulated neck with Velcro fasteners keeps water from getting inside the jacket*

**Safety harness**
*Good gear has an attachment for a safety harness*

## FOUL WEATHER GEAR

There are many types of foul weather gear available to suit all conditions. The main difference between gear designed for coastal sailing and that intended for offshore or ocean passages is in the weight and strength of its material. Ocean foul weather gear will probably have a better hood arrangement and more storm seals on cuffs, ankles, neck, and zip openings. It will also be more expensive. Be realistic about the type of sailing you intend to do, and buy your foul weather gear accordingly.

## △ FOUL WEATHER GEAR

*Some foul weather gear is made of breathable material, allowing condensation out but not letting water in. If you can afford the breathable gear, you will appreciate its benefits, but good conventional gear is adequate.*

**Non-slip sole**
*Grooved soles help the wearer get a grip on a wet deck*

**Thermal leggings**
*Thermals are light, warm, and comfortable to wear*

## △ BOOTS

*Boots are available in high or short styles; the short ones are lighter to wear and more useful for all-round wear. Non-slip deck shoes are ideal when conditions on deck are dry.*

## THERMALS ▷

*Thin, light, multi-layered thermals worn underneath foul weather gear will keep the wearer dry, warm, and well insulated from the elements.*

**Thermal socks**
*Wear these inside boots for added warmth*

# SAFETY EQUIPMENT

All cruisers should carry sufficient safety equipment to cope with an emergency involving either boat or crew. Danger can come in a number of ways: a crew member can fall overboard or be injured, fire can break out on board, or the boat can be holed and take on water. Safety equipment must be stowed in a location where it can be reached quickly when needed, and the crew must know how it works and the correct procedure for using it.

## STAYING OUT OF DANGER

It is important that all crew members are aware of the potential dangers on deck and down below and understand how to move safely around the yacht. The cockpit is the safest place on deck when underway, and offers security to the on-watch crew. There should be plenty of strong, dedicated attachment points for the crew's safety harnesses; crew members should clip on before leaving the companionway.

Jackstays (safety lines) should be fitted along each sidedeck so that it is possible to move all the way from the cockpit to the bow without unclipping the harness line. When moving on deck, each crew's line should, ideally, be short enough to prevent them from going overboard in the event of a fall. Remember that the jackstays and the fittings to which they are attached will take a tremendous load if a person does fall overboard, so ensure that their strength is sufficient.

When standing and sitting on deck, always be aware which sheets, blocks, and other fittings are under load at the time. Never place yourself in the way of a loaded sheet; if anything failed, it could whip toward you and cause injury. When walking on deck, do not stand on ropes or sails, as they may move under foot and throw you off balance.

In rough weather, only move from the cockpit to the deck if really necessary. Plan your movements in advance and, when possible, use the windward sidedeck to move fore and aft. A yacht's motion in rough weather can be very lively, so keep your weight low to aid balance; do not be ashamed to crawl along the deck and sit on the foredeck to reduce the risk of falling overboard.

Moving about down below can be hard in bad weather. There should be ample handholds at heights to suit all the crew. When the motion is rough, move from handhold to handhold and try to anticipate the boat's movements to avoid losing your balance and being thrown across the boat.

## PERSONAL SAFETY EQUIPMENT

The best way of keeping safe at sea is by staying on the boat. This makes a safety harness the most important item of personal safety gear. A life jacket will keep you afloat if you go overboard, but it is best to avoid falling in the water in the first place.

### HARNESSES AND LIFE JACKETS

There are several types of safety harnesses. Some waterproof jackets have a built-in harness to protect you whenever you are wearing the jacket. However, a separate harness may be more useful as it can be worn at any time – even in conditions where you do not want to wear a waterproof jacket. Some harnesses have an incorporated life jacket. These are popular as they are easy to put on, reasonably comfortable to wear, and do not require you to don two separate items of equipment. If you choose a separate life jacket, the most popular and practical are the inflatable type, either with manual or automatic inflation. If you buy separate items, try them on together over all the clothes you expect to wear in bad conditions. Make sure they fit well, do not interfere with each other, and are comfortable to wear.

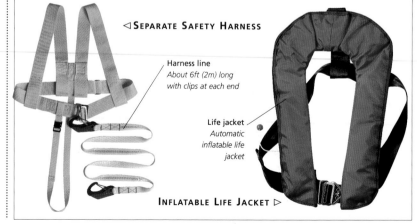

◁ **SEPARATE SAFETY HARNESS**

Harness line
*About 6ft (2m) long
with clips at each end*

Life jacket
*Automatic
inflatable life
jacket*

**INFLATABLE LIFE JACKET** ▷

## STOWING LIFEBUOYS

Lifebuoys must be stowed where they can be reached immediately in case someone goes overboard. They are only effective if they are thrown at once to the crew in the water. Stow the lifebuoys – most cruisers carry two – in quick-release brackets on the pushpit. A lifebuoy should be fitted with a flashing strobe light that works when it floats upright in the water; check the light regularly and replace the batteries before they run out. To increase the effectiveness of a lifebuoy, attach a marker buoy – a weighted, floating marker pole about 6ft (2m) high. Marker buoys are available in solid or inflatable form. They should be stowed along with the lifebuoy on the pushpit.

### △ LIFEBUOY AND MARKER BUOY

*A lifebuoy blows downwind in the water. It is therefore fitted with a nylon drogue to reduce its drift. A marker buoy – a brightly-colored pole (here, flying code flag O – Man Overboard) – is more visible than a person or a lifebuoy in the water. This makes it easier to locate a man overboard, particularly in large waves.*

---

## FIRE EXTINGUISHERS AND FLARES

Basic safety gear is essential on board. A fire may break out if there is an accident in the galley, or an engine or electrical fault. Flares are necessary for attracting attention in an emergency.

### FIRE EXTINGUISHERS

Fire can be a major danger on a yacht if it is allowed to get out of control. Extinguishers must be situated where they are most likely to be needed: close to the galley and the engine, in the saloon, and up forward. Use a foam extinguisher for oil or fat fires and a halon extinguisher for an electrical or engine fire; dry powder extinguishers work on all types. A fire blanket should be stowed close to the galley, where it is useful for smothering a pan fire. Make sure the crew know where the extinguishers are stowed and how and when to use them (p.300).

### FLARES

You should have a number of flares on board suitable for the type of sailing you do. If you are out sailing for the day in coastal waters, several red parachute flares and a few hand-held red flares, together with an orange smoke flare, will be sufficient. If you sail at night, carry a few white flares to signal your position in the event of a potential collision. If you sail further offshore, increase the number of parachute flares you carry and add a floating dye marker. Make sure that all the crew know how and when to use the flares (p.303).

---

## FIRST-AID KIT

Make sure that you have a well-stocked first-aid kit on board in case a crew member is injured. Most injuries on board involve nothing more than minor cuts and bruises, but there is always the possibility of a broken limb, severe impact injury, or burns. The first-aid kit should reflect the type of sailing you do. A simple kit containing some cold packs and bandages is all you need for day sailing and short cruises. Longer passages, however, will require a more comprehensive kit so that you can deal with any injuries on board until you can obtain professional medical assistance for the victim.

## CARRYING A LIFE-RAFT

If you sail offshore, you should carry either a dedicated life-raft or a dual-purpose tender that can serve in this important role. Life-rafts should be professionally serviced annually to ensure that they meet current safety standards. Carry an emergency grab-bag filled with food, water, flares, and other essential survival equipment in case you need to abandon ship in an emergency, and store it where you can find it in a hurry.

### △ LIFE-RAFT ON DECK

*A life-raft is packed inside a canister or valise. It is often stowed on deck, lashed down with quick-release fastenings.*

## WHIPPING

Whipping is used to prevent the end of a rope from unraveling. With modern synthetic ropes, you can accomplish this by heat-sealing the ends, but whipping using thin twine is stronger and neater.

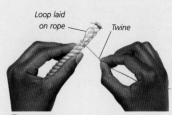

*Loop laid on rope*  *Twine*

**1** Form a loop in the end of the twine and lay it along the rope with the loop toward the end of the rope.

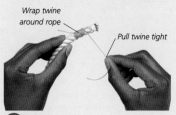

*Wrap twine around rope*

*Pull twine tight*

**2** Wrap the long end of the twine around the rope, moving toward the rope end. Pull each turn tight.

*End passed through loop*

**3** When the turns approach the end of the rope, pass the end of the twine through the loop.

*Tail buried under turns*

**4** Pull hard on the short tail of the loop to bury it under the turns. Trim both twine ends close to the whipping.

# CRUISER ROPEWORK

*Learning basic rope skills is an essential first step for anyone who aspires to become a good seaman. An experienced sailor will perform these skills naturally, as proficiency in rope-handling forms the basis for much of the work involved in sailing a yacht. It is not necessary to be a knot-tying expert to become a good seaman. However, you should know how to tie a few essential knots, how to coil, handle, and stow ropes of all sizes, and how to heave a line.*

## USING ROPES

A typical cruiser will have many different ropes on board, ranging from light line up to heavy mooring and anchor warps. Ropes found on cruisers are larger and heavier than those used on sailing dinghies and can be more difficult to handle because of their extra weight and length. Each rope has its use and place on board, and each will require handling in a way determined by its size and purpose. Practice tying a few essential knots, and coiling, cleating, stowing, and heaving these larger ropes. Proficiency in these skills can be critical when mooring, as well as in other situations. You should be able to complete these tasks quickly and efficiently, even in the dark when you cannot see the rope you are handling.

The basic knots and rope-handling skills described on pp.36–39 must become second nature. You should then extend your ability by learning the additional knots shown (*right*). Always ensure that ropes are coiled and stowed neatly to avoid tangles, and never leave mooring ropes lying around the deck or dock where someone could trip over them. Wash all ropes once a year with mild detergent to remove salt and grease.

### HEAVING A LINE

Sometimes you will need to heave (throw) a line to someone on another boat or on the quayside. If there is a tangle in the line, your throw will fall short. Do not rely on a previously coiled rope, but re-coil it before the throw. Make sure that the rope is long enough to reach your target.

On larger boats, there may be a dedicated heaving line of light rope with a weight spliced into one end to help it travel. Once caught, it is used to pull over a heavier mooring warp.

*Throwing hand*

◁ **READY TO THROW**
*Coil the rope neatly and split into two coils, half in your throwing hand and the rest in the other hand. Stand with your non-throwing*
**PREPARING** *shoulder toward the target.*

**The throw**
*Heave the line underarm and aim above the target, letting the line uncoil from your other hand. Hold on to the end*

**THROWING**

# KNOTS

Many of the knots used on cruisers are identical to those required to sail a dinghy, so re-acquaint yourself with them (*pp.36–39*). Two other knots – the fisherman's bend and the rolling hitch – are often used on board a cruiser, especially when mooring, and should be included in your rope-handling skills.

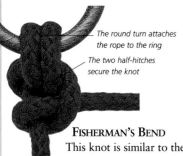

The round turn attaches the rope to the ring

The two half-hitches secure the knot

### FISHERMAN'S BEND
This knot is similar to the round turn and two half-hitches (*pp.38–39*), but is more secure. It can be used for tying an anchor warp to the anchor or a mooring warp to a ring.

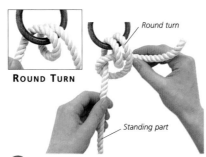

**ROUND TURN**

Round turn

Standing part

**①** Take a turn around a spar or rope, taking the working end up on the right side of the standing part. Bring the working end across the standing part.

Working end

**②** Take a second turn identical to the first turn. Take the working end up between the standing part and the second turn.

### ROLLING HITCH
The rolling hitch is a very useful knot when you want to tie a rope around a spar or to take the strain off another rope. It grips very tightly and is valuable in an emergency, when you can use it to take the load off another line to pull along the spar.

The three turns of this hitch secure the rope to a spar.

Rope pulls along spar

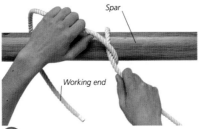

Spar

Working end

**①** Make a turn around a spar or rope, bringing the working end up on the right side of the standing part. Take the working end across the standing part.

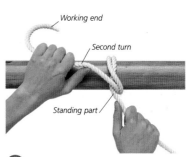

Working end

Second turn

Standing part

**②** Make a second turn identical to the first turn, bringing the working end up between the standing part and the second turn.

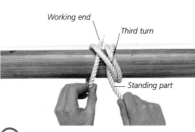

Working end

Third turn

Standing part

**③** Take a third turn, and then bring the working end up on the left side of the standing part. Next, tuck the turn under itself.

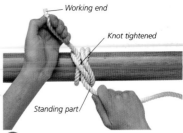

Working end

Knot tightened

Standing part

**④** Pull on both the standing part and the working end to tighten the knot. Pull the standing part over the first two turns before putting strain on the rope.

# USING WARPS

Warps are mooring ropes used to tie a boat to a dock, quayside, mooring buoy, piles, or other boat. Knowing how to use warps is an essential part of cruiser handling. The size of warp will depend on the size and, most importantly, the weight of your boat: large yachts will have big warps that are heavy to handle. All warps should be strong enough to hold your boat and long enough to allow for the rise and fall of the boat in tidal waters.

Nylon is the most common material for warps, since it is strong. It also stretches well to absorb shock and reduce loads on fairleads and cleats. Warps should always be coiled when not in use, and stored, preferably hanging up, in a locker from where they can easily be retrieved.

When mooring alongside, a number of warps are needed to hold the boat safely and to prevent it from ranging back and forth and causing damage. The precise arrangement depends on whether you are tied to a quayside (and have to allow for the tide), or to another boat or floating dock that also moves in response to changes in tidal height.

## AVOIDING PROBLEMS
The best way to avoid problems when mooring with warps is to have one rope for each job and to tie each one up on its own cleat. Always tie up the end to a cleat on shore or on the dock or a neighboring boat, and bring the rest of the warp back on board where it can be cleated and stowed. This avoids leaving rope on shore and makes it easy to adjust your warps on board when necessary. Sometimes you may make fast with a slip line led

## ▽ MOORING WARPS
*Each mooring warp has a different function, and it is important to know which warp does what. If you leave your boat alongside in tidal waters, make sure that there is sufficient slack in the warps to allow for the lowest level of tide, otherwise the boat will end up hanging from its warps and could be damaged.*

---

## TURNING WITH WARPS

There are times when it would be much easier to leave a berth if the boat was facing the other way, particularly if you want to leave under sail. This can be achieved by the use of warps.

### USING WARPS
The best way to turn a boat using warps is to make use of the tide or wind to help the maneuver. Start by placing fenders on the far side of the boat and at the bow and stern to protect the boat when it turns. The boat shown here is lying stern-to-tide, so the stern will be moved away from the dock to turn the boat. If the boat was lying the other way round, the bow would be turned first.

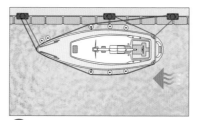

① Rig a stern line outside all rigging on the far side. Move the bow spring to a cleat on the far side, and the shore end to a cleat aft of the boat.

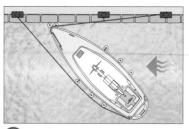

② Release the bow line and stern spring. Release the stern line and push the stern out, or pull on the bow spring. The tide will start to swing the boat out. Take up the slack on the new stern line.

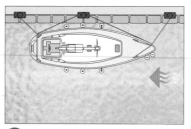

③ The turn will slow down as the boat lines up with the tide. Make fast the new bow and stern lines and rig new springs. For short stays, you need only rig a bow line and a stern spring.

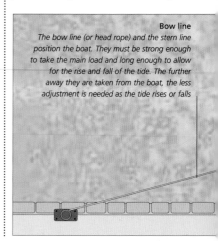

**Bow line**
*The bow line (or head rope) and the stern line position the boat. They must be strong enough to take the main load and long enough to allow for the rise and fall of the tide. The further away they are taken from the boat, the less adjustment is needed as the tide rises or falls*

through a ring or around a cleat on shore with both ends brought back aboard (*right*). This is only suitable for temporary stops, as a warp rigged in this way is liable to chafe where it passes through the ring or cleat. When chafe occurs in the middle of a long warp, it becomes useless unless you can cut it in half and make it into two shorter warps.

## CLEATS

All mooring cleats and fairleads must be large enough for the job. They should be securely bolted to the deck, and have smooth, rounded edges to prevent chafe on the warps. Generally, the larger the cleat, the less it will wear the rope and the easier it will be to tie off a rope with sufficient turns. Some yachts have a central bollard on the foredeck together with a pair of cleats, one on either side of the bow, and a pair at the stern. If there is no central bollard, there should be at least three cleats on the foredeck. A pair of midship cleats on the sidedecks is useful when mooring alongside.

## FAIRLEADS

Fairleads should be fitted either side of the bow and stern and alongside each midship cleat, if attached. Fairleads can be open or closed; the open

---

# SLIP LINES

A slip line is a warp led through a ring or around a cleat or bollard on shore, with both ends made fast on board. It allows the crew to release the warp from on board and is particularly useful when berthed alongside a quay wall. Never rig a warp permanently as a slip: this can lead to chafe in the middle of the warp and ruin it.

### USING RINGS

If a slip line is rigged through a ring on shore, it is important to lead it through the ring in the right way. Lead the end of the warp that will be released up through the ring if it is lying on top of the quay, or down through the ring if it is hanging on the quay wall. In this way, the warp lifts the ring away from the quay as it is pulled, preventing the warp from jamming as you pull it on board. Make sure that there are no knots or splices in the warp to snag, and pull the line steadily to avoid tangles.

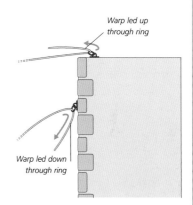

*Warp led up through ring*

*Warp led down through ring*

**SLIP LINES THROUGH RINGS**

---

variety is more versatile, but the closed type is more secure. All warps should be led through fairleads so that they cannot chafe on the deck edge or any other obstruction. Warps are particularly susceptible to chafe where they are led through fairleads or across the edges of quay walls.

They can be protected by feeding the warp through short lengths of plastic tubing, which can then be positioned at likely chafing points. Check that your fairleads do not have any sharp edges, or these will quickly damage your warps when they are under heavy strain.

---

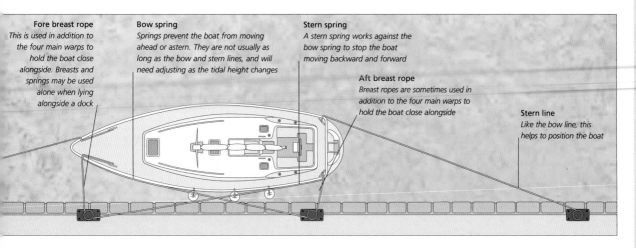

**Fore breast rope**
*This is used in addition to the four main warps to hold the boat close alongside. Breasts and springs may be used alone when lying alongside a dock*

**Bow spring**
*Springs prevent the boat from moving ahead or astern. They are not usually as long as the bow and stern lines, and will need adjusting as the tidal height changes*

**Stern spring**
*A stern spring works against the bow spring to stop the boat moving backward and forward*

**Aft breast rope**
*Breast ropes are sometimes used in addition to the four main warps to hold the boat close alongside*

**Stern line**
*Like the bow line, this helps to position the boat*

# BASIC SAIL SKILLS

*S*ails *on a modern cruising yacht are similar in most respects to those found on a dinghy, but they are both larger and heavier. Also, a cruiser's sail wardrobe is more extensive than a dinghy's, because it must have sails suitable for a wide range of conditions, from light airs to storm-force winds. Many modern cruisers are fitted with a headsail roller-reefing system, which allows one sail to be used in a range of wind strengths, but some follow the traditional approach of having several sails of different sizes.*

## BENDING ON SAILS

"Bending on" is the traditional term used to describe fitting the mainsail onto the boom. It is usually done only at the beginning of the sailing season, as the mainsail on most cruisers is stowed on the boom and removed only at the season's end. Headsails are traditionally bent on when needed, being stowed at other times, but many modern cruisers use a roller-reefing system that allows the headsail to be furled tightly around the forestay when the boat is not sailing. With this system the headsail is often left bent on throughout the season.

## MAINSAIL FOOT

Most cruiser mainsails are attached to the boom either by sliding the bolt rope out along the groove in the boom, as is done with many dinghies (*p.60*), or with slides that are attached to the sail and run in the boom groove. The tack is fastened to the gooseneck using a shackle or lashing. The clew is pulled toward the outer end of the boom using the outhaul, which, if it is adjustable, runs inside the boom, to a winch or cleat at the forward end.

## MAINSAIL LUFF

The luff is usually attached to the mast by slides that run in the mast groove. With a fully battened mainsail, the battens run from the leech to the luff. They fit into special low-friction sliders that enable the sail to be hoisted and lowered easily despite pressure from the battens.

## REEFING LINES

Lines to reef the mainsail (*p.185*) are usually led from the end of the boom through the reef cringles in the leech. They are then led back down to the boom before being led forward to a winch and cleat at the forward end of the boom, or through turning blocks back to a winch in the cockpit. Similar lines are sometimes rigged at the luff, unless the luff cringles are fixed onto inverted hooks known as ram's horns.

## HOISTING THE MAINSAIL

*Before hoisting the mainsail, make sure that the boat is facing head-to-wind. If it is not, the sail will fill as it is hoisted, making the job difficult, if not impossible, and the boat will start sailing before you are ready.*

**①** Check that the halyard is clear aloft. Remove the ties that hold the stowed sail in place on the boom, fully release the mainsheet, and pull on the halyard. As you hoist, keep an eye aloft to make sure that the sail does not snag on anything.

**②** If the halyard is led aft to a winch in the cockpit, as here, one crew member at the mast can pull on the halyard to help hoist the sail more quickly. The person at the winch takes in the slack, only winching the halyard when the sail is nearly hoisted.

**③** Put enough pressure on the halyard to pull a light crease into the sail parallel to the luff – this will disappear when the sail is full of wind. Cleat, coil, and stow the halyard, ease off the topping lift and leave it slack, and tighten the boom vang.

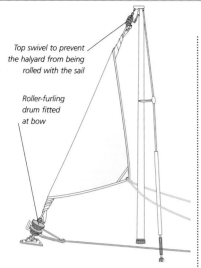

Top swivel to prevent the halyard from being rolled with the sail

Roller-furling drum fitted at bow

△ **ROLLER-FURLING HEADSAIL**
*The luff of a roller-furling headsail runs in a foil fitted to the forestay. The tack is fixed to a drum that turns to roll the sail.*

## FURLED HEADSAILS

In roller-furling and reefing headsail systems, a headfoil is fitted over the forestay. The headfoil has a groove in the aft edge, into which the sail's luff rope is fed. The sail's tack is shackled to the roller-furling drum at the base of the headfoil, and the head is shackled to a halyard swivel. The sheets are attached to the clew in the usual way, using a bowline on each. They are then led aft through their turning blocks or fairleads. Remember to tie a figure eight knot (*p.38*) in the end of each sheet. After the sail is hoisted, it is furled by pulling on the furling line wound around the furling drum. This rotates the headfoil, and thus furls the sail.

## OTHER HEADSAIL SYSTEMS

If a furling system is not used, the yacht will have a number of headsails of different sizes to suit a range of wind strengths. These sails are stowed in a sail locker, and are rigged when needed. This type of headsail is rigged exactly like the jib of a dinghy (*p.58*).

Remove the headsail from its bag and attach the tack to the stemhead fitting with a shackle, or by hooking it over a ram's horn. Next, clip the luff hanks onto the forestay and attach the sheets to the clew. Finally, shackle the halyard to the head. The sail is now ready for hoisting.

## HOISTING THE HEADSAIL

If you have a roller-furling headsail, it will already be hoisted and stowed in its furled state. To unfurl it, you simply release the furling line and pull on the jib sheet. If you have hanked-on headsails, you will hoist the sail using the halyard and halyard winch. Unlike the mainsail, the headsail can be hoisted in any wind direction. Ensure, however, that the sheets are free so that the mainsail can flap freely until you are ready to sheet in. Before hoisting, untie the sail ties securing it (*p.174*), and check that the halyard is not tangled aloft. Hoist the sail by hand with one turn around the winch drum (*p.172*), using the handle only when needed. Tighten the halyard until a small crease appears in the sail, parallel to the luff. This will disappear when the sail is full of wind. Cleat the halyard and coil and stow the tail.

---

### STOWING THE HALYARD

If your halyard winches are mast-mounted, you will have a long length of halyard when each sail is hoisted. The best way to stow them, after cleating (*p.36*), is to coil them and hang them on their cleats. If your halyards lead aft to winches in the cockpit, their tails are most effectively dealt with by stuffing them into bags mounted on the bulkhead for the purpose. Alternatively, coil them and hang them on their cleats or winches.

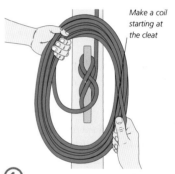

Make a coil starting at the cleat

**①** Once the halyard has been cleated, coil up the tail, starting the coil from the cleat end.

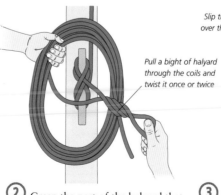

Pull a bight of halyard through the coils and twist it once or twice

**②** Grasp the part of the halyard that leads to the cleat and bring it through the coil center, twisting it once or twice.

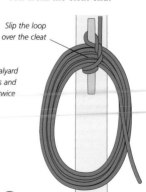

Slip the loop over the cleat

**③** Pull the twisted loop over the coils and drop it over the top horn of the cleat to hold the coils securely.

# USING WINCHES

The sails on a cruiser are larger than those on a dinghy, and, therefore, exert much more force on their sheets and halyards. Winches are an important part of the sail-handling equipment, as they are used to handle the loads on these lines. On traditional craft, however, tackles are sometimes used to perform the same function. Winches positioned in the cockpit are used for handling sheets, control lines, and halyards that are led aft. Mast winches are used for any halyards and reefing lines that are not led aft.

There are two types of winch – the standard winch and the self-tailing winch. Using a standard winch properly usually requires two people:

one to load and wind the winch, and the other to tail (pull) on the free end (the tail) of the sheet or halyard. On a self-tailing winch, there is a circular grooved cleat running around the top. This is used to retain the tail of the rope. It allows one person to operate the winch. Some winches have two or three speeds to enable the task to be carried out more easily and quickly.

## LOADING A WINCH

Loading a winch means putting turns of rope on it before it can be used. Usually, at least three full turns are needed to provide sufficient friction between the rope and the winch drum. The rope must be wound on in the

△ **SELF-TAILING WINCH**
*Most modern yachts have self-tailing winches for one-person operation. Load the rope onto the winch and feed it into the self-tailing jaws. Wind the handle with your shoulders positioned over the winch.*

## WINCHING-IN USING A STANDARD WINCH

*To use a winch, one person loads the rope and then holds it in place, while another inserts the winch handle to winch it in. If the sheet or halyard has any load on it, you must be careful to avoid trapping your fingers between the rope and the drum when loading the winch. The best way to protect the fingers on the hand nearest the drum is to keep the back of the hand facing the drum. To winch efficiently, adopt a stable stance with your shoulders over the winch. Use two hands on the handle whenever possible, because this will enable you to exert the maximum amount of force. Always watch the gear that you are winching. It is possible to apply a large amount of power with a winch, and sails and gear can be damaged by over-tightening sheets and halyards.*

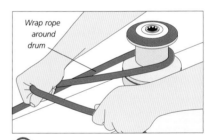

*Wrap rope around drum*

**1** If there is strain on the rope, use two hands to load the winch. Load in the direction that the drum rotates.

*Keep your hands clear of the drum*

**2** Make at least three full turns. As you wrap the rope around the winch, rotate your hand to make sure that you keep your fingers clear of the drum.

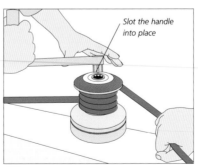

*Slot the handle into place*

**3** Insert the handle into the winch once the turns have been wound on. Make sure that the handle is fitted fully into the socket or it may slip as you wind.

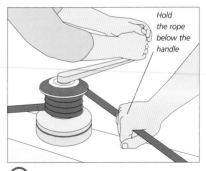

*Hold the rope below the handle*

**4** Turn the handle clockwise for high speed, and counterclockwise for slow speed. The person tailing must maintain a steady pull on the tail.

same direction that the winch drum rotates. Nearly all winches rotate clockwise, but you can quickly check a winch's rotation by seeing which way it spins freely.

## USING WINCH HANDLES

Once the winch is loaded, a handle, inserted in the top of the winch, is used to wind in the rope. Some winch handles have a locking arrangement that prevents them from being accidentally knocked out of the winch. With these, you must turn a small lever on the handle to insert and remove it from the socket.

Winch in the rope, and cleat it securely once you have finished. Cleating is not always necessary with a self-tailing winch, because, in that system, the rope is cleated on the top of the drum. However, it is safer to secure the rope on a separate cleat for added security. With the rope cleated, the handle should be removed and stowed where it will be easy to find when you need it. Never leave a handle in a winch when it is not being used.

## EASING A SHEET

Headsail sheets impart high loads on their winches, and you must be very careful when easing or fully releasing one. If you need to ease the sheet, undo it from its cleat, keeping it tight between your hand and the drum to prevent it from slipping prematurely. Press the heel of your other hand against the turns on the winch to increase the friction of the rope against the drum, and keep the sheet under control as you ease the turns slightly.

## RELEASING A SHEET

To fully release a loaded sheet (when you are tacking for example), do not unwind the turns from the drum or the sheet will kink and jam. Pull the sheet sharply upward and release it as the turns come off the drum.

Riding turns occur when the coils that are on the winch become crossed over each other. This will jam the rope and prevent it from being released. Riding turns usually happen on a sheet winch when too many turns have been put onto the winch drum before the slack in the sheet has been pulled in.

### CLEARING A RIDING TURN

To clear a riding turn on a sheet or halyard under load, you must first remove the load from the winch. To do this, tie another line to the sheet or halyard ahead of the winch. Attach this line with a rolling hitch (*p.167*), and then lead it to another winch (positioned in the direction in which you need to pull to relieve the load on the first winch). Load the second line onto the new winch and wind it in until it takes all the pressure off the riding turn. Now return to the jammed winch and release the riding turn. Reload the sheet and winch it in. Release the rolling hitch and the second line.

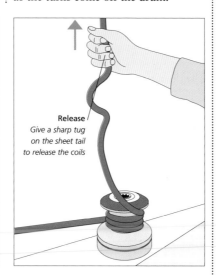

**Winch hand**
*Push the heel of your hand against the turns*

**Release**
*Give a sharp tug on the sheet tail to release the coils*

△ **EASING THE SHEET**
*To ease the sheet, release it from its cleat but maintain tension between the tail and the drum using one hand. Press the heel of your other hand against the turns on the winch. Allow the rope to slide gradually around the winch drum.*

△ **RELEASING THE SHEET**
*When you need to release the sheet from the winch, uncleat the tail and pull the sheet upward sharply so that the coils are freed from the drum without getting twisted or jammed. Let go of the rope end as soon as the coils leave the winch.*

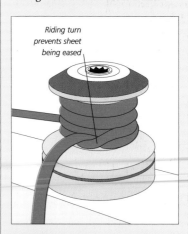

*Riding turn prevents sheet being eased*

△ **RIDING TURN**
*A riding turn occurs when the rope turns become crossed. The load on the rope locks the turns, preventing the rope from being released. If the load is light, it may be released by hand, but usually another line must be used to relieve the load.*

# LOWERING AND STOWING SAILS

Lower the sails by reversing their hoisting procedures. Before you lower the mainsail, remember to tighten the topping lift to take the weight of the boom if you do not have a solid boom vang that supports the boom. Otherwise, the boom will come crashing down onto the deck and may injure someone. Make sure that the boat is head-to-wind so that the sail is not full of wind, then ease the mainsheet and allow the sail to flap. Lower the mainsail, keeping the halyard under control so that it does not rush out. When the sail is down, secure the halyard and tighten the mainsheet to prevent the boom from swinging around. The mainsail can now be stowed.

If you have a headsail-furling system, you can roll the sail around the forestay simply by easing the sheet and pulling on the furling line. If you have a hanked-on headsail, lower it to the deck by easing the halyard. The headsail can be lowered with the wind in any direction. One crew member should go forward to gather the sail onto the foredeck to prevent it from falling in the water. Secure the halyard, and then stow the sail.

## STOWING THE MAINSAIL

During the sailing season, the mainsail is usually left stowed on the boom, shielded from the elements by a sail cover. Sailcloth is damaged by long-term exposure to ultraviolet light, so it is important to protect the sail with its cover whenever it is not being used.

A fully battened mainsail will stow itself neatly on the boom as it is lowered. As long as restraining lines (called lazyjacks) are correctly rigged from the mast to the boom to retain the sail, it will stack like a Venetian blind, requiring only the sail ties to secure it. The sail cover must be designed to fit around the lazyjacks, or they must be pulled forward out of the way before the cover is fitted.

A conventional mainsail does not stack neatly when it is lowered, and must be stowed by hand.

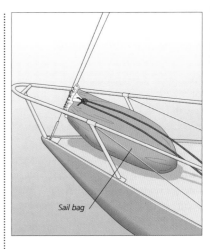

Sail bag

## △ TEMPORARY HEADSAIL STOW
*Hanked-on headsails can be temporarily stowed in their bag on the foredeck. The sail can remain hanked on, ready to hoist, with sheets attached. The bag protects the sail and keeps the decks clear.*

## STOWING THE HEADSAIL

A headsail that is stowed furled on the forestay needs protection from ultraviolet light, which will degrade the exposed part of the sail. Many sailmakers allow for this by building in a sacrificial strip of material along the leech. Alternatively, you can hoist a cover over the furled sail.

A furling headsail is easily stowed: you simply roll it away on the forestay. A hanked-on headsail requires another approach, however. If the sail is to be used in the near future, it can be stowed neatly on the foredeck. If not, it should be removed completely and stowed in its bag in the sail locker. To stow

## ◁ FULLY BATTENED MAINSAIL
*A fully battened mainsail will self-stow neatly on the boom if lazyjacks are properly rigged from the mast to the boom. Once the sail has been lowered, sail ties are secured around the sail and boom.*

the sail on the foredeck, pull the sail out along one sidedeck and furl it into a neat roll that can be secured to the lifelines with sail ties. Tie it to the top lifeline so that it is held clear of the deck. Alternatively, you can use the headsail bag to cover and protect it while it is still hanked to the forestay. Fold the sail in half by pulling the clew up to the tack and head. Now pack the bulk of the sail into its bag; you should end up with just the tack, clew, and head protruding. The sheets can be left attached, but the halyard should be removed. The halyard end should then be stowed on the pulpit to keep it out of the way.

Sometimes, when you are sailing with hanked-on headsails, you may need to change to a different sail. When you remove the old sail, it is best to stow it immediately in its bag in the sail locker. Occasionally, however, you may stow it temporarily on the foredeck if you are likely to use it again soon. Make sure that it is lashed securely to the stanchions so that it cannot slip overboard. Never leave a sail on deck in rough weather.

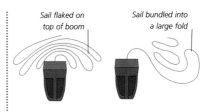

Sail flaked on top of boom

Sail bundled into a large fold

**FULLY BATTENED**    **CONVENTIONAL**

## △ STOWING MAINSAILS

*A fully battened mainsail will stow itself in Venetian blind-like folds as it is lowered. A conventional mainsail is pulled over to one side of the boom after being lowered and is stowed neatly.*

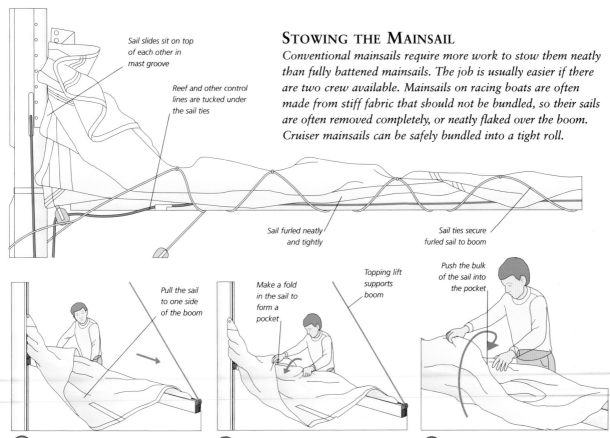

Sail slides sit on top of each other in mast groove

Reef and other control lines are tucked under the sail ties

## STOWING THE MAINSAIL

*Conventional mainsails require more work to stow them neatly than fully battened mainsails. The job is usually easier if there are two crew available. Mainsails on racing boats are often made from stiff fabric that should not be bundled, so their sails are often removed completely, or neatly flaked over the boom. Cruiser mainsails can be safely bundled into a tight roll.*

Sail furled neatly and tightly

Sail ties secure furled sail to boom

Pull the sail to one side of the boom

Make a fold in the sail to form a pocket

Topping lift supports boom

Push the bulk of the sail into the pocket

**①** Once the mainsail has been lowered, pull it over to the leeward side of the boom. Move around to the windward side of the boom so that you are in the best position to stow it neatly. Ensure that the mainsheet is pulled in and cleated before you start.

**②** Reaching over the boom, grab the leech of the sail some way up from the foot. Pull it aft and toward you to form a pocket. If there is more than one crew member available, one should stand at the aft end of the boom, where it is easier to create the pocket in the sail.

**③** Pack the rest of the sail into the pocket, pulling the leech aft as you go to create a neat bundle. When all the sail is inside, pull the pocket tightly around the sail and secure it with sail ties tied around the bundle and the boom. Fit the sail cover to protect the sail from UV light.

# PREPARING TO SAIL

*Before you go sailing, even for a short trip, you should check that the boat is ready for sea, that all its equipment is in place and in working order, and that all the crew understand its use. It is crucial that the safety equipment is fully functional, and that the crew know what it is for and how and when to use it. Problems can occur even on a short trip in good weather, so do not be complacent. Make sure you let someone on shore know of your plans and when you expect to return.*

## BEFORE YOU SET SAIL

Even if you are just heading out for a few hours in familiar home waters, spend a few minutes planning the trip and briefing the crew. Make an outline plan of where you expect to sail and when you will return. Check the weather forecast, and have a contingency plan prepared if the weather looks changeable. Make sure you know the state of the tide and what it will be doing over the period of your trip. Check that the tidal stream will help rather than hinder you on both outward and return trips. Make sure you have enough provisions on board for the crew, sufficient to last the length of the trip with some spare.

If you are heading off on a longer cruise, your pre-trip planning needs to be more thorough. You can gain much pleasure from planning a passage at home; work done at this stage makes it more likely that your trip will go smoothly and efficiently.

Before you set out, take some time to brief the crew on the overall plan for the trip and run through the safety equipment and procedures for its use. Make sure that everyone has suitable clothing and their own safety harness and life jacket. If any crew member suffers from seasickness, suggest that they take their chosen treatment before they set sail.

Decide on how you plan to leave your berth; make sure the crew know how the maneuver is to be performed, their roles in the procedure, and what jobs need to be done as soon as you have cleared the berth. If you are going to be out for more than a few hours, prepare a snack and a hot drink in a vacuum flask before you sail. If conditions are rough, you may not feel like preparing food once you are under way; it will make life much more pleasant for the crew if this has been done before you set sail.

## STOWING GEAR

The motion aboard a small boat in a seaway can be quite rough, and will dislodge all but the best-stowed gear and equipment. Nothing is worse than a boat's interior where gear has broken loose and is scattered around the cabin, especially if it gets wet. Spend some time before you set sail ensuring that everything is stowed securely and cannot move, however far the boat heels. Impress on your crew the need for tidiness below and on deck, give them some stowage space for their personal items, and make sure that they understand where all important equipment is stowed and how it should be secured. Take a final look around below and on deck before you leave your berth.

# USING THE TENDER

A tender is needed for when you are on a mooring or at anchor and want to go ashore. The vast majority of cruisers carry an inflatable dinghy, because it is easy to stow when deflated. An inflatable is, however, difficult to row even in ideal conditions and can be impossible in a strong wind and choppy water. This is why most cruisers carry a small outboard for the tender. A small, solid dinghy makes a far better tender if you have the space to stow it; a small RIB (rigid inflatable boat) with a solid bottom and inflatable topside tubes is another alternative. Some cruisers carry their tender in davits at the stern; an inflatable can also be carried on short trips by lashing it across the pushpit. Both these arrangements create a lot of air resistance, however, and can get in the way when in port. Most inflatables are therefore stowed deflated in a cockpit locker or on deck, and are inflated by a foot or electric pump when needed.

### GETTING IN AND OUT
More sailing accidents happen using the tender than on the cruiser itself. Always wear a life jacket when using the tender, and carry a flashlight at night to warn other boats of your presence. Be especially careful when getting into and out of the tender. Inflatables seem quite stable, but they can invert like any dinghy if you put your weight in the wrong place. Inflatables also flex and move as you shift your weight, as they are not as rigid as a solid dinghy. Some boats have a stern platform, from which the dinghy can easily be boarded in calm water. If your boat has this arrangement, tie the dinghy at the stern with its painter and a stern line so that it is held securely. If your dinghy has removable oarlocks, make sure that you remove the one on the side next to the cruiser when you are alongside, or it may damage the topsides.

### ROWING IN TIDES
When rowing in tidal waters, take note of the direction and strength of the tide to avoid getting swept downtide of your destination. If you are rowing across the current, aim uptide so that you are swept down to your destination. If you have to row against the tide, row into shallow waters where the tide is weakest. Head out into the current, if necessary, only when abreast of your destination.

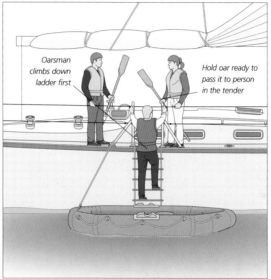

Oarsman climbs down ladder first

Hold oar ready to pass it to person in the tender

**1** The person rowing should get into the tender first. Step into the middle of the boat and sit down at once to get your weight low in the boat; sit on the middle thwart. Other crew members pass the oars down to the person in the boat and can then get aboard themselves.

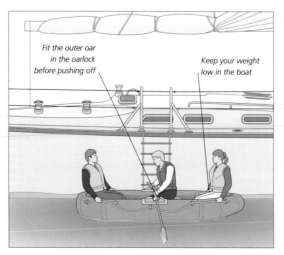

Fit the outer oar in the oarlock before pushing off

Keep your weight low in the boat

**2** Do not risk an accident by trying to cram too many people into the boat: make two trips if necessary. Once the rower has the outer oar in place, untie the tender and push it off before fitting the inboard oar into its oarlock. Reverse the procedure when coming alongside.

# HANDLING YOUR CRUISER

*The handling characteristics of a cruiser depend on a number of factors, including its hull and keel shape and its rig configuration. Every class and design of cruiser is different and will behave in its own particular way under sail and power. The differences are apparent when you are sailing at normal speed, but they are much more so when it comes to handling the boat at slow speeds and in confined spaces, such as when entering or leaving a harbor or berthing. It is these occasions that usually cause the most difficulty for inexperienced skippers and crews. The only way to become fully proficient in handling your boat is to learn how it behaves at all speeds, including when you are sailing and motoring very slowly.*

## DRIFTING CHARACTERISTICS

To start learning about your boat, take it to an area of clear water, away from other boats, and see how it behaves when left to drift. Go out under engine with the sails stowed. When you are clear of other boats, put the engine into neutral, turn the boat into the wind, and let it come to a stop. Let go of the tiller and see how the boat behaves. The bow will blow off downwind and the boat will pivot around its keel until it takes up its natural drifting position. Watch carefully to see how quickly the bow blows downwind – you will need to know this for situations when you must maneuver at slow speeds.

Some boats will lie naturally beam-on to the wind, but most point further downwind. If the wind is strong enough, you will find that you can steer the boat downwind with the windage of rig and hull giving steerage way. You should experiment to see how broad an angle either side of dead downwind you can sail under bare poles, and how quickly the boat moves through the water. Next, check to see how quickly your boat will stop

when put head-to-wind. Motor head-to-wind and put the engine in neutral. The boat will slow down and eventually stop. Note how far you have traveled before you lose rudder control and the boat comes to a complete standstill. You should repeat these exercises with a range of starting

speeds and in different wind and sea conditions to build up a complete picture of your boat's behavior.

## MAINSAIL ALONE

Once you have explored how your boat stops and drifts, hoist the mainsail alone and try sailing on all points of sailing. How well or badly your boat sails with only the mainsail will depend on the rig configuration and the underwater hull shape. Many modern cruisers sail well under mainsail alone. This is especially true of those with a fractional sloop rig, which has a proportionally larger mainsail and relies less on the headsail than a full masthead design.

You will probably find that the boat will sail downwind very easily with only the mainsail, but will perform less well on a reach or when close-hauled. The lack of a headsail will cause the boat to sail slowly on a reach. You will probably experience considerable weather helm as the boat tries to turn up into the wind and you are forced to counter this direction with a large amount of rudder.

You may find that sailing close-hauled is even more difficult. Try tacking the boat to see if it will turn through the wind and bear away onto the new tack. If your boat will tack and sail slowly to windward under mainsail alone, this will be helpful when you need to sail slowly in confined spaces. Try turning the boat in as tight a circle as possible.

◁ HEADSAIL ALONE
*Some well-balanced yachts will sail to windward under headsail alone. Try out different sizes of sails in different wind strengths to see how your boat responds.*

**MAINSAIL ALONE ▷**

*Knowing how your boat handles under mainsail alone can be particularly useful when dealing with rough weather. Here, a small cruiser is using a deep-reefed mainsail alone to sail comfortably in heavy conditions.*

You will find it easy to luff up, especially if you pull in the mainsheet rapidly as you start the turn, but bearing away will be more difficult without the headsail to assist the maneuver. The boat will need to be moving as fast as possible, and you must let the mainsheet right out before you try to turn, or the boat will respond very slowly, if at all.

Being confident in your ability to sail the boat slowly but in full control under mainsail alone is a valuable skill. It allows you to lower the jib and clear the foredeck before picking up a mooring, laying an anchor, or coming alongside, which makes life much easier for the foredeck crew.

## HEADSAIL ALONE

Now try sailing the boat under headsail alone. Set the largest headsail you can for the prevailing conditions, and put the boat on each point of sailing in turn. The boat will sail well downwind and should be comfortable all the way up to a beam reach. It will sail slower on a reach than it would with full rig, and will probably demonstrate lee helm. Try sailing on a close reach and then close-hauled, if possible, but do not be surprised if your boat will not respond well to sailing close-hauled under headsail alone. Much will depend on the amount of wind and the size of the headsail. Try changing down to a smaller headsail and see what difference that makes. Experiment with all your headsails in turn. You should repeat the exercise with different headsail sizes in as many different wind strengths and sea states as possible to determine how your boat handles. What works in ideal cruising conditions may not work in light or strong winds, or in rough seas. It is far better to find this out in an exercise than in a situation where the boat's safety – and that of the crew – depends on it.

Finally, try turning the boat in tight circles under headsail alone. The boat will bear away readily, but luffing up may be difficult as the headsail attempts to counteract the force of the rudder. Get the boat moving as fast as possible before luffing; pull in the headsail sheet slowly, letting it shake at the luff, to reduce its counter-effect on the rudder. You will probably not be able to turn a full circle, as the boat may not tack. However, at least you will find out how close to the wind you can luff while still retaining control. Beware of letting the boat slow down too much when trying to sail close-hauled under headsail alone. If it slows too much, the bow is likely to quickly blow off downwind, and you may find it difficult to regain control quickly.

# TACKING AND JIBING

*You use the same basic techniques to tack and jibe a cruiser as for a dinghy (pp.78–85). The main difference is that a cruiser is much larger and heavier and, therefore, subject to more power in the sails and greater loads on the sheets.*

### TACKING PROCEDURE
When tacking a cruiser, your aim is to turn the bow through the wind and sail the boat onto the new course with a minimum loss of speed. You will usually tack from a close-hauled course on one tack to a close-hauled course on the other in the process of beating to windward. There may be occasions, however, when you need to tack from a reach to a reach.

### CREW AND HELMSMAN
The cruiser's size and weight mean that tacking will be much slower than in a dinghy. There will also be more work for the crew because the sails are bigger. There may be more crew aboard, which will make the job easier, but they need guidance from the helmsman to coordinate their actions effectively. If you are a member of the crew, make sure that you know how the helmsman likes to perform the tack. If you are the skipper, brief the crew beforehand to avoid confusion. For example, if the boat's design makes it difficult to tack (as with a catamaran or some heavy-displacement long-keeled yachts), you may prefer the jib to be backed to help the bow turn through the wind.

### SLOWING THE TURN
By slowing down the turn once the bow has passed through the wind, the helmsman can give the crew more

## TACKING
*Prepare to tack by sailing on a close-hauled course. The skipper must ensure that the new course is clear. If there are enough crew members, it is best to have one manning each jib sheet winch. Otherwise, a single crew must prepare the new winch before releasing the old jib sheet.*

**①** The helmsman calls "ready about." A crew member puts two turns of the new sheet on its winch, and pulls in the slack. The other crew then uncleats the working jib sheet, but keeps it tight to prevent it from slipping on the winch.

**②** The crew call "ready," and the helmsman, calling "hard-a-lee," starts the tack by putting the tiller to leeward. The crew on the working sheet watches the luff of the jib, and, as it starts to flap, eases and releases the sheet.

**③** When the jib blows across to the new side, the new sheet is pulled in. When load comes on the sheet, the crew takes another turn or two on the winch. Then the handle is inserted and the crew winches the sheet in to trim the sail.

time to sheet in the jib before it fills with wind. If the helmsman is not careful or considerate, the boat may turn too far on the new tack, and it will be more difficult for the crew to sheet in the sail when it is full of wind.

## WINCHES

With self-tailing winches (*p.172*), it is easy for one crew member to sheet in the jib after tacking. The sheet is simply fed into the self-tailing groove on the top of the winch, and the handle is wound until the jib is sheeted home. With an ordinary winch, one person tails (pulls) the sheet while another winds the handle. If one person has to sheet in alone without self-tailing winches, he must tail and wind at the same time, which makes the job harder and slower.

## JIBING PROCEDURE

When jibing a cruiser, your aim is to turn the stern through the wind safely and smoothly. Although the same procedures apply to jibing a cruiser and a dinghy, a cruiser has much heavier gear. It is important therefore, to control the boom through the jibe. Do not allow it to sweep across from one side to the other (known as jibing all standing), except in light winds. If the jib is poled out, the pole must be removed before the jibe. The mainsheet traveler should be cleated in the middle of its track before the jibe. In small cruisers, or if you are sailing a larger boat in light winds, sheeting in can be done by hand. However, larger boats usually have a winch for the mainsheet to handle the high loads. Make sure the mainsheet is cleated before the jibe.

In medium and strong winds, the boat will try to turn to windward as soon as the mainsail is jibed. The helmsman should counteract the turn with the tiller by ensuring that it is on the centerline when the boom crosses the boat. If the boat still tries to turn, he must be ready to adjust the tiller once again. Once the boom has swung across under control, the mainsheet should be eased rapidly to set the mainsail at its correct angle. On all but the smallest cruisers, it is easier if a crew member handles the mainsheet.

## JIBING

*Prepare to jibe by sailing on a run. In strong winds, the boom should be pulled in tight to prevent it from sweeping across the boat as you jibe, which may cause damage or injury. On larger boats, the mainsheet is often led to a winch and the sheet must be winched in, except in light winds.*

**①** The helmsman warns the crew by calling "stand-by to jibe," and pulls in the mainsheet to bring the boom toward the centerline. If the mainsheet runs on a traveler across the cockpit, the traveler is cleated in the center before the jibe.

**②** While one crew member prepares the new jib sheet by taking a turn or two on the winch and pulling in any slack, the other uncleats the working sheet and prepares to release it. When the crew are ready they tell the helmsman.

**③** The helmsman pulls the tiller to windward, calling "jibe-oh." As the jib blows across the bow, the crew releases the old sheet as the new one is pulled in. The helmsman quickly lets the mainsheet out to set the mainsail on the new side.

# SAIL BALANCE

*Keeping a sailing boat balanced is as important in a cruiser as it is in a sailing dinghy. When a dinghy gets out of balance, it is usually quickly apparent as the boat heels, slows down, and develops more weather or lee helm (p.112). The same occurs in a cruiser, but, because of its greater size and weight, and its relatively slow response, you may find it harder to spot when the boat is not well balanced. Get to know your boat so that you understand the best sail trim for all conditions.*

## BOAT TUNING

Many cruising sailors think that boat tuning is only of interest to racing sailors. Nothing could be further from the truth. A well-tuned cruising boat will sail faster, heel less, and exhibit much less weather helm than a boat whose owner has not taken the trouble to ensure that the rig and sails are working in harmony. While ultimate speed is not the cruising sailor's main objective, achieving better speed while heeling less will allow the cruiser to make faster, and more comfortable, passages. Good balance can also be a distinct safety feature since it is easier to handle heavy weather in a boat that is balanced correctly. A cruiser's rig and sails are tuned using the same principles that apply to tuning a dinghy (*pp.136–39*). If you find it difficult to tune your boat, ask your sailmaker to sail it and advise you on any changes that may be required to mast rake, mast bend, and sail shape.

## WEATHER AND LEE HELM

Most yachts have a degree of weather helm, but it should never become so great as to require large amounts of rudder deflection to keep the boat on course. Similarly, lee helm should not be permitted as it makes it very difficult to keep the boat on course and it can be dangerous. If the boat has lee helm and the wheel or tiller is released for any reason, the boat will bear away and keep sailing, possibly

## ▽ GOOD SAIL BALANCE

*This cruiser is sailing fast with little heel while close-hauled in moderate to strong winds. The mainsail has been reefed and sail balance has been maintained by partly furling the roller-reefing headsail.*

## △ BEARING AWAY

*This crew are using the sails correctly to help the boat bear away smoothly without heeling. A crew lets out the mainsheet as the helmsman bears away, while the headsail is kept full to assist the turn.*

accelerating as it does so, rather than turning head-to-wind and stopping as it should. This can lead to accidents and should be avoided.

Try your boat on a close-hauled course in a good Force 3–4 breeze. With the boat sailing properly to windward, there should be a small amount of weather helm. If there is too much weather helm or, worse still, lee helm, you must tune your boat to get the desired balance.

## TURNING FORCES

The sails on a cruiser create exactly the same turning forces as they do on a dinghy (*pp.66–67*), but many cruising sailors fail to use (or to make allowances for) these forces. Instead, they rely solely on the rudder to turn the boat. This can lead to loss of control in strong winds, so you should always remember to use the sails to assist you when altering course. This is especially important when bearing away in strong winds.

## HEAVING-TO

Heaving-to can be a very useful technique in a cruiser. You can heave-to to stop the boat in order to prepare and eat a meal in comfort, or to take in a reef if the wind strength increases. Heaving-to is also often a good tactic for riding out rough weather.

### HOW TO HEAVE-TO

The procedure for heaving-to in cruisers is the same as that for dinghies (*p.88*). The headsail is sheeted to windward to balance the actions of the mainsail and rudder. The precise arrangement depends on the type of cruiser. Traditional long-keeled craft often heave-to very well, typically lying with the wind between 45° and 60° off the bow. Modern cruisers, with shallower hulls and shorter keels, do not always heave-to so steadily, but you should be able to achieve an angle of about 60° off the wind.

Experiment with your boat and try different combinations of mainsail and rudder position. A typical arrangement has the jib sheeted hard aback, with the mainsail eased slightly, and the tiller lashed to leeward. If the boat will not lie close to the wind, try using a smaller headsail. A boat hove-to drifts at between 90° and 135° to the wind direction, but it will lie much more quietly than if it were sailing.

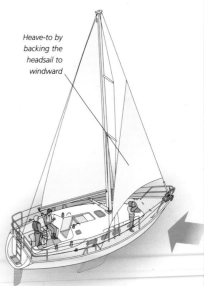

*Heave-to by backing the headsail to windward*

### △ HOVE-TO

*A cruiser is hove-to by tacking while leaving the headsail sheet cleated on the old side. The tiller should be lashed to leeward (or the wheel lashed to windward) so that if the boat does try to sail it will turn toward the wind and stop.*

# REDUCING SAIL AREA

*For all sailing boats, there is a certain wind strength in which the boat is fully powered up. Beyond this optimum load, the boat will be overpowered, will heel excessively, slow down, and be harder to steer. The wind speed at which this overpowering occurs varies according to boat type, size, rig, and keel shape. It also depends on sea conditions and air temperature. In smooth water and warm air, a yacht will be more comfortable at a higher wind speed than if conditions are rough or cold. Cold air is heavier and exerts more force on the sails. Rough seas throw the boat about, making it wetter to sail and harder to steer. Whatever the prevailing conditions, it is important to know when your boat is over-pressed and to take action by reducing sail area.*

## KNOWING YOUR BOAT

A relatively narrow, moderate- or heavy-displacement yacht with a long keel will sail to windward well-heeled, and will be comfortable with the lee rail down to the water. On the other hand, a wide, light-displacement yacht is designed to sail much more upright and will become uncomfortable if pressed beyond about 20°. Get to know your boat's idiosyncrasies, so that you can reduce sail in good time before the boat starts to struggle.

## REDUCING HEADSAIL SIZE

How you reduce sail area depends on the type of rig in your boat. In most Bermudan sloops, the first step is to reduce the size of the headsail, especially when you are carrying an overlapping genoa. If you sail with a roller-reefing headsail, you simply need to take a few rolls in the sail by easing the sheet and pulling in on the furling line. When sufficient sail has been rolled away, the furling line is cleated and the sail sheeted in again. The main problem with this system is that it rarely results in a well-setting sail once a few rolls have been taken

in. Roller-reefed headsails usually develop a baggy shape that makes them inefficient when sailing to windward and adds to the heeling forces (which is the opposite of what is required). Nevertheless, many

coastal cruising sailors choose to sail with this equipment because of the ease with which the sail can be reefed and furled on the forestay.

## CHANGING HEADSAILS

The alternative to a roller-reefing system is to have a number of headsails of various sizes to suit different conditions. These are hanked onto the forestay when in use. If you plan to sail far offshore, or expect to have to deal with rough weather on a regular basis, this system offers the advantages of being simple, efficient, and less prone to gear failure and jamming.

To change a hanked-on headsail, the old sail is lowered, unhanked, and the sheets removed from its clew. The old sail is stowed away in its bag, and the new sail is attached and hoisted in

---

### REEFING HEADSAILS

Some jibs designed for heavy weather have a row of reef points so that they can be reduced in size quickly and easily. To reduce their area, the sail is partly lowered and the new tack fitting attached to the bow. The sheets are moved to the new clew and the sail is set.

*Area of sail to be reefed*

△ **UNREEFED**
*A reefing headsail is made slightly heavier and stronger than a normal sail of the same size, but is set in the usual way if unreefed.*

*Line furls middle of sail*

△ **REEFED**
*When reefed, the upper tack and clew fittings are used. The bundle of loose sail along the foot is laced with a light line.*

△ **REEFED IN ROUGH WEATHER**
*This yacht has a deeply reefed mainsail and a small jib set to sail upwind in rough weather without undue heeling.*

the normal way. Changing a hanked-on headsail requires at least one crew member to go forward and work on the foredeck, which will be wet and moving quite violently in rough weather. The job is made easier if two crew are available to work together, one handling the halyard, and the other changing the sail at the bow.

If you are sailing upwind when you need to change a headsail, you should slow the boat down to make the task easier and safer before you send someone forward. This can be done by easing the sails or heaving-to. Alternatively, you could alter course downwind, which will bring the boat upright and reduce the strength of the apparent wind. The crew going forward should always move along the windward sidedeck and be clipped on. When moving a heavy sailbag, drag it rather than carry it. Move forward on your hands and knees if the motion is difficult. Once on the foredeck, brace yourself in a secure position before starting the job.

## REEFING THE MAINSAIL

*Once the headsail has been reduced, the next step is to reef the mainsail. If the reefing gear is properly organized, reefing should be a quick and easy operation. In many boats, the procedure can be carried out from the security of the cockpit. Slab reefing is the most common system, but there are other systems that roll the mainsail away inside the mast, or inside or around the boom. These systems, however, rely on additional mechanical equipment, and do not give such a good sail shape. They are unnecessary on most cruisers.*

**①** First, ease the mainsheet to spill all the wind from the mainsail. Then ease the boom vang. Take the weight of the boom on the topping lift, unless you have a solid vang that will safely support the boom.

**②** Ease the halyard to bring the first reef down to boom level. Pull the luff reef cringle down to the boom by using a reef line, or by hooking it under a ram's horn at the gooseneck, and tighten the halyard.

**③** Pull the leech reef line tight to pull the leech cringle down and out toward the boom end. There must be no wind in the sail while doing this, and the vang must be loose or the sail may tear.

**④** Keep winching in the leech reefing line until the reef cringle is pulled down tightly to the boom. Release the topping lift, trim the mainsheet, and tighten the vang. Check that the halyard tension is sufficient.

**⑤** There is now a fold of sail hanging down along the length of the boom. This can be left free, or tidied into a neat roll and secured by a light line laced through the reef cringles from leech to luff.

# INCREASING SAIL AREA

*T*he modern Bermudan sloop is the most efficient rig upwind, but it tends to be underpowered downwind in light and moderate breezes. In these conditions, it is necessary to increase the sail area to maintain performance. This can be achieved by hoisting a conventional or asymmetric spinnaker, or a gennaker (sometimes called a cruising chute). Many cruiser sailors worry about using a spinnaker, but it need not be a problem if the right techniques and equipment are used to control it.

## DOWNWIND SAILS

Cruiser spinnakers are bigger, more powerful, and made of heavier sailcloth than their dinghy equivalents. There is a range of sail shapes, cloth weights, and construction methods available. Many cruisers have a single, general-purpose spinnaker (usually a tri-radial sail; *pp.122–27*), used when reaching or running. For light weather, some cruisers carry a lighter cross-cut or radial headsail.

Cruiser-racers carry a number of different spinnakers for running or reaching in various wind strengths.

## ASYMMETRICS

Some modern, fast cruisers use asymmetric spinnakers rather than the conventional type. An asymmetric does not use a spinnaker pole, but requires a bowsprit – often made of carbon fiber for lightness – to hold the sail's tack ahead of the bow. The bowsprit is usually extended and retracted by control lines. The lack of a pole makes an asymmetric easier to use than a conventional spinnaker. An asymmetric uses two sheets, like a headsail, but the lazy sheet is led around the forestay rather than between the stay and the mast.

An asymmetric is efficient on a beam or broad reach but less so on a dead run, because it falls into the wind shadow of the mainsail. Cruiser-racers that use an asymmetric tend not to sail dead downwind. Their light weight and surfing ability make it more effective to sail downwind on a series of broad reaches.

## USING GENNAKERS

Like an asymmetric spinnaker, a gennaker does not use a spinnaker pole and is sheeted in the same way as a headsail. It is not usually as large or as powerful, however, and is attached at the tack to the bow-fitting rather than to a bowsprit. This makes it easy to use. However, a gennaker is inefficient on a dead run, as it is blanketed behind the mainsail. To overcome this, the gennaker's clew can be held out to windward with a pole.

◁ **SPINNAKER**
*The conventional, all-purpose spinnaker, as flown by this cruiser, adds considerably to the sail area and increases the boat's speed and efficiency downwind.*

**GENNAKER** ▷

*The gennaker is a useful sail to use to increase downwind speed. It is easier to handle than a spinnaker, but is less efficient, especially on a run.*

## SPINNAKER EQUIPMENT

A conventional spinnaker is flown from a spinnaker pole attached to a bracket on the mast. The bracket is usually fitted to a track to allow the height of the pole's inner end to be adjusted. On most small and medium-sized cruisers, the pole has two identical end fittings, each opened and closed with a plunger, to allow either end to be attached to the mast bracket. Larger boats usually have a single-ended pole with a plunger at the outer end and a ball fitting at the inner end that fits into a cup-shaped bracket that swivels on the mast track.

The pole is held horizontal by an uphaul and downhaul. On small cruisers, the spinnaker downhaul is attached midway along the underside of the pole and runs through a block at the base of the mast, and then to the cockpit for adjustment. On larger boats, the downhaul is often called the foreguy. It is attached to the outer end of the pole. The foreguy is led through a block near the bow, and then aft for adjustment.

The conventional spinnaker is controlled by a sheet attached to its clew and a guy attached to its tack. The guy is led through the end of the spinnaker pole. Except on small cruisers, twin sheets and guys are used, with one pair rigged on each side. Only one pair is used at any one time. The windward guy leads from the tack, through the pole end, then through a block ahead of the cockpit, and to a winch. The leeward sheet runs from the clew through a block at the stern and onto a winch.

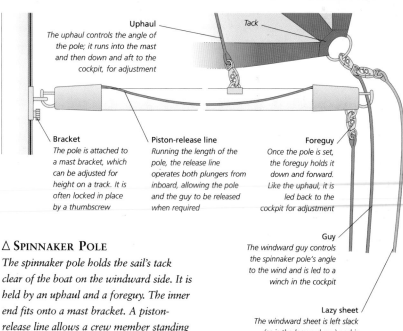

**Uphaul**
*The uphaul controls the angle of the pole; it runs into the mast and then down and aft to the cockpit, for adjustment*

**Tack**

**Bracket**
*The pole is attached to a mast bracket, which can be adjusted for height on a track. It is often locked in place by a thumbscrew*

**Piston-release line**
*Running the length of the pole, the release line operates both plungers from inboard, allowing the pole and the guy to be released when required*

**Foreguy**
*Once the pole is set, the foreguy holds it down and forward. Like the uphaul, it is led back to the cockpit for adjustment*

**Guy**
*The windward guy controls the spinnaker pole's angle to the wind and is led to a winch in the cockpit*

**Lazy sheet**
*The windward sheet is left slack (as is the leeward guy) and is called the lazy sheet.*

### △ SPINNAKER POLE

*The spinnaker pole holds the sail's tack clear of the boat on the windward side. It is held by an uphaul and a foreguy. The inner end fits onto a mast bracket. A piston-release line allows a crew member standing at the mast to release the guy from the pole.*

# HANDLING DOWNWIND SAILS

## PREPARING A CONVENTIONAL SPINNAKER

Before hoisting a spinnaker from its bag, check that the sail has been packed properly in the bag without twists. When you are ready to hoist the spinnaker, attach the bag to the pulpit or to the leeward guardrail. Then attach the halyard to the head. Fasten a guy to each clew, and a sheet to each guy shackle (not to the clews). Each guy is led outside all the rigging, through a block on the toerail forward of the cockpit, and then to a winch. Each sheet is led outside all rigging and through a block aft of the cockpit, before going to a winch. When the sail is hoisted, its windward sheet and leeward guy are left slack, or "lazy," while the sail is controlled by the "working" guy to windward and the sheet to leeward.

The spinnaker pole must be rigged before the sail is hoisted. Attach the inner end to the mast fitting and the uphaul and downhaul to the outer end. The working guy is then dropped into the outer-end fitting, and the pole is hoisted to a horizontal position with the uphaul.

## PREPARING AN ASYMMETRIC SPINNAKER OR GENNAKER

If the sail is to be hoisted from a bag, fasten the bag to the pulpit or the leeward guardrail. Attach two sheets to the clew, with the windward sheet led around the forestay. Each sheet is led through a turning block aft, then forward to a winch. Attach the tack to the stem fitting (for a gennaker) or to the end of a bowsprit (for an asymmetric). If a retractable bowsprit is used, this must be extended and the sail's tack attached to the line used to pull it to the end of the bowsprit.

## HOISTING

*To hoist any downwind sail from a bag, steer onto a broad reach with the headsail still hoisted. Then hoist the sail, and cleat its halyard. With a spinnaker, pull the guy to get the clew to the end of the pole as the sail goes up, but leave the sheet slack. Then trim the guy to bring the pole aft until it is at right angles to the apparent wind. Once the pole is in the correct position, cleat the guy and trim the sheet to fill the sail. Asymmetrics or gennakers are easier to set, as there is only a sheet that has to be trimmed.*

**1** Attach the spinnaker bag to the pulpit (as here), or, if you have a hanked-on headsail, to the leeward guardrail. Fasten the bag in position with its straps.

**2** Attach the halyard to the head of the sail and a sheet and guy to both clews. Check that the sheets and guys are led correctly and not caught under any gear.

**3** Rig the spinnaker pole with the windward guy led through the end of the pole, and check that the halyard is clear.

**4** Pull the halyard to hoist the sail to the masthead as quickly as possible. Pull the guy to bring the clew to the pole end.

**5** Once the spinnaker is hoisted and sheeted, furl or lower the headsail. Stow it ready to be hoisted again when needed.

## LOWERING

*When lowering a spinnaker, the sail must be kept under complete control until it is in its bag or below deck. The safest technique with any downwind sail is to steer first onto a run or broad reach so that the sail can be lowered in the wind shadow behind the mainsail. The sail's tack is then released from the guy by tripping its quick-release shackle. The sail is pulled in under the main boom, using the lazy guy, as the halyard is eased. The quickest option is usually to lower the sail straight into the companionway, packing it in its bag later when the sheets and halyards have been removed and stowed. Do not lower the sail faster than it can be gathered in: you may lose control and the sail will end up in the water.*

**①** The guy is eased to let the pole forward, and the uphaul is eased to lower it to within reach of the foredeck crew. He should brace himself securely and keep his head safely below the pole. He releases the sail by tripping the shackle that attaches the guy to the tack.

**②** As soon as the sail has been tripped from the working guy, the cockpit crew begin pulling in the lazy (leeward) guy to bring the sail over the lifelines and under the boom. The halyard is eased as fast as the crew can pull in the sail and bundle it down the companionway hatch.

## USING A SOCK

The trick to handling all lightweight, downwind sails is to keep them under full control during hoisting and lowering. The easiest way to do this on a short-handed cruising boat is to use a sock. This is a lightweight nylon tube, with a bell-shaped opening at the lower end, and two light control lines to pull the bell up and down. The sock can be used with a conventional spinnaker, an asymmetric spinnaker, or a gennaker. The sock covers the sail during hoisting and lowering, being pulled up out of the way when the sail is set.

### HOISTING WITH A SOCK

With the sail stowed in its sock, the top of the sock is attached to the halyard, and the sail's sheets and guys are rigged. The head of the sock is then hoisted to the masthead. When the halyard has been cleated, pull the sock up clear of the sail using its uphaul, and set the sail in the normal way.

on a gennaker. Then pull the sock down using the sock's downhaul until it encases the sail. Once all of the sail is in the sock, lower the halyard and gather the sock tube onto the foredeck. Remove and stow the sheets, guys and halyard. The sock is stowed with the sail left inside it ready for use.

### LOWERING WITH A SOCK

To lower the sail, first steer onto a broad reach and hoist the headsail. The object is to collapse the downwind sail in the lee of the mainsail. To collapse the sail, ease the guy of a spinnaker, the tack line on an asymmetric spinnaker, or the sheet

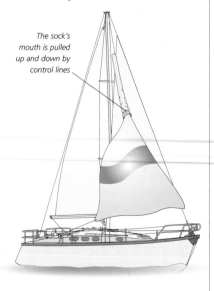

*The sock's mouth is pulled up and down by control lines*

**USING A SOCK ▷**
*A sock makes it far easier to hoist and lower any downwind sail because the sail is held under control, inside the sock, during these tricky procedures. Make sure that the sail is fastened firmly to the top of the sock and fit a swivel between the sock and the halyard to prevent the sock from twisting in use.*

# TRIMMING DOWNWIND SAILS

The secret to trimming all downwind sails is to ease the sheet as much as possible without collapsing the luff of the sail. With a gennaker or an asymmetric spinnaker, the tack is fixed to the bow or to the end of a bowsprit, and only the sheet needs adjusting. A conventional spinnaker is more complex, as both the guy and sheet must be adjusted to trim the sail.

## ADJUSTING THE POLE

With a conventional spinnaker, the pole is trimmed aft by pulling on the guy. Remember to ease the foreguy first or the pole will be held forward. Trim the guy until the pole is just forward of a position at right angles to the apparent wind. Cleat the guy, tighten the foreguy, and use the sheet to trim the sail. If the apparent wind moves forward or aft, the pole angle must be adjusted using the guy to put it back in the correct position. In light winds, the pole can be lowered to keep the clews level and help the sail set. In medium winds, you need to make sure that the pole is kept horizontal by adjusting the uphaul and foreguy. In strong winds, the pole can be set higher to move the sail's foot further away from the mainsail.

## PLAYING THE SHEET

For maximum performance, the sheet on all downwind sails should be constantly adjusted to keep the sail eased as much as possible without it collapsing. Most well-cut downwind sails can be eased until they curl at the luff. This will happen when the sail is perfectly trimmed. You will still be able to ease more sheet before the sail collapses. If it does collapse, it will be necessary to pull the sheet in quite vigorously before the sail fills again.

Once the sail has filled, ease out most of the sheet you have just pulled in. Unless you do this, the sail will be over-trimmed, and the boat will slow down, heel more, and be harder to steer, possibly leading to a broach in stronger winds (*below*).

In most situations, a cruiser's crew will not wish to constantly play the sheet. In this case, the sheet should be slightly overtrimmed and then cleated.

## JIBING A GENNAKER OR ASYMMETRIC SPINNAKER

Jibing a gennaker or an asymmetric spinnaker is quite easy, as both are controlled by two sheets (just like a headsail). The lazy, windward sheet of the gennaker leads from the clew forward around the back of the sail and around its luff, and back to its fairlead and winch. The asymmetric's windward sheet can be rigged in the same way. Alternatively, it can lead inside the sail's luff (but outside the forestay), in which case it will jibe inside its luff (like a headsail), rather than outside it. In either case, the sail is jibed by easing the old sheet as the boat jibes, and pulling in the new one. Where an asymmetric has to pass inside its luff, the new sheet should be pulled in as much as possible before the old one is completely eased.

---

## BROACHING

Broaching may occur when the boat is sailing under a downwind sail in moderate to strong winds and the sail is sheeted in too hard. The boat heels, and rounds up very quickly toward the wind.

### AVOIDING A BROACH

The best way to avoid a broach is to reduce sail area in good time when sailing in moderate to strong winds. A broach occurs when the boat is pressed too hard and turning forces develop that overcome the effect of the rudder. A broach is most likely to occur in large waves, which make it difficult to keep the boat balanced. Once a broach begins the helmsman will have no control of the boat's direction as the boat spins round toward the wind and heels violently. Even in moderate winds, a broach can occur when sailing on a reach under spinnaker if the sheet is pulled in too much, causing the boat to slow down and heel – the first signs of a broach. Drop the spinnaker if a rising wind threatens a broach, and sail under mainsail and jib (*right*).

△ **REGAINING CONTROL**
*This cruiser-racer has broached violently under spinnaker. Now beam-on to the strong wind, with her boom end in the water, the boat is heeling heavily. In order to regain control, the crew must let go of the boom vang and spinnaker sheet.*

## JIBING A SPINNAKER

*Jibing a conventional spinnaker is complicated by the need to move the pole from the old to the new windward side. It is important that both the spinnaker and the pole are kept under full control throughout the maneuver. Small cruisers may have a dinghy-like double-ended pole system, in which case the jibing method for dinghies (pp.120–21) is used. Larger cruisers often have a single-ended pole, with the uphaul and foreguy led to the outer end of the pole. With this system, the dip-pole method of jibing is used, as here. This is complicated for the crew, and requires practice.*

**(1)** The foredeck crew releases the guy from the pole end by pulling the piston-release line. The inner end of the pole is raised, and the uphaul eased, to drop the outer end of the pole inside the forestay.

**(2)** The foredeck crew takes a bight of the old lazy guy forward, and guides the pole end inside the forestay. He clips the guy into the pole end fitting.

**(3)** The inner end of the pole is now lowered to its normal position and the outer end is raised with the uphaul. The guy is trimmed to pull the pole end aft.

**(4)** The mainsail was sheeted near the centerline during the spinnaker jibe to avoid it blanketing the spinnaker. The mainsail is now jibed (*p.181*).

**(5)** With the boat on its new course, the mainsail is let out to its correct position. The guy is used to set the pole angle, and the spinnaker is trimmed with the sheet.

## MAINSAIL AND HEADSAIL

In moderate to strong winds, most cruisers will not use additional downwind sails, but will sail downwind under mainsail and a headsail. Many cruisers suffer from a rolling motion sailing downwind if these sails are not set correctly.

### MAINSAIL CONTROL

Set the mainsheet so the boom is just clear of the shrouds. Then tighten the vang. This prevents the boom from lifting, and stops the mainsail from twisting forward at the top. This will reduce rolling. In light to moderate winds, ease the mainsail outhaul to make the sail fuller. In strong winds, tighten it as much as possible to flatten the sail. When sailing in strong winds, rig a line as a boom preventer to avoid an accidental jibe. Run it from the end of the boom, outside all the gear, to a block on the foredeck, then back to a cleat in the cockpit.

*Pole holds headsail to windward to increase effective sail area*

### △ POLING OUT

*If the wind is too strong for a spinnaker, pole the headsail out to windward when on a run or broad reach, to add speed and reduce rolling.*

# HANDLING UNDER POWER

*P*ressures of time, busy sailing areas, and crowded marinas mean that most cruisers are now fitted with engines. Modern marine engines are far more reliable than their predecessors, and usually work when required. However, you should still allow for a possible engine failure. Have an anchor ready to let go, and sails ready to hoist, whenever engine failure could cause problems. A boat under power does not steer like a car, and factors, such as prop walk, will affect the boat's handling.

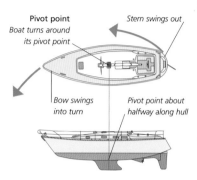

Pivot point
*Boat turns around its pivot point*

Stern swings out

Bow swings into turn

Pivot point about halfway along hull

### △ THE WAY BOATS TURN

*When a boat is turned, its stern does not follow the bow through the turn. Instead, the boat pivots and the stern swings out.*

## BOAT HANDLING

People who are new to sailing often make the mistake of assuming that a boat steers in the same way as a car. In fact, when a boat turns, it pivots about a point near its center, and the stern swings out away from the direction of the turn. When handling the boat in a confined space, you should be aware of the stern's swing as you turn the boat.

## PROPELLER EFFECTS

The key to handling a boat well under power is understanding the propeller effect called "prop walk." Water density increases with depth, so the lower blade of a turning propeller is always in denser water than the upper blade. This creates a paddlewheel effect, which tends to push the stern sideways in the same direction in which the propeller rotates. A typical

right-handed or clockwise-rotating propeller tends to "walk" the stern to starboard when moving forward. With most gearboxes, the direction of rotation reverses when going astern, so the propeller tends to "walk" the stern to port.

When going ahead, the rudder is more efficient and will easily counter prop walk as soon as you have steerage way. When going astern, however, the rudder is less effective on most boats, especially at the slow speeds normally used in reverse, and prop walk will be more apparent. You can discover the extent and direction of prop walk in reverse before you leave your berth. With the boat tied up securely, put the engine in reverse at half throttle. Look over the side to see from which direction water turbulence appears. This is the flow off the propeller. If free to move, the stern will swing away from the disturbance.

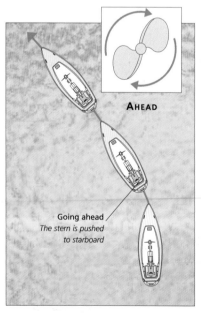

**AHEAD**

Going ahead
*The stern is pushed to starboard*

### △ PROP WALK AHEAD

*With a clockwise-rotating propeller, the stern will tend to move to starboard when the engine is running ahead.*

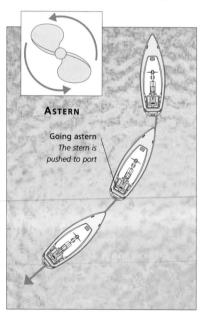

**ASTERN**

Going astern
*The stern is pushed to port*

### △ PROP WALK ASTERN

*With a conventional gearbox, the propeller rotates counterclockwise when running astern and pulls the stern to port.*

## BOAT CHARACTERISTICS

How a boat handles under power depends on a number of factors. These include engine size, propeller location and direction of rotation, type of keel and rudder, and the amount of wind resistance above decks. A long-keeled boat with its rudder hung on the back of the keel is usually difficult to steer when going astern. In some cases, it may be impossible to get such a boat to go astern in a straight line. It is important to know your boat's limitations so that you can plan your maneuvers to avoid such situations. The effect of wind on the boat can also help or hinder your maneuvers. A wind blowing from the side tends to push a boat's bow downwind when moving at slow speed. If this effect counteracts the effect of prop walk, you may be able to reverse in a straight line. If the wind contributes to the prop walk effect, you will not be able to stop the bow from turning rapidly downwind.

## STEERING UNDER POWER

Many modern fin-keeled cruisers, especially those with a spade rudder, steer astern well, even at slow speeds. If you are steering this sort of boat using a tiller, however, beware when motoring quickly astern. The forces on the rudder can be strong and will be transmitted to the tiller. Unless you hold it firmly and avoid large movements, the tiller may be wrenched from your grasp and swing violently to one side. If this happens, the boat will turn rapidly, and you may be trapped by the tiller unless you stand clear of its end.

You will be using the engine to maneuver in confined spaces, so you must learn how your boat behaves in different conditions. Experiment in a stretch of clear water to find out how it handles. Try steering in a straight line astern at different speeds, check the extent of prop walk, and see how tight a turning circle you can achieve under full power, half power, and at

low speed. Prop walk will result in a tighter turning circle in one direction, often when turning to port going ahead or astern. When motoring astern, remember that the effect of moving the tiller is reversed: the bow will swing in the direction in which the tiller is moved, whereas the stern moves in the opposite direction. Keep practicing your handling skills until you are fully proficient at turning the boat in tight spaces. Even then, always plan for the unexpected, and have an anchor and sails ready for instant use.

---

### TURNING UNDER POWER

Turning in a confined space is usually the most difficult maneuver under power. Unless you have the space to execute a power turn with the helm hard over, you will need to use your slow-speed handling skills and any wind effects to help you turn safely under full control. Prop walk can also be very helpful.

#### PROP WALK

If the stern moves to port under prop walk when you go astern, start your turn to starboard. Put the tiller hard over to port and hold it there. Power the engine for a few seconds to start the boat turning. With the rudder hard over, the water pushed by the propeller is deflected by the rudder. This makes the stern move in the opposite direction. Shift to neutral when the boat moves forward. Reverse and give another burst of power, keeping the tiller hard over to port. Prop walk in reverse moves the stern to port. As the boat moves astern, shift into forward gear and give another burst of power.

#### ▽ TURNING WITH PROP WALK
*Use alternating ahead and astern bursts of power from the engine to turn, with the tiller held hard over. The aim is to use the propeller thrust to turn without moving the boat forward or backward significantly.*

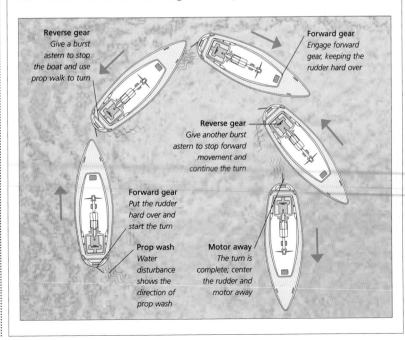

**Reverse gear**
*Give a burst astern to stop the boat and use prop walk to turn*

**Forward gear**
*Engage forward gear, keeping the rudder hard over*

**Reverse gear**
*Give another burst astern to stop forward movement and continue the turn*

**Forward gear**
*Put the rudder hard over and start the turn*

**Prop wash**
*Water disturbance shows the direction of prop wash*

**Motor away**
*The turn is complete; center the rudder and motor away*

# ALONGSIDE BERTHS

*I*t is very common for cruisers to berth alongside a dock or quay. Floating docks tend to be preferred in tidal waters because they float and are thus able to move up and down with the rise and fall of the tide. This means that you do not have to adjust your warps to allow for changes in the water level. With quay walls, however, your boat will rise and fall in relation to the wall as you lie alongside, and may even dry out if the harbor is shallow. In addition, quays are often busy with fishing boats and other craft. This makes maneuvering more difficult, and yachts may have to raft alongside one another in order to save space. All alongside berths present different challenges, but the basic methods of coming alongside and leaving are the same.

## CHOOSING A BERTH

Your choice of berth will determine the comfort of your stay. If possible, choose a berth that is sheltered from the wind and any swell. If the berth is affected by a swell rolling into the harbor, the boat could be damaged. Always lie on the lee side of a dock or quay if possible, so that the yacht is pushed off by the wind rather than being pressed against the berth. This will make it easier to leave and will provide a more comfortable stay. If you cannot lie on the leeward side of a berth, the next best option is to lie head-to-wind, as this keeps the companionway sheltered. If strong winds are forecast and you need to be able to leave quickly, avoid lying on the windward side of a dock.

Be aware of your boat's handling characteristics at slow speed, and do not attempt to enter a tight marina berth if it is too difficult to leave safely. Alongside berths have obvious attractions, but it is often safer, more comfortable, and cheaper to anchor or pick up a mooring elsewhere.

### EFFECTS OF WIND AND TIDE

When approaching or leaving an alongside berth, the most important factor is the combined effect of wind and tide on your boat. As usual when handling a boat in close quarters, you should always try to leave or arrive at a berth pointing into the strongest element. If in doubt, assume that the tide will have the greatest effect. When approaching a berth under power or sail, the aim is to stop the

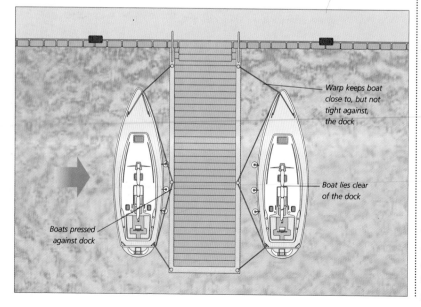

Warp keeps boat close to, but not tight against, the dock

Boat lies clear of the dock

Boats pressed against dock

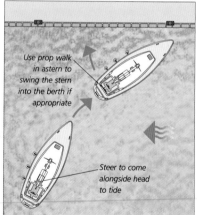

Use prop walk in astern to swing the stern into the berth if appropriate

Steer to come alongside head to tide

### △ HEAD-TO-TIDE

*Approach a berth into the tide, using it to stop the boat by the quayside. Use prop walk to swing the stern into the berth.*

### ◁ LEEWARD BERTH

*It is more comfortable to berth on the leeward side of the dock, where the boat is held off by the wind instead of being pushed against the dock.*

boat in the chosen position alongside the berth so that the crew can step – not jump – safely ashore and secure the lines. In the absence of any tide, head into the wind, if possible, and use the boat's wind resistance to help you slow down and stop. When a tidal stream is present, this will usually have the strongest effect on the boat. Except in a strong wind and weak tide, you should choose to stem the tide in your final approach.

Never attempt to come alongside a berth downtide in a strong stream. Even with a powerful engine, it will be very hard to stop the boat where you choose. The same considerations apply to leaving a berth: always leave pointing into the strongest element if possible. Sometimes you will find that you are berthed stern-to a strong tide. In this situation, you will have to leave astern or turn the boat in its berth using warps (*p.168*).

## USING FENDERS

Fenders are used to protect the boat from contact with whatever it is lying alongside. They should be concentrated around the point of maximum beam, not spaced at even intervals along the hull.

### TYPES OF FENDERS
Plastic fenders are made in a variety of shapes and sizes. You should use at least four when lying alongside, and have some spare in case someone berths alongside without enough fenders to protect both craft. The movement of fenders can itself damage the gelcoat or paint on the hull. You can avoid this by hanging a fender skirt between the hull and the fenders. When mooring alongside an uneven quay wall, it can be difficult to keep the fenders in position; a fender board (a wooden plank) hung outboard of the fenders solves this problem.

△ **ATTACHING FENDERS**
*Attach the fenders to the coach-roof handrails or the toe rail. Avoid attaching them to the lifelines or stanchions, which may by damaged by their movement.*

## DRYING OUT ALONGSIDE

It is sometimes necessary to dry out alongside a quay, either to work on the hull or because the harbor dries at low tide. How well a boat behaves depends on its keel shape and configuration. Multihulls sit happily upright on their hulls, and long-keeled boats dry out well sitting on their keel and leaning against a wall. Fin-keeled boats with narrow keels are less stable and are prone to tipping down at bow or stern.

### INITIAL CHECK
Ask the harbor master about the state of the bottom before you dry out. Debris on the seabed can damage a hull or keel. If the seabed slopes steeply away from the wall, the keel could slip outward and cause damage to the hull.

### CORRECT ANGLE
Once in the berth, ensure that the boat leans slightly in toward the wall as it drops on the ebbing tide. Achieve this by placing heavy gear, such as the anchor and chain, on the sidedeck nearest to the wall, or by leading a halyard to a strong point on shore.

Tighten the halyard as the boat drops to keep it heeling slightly toward the wall. You must also ensure that the mooring warps are arranged so that the boat cannot move too far from the wall as it drops, otherwise it will lean in at a large angle and could damage its topsides or rigging. Make sure that all warps lead out through fairleads and not under the lifelines; lash the warps into any open fairleads if there is a danger of lines lifting out of them. The further you can lead your warps fore and aft of the boat, the less you will need to adjust them as the tide rises and falls.

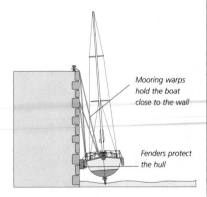

*Mooring warps hold the boat close to the wall*

*Fenders protect the hull*

△ **DRYING BERTH**
*Secure your boat close to the quay wall with warps and use plenty of fenders to protect the hull while drying out.*

# LEAVING A BERTH

When you are preparing to leave an alongside berth, make a careful observation of all the factors that could affect the maneuver. Assess the strength and direction of wind and tide and their relative effects on your boat. Sound knowledge of your boat's handling characteristics will be of value here, especially with regard to its behavior at slow speed, its drifting characteristics, and how it reacts to wind on the beam. Look out for any obstructions in the vicinity, and decide how to clear them. Consider the strength and experience of your crew. If the wind is light, there is little tide running, and there are no obstructions nearby, it is often easy to untie the warps, push the boat off, and sail or motor away. Most situations are more complex, however, and it takes careful preparation and execution to avoid damaging the boat.

## PREPARING TO LEAVE
After taking all the factors into consideration, decide on a plan to leave the berth and brief the crew. The task will be easier with a full crew, but if you sail single-handed or with just one other person, you should work out routines that suit your particular boat and crew.

In many cases, it is easiest and safest to leave under power, as this can give you greater control. Do not, however, assume that you must always use the engine. Many berths can be left safely under sail, and it is satisfying and instructive to do so when possible. If you do need to use your engine, start it and leave it running in neutral to give it time to warm up before departure. Check which warps are under the most load, and plan to cast these off last.

## LEAVING UNDER POWER
If the tide is the strongest element affecting you and it is on the bow, then you should leave bow first. If the tide is from astern, then leave stern first or turn the boat using warps. If the tide is not significant, leave into the wind if possible: bow first if the wind is forward of the beam, stern first if it is aft of the beam. These rules cannot be rigidly applied, however, since much depends on the boat's particular configuration, its engine power, and the strength of the wind.

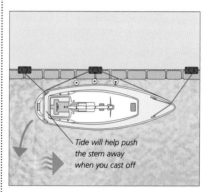

Tide will help push the stern away when you cast off

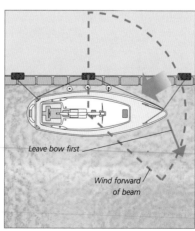

Leave bow first

Wind forward of beam

### △ WIND AHEAD
*If the wind is the significant factor, and it is forward of the beam, leave bow first. If the wind is off the quay it will push the bow away. If it is onshore, spring off.*

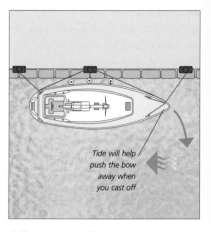

Tide will help push the bow away when you cast off

### △ BOW INTO TIDE
*When the boat is facing into a tidal stream, leave bow first. The bow line and stern spring will take the load of the boat; the stern line and bow spring will be slack and can be cast off first when you are preparing to leave the berth.*

### ◁ STERN INTO TIDE
*When the stern is facing into a tidal stream, leave stern first. If your boat does not handle well in reverse, turn the boat using warps (p.168) and leave bow first, as above. If leaving stern first, cast off the bow line and stern spring first.*

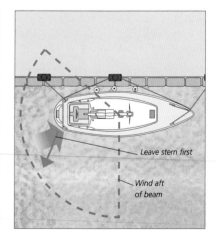

Leave stern first

Wind aft of beam

### △ WIND ASTERN
*If the wind is aft of the beam, leave stern first, or turn the boat using warps if handling astern is a problem. If the wind is onshore, use a spring to help you.*

## PUSHING OFF

If you were to try to leave – even with no wind or tide to cause problems – by casting off your lines and motoring away, the boat's stern would hit the quay as you turned. The way to avoid this is to turn either end of the boat away from the quay before motoring off. In small, light boats, this can often be achieved by simply pushing the bow or stern off with a boathook. In strong, offshore winds, the boat will drift clear of the quay once the warps are released, making it a simple matter to motor away.

## USING SPRINGS

A more controlled departure can be achieved by using one of the springs to help turn the boat, enabling you to leave bow or stern first. Once you have cleared the berth and are in open water, stow the warps and fenders, making sure that all lines are kept out of the water and clear of the propeller.

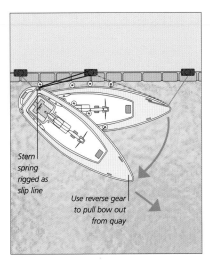

Stern spring rigged as slip line

Use reverse gear to pull bow out from quay

### △ LEAVING BOW FIRST

*Rig the stern spring as a slip line (p.169) and position a fender right at the stern. Cast off the other warps and motor gently astern, steering the stern in toward the quay as the bow begins to swing out. Once the bow has swung far enough to clear any obstructions, engage neutral gear, slip the spring, and motor away slowly in forward gear.*

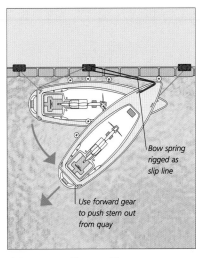

Bow spring rigged as slip line

Use forward gear to push stern out from quay

### △ LEAVING STERN FIRST

*Rig the bow spring as a slip line, position a fender at the bow, and cast off the other warps. Motor slowly ahead and steer carefully toward the quay. When the stern has swung out far enough, engage neutral, slip the spring, and motor slowly astern until you are away from the quay and able to engage forward gear.*

## LEAVING UNDER SAIL

It is often possible to leave a berth under sail, but if the wind is light and the tide is strong, you will have reduced control: it is usually easier to leave under power. If the wind is blowing onto the berth you will not be able to sail off at all. Use an engine, warps, or lay an anchor using the tender, to get yourself out of the berth. If tide is present, always leave bow-into-tide for best control. If the boat is lying stern-to-tide, turn it using warps before you attempt to sail off.

Once you are lying head-to-tide, sail off under jib only if the wind is on or aft of the beam. If the wind is from ahead, sail off under mainsail alone, or mainsail and headsail together if the wind is light. If the wind is from directly ahead, hoist and back the headsail to push the bow off.

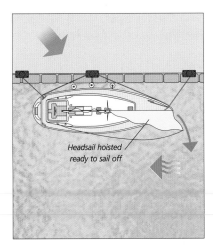

Headsail hoisted ready to sail off

### △ OFFSHORE WIND AFT OF BEAM

*Hoist the headsail but let it flap freely. First cast off the warps not under load, then cast off the others. Trim the headsail, and sail off under headsail alone. Once clear of the quay, turn head-to-wind before hoisting the mainsail.*

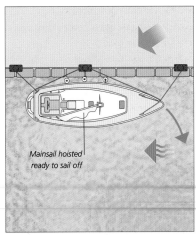

Mainsail hoisted ready to sail off

### △ OFFSHORE WIND AHEAD

*Hoist the mainsail and let it flap. Prepare the headsail for immediate hoisting. Cast off all warps, starting with those not under load, and push the bow off, with a boathook if necessary. Trim the mainsail and sail off, then hoist the headsail.*

# ARRIVING AT A BERTH

Approaching an alongside berth can be a complicated maneuver that requires thought, planning, and a well-briefed crew. If possible, make a dummy run to assess the situation. Check the wind and tide effects at the berth and look for any nearby hazards that you will have to avoid on the approach. Remember to allow for last-minute problems by planning an escape route that will take the boat safely back to clear water. Check which side will be alongside the berth. If it is necessary to raft alongside another boat, ask permission first.

Once you have decided on your tactics, brief the crew and give them plenty of time to get the gear ready, particularly the fenders and warps. If you have sailed into harbor but intend to come alongside under power, start the engine in plenty of time to allow it to warm up. Drop the sails and stow them before you approach the berth.

## PREPARATION

Get the warps ready on deck: when you are berthed you will normally lie to at least four warps (*pp.168–69*).

Rig fenders and prepare the bow and stern warps by leading an end out through their fairleads, pulling sufficient through and making them fast to deck cleats. Take the outer ends of the bow and stern lines outside everything to the middle of the boat just aft of the shrouds. The crew should normally step off from here when taking their lines ashore, as it is the widest part of the boat and should be closest to the berth when coming alongside. You may not need to rig the springs until you are alongside and secured by bow and stern lines. However, a stopping spring can be a very useful aid (*far right*), especially if the engine is not efficient in reverse. Once you are alongside, secure the bow and stern lines. The stern spring is usually rigged next, if the wind or tide are on the bow, as this warp will take much of the load and will hold the boat parallel to the berth. Finally, rig the other spring and tidy up all warps, making sure that there are no loose coils of rope left lying on the quay or dock where passers-by may trip over them.

## ARRIVING UNDER POWER

If wind and tide effects are not significant, choose to come alongside on the side toward which prop walk (*p.192*) will push the stern when you engage reverse gear to stop. This will help you end up alongside, parallel to the berth. Once the boat is close alongside, the crew steps ashore and makes fast. When the wind or tide are significant, however, approach by heading into the strongest element. This gives you greater slow-speed control and will help you stop accurately at the berth. Do not approach down-tide or with a strong wind behind, if it can be avoided (and never attempt this maneuver without a powerful engine).

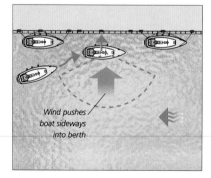

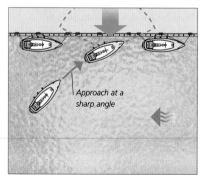

## △ WIND AND TIDE TOGETHER OR OPPOSED

*Use the tide to stop the boat by putting the engine into neutral as you approach the berth. Use reverse gear to help stop the boat if prop walk will act to pull the stern into the berth, but use it sparingly if prop walk acts in the opposite direction.*

## △ ONSHORE WIND

*Approach into the tide, but aim to stop your boat a few feet to windward of the berth. Allow the effects of wind resistance to push the boat gently sideways into the berth. If the bow blows quickly downwind, stop the boat with the bow slightly upwind to allow for the effect.*

## △ OFFSHORE WIND

*In a strong offshore wind, the bow tends to blow downwind when you stop alongside. Counter this by leading the stern line farther forward than usual, and approach at a sharper angle. The crew must get the lines ashore quickly and straighten up the boat in its berth.*

## ARRIVING UNDER SAIL

Berthing a cruiser under sail, especially in a confined space, requires skill and good judgment. The success of the maneuver will depend on your knowledge of your boat's handling characteristics and on the efficiency and speed of the crew. The choice of approach is much the same as when approaching under power. Always head into the strongest element of wind or tide so that you can use it to stop you when you reach the berth. If you approach too fast in the final stages, back the mainsail (if you are approaching into the wind), or lower the headsail (if you are approaching downwind). The crew will need to hold the leech of a partly lowered headsail to keep it drawing.

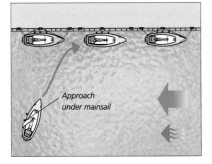

### △ WIND AND TIDE TOGETHER OR STRONG WIND OPPOSED

*If wind and tide are together, or if a strong wind is opposed by a weak tide, approach on a close reach under mainsail alone. Ease the mainsheet to slow down and turn into the wind when you reach the berth. Get the bow and stern lines ashore and made fast.*

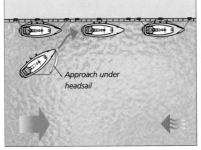

### △ STRONG TIDE OPPOSING WEAK WIND

*Approach from upwind under headsail alone. If the headsail alone will not push you over the tide, try hoisting just the top of the mainsail to provide extra drive. Slow down by letting the headsail flap. Get the warps ashore quickly.*

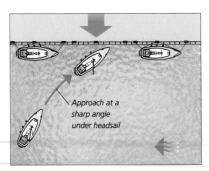

### △ OFFSHORE WIND

*Come in against the tide with the mainsail alone if the wind is forward of the beam. Use the headsail alone if the wind is on or aft of the beam. Approach at a sharp angle and lead the end of the stern line further forward so that the crew can step ashore from ahead of the shrouds. Get the warps ashore and made fast quickly.*

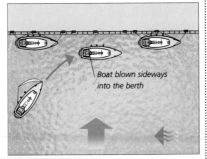

### △ ONSHORE WIND

*Approach downwind under headsail alone, turning into the tide to stop to windward of the berth so that the boat blows sideways into its berth. Stop the boat with the bow pointing slightly upwind to allow for it drifting faster downwind than the stern. Lower the headsail and get the warps ashore.*

## SHORT-HANDED TECHNIQUES

Approaching a berth is relatively easy with a full crew to handle all the warps, but it can be tricky with the typical short-handed crew – often only two people on board.

### USING AN AMIDSHIPS SPRING

One way of entering a berth when short-handed is to use an amidships spring to control the boat. A line is led from a sidedeck cleat just aft of amidships to a cleat ashore that is level with the stern or further back. This allows the boat to be held in position, parallel to its berth, by putting the engine slow ahead. If the boat swings toward or away from the berth, counteract this with the tiller. When coming alongside, all the lines are rigged as normal with the addition of the amidships spring. As the boat stops alongside, the crew steps ashore with the spring only and makes it fast on a cleat or bollard. The helmsman puts the engine into slow ahead and adjusts the tiller to hold the boat parallel to its berth. The boat is now secure and the shore crew can make fast the normal mooring warps.

### STOPPING SPRINGS

The amidships spring can be used as a stopping spring if the boat is moving too fast when it comes alongside. To do this, the shore crew takes one full turn around a cleat or bollard before strain comes onto the line. As the line becomes taut, he eases it under control (known as surging a line) to slow the boat down. Do not let the warp jerk tight as it may break. Surging a line is a good way to stop even a large boat. Using a bow spring as a stopping spring does not work as well. The spring is cleated at the bow, so it will pull the bow into the berth once strain comes on it, but the amidships spring will keep the boat straight.

# MARINA BERTHS

*C*ommon *in busy sailing areas, marinas provide a large number of sheltered berths in a confined space, usually with good shoreside facilities, such as fuel and fresh water, showers, shops, restaurants, pubs, supply stores, and repair yards. Marinas are therefore very popular and tend to be crowded in the busiest months of the sailing season. Boats are berthed very close together, on a network of floating docks, so maneuvering space is limited. Good boat handling is essential. You should always enter and leave a marina with caution, especially if your boat does not handle well under power. Be well prepared before you enter a marina, brief your crew, and have your warps and fenders rigged.*

### CHOOSING A BERTH

Before approaching a marina, it is vital that you know your boat's characteristics at slow speed and are able to turn in tight spaces using the effects of prop walk (*p.192*). If your boat does not handle well in reverse, you should avoid particularly tight or difficult berths. Marinas usually have a number of outside berths near the approach channel, with additional berths inside the network of docks. They are usually reached through narrow channels between docks that are often crowded with boats. If you are uncertain of the marina layout, or if your boat is difficult to handle, choose an outside berth if possible, perhaps maneuvering into an inside one later using warps. Most marinas have reserved berths for permanent berth holders, with others for use by visitors. Make sure that you select a visitor's berth when visiting a marina for the first time. It is not usually wise to attempt to sail into a marina because of the confined space, although you may be able to pick up an outside berth under sail.

### PREPARING TO BERTH

Before you arrive, contact the marina's berthing master by VHF radio to obtain directions to a suitable berth. Remember to ask which side of the boat you will berth on, so that you can prepare warps and fenders on the correct side.

If you have enough fenders, hang them on both sides of the boat so that you are well protected. This will also give you a choice of berthing on either side if the situation changes at the last moment or you find the planned berth too difficult to enter.

Marinas are often located out of the main tidal stream, so the effects of tide may not be significant in your final approach. Study the situation carefully however, because if a dock sticks out into the tide, it may have a significant effect that you will have to allow for. When preparing to berth, you should assess the situation and pick the best approach method (*pp.194–99*).

◁ **BUSY MARINA**
*Marinas are popular because they provide safe berths and numerous useful facilities. They can be crowded and noisy, however, and charges can be quite high.*

## TURNING IN A NARROW CHANNEL

Sometimes you may need to turn in a very narrow channel between docks, without enough space to execute a normal turn under power. On many occasions, you can use prop walk to turn the boat in nearly its own length (*p.193*), but a strong wind or poor boat performance under power may render this impossible.

### USING THE ANCHOR

Sometimes, when negotiating a marina to find a berth, you may find yourself heading down a narrow channel that turns out to be a dead end. In such circumstances, you need to be able to turn the boat or to reverse out the way you came. However, many sailing boats do not reverse well under power, and a strong following wind may make it difficult, or impossible, to turn in the space available. If you cannot use prop walk to assist you, you should consider using the anchor to help turn the boat. As you motor slowly along the channel, use the depth sounder to check the depth of water and prepare the anchor for dropping. When you reach the point at which you want to turn, drop the anchor but continue moving slowly ahead. Allow the anchor chain to run out freely until you have paid out about twice the depth of water. Now put the engine into neutral, start the boat turning in the desired direction and, at the same time, secure the anchor chain by taking a turn around a foredeck cleat or bollard. The anchor chain will draw taut and pull the bow around until the boat has turned through 180°. You can now motor slowly forward, recover the anchor, and make your exit safely.

### ▽ TURNING WITH AN ANCHOR
*Using an anchor to turn is an easy and effective technique. Most marinas are dredged regularly so there should be no bottom obstructions to foul your anchor.*

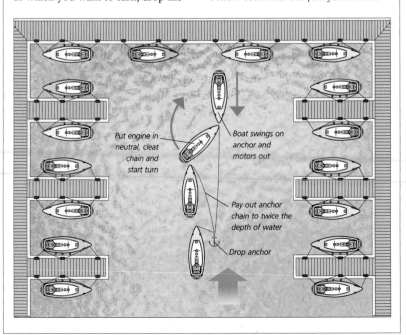

Put engine in neutral, cleat chain and start turn

Boat swings on anchor and motors out

Pay out anchor chain to twice the depth of water

Drop anchor

## DIFFICULT BERTHS

Marina berths in confined spaces can be very difficult to leave in certain conditions of wind or tide. If you are concerned about whether you have enough room to maneuver, or that the wind or tide may cause you to lose control, use your warps to help you arrive or leave safely.

### USING WARPS
The exact method of using warps will depend on the particular berthing situation; no hard and fast rules can be given. The skipper has to assess the effects of prop walk, wind, and tide on the boat while it is moving slowly into or out of its berth. He should plan to use the appropriate mooring warp to prevent or promote turning as required. A mooring warp used in this way should be rigged as a slip line so that it can be released quickly and easily from on board.

### INTO THE WIND
You may often find that you have to reverse out of a berth against a strong wind. Wind on the bow will tend to keep it downwind, and engine power may not be sufficient to turn in the space available. Use a spring to help you turn.

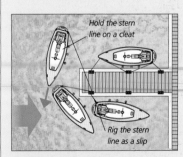

Hold the stern line on a cleat

Rig the stern line as a slip

### △ REVERSING OUT
*Rig the stern line as a slip with plenty of slack, and reverse slowly out. When the boat has cleared the berth, cleat the stern line to hold the stern as the bow swings out. Then slip the line and motor away.*

## LEAVING A MARINA BERTH

Before leaving the marina, start the engine and allow it to warm up in neutral while you assess the situation and plan your exit. Consider how the wind and tide will affect the boat as you leave the berth and as you maneuver within the marina. Brief the crew thoroughly and get them to prepare any slip lines you may need to control the boat as you leave. They should know in what order the lines are to be released, and must make sure that no warps are left in the water where they might foul the propeller. Take your time and proceed carefully.

## ▽ EXITING THE BERTH

*Your position in relation to the wind and tide, and whether you are bow-in or stern-in to your berth, will determine how you leave. Be aware of other boats on neighboring docks, and of boats entering or leaving the marina at the same time that may interfere with your plans.*

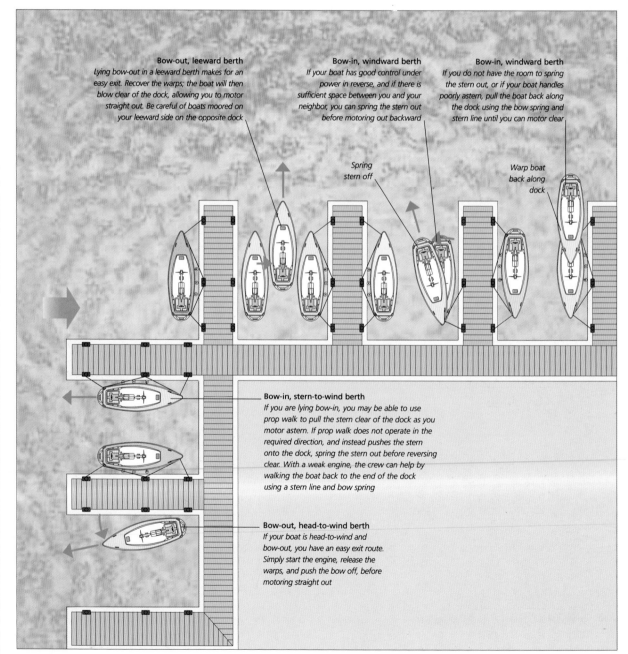

**Bow-out, leeward berth**
*Lying bow-out in a leeward berth makes for an easy exit. Recover the warps; the boat will then blow clear of the dock, allowing you to motor straight out. Be careful of boats moored on your leeward side on the opposite dock*

**Bow-in, windward berth**
*If your boat has good control under power in reverse, and if there is sufficient space between you and your neighbor, you can spring the stern out before motoring out backward*

**Bow-in, windward berth**
*If you do not have the room to spring the stern out, or if your boat handles poorly astern, pull the boat back along the dock using the bow spring and stern line until you can motor clear*

*Spring
stern off*

*Warp boat
back along
dock*

**Bow-in, stern-to-wind berth**
*If you are lying bow-in, you may be able to use prop walk to pull the stern clear of the dock as you motor astern. If prop walk does not operate in the required direction, and instead pushes the stern onto the dock, spring the stern out before reversing clear. With a weak engine, the crew can help by walking the boat back to the end of the dock using a stern line and bow spring*

**Bow-out, head-to-wind berth**
*If your boat is head-to-wind and bow-out, you have an easy exit route. Simply start the engine, release the warps, and push the bow off, before motoring straight out*

## ARRIVING AT A MARINA BERTH

Give yourself plenty of time to pick a berth. If necessary, sail past the marina a few times to get a good idea of its layout and the location of any likely berths. If reserved visitors' berths are not clearly marked, ask for advice to find a suitable berth. When you have found a berth, plan your entry with care. Brief the crew and give them time to prepare the gear. They should know which warps are to be secured first, and must check that no warps are trailing in the water where they might foul the propeller as you maneuver.

## ▽ ENTERING THE BERTH

*The direction of the wind and the angle of the berth to the wind will determine how you arrive at your berth. Your boat's ability to perform well at very low speeds and to prop walk will also have a bearing on your choice of berth and the way in which you enter it.*

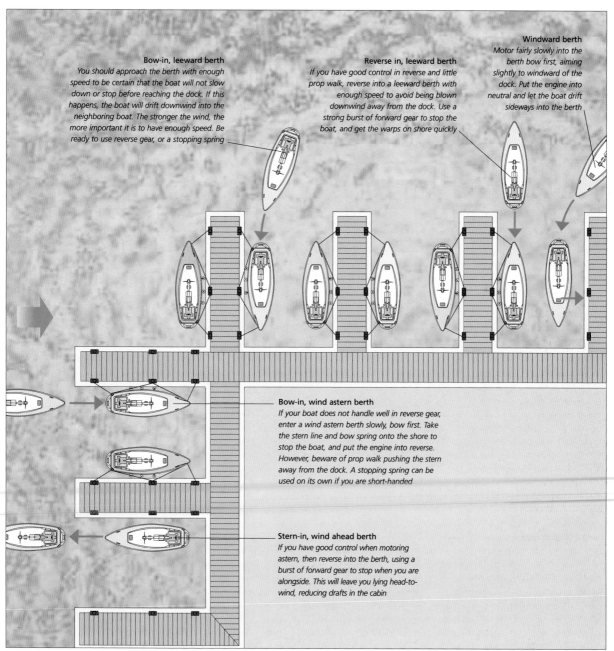

**Bow-in, leeward berth**
*You should approach the berth with enough speed to be certain that the boat will not slow down or stop before reaching the dock. If this happens, the boat will drift downwind into the neighboring boat. The stronger the wind, the more important it is to have enough speed. Be ready to use reverse gear, or a stopping spring*

**Reverse in, leeward berth**
*If you have good control in reverse and little prop walk, reverse into a leeward berth with enough speed to avoid being blown downwind away from the dock. Use a strong burst of forward gear to stop the boat, and get the warps on shore quickly*

**Windward berth**
*Motor fairly slowly into the berth bow first, aiming slightly to windward of the dock. Put the engine into neutral and let the boat drift sideways into the berth*

**Bow-in, wind astern berth**
*If your boat does not handle well in reverse gear, enter a wind astern berth slowly, bow first. Take the stern line and bow spring onto the shore to stop the boat, and put the engine into reverse. However, beware of prop walk pushing the stern away from the dock. A stopping spring can be used on its own if you are short-handed*

**Stern-in, wind ahead berth**
*If you have good control when motoring astern, then reverse into the berth, using a burst of forward gear to stop when you are alongside. This will leave you lying head-to-wind, reducing drafts in the cabin*

# RAFTING ALONGSIDE

*Stacking boats, one outside the other, beside a dock or quay, in between piles, or around a mooring buoy, is known as rafting. This is a common method of making the most of the limited space in crowded harbors. Although it is not an ideal method of berthing, rafting alongside may be the only option available to you in a busy harbor. It is advisable, therefore, to learn how to raft safely, making sure that you do not damage your own or anyone else's boat. You also need to know how to leave safely from the inside of the raft, as well as from the outside. Rafting can be a straightforward procedure, as long as you follow a few basic strategies and observe certain courtesies to other members of the raft.*

### RAFTING PROTOCOL

Always secure to the shore, dock, or piles with bow and stern lines, and to the boat next to you with springs and breast warps. Do not rely on your neighbors' shore lines to hold your boat – this is bad practice and also discourteous. Do not join a raft in which only the innermost boat has rigged shore lines. Such a raft will swing fore and aft under the effects of wind and tide, and will provide an uncomfortable and insecure berth.

A raft is more stable if the largest boat is on the inside and the smallest on the outside, so try to avoid rafting alongside a boat smaller than your own. When you join a raft, position your boat so that your mast is not in line with that of your neighbor. This will prevent them from clashing and causing damage as the boats roll. When going ashore across other boats in the raft, always cross by their foredecks, never their cockpits. This helps to preserve privacy.

### DISADVANTAGES OF RAFTING

One of the main disadvantages of rafting is that it can restrict your freedom to leave when you wish. When you are on the outside, it is inconvenient if an inside boat wants to leave before you. If you are on the inside, you have to put up with crews from boats outside you crossing your decks to get aboard or ashore. In an exposed location, the boats may rub and roll against each other, causing discomfort and sometimes damage.

### JOINING A RAFT

Although joining a raft involves coming alongside another boat, the method you use is exactly the same as when coming alongside a quay or dock (*pp.194–95*). Plan your approach, taking into account the effects of wind and tide. Always head toward the element that will have the most effect on your boat as you stop alongside. It does not matter if you are not facing in the same direction as the boat you are going to be beside. Brief the crew and prepare fenders and warps in the usual way. You will need three sets of warps – bow and stern lines led to the shore, and breasts and springs attached to your neighbor.

Coming alongside another boat, rather than a dock or quay, is harder for the crew. They will have to climb over two sets of lifelines and make their way along the other boat's sidedeck to find suitable cleats to secure the bow and stern breast ropes.

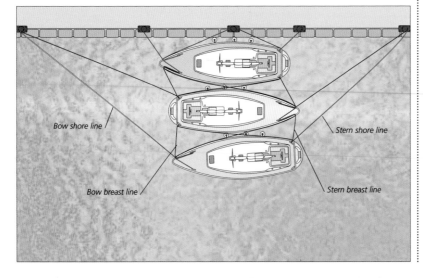

Bow shore line

Stern shore line

Bow breast line

Stern breast line

◁ **A TYPICAL RAFT**
*Boats rafted with bow and stern breast lines, and springs between each boat, Bow and stern shore lines are also rigged. Boats are arranged with masts not in line.*

It is important that these warps are attached as soon as possible, to bring the boat under control before rigging all the other lines.

The procedure can be made much easier if the other boat's crew are on deck. First, ask them for permission to come alongside. Then, if they are willing to help, your crew can hand them the ends of the bow and stern breast lines. Once they have been made fast, the lines can be adjusted from on board your boat. This means that your crew do not have to climb aboard the other boat. Rig the springs as quickly as possible, and then take your bow and stern lines ashore. Lead them outside all the boats between you and the shore or dock. Adjust them so that they are clear of the water, but have some slack in them.

## LEAVING A RAFT

If you are the outermost boat in the raft, leaving it is the same as leaving from a dock (*pp.196–97*), but you must recover your shore lines first. Before doing this, decide if the wind or tide is the strongest element, choose your exit strategy, and brief the crew. Then maneuver clear as you would if you were leaving an alongside berth.

When you are inside the raft, you must always leave with the strongest element. If you leave against it, there is a danger that the boats outside you will be at the mercy of wind or tide. To avoid problems, crew members may have to take control of other boat's warps as you leave. You will then have to pick the crew up at the outside of the raft once you are clear. Another raft close by may prevent you from departing until the boats outside you have left. If you are not sure that you can clear all nearby obstructions, either ask the outside boats to move to let you out or be prepared to wait until they leave.

## LEAVING FROM WITHIN A RAFT

*If you are on the inside or middle of a raft, leave with the strongest element – here, the tide. Otherwise, the boats outside you will become uncontrollable when their warps are released for you to leave.*

**1** Check whether the wind or tide is the most significant factor and plan to leave downtide or downwind. Also, check that there are no obstructions, such as another raft, in your line of departure. Next, recover your bow and stern shore lines so that your boat is now attached only to the boats to either side of it.

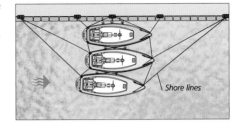

Shore lines

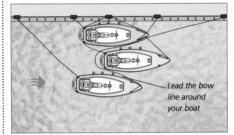

Lead the bow line around your boat

**2** Recover your warps from the boat that is outside you. Unfasten the outside boat's bow line and re-lead it around and behind your boat and back to the shore. Next, release your breast ropes and springs from the boat inside you, and allow your own boat to move out slowly with the strongest element.

**3** As your boat moves downtide out of the raft, the shore line of the boat outside is pulled in and secured, and the boat is secured to the inshore boat with breasts and springs. If your crew have been on the raft helping to secure the outside boats, circle back and come alongside the outside boat to pick them up when they are ready.

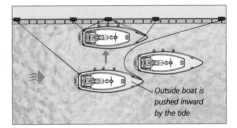

Outside boat is pushed inward by the tide

---

### RAFTING ON A BUOY

Boats are sometimes rafted on large mooring buoys, but usually only in areas where there are no significant tides or currents.

#### MOORING
Boats moor directly to the buoy and attach springs and breast warps to their neighbors. They leave stern-first simply by casting off. If necessary, a crew member stays on the raft to refasten the other boats' springs and breast warps, and is then picked up.

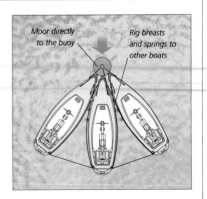

Moor directly to the buoy

Rig breasts and springs to other boats

**BUOY RAFT**

# BERTHING BOW- OR STERN-TO

*I*n areas without the complications of tide to consider, it is
common to moor by the bow or the stern to a dock or quay.
*An anchor (or, occasionally, a pair of small piles) is used to hold
the other end of the boat. This method saves space alongside, and
makes it easier for individual boats to arrive or leave without
disturbing others. It is usually simpler to come in bow first, which
also provides more privacy in the cockpit while you are berthed.
However, you may find it easier to get ashore if you are stern-to.*

### ARRIVING BOW-TO

Brief the crew, and prepare the warps,
fenders, and anchor well before you
approach the berth. Hang fenders on
both sides of the boat to protect it
from contact with neighboring boats.
For berthing bow-to, you will need
two bow lines and the kedge anchor
(*p.210*) with a long anchor warp or
chain. The anchor must be ready to
drop from the stern. If the kedge has
a length of chain between it and the
warp, stow the chain in a bucket to
keep it clear of the deck as it runs out,
to prevent damage. Make sure that
the chain and warp are led so that

they run out under the pushpit and
through a fairlead. It is important to
lay the anchor clear of other boats'
anchors. The best way to achieve this
is by making a long approach with
your boat lined up with the berth.
This gives you time to adjust your
line of approach, using tiller and
throttle as necessary, to give a steady
and straight run into the berth.

When you are about three to five
boat lengths from the berth, drop the
anchor over the stern and let its cable
run free. Continue your approach
until you are about half a boat length
from the berth, then snub the anchor

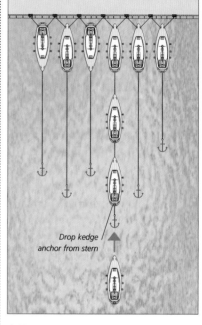

Drop kedge
anchor from stern

### △ BERTHING BOW-TO

*Approach in a straight line from some
way off. Drop the kedge anchor over the
stern about three to five boat lengths from
the berth. Stop just clear of the quay so
the crew can take the bow lines ashore.*

### TURNING USING WARPS

*If you wish to moor stern-
to but your boat does not
handle well in reverse, you
should first moor bow-to.
You then have to use the
anchor and the bow line
to turn the boat while
keeping it under complete
control. Ensure that your
crew understands how you
intend to complete the
maneuver, and keep an eye
out for a cross wind that
could push your boat onto
its neighbors.*

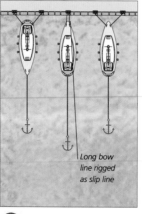

Long bow
line rigged
as slip line

**①** Rig the bow line as a long
slip line, making sure that you
have enough rope to complete
the maneuver.

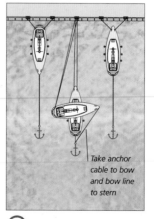

Take anchor
cable to bow
and bow line
to stern

**②** Pull on the anchor cable
to move the boat clear. Take
the anchor warp to the bow,
and the bow line to the stern.

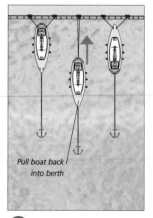

Pull boat back
into berth

**③** Turn the boat using the
warps and pull it back into
the berth stern first. Ease out
the anchor warp as you go.

cable. This is done by taking a turn of the cable around a cleat or bollard and holding the end tightly enough to put some load on the warp, while allowing it to slip slowly around the cleat. This will set the anchor and slow down the boat. Put the engine in reverse if necessary to stop the boat just clear of the quay or dock, so that the crew can step ashore with the bow warps and secure the boat.

## ARRIVING STERN-TO

If you wish to berth stern-to, you have two choices depending on how well your boat handles in reverse. If it handles well in reverse, approach from some way off, reversing in a straight line toward the berth. Drop your bow anchor about three to five boat lengths from the berth and allow the cable to run out. As your stern approaches the quay or dock, snub the bow anchor and give a burst ahead on the engine to stop the boat. The crew can then step ashore with

the stern warps and make them fast. If your boat does not handle well in reverse, but you still wish to berth stern-to, first berth bow-to then turn the boat using the bow line and anchor cable (*left*).

## LEAVING

Leaving a bow- or stern-to mooring is usually straightforward. Simply release the shore lines and pull on the anchor cable to move the boat clear of the berth, using the engine to help if necessary. Then recover the anchor (*p.214*) and motor clear. If a strong cross wind makes it hard to hold the boat straight as you leave, rig a long slip line to the shore to help control the boat. Keep the line under low tension as you move clear and it will stop the boat blowing downwind. Slip the line once clear of the berth.

When leaving a pile and dock berth, you can leave stern-first by simply releasing your bow warps and motoring out backward, provided that

you have good control in reverse and there is no strong cross wind. As you motor astern, release the pile lines as they come within reach.

If there is a strong cross wind blowing, however, you should release only the downwind bow and stern lines, rigging the two remaining warps as slips. Next, take the stern line forward to the middle of the boat. Motor slowly astern, or pull the boat back on the stern warp, gradually easing the bow warp. At the same time, keep some tension on the bow warp to prevent the bow from blowing downwind. When the middle of the boat is level with the piles, slip both remaining lines and motor clear.

If your boat does not handle well in reverse, rig both pile lines as slips and lead them forward to the middle of the boat. Release the bow lines and pull the boat back on the stern lines, slipping them when the piles are abeam and motoring clear.

---

# PILE AND DOCK BERTHS

Some harbors use a combination of piles and dock for berthing bow- or stern-to. Most resident berths have permanent lines attached to the dock and piles to make berthing easier. If you are entering a visitor's berth, however, you will have to use your own warps. These are best rigged as slips.

## ARRIVING

Although it is possible to berth stern-to if you have good control in reverse, most boats are easier to berth bow-to in this situation. Prepare two bow warps and two stern warps. The latter should be rigged like springs, with the port stern line running to the starboard pile and vice versa. Brief the crew and have a boathook ready. Make your approach slowly under power. Be careful of any beam wind that would cause the bow to blow downwind, and that could spoil your approach to the berth.

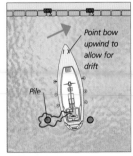

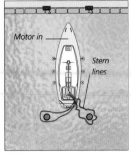

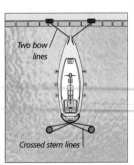

**①** If there is a cross wind, approach the upwind pile first under power. Lasso the pile with a loop of the stern line and leave slack.

**②** Lasso the second pile with the other stern line. Then motor in, taking care to keep the lines clear of the propeller.

**③** Stop the boat just clear of the dock and make fast on the shore using two bow warps. Position the boat just clear of the dock.

# PILE MOORINGS

*S*ome tidal harbors use pile moorings to provide fore and aft moorings along the edges of a channel, parallel to the main tide flow. Piles are large wooden or metal stakes driven into the seabed, with fittings to which mooring warps are tied. Boats often raft up between pile moorings, although there will usually be a limit to the number of boats allowed on each pair of piles. When rafted between piles, all the boats should secure to the piles as well as to their neighboring vessels.

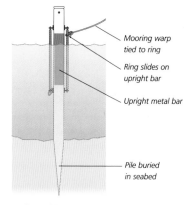

Mooring warp tied to ring

Ring slides on upright bar

Upright metal bar

Pile buried in seabed

**PILE MOORING**

## UNDER POWER

Leaving a pile mooring is generally quite a simple procedure. The main thing to consider is your exit in relation to any nearby hazards.

### LEAVING UNDER POWER

If you are lying alone between a pair of piles, leave into the tide, either bow or stern first. If you are inside a raft, recover your pile lines using the tender, then leave as for a raft (*p.207*). If you are the outside boat, recover your pile lines and leave as for an alongside berth (*pp.202–03*).

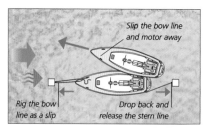

Slip the bow line and motor away

Rig the bow line as a slip

Drop back and release the stern line

△ **LEAVE INTO THE TIDE**
*Pull the boat up to the uptide pile while paying out the other line. To leave bow first, rig the bow line as a slip, drop back to the stern pile, and release the stern line. Motor ahead and slip the bow line.*

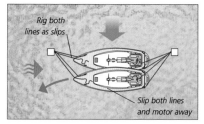

Rig both lines as slips

Slip both lines and motor away

△ **STRONG WIND ON BEAM**
*If a strong wind on the beam threatens to cause difficulties, rig both bow and stern lines as slips. Ease both out to allow the boat to blow to leeward, then slip both lines and motor away into the tide.*

### ARRIVING UNDER POWER

Picking up a pile mooring is quite simple. If you select empty piles you will only need two mooring lines, and can complete the operation from on deck. If you choose to come alongside another boat, approach as for an alongside berth. You will need six warps, plus fenders, and you will have to use the tender to attach the pile lines. The skipper should plan to approach into the strongest element and should brief the crew in advance. Have a boathook handy, as well as the mooring lines, and appoint your quickest knot-tier to attach the lines.

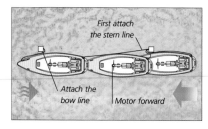

First attach the stern line

Attach the bow line

Motor forward

△ **RUNNING MOOR**
*Approach into the strongest element. Stop the boat alongside the rear pile. Keep the pile ahead of the shrouds when you have stopped. Attach the stern line. Motor forward to the bow pile and attach the bow line. Adjust both lines so you are positioned midway between the piles.*

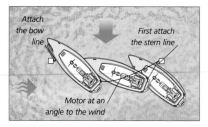

Attach the bow line

First attach the stern line

Motor at an angle to the wind

△ **STRONG WIND ON BEAM**
*Approach the stern pile from the leeward side. Stop with the pile alongside the windward shroud. Secure the stern line. Motor forward with the bow angled to windward. Stop with the bow pile on the leeward bow. Secure the bow line and center the boat between the piles.*

# UNDER SAIL

If the immediate vicinity is not too crowded with other boats, you can often leave a pile mooring under sail.

## LEAVING UNDER SAIL

It is a fairly easy maneuver to leave under sail if you are berthed alone between piles. If you are the outside boat in a raft on piles, you may be able to leave under sail if you are on the leeward side, after recovering your pile lines with the tender.

As pile moorings are usually found in tidal areas, it is best to leave bow into the tide; this gives you the most control. If you are lying stern to the tide, turn the boat using warps before you try to leave. With the bow pointing into the tide, your method of leaving will be determined by wind direction. As with other berthing

situations under sail, use the mainsail alone, or with the headsail, if the wind is forward of the beam, and the headsail alone if the wind is on or aft of the beam. Rig the bow and stern lines as slips before hoisting sails, and use them to turn the boat one way or the other if it helps you to sail off.

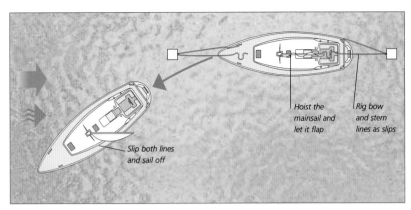

Hoist the mainsail and let it flap

Rig bow and stern lines as slips

Slip both lines and sail off

△ **WIND FORWARD OF BEAM**
*Rig both pile lines as slips and prepare the mainsail for hoisting. Plan your exit route and brief the crew. Hoist the mainsail and let it flap freely, then cast off the stern line. Pull in on the bow line to give the boat steerage way, then slip the line and sail away.*

## ARRIVING UNDER SAIL

If you choose to approach a pile mooring under sail, always make your final approach into the strongest element. This will usually be the tide. However, if a very strong wind opposes a very weak tide, you should plan your approach into the wind.

Brief the crew well in advance, and make a dummy run if necessary to assess the situation. Prepare bow and stern lines and have a boathook to hand. Your method of final approach will depend on the relative direction of the wind. If the wind is ahead of the beam, then make your final approach under mainsail alone. Approach on a close reach and aim to stop alongside the bow pile. Make the bow warp fast, then lower the mainsail and drop back to the stern pile to attach the stern warp. Center the boat between the piles. If the wind is on or aft of the

beam, approach under headsail alone, using the jib sheet to control speed. In this case, use a running moor (*above*). Let the jib flap to stop by the stern pile first to attach the stern warp, before sailing on to the bow pile to attach the bow warp. If the wind is light and you cannot make way over the tide, hoist the top part of the mainsail to get extra drive.

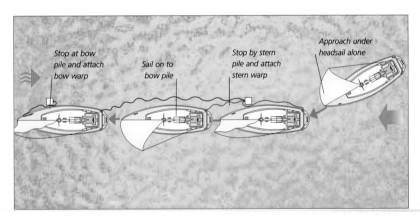

Stop at bow pile and attach bow warp

Sail on to bow pile

Stop by stern pile and attach stern warp

Approach under headsail alone

△ **WIND ON OR AFT OF BEAM**
*With the wind on or aft of the beam when you are pointing into the tide, sail upwind of the piles and lower the mainsail. Make your final approach under headsail alone, easing the sheet as necessary to spill wind and slow down. You should attach the stern line first, then sail on to the bow pile to attach the bow line.*

# MOORING AND ANCHORING

*T*wo ways of securing a boat without coming alongside a
quay or dock are mooring and anchoring. Moorings are
often laid in harbors, rivers, and bays to provide convenient
securing points for visiting or resident yachts. Anchoring is a
fundamental technique for a sailor to learn, although it is less
common in areas where marinas are plentiful. It allows you to
choose a remote anchorage for a quiet stop, or to wait out a
foul tide or ride out a gale in shelter.

## ABOUT MOORINGS

A mooring consists of one or more
heavy anchors or weights on the seabed attached to a heavy-chain riser.
This, in turn, is attached, sometimes
by rope, to a floating buoy. Moorings
intended for light craft usually have
a small buoy that is picked up and
brought on board through a bow
fairlead and secured to a cleat. Other
moorings have a larger buoy, either
with a ring on top to which the boat
is tied with a mooring line, or a
separate, smaller pick-up buoy that is
brought aboard to secure the boat.
Moorings are often laid in rows, called
trots, along the edges of river channels,
usually in line with the tidal flow.

## CHOOSING A MOORING

When you visit a harbor with visitors'
mooring buoys, choose a mooring
suitable for your boat. Ensure that
the mooring is strong enough, that it is
laid in water deep enough so that your
boat will still float at low tide, and
that there is enough room to swing
around the buoy with the wind and
tide. You should also consider how
sheltered the mooring is from both
wind and swell, especially if you are
planning an overnight stop.

It is also important to think
about how easily you will be able to
approach and leave the mooring under

power or sail, as well as the proximity
of the mooring to other boats and to
the shore. Be careful not to pick up
a permanent mooring, as its owner
may return at any time and claim
the berth. If you do have to pick
up someone else's mooring, never

leave your boat unattended in case
the owner does appear. If possible,
ask the harbor master or a local
sailor to advise you.

## ANCHORS AND CABLE

All yachts should carry at least two
suitably sized anchors, together with
appropriate lengths of chain or rope
cable. The choice of anchor and the
decision whether to use chain or rope
depend on the characteristics of your
boat and the areas in which you
normally sail. A typical setup will
include a main anchor, called the
bower anchor, and a lighter anchor,
called a kedge. The kedge is used for
short stops in good weather, or for

---

## FORE-AND-AFT BUOYS

Fore-and-aft mooring buoys are
usually laid in rows at the edges
of tidal and river channels.

You should use them just like pile
moorings, and secure your boat
between them.

### PICKING UP BUOYS

Picking up fore-and-aft buoys is the
same as picking up pile moorings
(*pp.208–09*): before you pick them up,
check that they are suitable for your
size of boat. Reaching the buoys from
the deck of a cruiser can be difficult.
The crew may have to lie on the deck,
so have a boathook handy. Some fore-
and-aft buoys have smaller pick-up

buoys attached to them to make it
easier to pick them up. When you
leave, tie the pick-up buoys together
to make recovery easier. Come
alongside the pick-up buoys and take
the forward buoy to the bow and the
other to the stern. Check the quality
of the line attaching them to the main
buoys; if it is suspect, rig your own
lines to the mooring buoys.

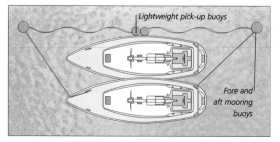

*Lightweight pick-up buoys*

*Fore and
aft mooring
buoys*

◁ **FORE AND
AFT BUOYS**
*Many pairs of fore and
aft mooring buoys have
lightweight pick-up
buoys attached to make
it easier to secure the
boat. Pick up the small
buoys and take their
lines to bow and stern.*

kedging-off after running aground. The Bruce, CQR, Danforth, and Fortress anchors are all good anchors. They are designed to bury themselves well into seabeds of shingle, sand, or mud. The Bruce is a popular choice as a bower anchor, and an aluminum Fortress a good option as a kedge. A Fisherman's anchor is better, however, when anchoring on a rocky seabed. For serious offshore sailing, always use the heaviest anchor you can fit on the boat, as nothing else will give you peace of mind in exposed anchorages.

The best material for anchor cable is chain. Although much heavier than rope, chain is stronger and does not chafe against underwater obstructions. A nylon rope cable is appropriate for the kedge. It may have to be used from the tender, where the lightness of rope will make the job much easier. It is advisable to place a short length of chain between the anchor and the rope to take the chafe from the seabed.

An anchor's holding power is dependent on the amount of cable you can pay out; this, in turn, will depend on the amount you can carry and the depth of water. The minimum scope for chain is 3:1 and for rope 5:1. However, it is much better to increase these ratios to 5:1 and 8:1 respectively if you have sufficient cable. In rough conditions in an exposed anchorage, you may have to pay out ten or more times the depth of water to avoid dragging. Remember to allow for the rise of tide if you anchor at low water.

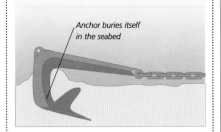

*Anchor buries itself in the seabed*

### △ BRUCE ANCHOR

*The Bruce anchor is a popular type of modern, burying anchor. In use, its large flukes dig into the seabed. As the load on the anchor increases, it buries itself deeper into the bottom.*

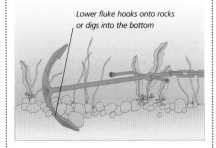

*Lower fluke hooks onto rocks or digs into the bottom*

### △ FISHERMAN'S ANCHOR

*The traditional Fisherman's anchor performs better than most other types of anchor when used in rock or weed. However, it is much heavier than modern designs and, because of its shape, is very awkward to stow.*

### ▽ SCOPE OF CABLE

*Pay out an absolute minimum of three times the depth of water if your anchor is attached to chain, and five times the depth if it is attached to rope. Increase these amounts if you have sufficient cable.*

## CHOOSING AN ANCHORAGE

When choosing an anchorage, you need to consider the amount of shelter from wind and waves, the depth of water, the type of seabed, and the ease of approach and departure under sail or power.

### CHANGING CONDITIONS

An anchorage that is sheltered from the wind when you anchor can become untenable if the wind swings and the anchorage becomes exposed. The same may happen if a tidal stream changes direction and causes a change in the sea state. Check the weather forecast before you anchor, and take into account any predicted changes in wind direction or strength. Consult the tidal atlas and tide tables to see if any changes will affect your anchorage. If you are anchoring in shallow water, check that there will be sufficient water at low tide to keep you afloat and to allow you to leave safely at any time.

### TYPES OF SEABED

Check the chart or local sailing directions for a description of the type of seabed. Be careful when anchoring on rock, weed, or coral covered by thin sand, as these bottoms provide poor holding for most anchors. If possible, choose to anchor in sand or firm mud.

### OTHER BOATS

Finally, consider any other yachts in the anchorage and the route you will take to approach and leave. Allow plenty of room between you and all the other boats, leaving enough space to swing clear of others if the wind or tide change direction. Try to anchor with boats of a similar type and size to your own, as they will react in much the same way as your boat to the effects of wind and tide.

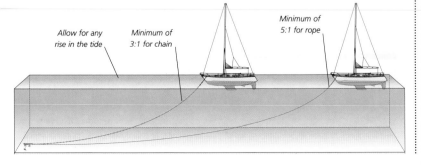

*Allow for any rise in the tide*

*Minimum of 3:1 for chain*

*Minimum of 5:1 for rope*

# ARRIVING AND LEAVING

The methods of approaching and leaving a mooring and an anchorage are similar. The only differences are in the equipment and crew procedures used. When arriving at either a mooring or an anchoring spot, decide on a method and route of approach. The aim is to stop the boat at the chosen spot in order to drop the anchor or pick up the mooring.

The precision required when anchoring is not as great as when picking up a mooring buoy. Aim to stop the boat in the chosen position, and move backward as the anchor is dropped. This prevents the chain from piling up on top of the anchor and fouling it. It is often impossible to hear spoken commands, so it will help if a system of hand signals has been worked out to allow easy communication between the foredeck and the cockpit.

## MAKING THE APPROACH

If you are approaching under sail, the first step is to decide how your boat will lie once it is anchored or moored. Check how other boats in the vicinity are lying, and decide if the wind or tide will have most effect on the boat. The secret is always to approach into the strongest element to retain control and be able to stop. If in doubt, approach into the tide.

You must now decide whether to make your final approach under mainsail alone or headsail alone. The rule is: if the wind is forward of the beam for your final approach, use the mainsail only; if it is on the beam or further aft, then approach under headsail only. If the mainsail is used with the wind on or abaft of the beam, you will not be able to let it out far enough to spill all the wind, so you will not be able to stop.

Sail around the area slowly to give yourself time to assess the situation and plan your approach and an escape route. If necessary, make a dummy run at the chosen spot. Brief the crew and give them time to prepare any equipment needed, such as a mooring line, or the anchor and cable. They will also need time to lower or furl whichever sail is not going to be required.

If you decide to approach under power, lower and stow the sails in plenty of time. Then motor slowly around the mooring area or the anchorage while you plan your approach and check the depth of water. Make sure that the crew are fully briefed and understand your intentions, and give them time to prepare the gear. If there is a tidal stream present, make your final approach head to tide, motoring slowly up to the chosen mooring buoy or the spot where you plan to drop your anchor.

## ARRIVING UNDER SAIL

With the wind forward of the beam, approach under mainsail alone to keep the foredeck clear of a flapping headsail. If you are anchoring, wait until the boat stops before dropping the anchor. Lower the mainsail when the boat has dropped back and the anchor is set.

If the wind is aft of the beam, sail upwind of the mooring or anchoring spot, lower the mainsail, and sail slowly toward the mooring buoy or anchoring spot under headsail alone. In strong winds, if the boat moves too fast even with the headsail sheet eased, you may have to lower or furl the headsail and sail under bare poles. In light winds, you may have to partly hoist the top of the mainsail to create enough power to counter the tide.

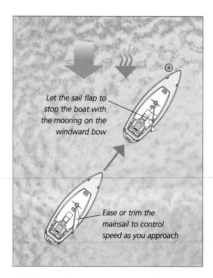

Let the sail flap to stop the boat with the mooring on the windward bow

Ease or trim the mainsail to control speed as you approach

△ **WIND AHEAD OF THE BEAM**
*Approach on a close reach under mainsail alone. Let the sail flap in your final approach to stop the boat. As soon as the mooring is secured, drop the sail.*

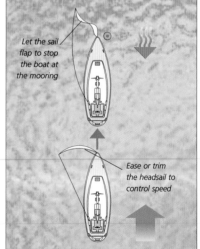

Let the sail flap to stop the boat at the mooring

Ease or trim the headsail to control speed

△ **WIND AFT OF THE BEAM**
*Sail upwind of the mooring or anchorage, lower the mainsail, and sail slowly back toward the mooring under headsail alone. Pick up mooring or drop anchor.*

## LEAVING UNDER SAIL

The same rules apply to leaving under sail as arriving. How you leave will be determined by the wind direction. If the wind is from ahead of the beam, you should leave under mainsail only, or mainsail and headsail together. If it is on or abaft the beam, leave under headsail alone. Decide on the route you will take, check for obstructions, then brief the crew.

If you are lying to a mooring, the boat can be given steerage way, and turned in the desired direction by pulling the buoy aft along one side of the boat before releasing it. If an anchor is being recovered, steerage way is provided by pulling the boat up to the anchor. When the wind is aft of the beam, break the anchor out before hoisting the headsail, then sail slowly while the anchor and cable are stowed and before you hoist the mainsail.

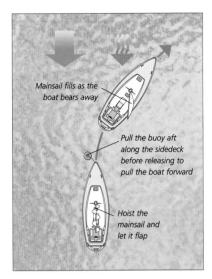

*Mainsail fills as the boat bears away*

*Pull the buoy aft along the sidedeck before releasing to pull the boat forward*

*Hoist the mainsail and let it flap*

### △ WIND AHEAD OF THE BEAM

*Hoist the mainsail and prepare the headsail. If the wind is light, or if your boat does not handle well under mainsail alone, hoist both sails. Drop the mooring and bear away to your chosen course.*

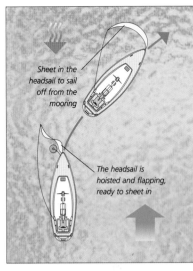

*Sheet in the headsail to sail off from the mooring*

*The headsail is hoisted and flapping, ready to sheet in*

### △ WIND AFT OF THE BEAM

*Hoist the headsail; when you are ready to drop the mooring, sheet it in and sail away. Sail into clear water before turning head-to-wind to hoist the mainsail and sailing off on your preferred course.*

## ARRIVING AND LEAVING UNDER POWER

Under power, approach a mooring or anchorage into either the wind or the tide (whichever is the stronger). This will give you maximum control over where you stop. If you are not sure which is the stronger element, look at other boats of a similar type to yours that are moored or anchored in the vicinity. Plan your course clear of other boats or obstructions and have an escape route planned in case of unforeseen circumstances. Brief the crew and give them time to prepare a mooring warp or anchor and cable.

When you leave, your boat will be pointing toward the wind or tide, whichever is the stronger. This is the direction in which you will set off, unless an obstruction requires you to steer another course. As when you arrived, brief your crew to prepare them for departure.

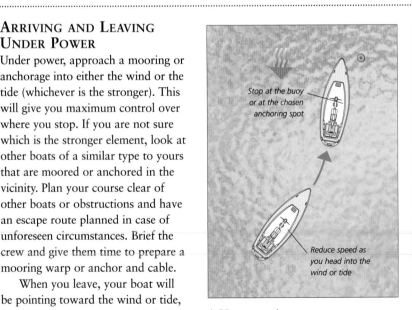

*Stop at the buoy or at the chosen anchoring spot*

*Reduce speed as you head into the wind or tide*

### △ HOW TO APPROACH

*Motor slowly into the wind or tide toward the mooring buoy or your chosen anchorage spot. Reduce speed until you are stationary alongside the buoy or at the anchoring spot.*

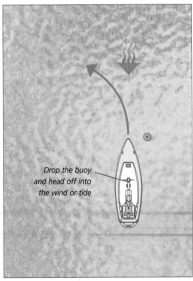

*Drop the buoy and head off into the wind or tide*

### △ HOW TO LEAVE

*Drop the mooring buoy or motor forward to pick up the anchor. Head initially into the wind or tide, whichever is stronger, as this will give you maximum control before turning to your preferred course.*

# SECURING TO A MOORING OR ANCHOR

It is simpler to pick up a mooring than to come alongside, but be prepared before approaching. Detail one or two crew members to pick up the mooring; they should have a mooring line and boathook ready. Make a dummy run up to the mooring to check the approach and inspect it closely, particularly its pick-up arrangement.

On larger cruisers, the bow may be quite high out of the water, making it difficult to pick up the buoy or thread a mooring line. In this case, come alongside the buoy just forward of the shrouds, where the freeboard is usually less. As you make your final approach, the foredeck crew should indicate the position and distance of the buoy by hand-signals, as the helmsman may lose sight of it in the last few yards.

Once the buoy is alongside, the foredeck crew can either pull the pick-up buoy on board or tie the mooring

### ▽ PICKING UP A BUOY
*The foredeck crew should be equipped with a boathook and have a mooring warp available. Hook the buoy with the boathook and tie up with a mooring line.*

line to the ring on the buoy or to the chain under the buoy. Take a round-turn through the ring, then tie a bowline (p.39). If a pick-up buoy is pulled aboard, check the condition of the rope or chain between it and the main riser. If the rope or chain looks at all suspect, use a warp to tie to the main chain. Make sure that the mooring line is led through a fairlead.

To leave a mooring, the foredeck crew must prepare the gear to allow them to drop it immediately on command. If a pick-up buoy has been brought aboard, its line should be uncleated and held with a turn around the cleat. If a mooring rope has been tied to the buoy or chain, it should be re-led as a slip line, with both ends on board; it can then be easily released and recovered. When the buoy is dropped, make sure that the skipper knows it is clear of the boat.

## DROPPING AN ANCHOR
Prepare the anchor and cable before the final approach to the chosen spot. With the anchor stowed in its bow roller, release any lashings or securing pins. Make sure that the anchor

cannot drop before you are ready. Check the depth of water and allow at least three times the depth for the amount of cable required. This length should be pulled on deck, so that it is ready to run without snagging, and then cleated. When the boat reaches the chosen spot, and has stopped or is moving astern, give the order to let go. The anchor should be lowered, not dropped free, into the water, and the cable allowed to run out under control until the anchor reaches the bottom. Pay out the rest of the cable as the boat drifts away from the anchor and snub to set. When the cable is under strain, take a series of bearings on two or more points on shore to make sure that the boat is not dragging its anchor. If the anchor drags, let out more cable. If this does not work, haul the anchor up and try another spot.

## WEIGHING ANCHOR
The ease with which an anchor can be recovered depends on the weight of anchor and cable, the depth of water, wind and sea conditions, and the strength of the crew or the anchor windlass. The first step is to bring the boat over the anchor by pulling in the cable. In stronger conditions, you may need the help of the engine or sails. When the boat is over the anchor, the crew must inform the skipper that the anchor is ready to break out. Haul up the cable by hand or windlass until the anchor breaks out of the seabed.

At this point, motor or sail slowly until the foredeck crew have stowed the anchor and cable. If the anchor cannot be broken out by hand or with the windlass, you may have to haul the cable as tight as possible, then cleat it, and use the power of the engine or sails to break it out.

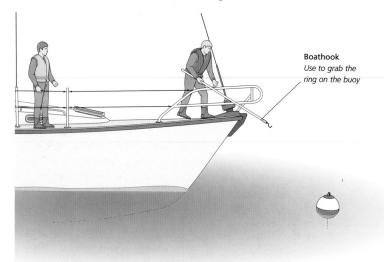

**Boathook**
*Use to grab the ring on the buoy*

## LAYING TWO ANCHORS

To provide extra security, lay two anchors, either both in line on one cable, or at a 30-45° angle to each other using two cables. To stop your boat swinging far when the tide changes, lay two anchors ahead and astern of the boat. To do this, drop the main anchor and reverse the boat while paying out twice the length of cable needed. Drop the second anchor (the kedge) from the bow, and pull in the main cable while letting out the kedge cable to position the boat midway between the two anchors. Join the two cables with a shackle, and let out both to lower the joint below the boat's keel. Secure both cables on cleats.

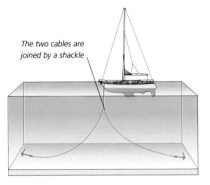

*The two cables are joined by a shackle*

*Set the anchors at about 30-45° to each other*

### △ REDUCED SWING

*Two anchors dropped ahead and astern of the boat will restrict its swing to a much smaller radius than on just one anchor.*

### △ EXTRA SECURITY

*If you may have to ride out a strong wind from a certain direction, lay two anchors in the direction of the expected wind.*

## TRIPPING LINES

It is very easy for an anchor to become fouled by an obstruction on the seabed. Motoring around the anchor and pulling its chain from several directions may free it, but it is best to avoid the problem in likely areas of foul ground by using a tripping line.

### USING A TRIPPING LINE

A tripping line is a light line tied to the crown of the anchor. The other end of the line is either brought back on board, where it is left slack but secured on a cleat, or it is attached to a small buoy to float over the anchor. Beware of using a buoy on the tripping line in crowded anchorages, as it may get caught by another boat's propeller or be mistaken for a mooring buoy and picked up. In such cases, it is better to bring the end back aboard, although a longer length of line will be needed.

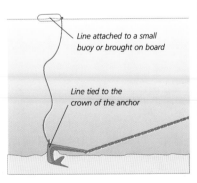

*Line attached to a small buoy or brought on board*

*Line tied to the crown of the anchor*

### △ RETRIEVING A FOULED ANCHOR

*If an anchor is fouled, it can be retrieved by pulling on the tripping line. This will capsize the anchor and bring it up upside down.*

## USING THE TENDER

Sometimes it will be necessary to use the tender to lay or recover an anchor. This is easier to do with a solid dinghy than with an inflatable. It is also easier if rope cable is used rather than chain.

### LAYING AN ANCHOR

To lay an anchor from the tender, tie the tender securely alongside the cruiser and transfer the anchor and all the cable required into the dinghy. Coil the cable in the stern of the tender so that it will run out smoothly. Make the end fast aboard the cruiser. It is much easier to handle the anchor if it is hung over the tender's stern and held by a length of line tied to the thwart with a slip hitch. This allows you to release the anchor while seated and is much safer than trying to manhandle the anchor over the side. Row or motor the tender in the direction you want to lay the anchor. Then, when all the cable has run out, slip the retaining line to release the anchor. The crew left on board can now pull in the slack to set the anchor.

### RETRIEVING AN ANCHOR

On some occasions you may have to recover an anchor using the tender, usually when you have set two anchors and you cannot recover them both from the yacht. Recovering an anchor can be hazardous in an inflatable and is easier and safer in a rigid dinghy. Pull the tender along the anchor cable, with the cable running over the tender, until the cable leads vertically down into the water. The tender's buoyancy, combined with a strong pull on the cable, should be enough to break out the anchor, which can then be pulled up and into the tender. Return to the cruiser by pulling on the cable, coiling it into the tender as you go.

# PASSAGE MAKING

*There are few things more pleasurable for the cruising sailor than a well-executed passage culminating in a safe arrival at the destination. It does not matter if you arrive at a harbor you know well; the sense of satisfaction cannot be equaled by any other form of travel. As skipper, you alone are responsible for the safe handling of the yacht and the welfare of the crew. If your experience is limited, start with short day trips, building up to a longer cruise lasting several days.*

## ROLE OF SKIPPER

All aspects of the running of the yacht, its safety, and the welfare of the crew are the skipper's responsibility. He should be comfortable with every area of sailing, inspire confidence in his crew, and be a good communicator. He should be able to keep on top of all his duties and give the crew tasks that are appropriate to their level of ability and experience, so that they are neither underworked nor overburdened.

It is important, when you are learning the skipper's role, that you do not undertake passages that are beyond your level of experience. Although ultimate responsibility lies with the skipper, his job will be easier if some of the crew have offshore passage-making experience. Passage making with an inexperienced crew puts great demands on a skipper, who may feel under immense pressure if there is not an experienced crew member to

whom some tasks can be delegated. If you cannot find an experienced sailor to come with you, adjust your plans to suit the crew's level of experience.

## ROLE OF CREW

Good crew are worth their weight in gold. The most important qualities are a positive attitude, a sense of humor, and the ability to get on with others in the confined space aboard a cruiser. If the crew also have good sailing or navigation skills, the skipper can consider himself fortunate. The crew should be fully involved in the boat's management and passage planning, and the skipper should always listen to their opinions. The crew must remember, however, that a vessel at sea is not a democratic environment; ultimately, the skipper is in charge and must make the final decisions.

## PASSAGE PLANNING

Planning for a cruise or passage starts some time before the day of departure. The skipper, or navigator if there is one, prepares a detailed navigation plan (*pp.258–59*). From this you can estimate the number of hours for which you will be sailing and whether the passage involves night sailing. Remember to have an alternative plan in case the weather or other factors require a change of plan. Also, build in days for rest and shoreside recreation, especially if there are children on board.

Using the passage plan, you will be able to work out your fuel, food, and water requirements, and can allow for stops to replenish supplies if necessary.

◁ DISCUSSING PLANS
*Plan your passage in detail before you set sail, and make sure that the crew are involved in the planning. Include back-up plans to allow for bad weather.*

# WATCH SYSTEMS

When passage making, it is essential that all members of the crew, including the skipper, get sufficient rest so that they continue to perform at their optimum. When setting out on a passage of more than a few hours, you should operate a watch system that allows all crew members to have time off watch for rest and sleep.

## APPORTIONING TASKS
Sailing offshore can be mentally and physically tiring, especially in rough weather. If everyone is to enjoy the passage and be able to contribute to the sailing of the yacht, you need to ensure that the crew stay alert and are well fed and rested throughout. A watch system divides the crew into two or more watches, one of which is responsible for the sailing of the yacht, while the other rests or prepares meals.

## TRADITIONAL SYSTEM
A traditional watch system has one watch on duty for four hours, followed by four hours off-watch. To prevent each watch having the same periods on watch each day, the watches are staggered by two dog watches of two hours each in the late afternoon and early evening, during which everyone is usually awake.

## IMPROVIZED SYSTEM
There is no need to use a traditional system. Many experienced skippers devise their own system to suit the particular needs of their crew and the length of the passage. What is important is that everyone gets sufficient rest, and that light and noise are kept to a minimum below when the off-watch crew are sleeping.

## KEEPING TIME
Make sure that everyone understands the importance of being on time for their watch. In the confines of a small yacht, when people are tired on passage, it is very easy for tempers to fray if the watch on deck is not relieved on time because the new watch has overslept. In some watch systems, when the crew is large enough, the skipper stays outside the watch system but remains on call at all times, and is usually on deck at each change of watch.

**TRADITIONAL WATCH SYSTEM ▷**
*Watch systems are arranged to run from midnight to midnight, splitting the twenty-four hours into periods of on-watch duty and off-watch rest. The traditional system demands four-hour watches at night, which may be too long in poor conditions.*

**KEY**

ON WATCH    RESTING    MEALTIMES

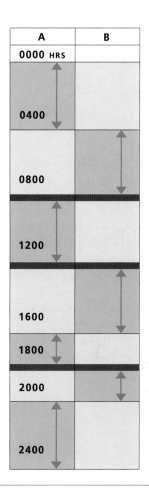

| | A | B |
| --- | --- | --- |
| **0000 HRS** | | |
| **0400** | | |
| **0800** | | |
| **1200** | | |
| **1600** | | |
| **1800** | | |
| **2000** | | |
| **2400** | | |

Check your yacht's insurance details to ensure that you are covered for the passage and, if you are going abroad, make sure that all your crew bring their passports and make any visa arrangements that may be necessary. Check that your yacht's registration papers are on board. Many countries now require a small-boat skipper to possess a certificate of competence, so make sure that you have it with you.

## COASTGUARD SERVICES
In many countries, the Coastguard Service is responsible for managing rescue operations at sea, either using its own resources or those of the navy, air force, lifeboat service, or any shipping in the vicinity. Many coastguards operate a system in which a yacht setting out on passage can inform the coastguard of its passage plan, destination, and estimated date and time of arrival. On reaching the destination, the skipper then notifies the coastguard of his boat's safe arrival. This system allows the coastguard to begin a search-and-rescue operation if a yacht is overdue. If the coastguard in your sailing area operates such a service, it is wise to take advantage of it. Always remember to inform the coastguard on arrival or if your plans change.

# AVOIDING COLLISIONS

*The International Regulations for Preventing Collisions at Sea (Col Regs) specify the responsibilities of all types of craft. They apply to all vessels on the high seas and connected waters, and it is essential that you learn the most common rules. As the skipper of a small boat, you have exactly the same responsibility for avoiding collisions as the skipper of the largest liner or supertanker. Ignorance of the rules is no defence, and the penalties for lack of observance can be severe.*

## RULES OF THE ROAD

In addition to the Col Regs, national governments and local authorities can impose their own regulations covering harbors, rivers, or inland waterways. Details of these are found in local pilot books. Make sure that you know and understand the basic "rules of the road" (pp.44–45), and study the full regulations for a more complete understanding. Have a ready reference to the rules on board so that you can check any situation with which you are unfamiliar.

Confusion sometimes arises when judging which boat is the stand-on or give-way vessel in any situation. When under power, this can be most easily understood by reference to the sectors of the basic navigation lights. When under sail and sailing to windward on port tack, it can sometimes be difficult to decide, especially at night, if a boat to windward of you and running downwind is on port or starboard tack. If it is on port tack, you have right of way and should stand on, but if it is on starboard tack, it has right of way and you must keep clear. In this situation and others where there is any doubt, you should assume that you have to give way and take evasive action in good time before a danger of collision arises.

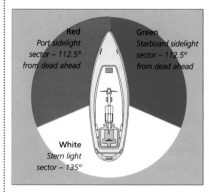

*Red*
*Port sidelight sector – 112.5° from dead ahead*

*Green*
*Starboard sidelight sector – 112.5° from dead ahead*

*White*
*Stern light sector – 135°*

△ **NAVIGATION LIGHT SECTORS**
*Under power, use another power boat's light sectors to decide when to give way or stand-on. In the white or red sectors, give way; in the green sector, stand-on.*

## TRAFFIC-SEPARATION ZONES

In busy shipping areas, traffic-separation schemes are in place to keep local traffic separate from through traffic, which is split into two lanes according to its direction. Separation zones between the traffic lanes are restricted to fishing vessels, ships in a state of emergency, and those crossing the lanes.

### TRAFFIC LANES

Boats entering a traffic lane should do so at the ends of the lane where possible, or at a shallow angle so that they blend into the traffic flow. Local traffic must use the inshore zones and keep out of the lanes. If you have to cross a traffic-separation scheme, it is important that you do so as quickly as possible. Steer a course at right angles to the lane; do not adjust your course to allow for any sideways tidal effect, as doing so would increase the time that it takes to cross the lane.

**SEPARATION ZONES** ▷
*Traffic-separation zones are used in areas of heavy shipping traffic and in constricted or dangerous waters. Vessels that are crossing a separation zone must do so at right angles.*

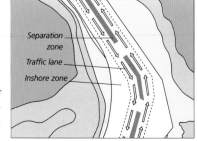

*Separation zone*
*Traffic lane*
*Inshore zone*

## TAKING EVASIVE ACTION

The crew on a cruiser may be small and inexperienced, but it is vital that a lookout is kept at all times. As skipper, you should instruct your crew to alert you whenever an approaching vessel is seen. When yours is the give-way vessel, or you are uncertain of the situation, take evasive action well in advance of any potential collision. In a crossing situation with a large ship, you may be uncertain as to whether you are on a collision course. Use a hand bearing compass to take a bearing of the approaching ship. Record the bearing and then take a series of bearings at frequent intervals. If the bearing remains the same, then you are on a collision course and must take immediate action.

Once you have decided to take avoiding action, make a significant change of course so that your intentions are obvious to the other vessel. Avoid crossing the bows of another craft, especially a large ship, which may be moving much faster than you think. Where possible, alter course to pass astern of the other vessel. If in doubt, turn onto a parallel course in the same direction as the other vessel and wait for it to pass.

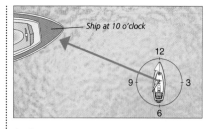

Ship at 10 o'clock

△ **CLOCK-NOTATION SYSTEM**
*Use a clock-notation system to tell the skipper where an approaching vessel is in relation to your yacht – here, the ship is at 10 o'clock. If possible, also give an estimate of the distance of the ship and its direction of travel. In this case, the vessel is moving from left to right.*

---

## SOUND SIGNALS AND DAYLIGHT SHAPES

Sound signals are used in clear visibility to indicate that a vessel is carrying out a maneuver. When vessels under power are in sight of each other, and one is altering course, it must indicate its intentions by the use of horn signals. At night, an all-round white light can be flashed for the appropriate number of times.

During the day, vessels must use shapes to make identification easier. A yacht should hoist an inverted cone shape up the forestay to indicate that it is motor-sailing, and hoist a ball shape into the rigging when at anchor. Only the basic signals are shown here: refer to the Col Regs for a full list of all the signals used.

| SOUND SIGNALS | ( ■ = SHORT BLAST; ▬▬▬ = LONG BLAST) | DAYLIGHT SHAPES | |
|---|---|---|---|
| ■ | Altering course to starboard | ▼ | Vessel under sail and power |
| ■ ■ | Altering course to port | ● | Vessel at anchor |
| ■ ■ ■ | Engine going astern. Large ships take time to stop; they may still be moving ahead even when their engine is running astern | ▼▲ | Vessel fishing or trawling |
| ■ ■ ■ ■ ■ | Vessel indicating that another's intentions are not clear | ▮ | Vessel constrained by its draft |
| ▬▬▬ ▬▬▬ ■ | Wishes to pass another vessel to starboard in a narrow channel | | |
| ▬▬▬ ▬▬▬ ■ ■ | Wishes to pass another vessel to port in a narrow channel | ●◆● | Vessel restricted in its ability to maneuver |
| ▬▬▬ ■ ▬▬▬ ■ | Vessel agreeing to be passed in narrow channel | | |

# RUNNING AGROUND

*There are very few experienced sailors who have never run aground. In theory, careful navigation and good seamanship will avoid a grounding, but, in the real world, it is an occupational hazard. Most groundings result in little more than wounded pride, but the situation is potentially dangerous. Quick and effective action is required to refloat the boat immediately if possible, or to minimize the danger and potential damage if you are stuck fast.*

### ASSESSING THE SITUATION

If you run aground, the amount of danger that your boat is in will depend on the bottom and on the sea state. Grounding on rocks in a heavy sea will wreck the strongest boat, but grounding on sand or mud in settled conditions should present little threat. Check your charts and test around the boat with the spinnaker pole or boathook to find out what the bottom is like. If weather conditions are forecast to deteriorate, try everything possible to get the boat off quickly.

### TAKING ACTION

The first action you take on running aground can be crucial if you are to get off quickly. It is important to know whether the tide is rising or falling. If it is rising, the situation is less serious: the tide will soon float you off, as long as you can prevent the boat from being driven further into shallow water. If the tide is falling, however, you may have only a few moments to get off before you are stuck until the tide rises again. In the worst case – running aground at the top of a spring tide – you may have to wait a fortnight or more until the tide returns far enough to float the boat. If you

ground under sail, you must decide immediately if you can use the sails to help you get off. If you ground on a lee shore, the wind will push the boat into the shallows, and you will not be able to use the sails to get off.

When the sails cannot help, drop them and, under power, try reversing off the way you went on. If the bottom is muddy, the keel will have plowed a furrow. It will be easier to reverse out than to turn the boat and motor off forward.

### GROUNDING IN CHANNELS

Grounding can easily occur when tacking up a channel with shallow water on each side. If you hold a tack too far, the boat will touch bottom. In this situation, you should immediately try to tack the boat so that it is pointing back into deep water. If you are successful, and the sails fill on the new tack, sheet them in very tight and the boat may heel far enough to reduce its draft and sail clear into deep water. You can avoid this situation by checking the depth sounder frequently when tacking along a channel.

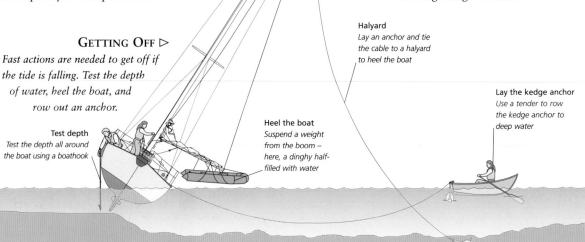

**GETTING OFF ▷**
*Fast actions are needed to get off if the tide is falling. Test the depth of water, heel the boat, and row out an anchor.*

**Test depth**
*Test the depth all around the boat using a boathook*

**Heel the boat**
*Suspend a weight from the boom – here, a dinghy half-filled with water*

**Halyard**
*Lay an anchor and tie the cable to a halyard to heel the boat*

**Lay the kedge anchor**
*Use a tender to row the kedge anchor to deep water*

## TURNING THE BOW

In a small boat with a shallow draft, you may be able to send a crew member over the side to push the bow round. If a crew member goes over the side, first check the depth of water around the boat with the spinnaker pole or boathook, and tie a line to keep him attached to the boat. Alternatively, you could try pushing off with a spinnaker pole or boathook from the deck.

## REDUCING DRAFT

Sometimes, you may be able to reduce draft to enable the boat to sail or motor clear. If your boat has a centerboard, raise it immediately and head for deep water. In a deep-keeled boat, you can try heeling the boat to reduce its draft. If the wind is blowing off the shallows, try sheeting the sails in tightly to increase the heeling force. Alternatively, have the crew sit on the end of the boom and swing it out over the side of the boat. Make sure that the topping lift is strong enough before you do this, however. If the crew is reluctant to sit on the boom, try hanging a heavy weight, such as an anchor, from its end and swinging it over the side. This weight should be sufficient to heel the boat and reduce its draft. This may be enough to allow you to sail off.

Many boats have their deepest draft at the aft end of the keel. In this case, draft can be reduced slightly by putting all the crew on the bow to lift the stern. A bilge keel boat draws more when heeled than upright because of its keel configuration, so you should bring it upright in order to minimize its draft.

## RETURNING TIDE

If you are stuck fast until the tide returns, try to lay the boat over with the mast pointing toward shallow water. If you have grounded on a slope and the boat lays over toward deep water, it may flood through the deck openings, such as hatches and ventilators, before the boat can rise on the returning tide. If the boat has already settled heeling the wrong way, try shifting weight to the side you want it to heel toward. Alternatively, push the bow or stern round, or pull it with an anchor line, to point the boat in the right direction. If the bottom is rocky or uneven, pad the outside of the hull before it lies on its side. This will help protect the boat from crashing on the seabed as it rises and falls on the returning tide. Use bunk cusions, sail bags, or a partly inflated dinghy.

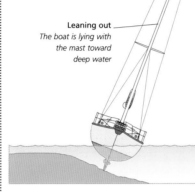

Leaning out
*The boat is lying with the mast toward deep water*

△ **LEANING WRONG WAY**
*If the boat is heeled with the mast lying toward deep water when the tide is rising, try to correct it or the boat may flood.*

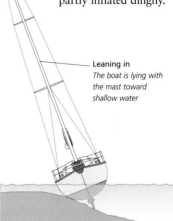

Leaning in
*The boat is lying with the mast toward shallow water*

△ **LEANING RIGHT WAY**
*If the boat is heeled with the mast lying toward shallow water, lay an anchor and wait until the tide rises and floats it off.*

## USING A KEDGE ANCHOR

If the tide is not falling quickly, you may have time to launch the tender and row out the kedge anchor toward deep water. Try using it to winch the boat into water deep enough to float in.

### LAYING THE ANCHOR

Lay the anchor on the longest cable possible. Back aboard, take the cable to the bow or stern, depending on which end you are going to try to pull toward the deep water. Lead the cable through a fairlead and then to an anchor windlass or sheet winch. If necessary, lead the cable around two winches and wind on both of them. If your gear is strong enough, you may be able to winch the boat into deep water, recover the anchor and motor or sail away. It can help to free the boat if the crew who are not required to winch the cable try to heel the boat, or rock it from side to side, to break the suction if the keel is trapped in mud.

### STUCK FAST

If you are stuck fast, lay the anchor as far as possible toward deep water to prevent the boat from being pushed farther into the shallows by breaking seas, and to assist you in getting off when the tide returns.

# MAN-OVERBOARD RECOVERY

*Having a man overboard is one of the greatest fears of any skipper. As soon as a person falls overboard, he or she is in grave danger. Only the prompt and efficient action of the crew left on board can prevent a fatality. It is best to try to prevent people falling overboard in the first place: safety harnesses must be available and worn when necessary. If a man-overboard situation still occurs, it is vitally important to keep the person in sight and pick them up as quickly as possible.*

## FIRST ACTIONS

The immediate priority when a person falls overboard is to alert the rest of the crew with a cry of "man overboard." Keep the casualty in sight and deploy the lifebuoy and marker buoy immediately. If possible, the lifebuoy should be thrown upwind of the casualty so that it will drift toward him. If a dye marker is available, it should be thrown overboard to help mark the person's position. Any delay will result in the boat sailing further away from the casualty, reducing his chances of reaching the lifebuoy. On a fully crewed boat, one person should be detailed to keep a continuous watch on the person overboard. This may not be possible on a short-handed cruiser, but it is imperative to try to keep the person in sight if you are to have any chance of a successful recovery. The next step is for the skipper to decide on a recovery procedure, and quickly to brief the crew. If enough people are available, one should note the time and position in the log book and activate the MoB position function on the GPS unit (*pp.240–41*). This information will be needed to conduct a search if the victim is lost from sight.

## PREVENTION

By far the best way of dealing with this emergency is to prevent it occurring in the first place. The skipper must ensure that the appropriate safety equipment is carried on board.

### SAFETY HARNESSES
Every cruiser should have sufficient safety harnesses aboard for all the crew. Each crew member should adjust theirs so that it fits comfortably, and ensure that it is always accessible when needed. The skipper must set the rules for wearing a harness depending on the boat, the strength of the crew, and the weather conditions. There are no hard and fast rules, but, in general, harnesses should always be worn and clipped on in the following situations:

- When sailing at night or in fog
- When the boat is reefed or when a reef may be needed
- In areas of rough water
- When a crew member is working alone on deck

## RECOVERY UNDER SAIL

There are no set rules as to whether you recover a casualty under sail or power. All that matters is that you keep the casualty within sight and return to him under full control, without hitting him with the boat. The size of the boat, the number and experience of the crew, and the weather will dictate the best course of action. If you maneuver under sail, start the engine anyway, leaving it in neutral so that it is ready if needed.

The man-overboard recovery method for sailing dinghies (*pp.102–03*) is often taught for use in cruisers. It can work, especially with a full crew aboard. It requires you to sail away from the casualty to gain sea room, however, which means that you risk losing sight of the person. In very rough conditions or at night, it will be virtually impossible to keep the casualty in sight among the waves, and boat handling will be difficult.

## CRASH STOP

Another method to consider is the crash stop. This has the advantage of keeping the boat close to the casualty. With this technique, the helmsman should push the tiller hard to leeward as soon as the person goes over the side. Whatever the point of sailing you are on, this action usually results in the boat tacking. Leave the jib sheet cleated as the boat tacks, and the boat will end up hove-to. Push the tiller to the new leeward side to keep the boat stopped. There will be much flapping of sails and temporary disorder, but the boat will stop and lie relatively steadily. This will give you time to assess the situation and plan what to do without sailing away from the casualty. This method can work even

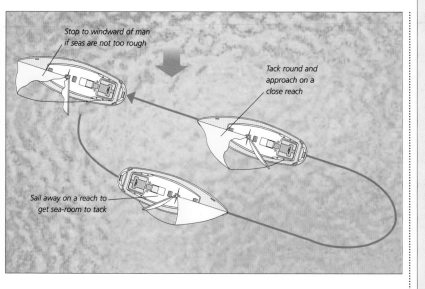

Stop to windward of man if seas are not too rough

Tack round and approach on a close reach

Sail away on a reach to get sea-room to tack

if you are sailing under spinnaker. The boat will almost certainly not tack, however, and the situation will be chaotic until you lower the spinnaker. Nevertheless, the boat will still be relatively close to the man overboard.

After a crash stop, you may be close enough to the casualty to throw him a line. If not, try to work the boat closer by adjusting the sheets and tiller. Alternatively, lower the headsail, sheet the main in tight, and use the engine to approach the person overboard.

Whichever method you use to return to the man overboard under sail, you should aim to make the final approach on a close reach. This allows you to adjust your speed easily by easing or trimming the mainsail. If possible, lower or roll up the jib to keep the foredeck clear of flapping jib sheets that can cause injury. In moderate conditions, aim to stop the boat with the bow to windward of the casualty so that it drifts to leeward as it slows down. This allows the casualty to be grabbed and brought aft to just behind the leeward shrouds. In heavier conditions, it is safer to stop to leeward of the casualty so that the boat is not pushed onto him by a

### △ RETURNING UNDER SAIL

*Sail away from the man overboard on a beam reach (to the apparent wind), tack round and approach the casualty on a close reach, stopping to windward of him.*

wave, causing injury. Have a rope ready to throw in case you cannot get alongside the man, and have another ready to tie him to the boat as soon as you have contact with him.

## RECOVERY UNDER POWER

If you are motoring when a person falls overboard, immediately turn the boat toward him. This will swing the stern away from the casualty as he passes down the side, and prevent him from being caught by the propeller. As soon as the person has cleared the stern, put the helm hard over the other way and start the boat turning back toward the casualty. Keep the person in sight and approach upwind. Aim to stop the boat with the person just forward of the shrouds, to keep him as far away as possible from the propeller. Once the casualty has been secured to the boat with a line, stop the engine while he is brought aboard.

## GETTING THE PERSON ABOARD

Once you are alongside the casualty, immediately secure him to the boat with a line tied under his armpits using a bowline (p.39).

### FACTORS TO CONSIDER

How you get the casualty aboard will depend on his ability to help himself (if conscious), the height of the boat out of the water, and the crew strength on board. Bear in mind that it is much easier to recover a man overboard on the leeward side, where the boat's heel reduces the freeboard.

### LIFTING TACKLE

It is nearly impossible to physically pull a wet, heavy, and unconscious person out of the water, so some form of lifting tackle will be necessary. Make up a sling and tackle ready for this purpose, or buy a ready-made system. Stow it where it can be reached quickly. The tackle can be attached to a spare halyard or to the end of the main boom. Use an arrangement appropriate for your boat, and practice using the system before it is needed in a real-life situation.

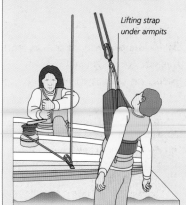

Lifting strap under armpits

### △ SLING AND TACKLE

*A ready-to-use lifting sling and tackle is the best solution for lifting a person out of the water. Attach the top of the tackle to a halyard or the boom end, whichever is most appropriate for your boat.*

# SAILING AT NIGHT

*In good conditions, sailing at night can be very rewarding. It reinforces a sense of solitude and of being solely responsible for your boat and crew. Moonlight and phosphorescence can make for a beautiful night-time passage, and dawn at sea is one of the most exquisite experiences afloat. To fully enjoy the experience, however, you and your crew must make preparations before darkness falls. For your first night-time passage, try to have at least one crew member who has had experience at night sailing. At night, all vessels must display navigation lights according to their size and type. Make sure that you have a suitable reference book aboard to look these up, as it can be difficult to remember all the possible light combinations.*

### ADVANCE PREPARATION

All crew who work on deck during the night must be familiar with the equipment and be able to find and use it in the dark. Retaining night vision on deck is important. This is made easier if red lights, or at least very dim white ones, are used below in the galley and navigation area. Work out a watch system (*pp.216–17*) and ensure that the crew keep to it so that they get enough rest. As skipper, ensure that the crew on watch call you if they are concerned about anything, or at any times or in any situations that you specify. Watch-keepers must dress warmly and wear foul weather gear if necessary. Insist that safety harnesses are worn and clipped on when in the cockpit or on deck, even in calm weather.

### BEFORE NIGHTFALL

Prepare and eat a hot meal before dark, and wash up immediately. Stow all loose gear below. Check the deck and stow any unnecessary equipment. Make sure that at least one flashlight is on hand in the cockpit.

Complete any sail changes before darkness makes the job harder. It can be helpful to change to a smaller headsail, or roll away part of a rolling headsail, to improve the helmsman's visibility. However, do not sail the boat under-canvassed in light weather. Sail with a spinnaker at night only if the crew is experienced, as spinnakers can be difficult to take down in the dark.

At dusk, switch on and check the navigation lights, update your position on the chart, and plan your passage to cover the hours of darkness. Write instructions for the on-watch crew in the logbook or on a deck slate. Include the course to steer and any light signals that you anticipate seeing.

### RECOGNIZING LIGHTS

The International Regulations for Preventing Collisions at Sea (the Col Regs) specify the type, size, layout, arc, and distance of visibility of lights to be used by all types of vessels. Various combinations indicate, among other possibilities, whether a boat is anchored or under way, under sail or power, or fishing or trawling. Make sure that you know all the common arrangements of lights and check that your own lights conform to the Col Regs. When using your engine rather than sailing, you must display the correct lights for a vessel under power. Incorrect use of lights can lead to a collision, for which you may be held responsible.

---

## COPING WITH THE DARK

It is important to know about some of the effects of night sailing. The boat's behavior does not alter, but the crews' perceptions of it may well change. Conditions may feel rougher than they really are, and it will be more difficult to judge distances accurately.

### CREW AND HELMSMAN

Inexperienced crew may feel nervous and disoriented at night. Wherever possible, they should be paired with a more experienced crew member. To avoid eyestrain through staring at the compass, the helmsman should use a star, the moon, a cloud, or other reference point ahead of the boat to steer towards, checking the course by the compass at frequent intervals.

Remember to keep a good lookout all around the boat, including immediately astern.

### SAIL SETTING

Checking the set of the sails is hard at night. Shine a flashlight on the luffs periodically to check that the sails are set properly. Do not shine a flashlight in someone's eyes, as this will ruin their night vision for up to 20 minutes.

# NAVIGATION LIGHTS

All vessels display basic navigation lights. They may also show one or more steaming lights. These lights identify whether a vessel is under power or sail, its direction of travel, and its likely size. Many vessels also have a set of extra lights to show that they are engaged in a particular job or have a specific restriction. The most common lights and their required arcs of visibility are shown here.

## BASIC NAVIGATION LIGHTS

### WHITE LIGHT
A dinghy (of less than 23ft/7m) under sails or oars must carry a flashlight to show a white light when required.

### ALL-ROUND WHITE LIGHT
A boat of up to 23ft (7m) long, under power but incapable of more than 7kn, must have a fixed all-round white light.

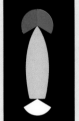

### STERN AND COMBINED SIDELIGHTS
A sailing vessel that is over 23ft (7m) long must show red and green sidelights, each covering an arc of 112.5°. Under 65ft (20m), the sidelights can be combined in one lantern at the bow. The stern light must be visible over an arc of 135°. Alternatively, a tricolor masthead light may be used (*below*).

### MASTHEAD LIGHT
Sailing yachts under 65ft (20m) may combine the sidelights and stern lights in a tricolor light at the masthead. The height of the masthead offers greater visibility. However, a separate stern light and sidelights (or a combined sidelight) must still be fitted in case of failure of the masthead light and for use under power, with a steaming light (*right*).

### SEPARATE LIGHTS
Yachts over 65ft (20m) in length are required to use two separate sidelights and a stern light. They may not use a tricolor masthead light, but they can show the optional sailing lights (*right*). These all-round, red over green lights are often used on large sailing vessels.

## STEAMING LIGHTS

### COMBINED LIGHT
A power craft under 65ft (20m) can have a combined masthead and stern light. The sidelights may be combined at the bow.

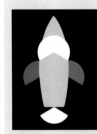

### SINGLE STEAMING LIGHT
A power-driven vessel that is less than 160ft (50m) long must show a masthead steaming light that is visible over a 225° arc, as shown. This is positioned above the sidelights. Over 65ft (20m), the sidelights and stern lights should be separate.

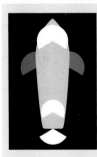

### TWO STEAMING LIGHTS
Larger power vessels that are more than 160ft (50m) in length must show two masthead steaming lights. The forward light should be positioned lower than the aft light. Both lights must be visible over an arc of 225°. The sidelights are separate, as is the stern light.

## EXTRA, ALL-ROUND LIGHTS

| | | | |
|---|---|---|---|
|  | Optional lights when under sail |  | Vessel fishing |
| | Vessel trawling |  | Minesweeper |
| | Vessel constrained by draught | | Pilot vessel on duty |
|  | Vessel restricted in ability to maneuver | | |

# SAILING IN FOG

*F*og can represent a greater danger than rough weather to a small boat. Your visibility can be reduced to near zero, making you vulnerable to collision with another craft or with the shore. Do not put to sea unless you are sure that the fog is land-bound and that conditions at sea are clear. If you are at sea when fog descends, you must take steps to preserve your safety. Increase your boat's visibility, use the appropriate sound signals, and avoid any other vessels in the vicinity.

△ **RADAR REFLECTOR**
*Increase your boat's visibility by fixing, or hoisting when needed, a radar reflector as high up in the rigging as possible.*

## IMMEDIATE ACTIONS

If fog appears when you are at sea, the safety of your crew and boat must be your first consideration. Plot your boat's present position on the chart by taking a fix, if possible, or working up an estimated position (*pp.254–55*). Unless you have one permanently fitted, hoist a radar reflector as high up the rigging as possible. All commercial vessels and many yachts use radar as a primary means of collision avoidance, so it is in your best interests to ensure that you help them to see you by using a reflector.

Turn on all navigation lights and delegate a member of the crew to make the appropriate sound signals. Station extra lookouts. If you are motoring, place a lookout on the foredeck as far away as possible from the noise of the engine.

## PERSONAL SAFETY

Make sure that all the crew put on lifejackets, as there will be no time to do this if a collision occurs. Recovering a person fallen overboard is likely to be impossible in fog. Think carefully before making the crew clip on safety harnesses, however, as they must be able to jump clear in a collision. If the weather is rough, the greater danger of falling overboard may require harnesses to be used. Crew members down below should wear lifejackets and remain fully clothed, so that they can get up on deck instantly if necessary. Check that the life-raft is ready for instant release if needed, and have some red and white flares on hand. If the weather is

◁ **FOG AT SEA**
*In fog, it is very difficult to estimate the size and speed of another boat and the direction in which it is travelling. When visibility is very poor, the risk of collision with another boat may be extremely high.*

calm, consider putting the dinghy over the side and towing it astern so that it is available in the event of a collision.

It is helpful to have an idea of your visibility. Sighting a buoy or other object can give you a rough idea. Alternatively, drop a bundle of paper over the side and monitor the time it takes before it disappears from sight; knowledge of your boat's speed allows you to work out the distance.

If your yacht is fitted with radar, turn it on as soon as visibility deteriorates. Station a crew member with experience at reading a radar screen to monitor it. Do not rely completely on radar, however; you must still have lookouts on deck.

## TACTICS

Your choice of tactics will depend on whether you are close to land, in a busy shipping area, or well out to sea. If out to sea, continue on course, keeping a good lookout and making the appropriate sound signals. Where possible, proceed under sail, as the noise of an engine will limit your ability to hear other boats. If it is calm and you have to motor, move under power at a reasonable speed so that you have good steerage way and can turn quickly if necessary. Stop the engine at regular intervals to listen out for other vessels or navigation aids. Keep the mainsail hoisted, as this will make you more visible to another vessel.

## SHIPPING LANES

If you are in or near a busy shipping lane, your first priority is to get clear of it as soon as possible. Plot a course to take you into shallow water, which will be free of large vessels. If you have to cross a shipping channel, do so at a right angle and as quickly as possible. Once in shallow water, either heave-to or anchor until the fog lifts. Remember that other yachts may have had the same idea, so keep a lookout and make the appropriate sound signals.

If a harbor with a safe entrance is close at hand and you are confident in your navigation skills, make for it. Do not rely solely on electronic aids such as GPS to ensure your safe entry.

## SOUND SIGNALS

Vessels in fog employ sound signals to indicate their presence to other boats. Many navigational aids such as buoys and lighthouses are also fitted with sound signal equipment to help you identify them. The type of signal that they emit is marked on charts and in pilot books. Sound can be distorted by fog, so do not assume a direction for the sound. Stop to double-check, and proceed with caution. Craft indicate their presence, size, and activity with a combination of foghorn, bell, and gong signals. A boat under 39ft (12m) is required to carry only an "efficient sound signal." Most use some form of compressed-air or aerosol foghorn. Larger boats over 39ft (12m) must also carry a bell, and vessels over 328ft (100m) will also use a gong.

# SOUND SIGNALS

In foggy conditions, you must use the appropriate sound signals to indicate whether you are sailing or motoring, aground, or at anchor. Foghorn signals are either prolonged (four to six seconds) or short (one second). A bell can be sounded as a single ring or as a rapid ringing for five seconds, and a gong is rung rapidly. The most common signals are shown here. You should also keep a reference book on board detailing the full list of signals as required by the International Regulations for Preventing Collisions at Sea (Col Regs; *pp.218–19*).

| | |
|---|---|
| ▬▬▬▬ ■ ■ | Under sail: One long and two short foghorn blasts every two minutes. |
| ▬▬▬▬ | Making way under power: One long foghorn blast every two minutes. |
|  ▬▬▬  ▬▬▬ | Under way but not making way: Two long foghorn blasts at two-minute intervals. |
|  ▲▲▲ ▲▽▲▽▲▽ ▲▲▲ | Aground – under 328ft (100m): Three bells, rapid ringing, three bells, at one-minute intervals. |
|  ▲▲▲ ▲▽▲▽▲▽ ▲▲▲ ○ | Aground – over 328ft (100m): Three bells, rapid ringing, three bells, a gong sounded aft, every minute. |
|  ▲▽▲▽▲▽▲▽ | At anchor – under 328ft (100m): Rapid ringing of bell forward in boat at one-minute intervals. |
|  ▲▽▲▽▲▽▲▽ ○ | At anchor – over 328ft (100m): Rapid bell ringing forward, gong sounded aft, at one-minute intervals. |
|  ■ ■ ■ ■ | Pilot boat on duty: Four short blasts (after under way or making way) every two minutes. |

| KEY | | | | |
|---|---|---|---|---|
| | ▬▬▬▬ ■ | ▲ | ▲▽▲▽▲▽ | ○ |
| | FOGHORN | BELL | RAPID BELL-RINGING | GONG |

# ROUGH-WEATHER SAILING

*The definition of rough weather depends less on the wind strength than it does on the experience of the crew, the type of boat, the state of the sea, and the course you are sailing. A novice crew in a small cruiser may have a rough ride upwind in a Force 5, whereas an experienced crew in a large yacht would be comfortable in much heavier conditions. Every skipper must know the strengths and weaknesses of the boat, its gear, and its crew, and must have tactics for dealing with heavy weather.*

### PREPARING THE BOAT

As soon as you know that bad weather is on its way, begin preparing for it, even if you plan to get to a harbor before it arrives. Ready the boat for heavy seas by clearing the decks of loose gear and double-checking the lashings on the life-raft and tender. Close all ventilators and fit the washboards in the companionway. Pump the bilges before bad weather arrives and then at regular intervals.

Navigation will be harder in rough weather, so bring the logbook up to date. Plot your position on the chart and, by studying the chart and pilot book, decide on a course of action. Turn on navigation lights if visibility is poor. If you do not have a permanent radar reflector, rig a removable one to increase your visibility to shipping.

As the wind strength increases, be prepared to reduce the sail area. Reef the mainsail, and change or reef the headsail (*p.188*) to keep the boat moving quickly but comfortably and without excessive heel.

### PREPARING THE CREW

A warm, dry, and tidy cabin in which to rest, cook, navigate, and sleep is vital. Ensure that everything is stowed securely and make every effort to prevent water getting into the cabin. Put on warm layers (and gloves and a hat in cold weather) and wear foul weather gear and boots. All crew must wear safety harnesses; the skipper ensures that these are properly

### ▽ HEAVY SEAS

*In heavy weather, rough seas are usually more of a problem than the wind. Here, a cruiser rises to a steep sea under a reefed mainsail and small jib, and the crew wear foul weather gear and safety harnesses.*

△ **SAFETY HARNESS**
*Safety harnesses must be used in rough weather to ensure the safety of the crew. Adjust them so that they are comfortable, and clip the lifeline only to strong fittings.*

adjusted and that the crew clip on whenever they are in the cockpit or on deck. A strong securing point near the companionway allows a lifeline to be clipped on before coming on deck.

Cook and eat a hot meal before the bad weather arrives, and prepare vacuum flasks of soup or hot drinks, together with nutritious snacks for consumption during the storm. Take anti-seasickness tablets if required.

## DECIDING ON TACTICS

Your plan of action for rough weather should be based on the capabilities of the boat and crew, the severity of the expected weather conditions, and the proximity of the shoreline.

The most important thing to remember is to stay away from lee shores. Head for harbor only if you are certain your chosen refuge is safe to enter in strong winds. Ensure that there are no off-lying shallows or other navigational dangers, and that there is no risk that you could end up on a lee shore. A windward shore with a sheltered anchorage can offer protection, but you must be certain that the wind will not shift to turn it into a lee shore. Seeking open water to ride out the bad weather clear of the shore is often the best option. Head offshore and get as much sea room as possible between your boat and any potential lee shore.

## TAKING ACTION

If conditions become too rough to hold your chosen course, keep the boat as safe and comfortable as possible, while still making progress toward your destination if feasible. The procedure you choose depends on the handling characteristics of your boat; however, the standard first step is to heave-to (*p.183*) under a deeply reefed mainsail and storm jib. Many cruisers will heave-to at an angle of about 60° to the wind, their motion will be considerably reduced, and they will rise to the seas while drifting slowly to leeward.

Depending on conditions and the type of boat, you can remain hove-to until or unless the boat starts being knocked down by the waves, when it will become too uncomfortable or dangerous. It is now time to take another course of action. If you have plenty of sea room to leeward, consider running before the wind, either under bare poles or with a storm jib. Many modern, shallow-hulled, fin-keeled cruisers will surf downwind comfortably under an experienced helmsman. If your chosen course is downwind, this might be the safest procedure. However, if you have a heavier boat that does not surf easily, you must slow it down as much as possible for safety (*below*).

---

### SLOWING THE BOAT

Trailing warps or lying a-hull are two ways of slowing a boat. To lie a-hull, lower all sails and lash the tiller to leeward. This makes many boats lie approximately beam-on to the seas. It is comfortable unless the waves start breaking, when there is a danger of the boat being knocked down or rolled.

**TRAILING WARPS** ▷
*While running downwind without sail, or with just a small storm jib, secure your longest warp to the headsail winches and cleats, and trail the bight (loop) over the stern. This will slow the boat and help keep it in line with the seas. An anchor in the middle of the bight adds weight.*

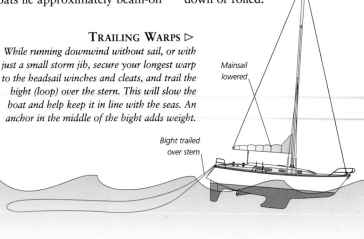

Mainsail
lowered

Bight trailed
over stern

# NAVIGATION

To gain the true freedom of the oceans,

a sailor needs to learn the art of navigation. It

may appear to be a complex subject, but anyone

who can work out a weekly shopping bill

will be able to cope with the mathematics

required to navigate proficiently. The immense

satisfaction gained when a planned destination

appears out of an empty ocean at the end of

a sailor's first offshore passage is ample

reward for the small effort involved.

*Navigating a small yacht on offshore passages
is a readily achievable skill, and is one of the
most rewarding aspects of offshore cruising.*

# STARTING TO NAVIGATE

*You need to understand only a few basic concepts to begin navigating. Once you understand the meaning of some simple terms – such as position, direction, distance, and depth – you will be able to apply them to practical navigation.*

## POSITION

The position of any spot on the earth can be described by its latitude and longitude – the lines of an imaginary grid laid on the earth's surface. The grid lines running east to west and parallel to the equator are known as parallels of latitude (the equator itself is 0° latitude). The lines running north to south, between the North and South Poles, are called meridians of longitude. The prime meridian (0° longitude) runs through the Greenwich Royal Observatory in the UK, from which it takes its name. Lines of latitude and longitude are measured by the angle that they form at the center of the earth, in degrees (°), minutes ('), and tenths of a minute. There are 60' in 1°, and 360° in a circle.

## LATITUDE AND LONGITUDE ON NAUTICAL CHARTS

Navigational charts have latitude and longitude scales printed at their edges, with grid lines going across them. This allows positions to be easily measured and plotted. When positions are described, latitude is given first in °N or °S, followed by longitude in °E or °W. For example, 50° 48'.7 N 1° 17'.3 W.

## DIRECTION

When coastal sailing, you will often find it easier to give a position with reference to a fixed sea- or landmark using direction and distance than to use latitude and longitude. Direction is measured clockwise as an angle relative to north. When describing the direction of an object in relation to your boat's position, or between two objects such as buoys, it is called a bearing. When describing the direction in which your boat is sailing, it is known as a heading.

## NORTH

Direction is defined relative to north. However, "north" can have three meanings. True north is the direction of the geographic North Pole, to which a chart's lines of longitude are aligned. Magnetic north is the direction of the magnetic North Pole. This is not in the

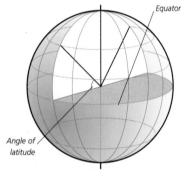

### △ LATITUDE
*The angle of latitude is measured at the center of the earth along the prime meridian from the equator (0°), and ranges from 0° to 90° north or south.*

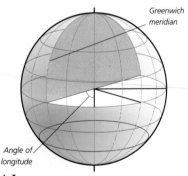

### △ LONGITUDE
*The angle of longitude is measured at the center of the earth along the equator from the prime (Greenwich) meridian (0°), and ranges from 0° to 180° east or west.*

### ▽ MEASUREMENTS ON CHART
*A position on the chart is measured on the latitude and longitude scales. Use a pair of dividers to transfer the distance from convenient grid lines to the scales.*

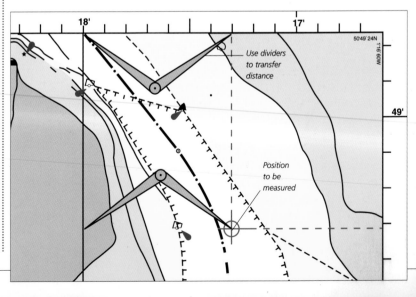

# NAVIGATIONAL TERMS

A variety of terms is used to record information on charts and to write down bearings, headings, and other important navigational data. The terms are recognized universally, eliminating (as far as possible) the risk of misunderstandings and enabling all navigators to understand the calculations. You need to know and understand these terms to be able to navigate successfully.

| SYMBOL | MEASUREMENT | DEFINITION |
|--------|-------------|------------|
| °T | Degrees true | Suffix attached to a direction measured relative to true north, e.g, 095°T. |
| °M | Degrees magnetic | Suffix attached to a direction measured relative to magnetic north, e.g, 135°M. |
| °C | Degrees compass | Suffix attached to a direction measured by the compass and not converted to °T or °M, e.g, 110°C. |
| M | Nautical mile | The unit of distance at sea. A nautical mile is equal to one degree of latitude (standardized at 6076ft/1852m). It is divided into 10 cables (ca) or tenths of a nautical mile. Each cable is 200yd (185m). |
| Kn | Knot | The unit of speed used at sea. One knot is one nautical mile per hour. |
| m | Meter | The standard meter is used to display depth and height on charts. Meters are divided into decimeters; 7.1m is shown on charts as $7_1$. |
| fm | Fathom | The old unit of depth, equal to 6ft (1.8m), sometimes found on older charts. Parts of a fathom are shown in feet, e.g, 38ft is shown as $6_2$. |

same place as the geographic North Pole. The difference between magnetic and true north is known as variation. This changes slightly every year, as the magnetic North Pole moves. Compass north is the direction in which your compass points. If there is no local magnetic interference, it will point to magnetic north. Navigators often have to convert between true, magnetic, and compass north (*pp.236–37*).

## DISTANCE AND SPEED

The unit of distance used at sea is the nautical mile, which is defined as one minute (1') of latitude. The earth is not a perfect sphere, so the actual length of a nautical mile varies, being shorter at the equator and longer at the poles. However, it is standardized to 6076ft (1852m) – slightly longer than a standard mile. The unit of speed used at sea is the knot. This is defined as one nautical mile per hour.

## DEPTH AND HEIGHT

Depth and height are measured in meters. Depth is shown on charts relative to a fixed datum, usually the lowest astronomical tide (LAT). This is the lowest water level ever expected. Usually, the water will be deeper than shown because of the height of tide (*p.247*). The datum from which heights are measured depends on the type of object measured (*p.247*).

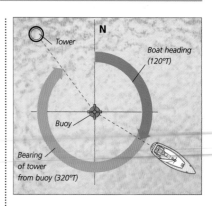

## △ HEADINGS AND BEARINGS

*A heading is a direction in which you steer your boat. A bearing is the direction of an object from you, or between two objects – here, a buoy and a tower. Both are measured in degrees relative to north.*

# CHARTS

A chart is an essential tool for navigation at sea. Charts are produced by the hydrographic agencies of most maritime countries. They were originally produced for professional sea-goers. Today, many hydrographic agencies, and some specialist publishers, also produce special yachting charts, derived from the official data but tailored to suit the yachtsman's needs. These are often available in folios covering the most popular sailing areas, and many include harbor plans and information.

## PROJECTION

A chart is a representation of a curved surface on a flat sheet of paper, which presents the cartographer with several problems. The main consideration is how best to represent (or project) the curve of the earth while minimizing distortion of the shape and size of land masses. The Mercator projection is the most common form found on nautical charts. It results in the parallels of latitude being drawn further apart toward the poles, whereas the meridians of longitude are drawn as parallel and equidistant.

Some charts use the gnomonic projection. These may be used for small-scale ocean passage charts or very large-scale harbor charts. On small-scale gnomonic charts, the meridians converge at the poles, whereas on large-scale gnomonic charts the area covered is so small that the meridians appear to be parallel. The type of projection that has been used on any particular chart is shown near its title.

## SCALE

Charts are available at various scales. Small-scale charts cover whole seas or oceans. They are used for overall planning and for plotting position on long passages. Medium-scale charts are typically used to cover sections of coastline. These are useful for coastal and offshore information around your departure point and destination. Large-scale charts cover small areas in great detail. They are essential when you are entering an unfamiliar harbor or are navigating a difficult stretch of water. The scale of the chart and other details, such as the units used for soundings (depths), and the date on which the chart was last corrected, are shown close to its title.

## SYMBOLS

Charts use many symbols to depict important features and potential hazards. Learn the common symbols on your charts, and keep a reference guide on board containing all the symbols used by the relevant chart-issuing agency.

## CHART CORRECTIONS

Charts are prepared from surveys conducted at regular intervals, depending on the importance to shipping of the area covered. As man-made features (and, occasionally, geographic ones) change, the chart is brought up to date with published corrections and a new one is issued periodically. Chart authorities issue regular corrections so you can update your charts, or you can return them to a chart agent for correction.

## NAUTICAL CHART

An up-to-date chart is essential for safe navigation, especially in a confined and congested area. The area illustrated here is an extremely busy channel that is used by commercial shipping and yachts.

Symbols

*Symbols are used on charts to indicate dangers and areas of particular importance. Learn the most common ones and carry a reference guide to the complete list of symbols*

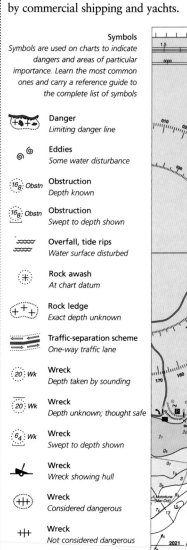

| | Danger | Limiting danger line |
| | Eddies | Some water disturbance |
| 16₈ Obstn | Obstruction | Depth known |
| 16₈ Obstn | Obstruction | Swept to depth shown |
| | Overfall, tide rips | Water surface disturbed |
| | Rock awash | At chart datum |
| | Rock ledge | Exact depth unknown |
| | Traffic-separation scheme | One-way traffic lane |
| 20 Wk | Wreck | Depth taken by sounding |
| 20 Wk | Wreck | Depth unknown; thought safe |
| 6₄ Wk | Wreck | Swept to depth shown |
| | Wreck | Wreck showing hull |
| | Wreck | Considered dangerous |
| | Wreck | Not considered dangerous |

Depth soundings

*Depths shown are related to chart datum (p.247), which are the lowest depths to which the water can usually be expected to drop. Contour lines join points of equal depth. Here, areas that dry out at low water are green, depths 0–15ft (0–5m) are blue, and depths 15–30ft (5–10m) are light blue. An underlined figure in areas that dry at low water indicates their drying height above chart datum*

# ELECTRONIC CHARTS

Charts are available in electronic form for use with a chart plotter (*pp.240–41*). They allow navigation to be done on screen and to incorporate data from other instruments.

## THE BENEFITS
Chart plotters display chart information on screen and allow the user to identify positions, courses, and distances by manipulating a cursor. The user can zoom in or out to alter the area covered, and can overlay data from a GPS set (global positioning system, *p.240*) and radar (*p.241*) onto the chart. The position shown by the GPS set can be shown directly on the chart, and the radar image can be compared with the details on the chart. The best systems allow the navigator to select the information he requires and to display it all on the plotter's screen.

## THE DISADVANTAGES
Electronic systems can be costly and susceptible to power failure, particularly in smaller yachts. Navigators must learn how to use them properly, and must understand how to interpret the information they provide accurately. Although digital systems give the impression of great accuracy, this should not be assumed unless information can be checked using another source. Using these systems is not an alternative to learning to navigate using simple manual tools and techniques. Paper charts must be on board as a back-up in the event of equipment failure.

**Latitude and longitude**
*Horizontal lines of latitude and vertical lines of longitude are used to plot position. Distance is measured using the latitude scale at the sides of the chart. The grid formed by the lines of latitude and longitude can be used in conjunction with plotting instruments (pp.238–39) to measure direction*

**Tidal stream information**
*Tidal diamonds located at key points relate to an information panel on the chart. From this, you can calculate the direction and strength of the tide at the tidal diamond at any time*

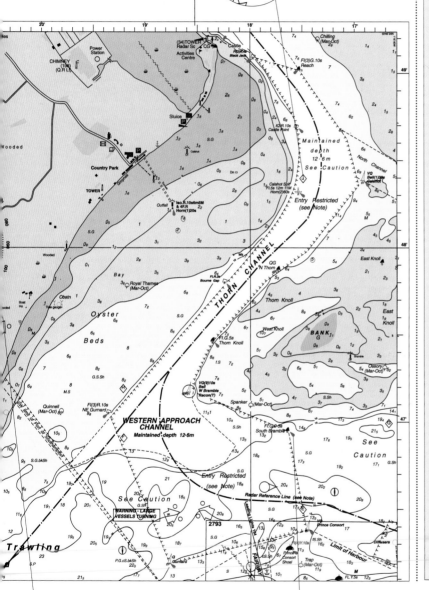

**Compass rose**
*There are several compass roses located on the chart. They allow true (°T) and magnetic (°M) bearings to be read directly from them. Information given in the rose provides details of the magnetic variation (pp.236–37)*

**Buoyage**
*Buoys are marked on the chart, together with details of their light characteristics (pp.242–43). The direction of buoyage may also be marked, especially when two channels meet that could otherwise cause confusion*

# THE COMPASS

*A compass is the most important navigation instrument on board a yacht. It is the primary means of identifying direction, enabling you to steer a course and to plot position by taking bearings of navigational marks and shore objects. The compass is also used to check the bearing of other vessels to help avoid collision. Two types of compasses are usually used – a steering compass for steering a course, and a hand bearing compass for taking bearings of objects and other vessels.*

## CONVENTIONAL COMPASSES

Conventional compasses have two or more bar magnets attached to the underside of a circular card, marked in degrees around its edge. The card is mounted on a pivot and is encased in a glass or plastic bowl filled with a damping liquid to slow down its rotation. Internal or external gimbals keep the card level when the boat heels. As the compass is turned, the bar magnets align with magnetic north and south. A reference mark, called a lubber line, is marked on the inside of

GETTING BACK ON COURSE
If you go off course, use this simple rule to get back. If the number on the compass is higher than the required course, turn to port. If it is lower, turn to starboard.

the bowl. The course or bearing is read against the lubber line. A light should be fitted to allow the compass to be used at night.

## FLUXGATE COMPASS

Fluxgate compasses dispense with cards, pivots, and liquids and use an electronic circuit to sense the lines of magnetic force. Their reading is displayed as a digital readout to the nearest degree. The apparent accuracy implied by a digital readout should be treated with caution. Fluxgate compasses must be kept level, or significant errors can occur that will not be obvious from the display. Fluxgate compasses are often used to automatically provide heading information to other electronic instruments, such as chart plotters, GPS, and radar sets.

## STEERING COMPASS

Fit your boat with the best quality steering compass you can afford. Choose one that has a large card, or display, with easy-to-read markings. When siting the steering compass, it is important that it can be seen directly by the helmsman. It should be mounted with the lubber line on, or parallel to, the boat's fore-and-aft line. For this reason, wheel-steered boats usually have the steering compass in a binnacle (casing) on top of the wheel pedestal. Tiller-steered boats often use two bulkhead-mounted compasses on the cabin bulkhead, either side of the

---

## MAGNETIC VARIATION

The angular difference between magnetic and true north (pp.232–33) alters year by year. It is called variation, and its amount and direction – either east or west – depend on where you are.

### ALLOWING FOR VARIATION

All charts display a compass rose aligned with true north, along with a concentric inner rose aligned to magnetic north. Local variation and its annual rate of change are also marked on the rose. When shaping a course or plotting a position, you will often have to convert between true and magnetic bearings. Do this using the rose, or by simple addition or subtraction (below). Be consistent in your methods to avoid mistakes.

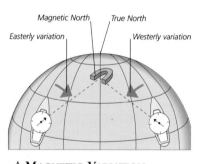

*Magnetic North   True North*
*Easterly variation   Westerly variation*

### △ MAGNETIC VARIATION
*The magnetic poles move over time, but their position and annual rate of change are known and can be allowed for.*

### TRUE TO MAGNETIC
ADD WESTERLY variation, or SUBTRACT EASTERLY variation
e.g, 150°T + 5°W = 155°M

### MAGNETIC TO TRUE
ADD EASTERLY variation, or SUBTRACT WESTERLY variation
e.g, 155°M − 5°W = 150°T

## △ CONVENTIONAL STEERING COMPASS

*A conventional steering compass designed for bulkhead mounting, usually on either side of the companionway.*

## △ FLUXGATE HAND BEARING COMPASS

*A fluxgate hand bearing compass designed to be held level, and used at arm's length. It displays results using a digital display, to the nearest degree.*

companionway. In either case, in order to minimize the effects of deviation (*above*), the compass must be at least 6ft (2m) away from the engine. It must also be as far as possible from any other large ferrous-metal object and the ship's wiring system. Keep moveable magnetic items, such as some drinks cans, well away, too.

## HAND BEARING COMPASS

Most steering compasses are not sited in a position that allows bearings to be taken all around the boat, so a portable hand bearing compass is often used. To use a hand bearing compass, line up the lubber line with

## COMPASS DEVIATION

Compass alignment may differ from magnetic north due to on-board magnetic fields. This is called deviation. It varies with the course, and is measured in degrees, east or west of magnetic north.

### DEALING WITH DEVIATION

Check your steering compass for deviation at least once a season (*below*). If any exists, plot a deviation card. If deviation on any course is more than about 6°, have a compass adjuster fit corrector magnets. Use your deviation card to convert between magnetic courses and compass courses. When using a hand bearing compass, pick a spot well away from any possible magnetic materials. Ensure that there is no deviation at your chosen spot, by taking a bearing of a charted transit (*p.244*) and checking it on the chart.

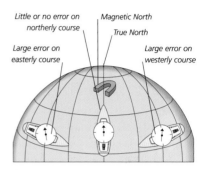

### △ MAGNETIC DEVIATION

*The amount of error depends on the boat's heading and the relative positions of the interfering magnetic materials (here, the engine), the compass, and magnetic north. It is largest on easterly or westerly courses.*

**MAGNETIC TO COMPASS**
ADD WESTERLY deviation, or SUBTRACT EASTERLY deviation
e.g, 204°M + 4°W = 208°C

**COMPASS TO MAGNETIC**
ADD EASTERLY deviation, or SUBTRACT WESTERLY deviation
e.g, 208°C – 4°W = 204°M

the object for which the bearing is being measured, such as a vessel or buoy, and read off the bearing.

There are three types of hand bearing compass: the traditional bowl compass, which is best held at arm's length; the smaller mini compass, which can be held close to the eye; and the fluxgate compass, which are also held at arm's length.

The type you choose depends on personal preference; all will deliver good results if used properly. Try to use a few afloat to decide which suits you best before buying one. Always brace yourself in a secure, comfortable position when using a compass.

## MAKING A DEVIATION CARD

Have the helmsman steer an accurate course of due north (000°C) and use a hand bearing compass to sight along the centerline of the boat while standing at the stern, well clear of any possible interference. Note the course steered and the reading from the hand bearing compass. Turn to 030°C and repeat the procedure. Continue recording bearings every 30° until you have completed a full 360°. Plot the results on graph paper to produce a curve giving the amount and direction of deviation for any course steered. Use the card, or the rules above, to convert compass to magnetic courses.

# PLOTTING EQUIPMENT

*Before you can do any plotting work on charts, you will need to obtain a few navigation tools and learn how to use them. Practice with these basic tools leads to confident chart work and accurate navigation, which will give you great satisfaction.*

## A CHART TABLE

A secure place to work is a major help in navigation. The best solution is to have a permanent chart table with a horizontal surface large enough for a chart to be laid out with no more than one fold. A typical chart table has either a lifting top with chart storage space underneath, or a drawer. Either type should allow the charts to be stored flat when folded in half.

## SITING A CHART TABLE

Some people prefer to stand up at a chart table that is arranged fore and aft, but more usually chart tables are built athwartships with a seat for the navigator. Ideally, the chart table is situated near the companionway, where there is least motion in the boat, with the seat facing forward. This position makes communication with the helmsman and access to the cockpit fairly easy. There should be shelf space for essential reference books, some of which will be quite large, and bulkhead space for instruments and communication equipment. A small compass, mounted with the lubber line fore and aft, is useful for keeping an eye on the course being steered.

If your boat is too small for a permanent chart table, use a flat board that is large enough to take a folded chart but that can be stowed away when not in use. Clip the chart to the board and use it on your knees, either down below or in the cockpit when conditions are suitable.

## LIGHTING A CHART TABLE

The chart table should be lit so that the navigator can work on charts without disturbing any sleeping crew or affecting the helmsman's night vision. A small, flexible stalk-light can be useful for lighting the chart. Fitting a low-power red bulb can also help minimize loss of night vision.

## PARALLEL RULERS

A navigator uses parallel rulers to transfer a direction from the chart's compass rose to the part of the chart on which he is working. First, the ruler is lined up on either the true or the magnetic compass rose. Depending on its design, the ruler is then either rolled or "walked" across the chart to the appropriate area. Lines can then be drawn to indicate a course to steer or a bearing on an object.

When you are choosing a parallel ruler, it is best to try out a range of both roller and walking designs at sea, to find out which most suits you. Generally, roller types are impractical on a yacht and walking types can be awkward on small chart tables.

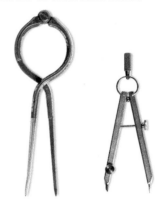

**DIVIDERS**       **COMPASS**

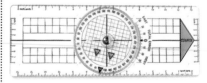

**PLOTTER**

◁△ **CHART TABLE**
*The chart table should be a secure spot to work, with space for spreading out a chart and mounting instruments within easy reach. A plotter, dividers, and a pair of compasses are all essential, basic tools.*

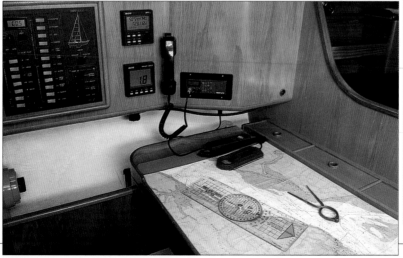

## LOGBOOK

A logbook is used for recording position, course, distance run, and other crucial information. You are required to keep one by maritime law, and might have to produce it in the event of an incident at sea.

### MAKING A LOGBOOK
You do not need to buy a printed logbook. There is no standardized format for logbooks, and many commercial ones include space for quite unnecessary information. Many experienced navigators produce their own, simply by ruling a few columns in a notebook or on loose-leaf sheets inserted into a ring binder. The column headings can be adapted to suit your individual requirements.

### KEEPING RECORDS
Try to keep your entries as neat as possible because you may need to refer back to them. Record the key data half-hourly or hourly when you are cruising close to shore, and less often when you are well offshore. A rough notebook is handy for making notes and calculations; some skippers have a deck log for use by the crew on watch, transferring the information at regular intervals to the main logbook.

## PLOTTERS

A plotter achieves the same result as a parallel ruler, and most people find it easier to use on a small boat. The Breton, Hurst, and Portland plotters are among the most popular makes.

All types of plotters are used in conjunction with the grid of latitude and longitude lines marked on the chart, rather than with the compass roses. The plotter is engraved with a compass rose and a square grid of lines, any of which are lined up with a line of latitude or longitude on the chart to orientate the plotter with true north. The plotter's straight edge is then lined up with the required bearing to be measured, and the bearing is read off from its compass rose. Some plotters enable variation and deviation to be set on their compass rose, thus allowing magnetic bearings to be read or plotted directly. A plotter does not need to be used in conjunction with a compass rose, so it does not have to be moved across the chart. This makes it easier to use and more accurate than parallel rulers.

## DIVIDERS

Used to measure distances on the chart, dividers are usually made of brass with steel tips. Buy a pair of dividers that is at least 6in (15cm) long so that it has a reasonable span. The single-handed type, which has a bowed top, is easier to use than the straight type, which needs two hands to open and close it.

Open the dividers to span the appropriate area, then read off the distance using the chart's latitude scale. If the span of the dividers is not large enough, set it to a convenient width using the latitude scale, then step the dividers across the area.

A simple pair of compasses should also be carried for use when plotting curved lines of position (*p.256*).

## PENCILS

Use soft pencils, such as 2B, on charts to avoid permanently marking them. Hexagonal pencils are less likely to roll off the table when the boat heels. You will also need a pencil sharpener and a soft eraser.

## REFERENCE BOOKS

Every navigator requires a selection of reference books to provide information that is not included on charts. These books should be stored somewhere conveniently close to the chart table for easy reference, and should be kept as up-to-date as possible.

### NAUTICAL ALMANAC
The principal reference book you require is a current copy of the nautical almanac that covers your sailing area. This provides tidal information, harbor plans and details, and other useful material.

### PILOT BOOKS
The navigator may want pilot books to cover the area being cruised. These vary from publications produced specifically for yachting, to those published by hydrographic agencies and intended for all types of seafarers.

### TIDAL ATLASES
Although tidal information is available from nautical almanacs and charts, tidal atlases of your sailing area showing the direction and rate of the tidal stream in pictorial form may be useful, depending on how you like to see the information presented.

### INSTRUCTION MANUALS
Electronic navigation instruments are often quite complicated to use. Make sure that you have a full set of instruction booklets and study them carefully to get the best out of your equipment.

### LIGHTS AND RADIO SIGNALS
If you are sailing long distances, you may also want to carry published references for lists of lights and radio signals, especially if you do not have a full set of large-scale charts for the area.

# NAVIGATION INSTRUMENTS

*For successful navigation, you require some form of log to measure distance sailed. Along with your compass, this will give you the minimum information you need, although it is also prudent to carry a depth sounder. Sophisticated instruments for performance enhancement and position fixing are useful, but they do not remove the need to use the basic skills. Nor are they failsafe – you must always be prepared to double-check their readings, and be able to do without them if necessary.*

## LOGS

The simplest and most reliable log is a mechanical trailing log. It consists of a rotator that is towed on the end of a long line, the boat end of which is attached to a recording head that counts the number of rotations. The distance sailed is shown in nautical miles and tenths of a nautical mile.

Most yachts, however, are fitted with some form of electronic log. Most of these use a small paddle-wheel impeller mounted through the hull and connected to the electronics in the display head. The impellers are usually retractable so they can be cleared of weed when necessary. The instrument often displays speed and total distance run, and has a trip meter that can be reset; some also have a timer function, which is useful when racing.

## CALIBRATING LOGS

Whatever type of log you use, it should be calibrated for accuracy. Find a measured distance on the chart and make two runs along it under power

in opposite directions when the tidal stream is slack. Note the distance for each run from your log, add them together, and divide by two to get the average. The difference between this figure and the distance marked on the chart is the log error. Electronic logs can often be corrected by inputting the error, or you can simply record the error and apply it to each log reading.

## DEPTH SOUNDERS

A lead line about 50ft (15m) long is the simplest form of depth sounder. You should carry one even if you have an electronic depth sounder: it makes a useful back-up and is handy for measuring depth all around the boat or for use from the dinghy.

Traditionally, a lead line is marked with specific types and colors of material at certain depths, but you can devise any marking system that suits you. The traditional lead has a hollow in the bottom that can be armed

(filled) with tallow or grease to collect a sample of the bottom, which can be useful when selecting an anchorage.

Most yachts use an electronic depth sounder, which sends out pulses of sound toward the bottom and measures the time for them to be reflected back. They usually display depth in feet, meters, or fathoms, and many have deep- and shallow-water alarm settings. The display head should be mounted in the cockpit where the helmsman can see it easily.

## WIND INSTRUMENTS

Wind instruments consist of a small vane and anemometer fitted at the masthead, connected to a display head in the cockpit. On its own, a wind instrument will display the strength and direction of apparent wind (*p.30*) in relation to the yacht's head. Adding an electronic log will enable it to compute true wind strength and relative direction, and plugging in a fluxgate compass (*p.236*) will enable it to read the actual direction (in °M) of true or apparent wind.

## GPS

Global positioning system (GPS) receivers calculate position using information from a network of satellites. They are typically accurate to within 300ft (100m). Enhanced, Differential GPS units (DGPS) are

### RANGE OF INSTRUMENTS ▷

*A typical instrument arrangement includes depth sounder, log (distance and speed), and wind direction and strength. Integrated instruments like these share information and calculate additional data.*

**DEPTH SOUNDER**

**SPEED**

**WIND**

### △ Chart Plotter
*When connected to a GPS set, the chart plotter can display waypoints, and your boat's position and track, superimposed on the chart.*

accurate to within 30ft (10m). They provide a digital readout in latitude and longitude or as a bearing and distance from a chosen site. The latter is often easier to use for plotting position. Receivers can also be programmed with 100 or more waypoints – positions of charted objects or turning marks on your course. Routes, consisting of many waypoints, can also be stored in the unit's memory. GPS units usually have many other functions, enabling you to calculate useful information about your progress and course sailed.

### Radar
On boats larger than 35ft (11m), radar can be the most useful electronic aid, and is the only one with position-fixing and collision-avoidance capabilities. Ideally, you should attend a course to learn to use radar properly.

A radar set consists of a display screen linked to an antenna that transmits signals and receives reflections from the shore, buoys, or other vessels. It provides a bearing and distance between the yacht and any objects displayed on the screen. If the object is marked on a chart, you can use the

range and bearing to plot your position. Radar is far more accurate at determining range than bearing, however, so the best radar fix uses three ranges of charted objects. If the object is another vessel, you can determine its course and speed and whether it represents a collision risk. This is particularly useful in restricted visibility or in crowded shipping lanes.

### Chart Plotter
A chart plotter displays an electronic form of the chart on a screen, which allows you to scroll around it and work on it as you would on paper. A chart plotter and GPS unit can be connected to an electronic self-steering system to steer between waypoints on the electronic chart, using GPS information to keep the boat on track and manage any required course alterations.

### Communication Systems
Most yachts carry a VHF (Very High Frequency) radio for short-range communication with shore stations or other boats. Cruisers sailing a long way from home also often have more sophisticated medium- and long-range ship radios or Ham sets installed to allow them to stay in touch. Satellite systems are also available, for voice, data and fax transmissions, and for GMDSS safety signals (*pp.302–03*).

Navtex and Weatherfax systems, often combined into one unit, are useful information sources. Navtex provides up-to-date navigational and safety information for a selected sea area, and Weatherfax delivers weather forecasts and synoptic charts. If you connect your radio to a portable PC, the information can be delivered to the PC without the need for separate units. With a satellite communication system, you can also use the PC to obtain satellite weather images.

## INTEGRATED SYSTEMS

The continuing trend toward integration of electronic aids gives the navigator information that would otherwise require considerable calculation, knowledge, and skill. Integrated systems can now calculate course and speed, true wind speed and direction, velocity made good to windward or downwind, and ETA.

### Unlimited Possibilities
Most manufacturers offer systems that integrate log, wind, and depth instruments. Usually a fluxgate compass, a GPS, chart plotter, and a radar can be hooked in too, so all the information is available to the computers in the individual instruments. It is also possible to add a PC with yet more calculation possibilities. The dedicated racing navigator will get much satisfaction from all this information, but most of it is not necessary for the cruising navigator who simply wants to enjoy sailing while ensuring a safe arrival at his destination.

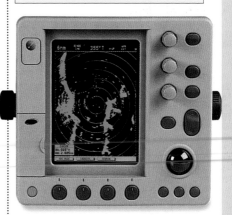

### △ Radar
*A radar display presents its information in the form of a picture that requires skill to interpret. Attend a course to help you make the best use of this equipment.*

# BUOYAGE

*A system of navigation marks is used to identify dangers and safe channels. Buoyage is organized by the International Association of Lighthouse Authorities (IALA). There are two systems: IALA system A is used in Europe, Africa, Australia, India, and most of Asia; IALA system B is used in North, Central, and South America, Japan, Korea, and the Philippines. IALA system A uses red port and green starboard lateral marks, whereas in IALA system B the colors are reversed.*

## LATERAL MARKS

The edges of channels are indicated with lateral marks. These are arranged according to the direction of buoyage, which is marked on charts. In the US, the rule "red right returning" usually applies. When you are headed for a harbor or moving along a channel toward a more protected area, you must keep red buoys on your right side. Lateral buoys are often numbered, starting from seaward with even numbers on red marks and odd numbers on green marks.

Around coastlines, buoyage is typically arranged in a clockwise direction. If the direction of buoyage is not obvious, check on your chart; it will be marked using an arrow with two dots (*pp.234–35*).

Preferred channel marks are modified lateral marks. They are used where a channel divides to indicate the main channel.

## CARDINAL MARKS

Large or individual hazards are indicated with cardinal marks. They are named after the points of the compass to indicate which side you should pass by them to avoid the danger. In other words, you should keep to the north of a north cardinal and south of a south cardinal. They are always pillar- or spar-shaped and are painted black and yellow. They all have two black cone top marks variously arranged one above the other, and at night their white lights flash in a sequence that indicates which quadrant they are in.

## OTHER MARKS

An isolated danger mark is used to indicate a small, solitary danger with safe water all around. A safe-water mark is used for mid-channel or landfall marks. It indicates safe water all around the position.

Various other marks are used to indicate a special area or feature, such as water-ski sites or military-exercise areas, but they are not primarily intended to assist in navigation. All these special marks are yellow. Where cones, cans, or spheres are used, they show the side on which to pass.

## BUOYAGE AT NIGHT

Navigation at night is made much easier through the use of lights that identify buoys, shore beacons, leading marks, and lighthouses. Buoys are usually lit with short-range lights, while medium-range lights may be found on shore beacons, and long-range lights are normally used on lighthouses. It can be difficult to identify marks at night, especially in the vicinity of ordinary shore lights.

To make it easier, different characteristics are used to light specific marks and aid identification. The characteristic of each light is noted on the chart of the area and in sailing directions. Usually, lights are white, red, green, or yellow, but purple, blue, and orange may also be used.

## LIGHT SEQUENCES

In addition to the color, the flashing pattern of the light and the time taken to complete one sequence are used as ways of identifying buoys. Using a stopwatch, check the timing of the flashing through three full sequences to ensure that you have correctly identified the light.

Some of the most common light sequences are shown in the diagram (*right*). The abbreviations used in the diagram are also found on charts. You should familiarize yourself with the abbreviations and the patterns associated with them. Some terms may be unfamiliar: "isophase" means that there are equal periods of light and dark in the sequence; "occulting" means that the periods of darkness are shorter than the periods of light.

Approaching a harbor with a lot of shore lights can make it difficult to pick out the buoy you are looking for at night. Using the hand bearing compass to sight along the expected bearing of a buoy can make it easier to find. Never assume that the light you see is the one you are expecting; you may not be where you think you are. Always double-check.

Lighthouses, and some other beacons, often use colored sector lights to indicate safe and dangerous areas. The chart will show details of the colors and sector angles. The edges of the sectors are often given in pilot books as bearings, and are always from seaward toward the lighthouse in degrees true (°T).

# BUOYAGE MARKS AND LIGHT SEQUENCES

To make them easy to recognize, buoys have different shapes and colors – and usually one or two top marks. Buoys do not always have lights fitted, but those that do flash in designated rhythms so that they can be easily identified at night. For example, the light on an isolated danger mark is white and flashes in groups of two.

## IALA B LATERAL MARKS

**STARBOARD-HAND MARKS**
Light red, any rhythm.

**PORT-HAND MARKS**
Light green, any rhythm.

## IALA B PREFERRED CHANNEL MARKS

**MAIN CHANNEL TO PORT**
Light red, Fl (2+1).

**MAIN CHANNEL TO STARBOARD**
Light green, Fl (2+1).

## CARDINAL MARKS

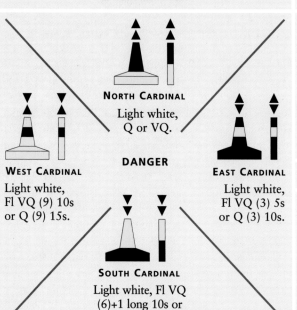

**NORTH CARDINAL**
Light white, Q or VQ.

**DANGER**

**WEST CARDINAL**
Light white, Fl VQ (9) 10s or Q (9) 15s.

**EAST CARDINAL**
Light white, Fl VQ (3) 5s or Q (3) 10s.

**SOUTH CARDINAL**
Light white, Fl VQ (6)+1 long 10s or Q (6)+1 long 15s.

## OTHER MARKS

**ISOLATED DANGER MARK**
Light white, Fl (2).

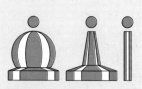

**SAFE-WATER MARK**
Light white, Iso, Oc, or long Fl 10s.

## SPECIAL MARKS

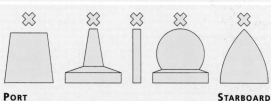

**PORT**　　　　　　　　　　　　　　**STARBOARD**

Light yellow, any rhythm but different from any rhythm on other (white light) buoys.

## COMMON LIGHT SEQUENCES

⊢――――⊣ PERIOD OF LIGHT SEQUENCE

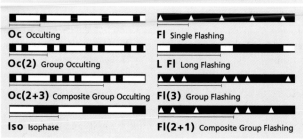

**Oc** Occulting

**Oc(2)** Group Occulting

**Oc(2+3)** Composite Group Occulting

**Iso** Isophase

**Fl** Single Flashing

**L Fl** Long Flashing

**Fl(3)** Group Flashing

**Fl(2+1)** Composite Group Flashing

**Q** Continuous Quick

**Q(3)** Group Quick

**IQ** Interrupted Quick

**VQ** Continuous Very Quick

**VQ(3)** Group Very Quick

**IVQ** Interrupted Very Quick

**UQ** Continuous Ultra Quick

**IUQ** Interrupted Ultra Quick

# PILOTAGE

Navigation by eye, compass, and chart, when in sight of land is known as pilotage. The art of pilotage is to determine a series of safe tracks, in between hazards, to your destination and to be able to confirm at any time that your boat is on or close to these tracks, without having to plot a position on the chart. Pilotage skills are used when entering or leaving harbor, occasions when you do not have time to plot fixes on the chart and where an error of a few boat's lengths can be critical.

## BEARINGS

Two types of bearings are useful when piloting. One is the bearing of the safe track between hazards, and the other is a clearing line. The safe track is the course you follow through constricted water, while clearing lines define the boundaries of a safe zone and are used to keep the boat clear of potential hazards. Once they have been identified on a chart or harbor plan, bearings of a safe track or a clearing line can be measured using the hand bearing or steering compasses

---

### BINOCULARS

A cruising yacht should have at least one pair of good binoculars aboard. They are essential when you are in constricted waters and need to be able to navigate by eye rather than using a chart.

**CHOOSING BINOCULARS**
Buy the best binoculars you can afford, perhaps having a cheaper second pair for general crew use. Strong, waterproof binoculars with a rubber coating are best on yachts to protect against inevitable bumps.

Binoculars are categorized by their magnification and the size of the object lens, which determines how much light is admitted. A pair of 7 x 50 binoculars makes a good choice. A magnification higher than 7 makes the binoculars difficult to hold steady, and an object lens smaller than 50mm will not work well in low light levels.

Some types have a built-in compass that makes taking bearings on distant objects easier, and some even incorporate a range finder.

**USING BINOCULARS**
When using binoculars on a moving boat, try to brace the lower half of your body and allow the upper half to move with the roll to keep the binoculars as steady as possible.

*Resilient, waterproof casing*

**BINOCULARS**

---

(pp.236–37). If the boat can be pointed at the object, the steering compass can be used; otherwise, the hand bearing compass must be used. However, using transits (right) is simpler than taking compass readings and can be more accurate.

## TRANSITS

When two objects are in line, they are said to be in transit. If you see two objects in transit, your boat must be somewhere on the extension of the imaginary line that joins them. If the objects can be identified on the chart, you have a very useful single line of position. However, transits do not need to be in line to be useful. A clearing line can be defined by two objects not quite in line, said to be open or closed (right). When using an open or closed transit as a clearing line, the boat is steered to keep the objects open or closed, as necessary, in order to avoid a danger to the side of the safe track.

## CHOOSING TRANSITS

Transits are often man-made objects, for example posts or beacons, that are specifically constructed to mark safe passages (leading lines) into and out of harbors. Natural objects, such as rocks or headlands, may also be used as transits, as long as they are clearly visible and are identifiable on the chart. They must also be a reasonable distance apart from each other and not too close to your boat.

If you select objects that are in the water, such as rocks or posts, you must allow for their appearance changing with tide height. Remember, too, that individual rocks may be difficult to identify with any certainty in rock-strewn areas. Even man-made leading marks can be difficult to identify against the background clutter of shore-side buildings.

# USING TRANSITS TO NEGOTIATE HAZARDS

One or more sets of transits can often be employed to navigate along safe tracks between hazards. Examine the chart to identify natural or man-made marks or features that can be used as transits or clearing lines. The appearance of rocks and headlands will alter with the tides; take this into account when using transits.

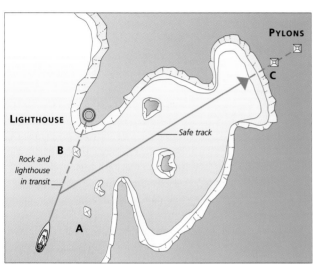

△ **FOLLOWING A SAFE TRACK**
*To stay clear of rocks at the entrance (A) to the anchorage, keep the rock (B) closed, or in transit with the lighthouse. When the leading marks (pylons) come on transit (C), turn onto the safe track into the harbor.*

◁ **CLOSED TRANSIT**
*The rock is described as closed in relation to the lighthouse. In the diagram, this means that the yacht must be clear of the dangerous rocks off the entrance.*

◁ **IN TRANSIT**
*The rock and the lighthouse are in transit. If the yacht steers to keep them in transit, it will follow a safe track clear of the rocks until it is able to turn into harbor.*

◁ **OPEN TRANSIT**
*The rock is described as open in relation to the lighthouse. In the diagram, this means that the yacht could be in danger of hitting the rocks off the entrance.*

## PRE-PLANNING

The key to accurate and safe pilotage is to prepare thoroughly. Before you reach the pilotage area, study the chart and harbor plans to determine the safe tracks and find suitable transits near your course. The best and most prominent transits are usually marked on charts or described in harbor plans. Identify all the navigation marks you expect to see on the route, draw in your intended track, and check for dangers close to your course. When piloting at night, make a note of all the light buoy characteristics near your course. Do not trust your memory to retain all this information – jot down the key details for use in a pilotage plan.

## PILOTAGE PLANS

When piloting, try to avoid using the chart on deck because it will be difficult to keep under control in a breeze and may quickly be ruined. In addition, if your course is from north to south, it can be difficult to interpret the chart upside down. The best solution is to prepare a pilotage plan for use on deck. Plan it to suit your particular way of working, and include courses to steer for each leg of the route, with distances between turning points and navigation marks. Use a suitable-sized notepad. Start the pilotage plan at the bottom of the page and work up. This way, the information on courses, navigation marks, and other important details, is clearly presented in relation to the direction in which you are traveling. Write down all the marks or other significant features you expect to see, together with their distance off the track. Also note the bearings of any clearing lines. If you are going to pilot at night, make a note of the characteristics of all the lit marks that are in the area.

You can never plan too carefully. Once pilotage is under way, you should double-check each piece of information. Avoid complacency, and the temptation to make the facts fit your expectations. Aim to move only from one known safe location to the next so that you do not stray from the safe track.

# TIDES AND TIDAL STREAMS

*When you sail in tidal waters, knowing the height of the tide and the direction of the tidal stream is important for safe and accurate navigation. Some areas, such as Canada's Bay of Fundy, have enormous tidal ranges of 35ft (11m) or more, whereas others, such as the West Indies, have very small ones. Areas with large tidal ranges may seem daunting, but they are not difficult to cope with once you know the relatively simple procedures for calculating tidal heights and streams.*

## TIDAL INFORMATION

Tides are the vertical rise and fall of the surface of the sea, caused by the gravitational attraction of the moon and, to a lesser degree, the sun (*p.49*).

Rotation of the earth causes a semi-diurnal tide in most parts of the world. In other words, there is a tide with two high waters and two low waters every 24 hours, 50 minutes (the length of the lunar day).

Some parts of the world, however, experience a different effect, due to the path of the moon and other, geographical, factors, and have only one high and low water every day. This is called a diurnal tide and occurs mostly in the tropics. Diurnal tides usually feature small tidal ranges (vertical movement). A few other places experience a combination of diurnal and semi-diurnal tides, called mixed tides, in which there are two high and low waters every day but their heights vary considerably.

Changes in the height of the sea's surface are of little account in the open sea, but near coastlines they become crucially important. In some areas, the shape and orientation of the coastline causes very large tidal ranges, and these huge movements of water create powerful tidal streams.

### INFORMATION SOURCES

The navigator can find information on tide heights, ranges, and times of high and low waters from a number of different sources. You can buy tide tables for local areas. These are issued by harbor authorities and give tidal time and height information for every day of the year. The most useful information, however, will be found in nautical almanacs. These cover a wider area and include tidal data for every port within it. It would be impractical for the almanac to include full details for all the ports within its area, so a system of "standard" and "secondary" ports is used. The almanac provides a complete tide table for each standard port, showing the times and heights of high and low water for every day of the year. A diagrammatic tidal curve is also given to allow calculation of tide height for any time between high and low water.

Tidal information for smaller, secondary ports is given as corrections, known as tidal differences. These can be applied to the time and height data from the standard port to find time and height at the secondary port. If the tide you are calculating falls between springs and neaps, you will have to interpolate between the figures given to achieve the best accuracy (*p.249*).

#### ▽ NAUTICAL ALMANAC
*This nautical almanac shows tidal differences to be added or subtracted to the times and heights at the standard port (Dover), to calculate the times and heights of tide at the secondary port (Deal).*

---

### TIDES
0000 Dover; ML3.7; Duration 0505; Zone 0 (UT)

### Standard Port DOVER

#### Times

| High Water | | Low Water | | MHWS | MHWN | MLWN | MLWS |
|---|---|---|---|---|---|---|---|
| 0000 | 0600 | 0100 | 0700 | 6.8 | 5.3 | 2.1 | 0.8 |
| 1200 | 1800 | 1300 | 1900 | | | | |

#### Differences DEAL

| +0010 | +0020 | +0010 | +0005 | –0.6 | –0.3 | 0.0 | 0.0 |
|---|---|---|---|---|---|---|---|

## TIDAL CALCULATORS

Electronic calculators and software for PCs are available to calculate tidal times and heights at thousands of ports around the world. Using these allows the navigator to find the time and height of tide at any time and place without using tables and calculations. The information is accurate enough for most purposes.

## TIME ZONES

Tide tables usually give the times of high and low water in the port's zone time or standard time, although some local tables show times as clock time, already corrected for daylight savings time when it is in force. Make sure you know which system your chosen almanac uses, and be prepared to convert to clock time if necessary. Remember, when sailing between two countries, that they may be in different time zones, or use different amounts of daylight-savings time.

Tide tables usually show their base time zone on each page. They also show the correction that must be applied to convert to local clock time. When working out secondary port information from standard port data, do the calculations in zone time and convert the answer to local time, otherwise significant errors may occur.

## TIDE HEIGHTS AND CHART DATUM

The depth of water shown on charts, and some heights, are calculated from chart datum, which is the lowest astronomical tide (LAT) – the lowest level to which the tide is expected to fall.

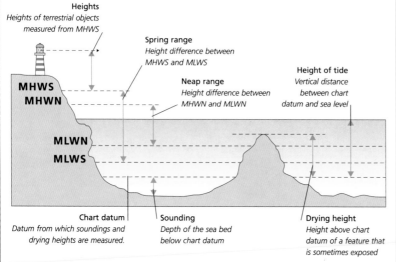

**Heights**
*Heights of terrestrial objects measured from MHWS*

**Spring range**
*Height difference between MHWS and MLWS*

**Neap range**
*Height difference between MHWN and MLWN*

**Height of tide**
*Vertical distance between chart datum and sea level*

MHWS
MHWN

MLWN
MLWS

**Chart datum**
*Datum from which soundings and drying heights are measured.*

**Sounding**
*Depth of the sea bed below chart datum*

**Drying height**
*Height above chart datum of a feature that is sometimes exposed*

### HEIGHT AND DEPTH INFORMATION
On charts, soundings (depths) and drying heights are measured from chart datum. Almanacs give figures for the height of an average spring (or large) tide's high and low waters – Mean High Water Springs (MHWS) and Mean Low Water Springs (MLWS). They also give the equivalent heights for an average neap (or small) tide (MHWN and MLWN). Heights of terrestrial objects are measured from the MHWS level. At all times other than MHWS, heights will be greater than shown, so the navigator must be able to calculate the difference.

## ESTIMATING TIDAL HEIGHTS

Tide tables show the height of the tide only at high and low water, and you will often need to know its height at other times. For an accurate figure, it is best to use the almanac's tidal curve (*p.248*), but for a rough guide you can estimate the height using the Rule of Twelfths.

### THE RULE OF TWELFTHS
This method of estimating tidal height assumes that it rises and falls symmetrically and that the duration of the rise or fall is six hours. This is suitable for many areas where high accuracy is not required, but it should be used with caution.

### THE RULE
The rule divides the tidal range (from high water to low water and vice versa) into twelve and assumes that the tide rises or falls as follows:
1st hour $\frac{1}{12}$ of the range
2nd hour $\frac{2}{12}$ of the range
3rd hour $\frac{3}{12}$ of the range
4th hour $\frac{3}{12}$ of the range
5th hour $\frac{2}{12}$ of the range
6th hour $\frac{1}{12}$ of the range

### AN EXAMPLE
To find the height of the tide at 15:15, or three hours after high water when the tide table gives HW at 12:15 and 4.8m high and LW at 18:20 and 1.2m high. First calculate the range 4.8 – 1.2 = 3.6m, then divide it into twelfths:

- In the first hour (to 13:15) the tide drops $\frac{1}{12}$ of 3.6m = 0.3m
- In the second hour (to 14:15) the tide drops $\frac{2}{12}$ of 3.6m = 0.6m
- In the third hour (to 15:15) the tide drops $\frac{3}{12}$ of 3.6m = 0.9m
- The tide will fall by 1.8m (0.3 + 0.6 + 0.9) from HW by 15:15, so the height of tide (above chart datum) is 4.8m – 1.8m = 3.0m

# TIDAL CURVES

There are often occasions when you need to find out the depth of water at a time other than high water and low water. For example, if you want to cross a shallow bank, you will need to know exactly when the tide is high enough to do so without grounding the boat. The most accurate way to calculate depth of water is to use the tidal curves that are provided in the nautical almanac. Alternatively, an electronic tidal calculator can be used for even quicker results.

## HOW TIDAL CURVES WORK

A tidal curve is represented on a graph that plots the progress of a tide over a complete tidal cycle. Where the cycle varies between spring and neap tides, two curves are shown. Spring tides are represented in the example (*right*) by a solid line, and neap tides by a dotted one. You can use the appropriate curve to find out what time the tide will reach a specific height, or what the tide's height will be at a specific time (*right*).

In some locations, the time of low water can be more accurately predicted than that of high water. For these areas, tidal curves are provided based on low-water times. Use them in the same way as in the diagram, but substitute the time of low water for that of high water.

## SECONDARY PORTS

The nautical almanac usually provides curves for each standard port. These can also be used to obtain the time or height of tide at the secondary ports, simply by entering the tidal data given for the secondary port.

First calculate the time of high water, and the height of high and low waters at the secondary port. Then enter these into the tidal curve, and proceed exactly as for a standard port.

# USING A TIDAL CURVE

*Before using a tidal curve, use tide tables to find tide times and heights for the day. Then use the steps below to find the height of the tide at a specific time. To find the time the tide reaches a specific height, reverse steps 3–5: draw a line down from the desired height on the top scale; where this line intersects the diagonal line draw a horizontal line to the curve; at the curve draw a line down to the timescale grid. Count up or down from the time of high water to read the time the tide reaches the required height.*

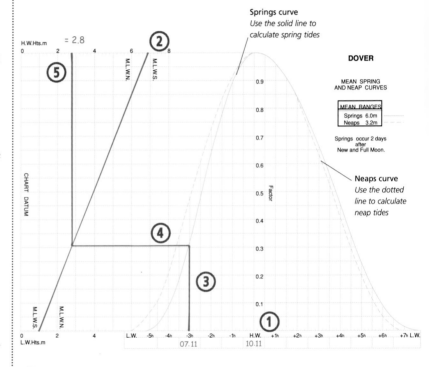

**1** Enter the time of the day's nearest high water (from the tide tables) in the timescale box marked HW.

**2** Enter the height of low water on the lower scale, marked LW Hts, and the height of high water on the upper scale, marked HW Hts. Draw a straight line to join the two marks together.

**3** To find the height of tide at a particular time, enter the required time on the timescale grid, counting up or down from the time of high water. Then draw a line from this time up to the curve. If the day's tidal range is close to the spring range, draw the line to the spring curve. If it is close to neaps, take the line to the neap curve.

If the day's tidal range is in between neaps and springs, it is usually sufficient to interpolate by eye – estimating the position between the two curves according to the size of the day's range compared with the spring and neap ranges.

**4** From the intersection of the curve and the vertical line, draw a horizontal line across to meet the angled line drawn in step 2.

**5** From here, draw a line up to join the top scale. The figure at this point is the height above chart datum of the tide at the required time. To obtain the total depth of water at your position, you need to add this figure to the depth shown on the chart.

# TIDAL STREAMS

The rise and fall of the tide causes a horizontal flow of water known as a tidal stream. Tidal streams are at their strongest during spring tides and their weakest during neap tides. The direction of the tidal stream at any time is called its set, and the strength of the stream is called its drift. When a navigator is shaping a course or plotting a position, he needs to know both the set and the drift for the area. Information about tidal stream set and drift can be obtained from the chart, an almanac, or a tidal atlas covering the area in which you are sailing.

## USING THE CHART

On charts, positions at which tidal streams have been measured are marked by a letter within a diamond, and are known as tidal diamonds (*pp.234–35*). A table on the chart shows the set and drift for spring and neap tides at every tidal diamond for each hour before and after high water at the standard port.

To use the information in the table, you need to know the time of high water at the standard port for the day in question and the tidal diamond that is nearest your position. High tide is shown as zero on the table. Select the hour (before or after high water) in which you are interested, and read across the table to the column headed by your tidal diamond letter. Here, you can read off the strength of the drift (written in knots and tenths of a knot) and the set of the stream, in °T. Select the spring or neap rate, or interpolate between the two if necessary (*above, right*).

If your position on the chart is between two tidal diamonds, plot the results for both on the chart and interpolate between the two by eye.

## TIDAL ATLASES

A tidal atlas provides tidal stream information for a specific area in the form of a separate page for each hour before and after high water at a standard port. Each page shows the set of the stream using arrows and the drift at spring and neap tides in figures. Drift may be shown in knots and tenths of a knot, or it may simply be shown in tenths (thus 1.1 knots may be written as 1.1 or 11). The nautical almanac may also show tidal stream information using small chartlets that are similar to the pages in the tidal atlas.

## USING A TIDAL ATLAS

In the tidal atlas the high water page is marked up with the time of high water for the day at the standard port, and each page before and after it is marked up with the appropriate time. Turn to the page you need and find the tidal arrow nearest your position.

Direction can be measured with a plotter. Note the spring and neap rates shown by the arrow. If the tide is a spring or neap, use the appropriate rate given. If the day's tidal range lies in between the spring and neap ranges, interpolate between the two (*above*). An alternative to calculation is to use a computation of rates table, usually provided in the tidal atlas.

## ▽ TIDAL ATLAS

*Tidal atlases and almanacs show tidal stream information in pictorial form. Direction is shown by the arrows, with numbers indicating the speed.*

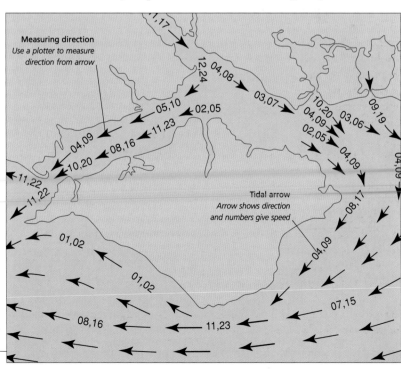

Measuring direction
*Use a plotter to measure direction from arrow*

Tidal arrow
*Arrow shows direction and numbers give speed*

# SHAPING A COURSE

*The essence of navigating is setting a course to steer that will take you from your departure point to your destination. Known as shaping a course, this process is a vital skill for accurate and safe navigation offshore. To shape a course, the navigator requires a chart of the area, plotting tools, tidal-stream information, and a compass. He uses this equipment to plot the course he wants to achieve on the chart, measure the distance to be sailed, and allow for tidal streams and leeway.*

## LEEWAY RULES

Use these rules to apply leeway.
Wind from Port side
Water track – Leeway angle
= course to steer.
Wind from Starboard side
Water track + Leeway angle
= course to steer.

## SYMBOLS

When plotting courses and positions on the chart, navigators use symbols in order to save space and avoid confusion. Standard symbols are shown below. You can devise your own if you wish, as long as everyone else doing chart work on your boat understands your symbols and uses them consistently. Time is usually written using 24-hour-clock notation (e.g. 14:15) and should include the relevant time zone (e.g. 14:15GMT).

| Symbol | Meaning |
| --- | --- |
| X | Dead Reckoning Position |
| △ | Estimated Position |
| → | Water Track |
| →→ | Ground Track |
| →→→ | Tidal Stream or Current |
| ⊙ | Fix |
| ←→ | Position Line |
| ←←→→ | Transferred Position Line |

## THE GROUND TRACK

The first step in shaping a course is to draw a line on the chart joining the departure point and the destination. This is called the ground track and is marked by two arrowheads. It is the course you want to follow, over the ground, to your destination. Check along it to make sure that it does not pass over or near hazards or restricted areas. Next, measure the length of the track using the dividers to transfer the length of the line to the latitude scale at the side of the chart (*pp.238–39*). If the length of the line is longer than the span of your dividers, set the dividers to a convenient length, using the latitude scale, and count the number of times you can step this length off along the line. Measure any odd length left over against the latitude scale.

The length of the line, A–B (*right*), is the distance to your destination. Dividing this distance figure by your anticipated speed will give you the expected duration of the passage and an estimated time of arrival (ETA).

In the absence of tidal stream, or leeway, the ground track you have marked on the chart is the course to steer. You can measure its direction on the chart using a parallel ruler or plotter (*pp.238–39*). You can use either °T or °M to measure direction, but be consistent in your choice and

make sure that others involved in chart work know what you are working in. Write the distance and bearing of A–B alongside the line.

## COURSE TO STEER

To allow for the effects of any tidal stream, you must obtain the set and drift of the stream from your chart or tidal atlas (*p.249*). Plot these on the chart in what is known as a vector diagram (*right*). This will give you the water track, marked by a single arrowhead, which denotes the course you want to follow through the water. Remember, however, that the boat does not actually follow the water track; it moves, relative to the seabed, along the ground track A–B, while pointing in the direction of the water track C–D. In the absence of leeway, the bearing of C–D is the course to steer. Measure its bearing using a plotter or parallel rules, and convert to °C (*p.237*) before giving the course to the helmsman.

## ALLOWING FOR LEEWAY

If you are sailing with the wind forward of the beam, or are under power in strong beam winds, you will have to allow for leeway. To estimate your boat's leeway angle, take a bearing on the wake of your boat using the hand bearing compass (*p.237*). Compare this bearing with the reciprocal of your compass heading (add or subtract 180° to or from the compass heading). The difference is the leeway angle. Adjust the line C–D to windward by the amount of the predicted leeway angle. The angle is usually between five and ten degrees. However, it will vary according to factors such as the shape of the hull, the type of rig, and the prevailing weather conditions. In practice, the adjustment is usually made by calculation (*left*) rather than being drawn on the chart, but, to avoid confusion, you may wish to pencil in the wind direction and adjust C–D towards it. After you have allowed for leeway in order to plot the course to steer, you will need to apply the corrections for variation and deviation to determine the compass course to steer in °C (*pp.236–37*).

## ALLOWING FOR TIDAL STREAMS AND LEEWAY

*In many situations, you will have to make allowances for a tidal stream. A tidal stream that is parallel to your ground track will not affect the course, but will affect the speed you achieve over the ground. For example, if your boat is sailing at 5kn against a 2kn tide, your speed over the ground will be reduced to 3kn. On the other hand, a 2kn tide running in the same direction as your course will give a speed over the ground of 7kn. Quite often, the tide will be at an angle to your ground track, and you will have to adjust your course to avoid being pushed off track. This is done by drawing a vector diagram.*

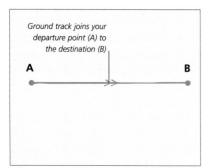

Ground track joins your departure point (A) to the destination (B)

A        B

**①** Draw a line from your departure point (A) to your destination (B). Mark it with two arrowheads. This is your desired ground track. Measure the distance A–B with dividers using the latitude scale at the side of the chart.

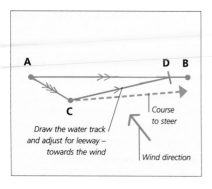

A        D   B

C

Draw the water track and adjust for leeway – towards the wind

Course to steer

Wind direction

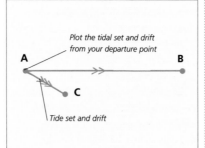

Plot the tidal set and drift from your departure point

A        B

C

Tide set and drift

**②** With information from the tidal atlas, plot the direction of the tide's set, starting from point A. Use dividers and the latitude scale to measure along the line the expected drift in the next hour (C). Mark the line with three arrowheads.

**③** Open your dividers to the distance that you expect to sail within the next hour. Then place one point at C, and scribe an arc to cut through the line A–B at the point D. Now join together the points C–D and mark the line with a single arrowhead. This is the water track required to offset the effects of the tide in the next hour. Now adjust the water track to windward by the amount of leeway to determine the course to steer. Finally, convert the calculation to °C.

## LONG PASSAGES

On a long passage in tidal waters you will encounter tidal streams that change hourly in set and drift. You can use one of two methods to deal with them.

### CHANGING TIDES

If there are no hazards near the track, you can use a simple plotting process. First, estimate how long the passage will take. From your departure point (A) lay off the first hour of tide. Then, from the end of this line, lay off the next hour of tide and continue the process for as many hours as you estimate the passage will take. Open the dividers to the distance you expect to sail, then put one point on C and cut the track A–B. The line C–B is the water track for the whole passage. It can then be adjusted for leeway, variation, and deviation as normal.

If there are hazards close to your track, you will need to keep the boat close to the track at all times. Mark the first hour's tide and plot the course to steer for the first hour. From point D, lay off the second hour's tide and plot the course to steer for the second hour. Continue this process for the length of the passage. Each hour will require a different course to steer, but the boat will proceed along the desired track.

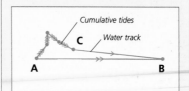

Cumulative tides

C   Water track

A        B

**NO HAZARDS**

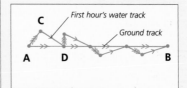

First hour's water track

C

Ground track

A   D       B

**HAZARDS**

# PLOTTING A POSITION

*On any passage outside local waters, the navigator must keep an accurate record of the course steered, distance run, times of course alterations, and the leeway experienced. These records are used to plot the estimated position (EP) on the chart at regular intervals of about half an hour or an hour, unless you are well offshore. This is important even if electronic fixing aids are available: it is only by comparing an EP with a fix (pp.254–57) that errors can be discovered and assessed.*

## USING THE LOGBOOK

The logbook (*below*) is a vitally important record and must be kept up to date throughout the passage. Do not neglect log keeping or plotting EPs just because you expect to get a fix from your electronic aids.

The logbook should be updated regularly and include distance run, course ordered and course achieved, estimated leeway, time of any course changes, and details of fixes. You may also want to record barometer readings, wind direction and strength, and general comments. The logbook must have two columns for course – required course and actual course – because it is often not possible to steer the ideal course to an objective. Each time the log is filled in, the helmsman should be asked for an honest assessment of the average course steered. If the destination is upwind, you will not be able to steer a direct course. In this case, you must log the course achieved and note the time, new heading, and log reading every time you tack.

## ▽ LOGBOOK

*A simple ruled notebook will make a perfectly adequate logbook. Rule off several columns and add column headings, then record your progress, neatly and clearly, at regular intervals.*

## DEAD RECKONING

A dead reckoning position (DR) is plotted on the chart by drawing the course steered from the last known position and measuring off the distance sailed according to the log.

If you work in °M on the chart, correct the course steered (°C) for deviation (*p.237*) before you plot it. If you work in °T, you must also correct for variation (*p.236*).

In theory, the DR position should be plotted before allowing for leeway (*p.251*). However, in practice, it is easier to allow for it before plotting the course but after correcting for deviation and variation. Remember to apply the leeway correction to leeward of the course steered.

Plot the corrected course steered on the chart and mark it with a single arrowhead to show that it is the water track. Measure off the

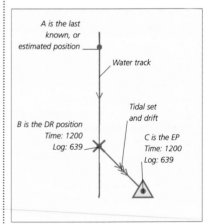

A is the last known, or estimated position

Water track

Tidal set and drift

B is the DR position
Time: 1200
Log: 639

C is the EP
Time: 1200
Log: 639

## △ DR AND EP

*From known point (A), plot the water track and mark it with one arrowhead. Measure off the distance sailed according to the log and mark the DR position (B). Plot the tidal set and drift and mark it with three arrowheads. Mark the final position with a triangle. This is your EP.*

| Time | Log | Course required | Course steered | Wind | Baro | Remarks |
|------|-----|-----------------|----------------|------|------|---------|
| 2230 | 574 | 060°C | 065°C | SW2 | 1005 | Extremely misty and damp |
| 0000 | 582 | 060°C | 060°C | SW4 | 1005 | Six knots regularly |
| 0045 | 588 | 060°C | 060°C | SW4 | 1005 | Yacht in sight starboard bow |
| 0200 | 594 | 060°C | 060°C | SW4 | 1005 | Watch change |

Time
Make log entries at regular intervals

Course
Detail course required and course actually steered

Remarks
Include any useful observations

Log
Use the log reading to measure progress

Wind
Record wind strength and direction

Barometric pressure
Can be used to forecast weather

distance sailed according to the log from the last known position, mark this DR position with a cross, and record the time and the log reading (*below left*). If there is no tidal stream or current, this is the yacht's position at that time.

## ESTIMATED POSITION

An estimated position (EP) is plotted from the DR position by applying the effects of any predicted tidal stream to the DR position.

Using the chart or tidal atlas, work out the set (direction) and amount of drift (distance) of the tide since the last known position (A, *below left*). From the DR position (B), plot the set of the tide by drawing a line on the correct bearing and marking it with three arrowheads. (Remember that tidal set is shown in °T; apply

variation if you do your chart work in °M). Using the dividers and latitude scale on the chart, measure the amount of tide (C) along the tidal line. Draw a triangle with a dot in the middle to mark the point and record the time and the log reading alongside it. This is your EP at that time.

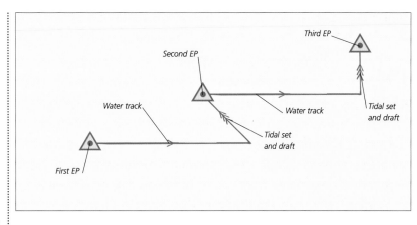

△ **PLOTTING SUCCESSIVE EPs**
*Once you have plotted your first estimated position and are satisfied that you have taken into account possible errors, you can use it to plot subsequent EPs. Plot the water track since the last EP. Measure the distance sailed since then, before plotting tidal set and drift.*

---

# ERRORS

Navigation errors arise for a variety of reasons – the difficulty of steering an accurate course, a log under-reading in calm conditions or over-reading in rough seas, uncalibrated instruments, or an inexperienced helmsman. Errors are inevitable, so you must learn how to take them into account when navigating.

## ASSESSING ERRORS

The longer the boat sails without a confirmed position fix (*p.254–57*), the more important it is that errors are allowed for. Otherwise, the resulting EP could become very unreliable.

Make a list of possible errors and estimate their maximum effect, concentrating on course steered, distance sailed, leeway, and tidal information. Pencil in any errors you think are possible and use them to create an area of likely position. This is a much more realistic approach than assuming you are at the single point suggested by your EP. Now, for safety, assume that you are at the point closest to any nearby hazard and shape your next course accordingly.

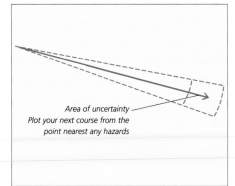

△ **PLOTTING ERRORS**
*Estimate possible errors in the course steered and the distance sailed. A course error would put you to one side or other of your track, whereas a log error would affect the distance you are along the track. Plot possible errors to get an area of likely position.*

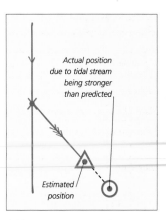

△ **ESTIMATED AND ACTUAL**
*This fix reveals that the set of the tide is stronger than predicted. Use this information to shape the course and plot the next EP.*

# FIXING A POSITION

No matter how accurately you plot your estimated position (EP) on a passage, errors will occur, making your exact position increasingly uncertain. To confirm position, a navigator periodically fixes the position of the yacht in relation to known objects. This is simplest to do when close to a charted sea- or landmark, when you can often determine your position by eye. In other circumstances, fixes can be obtained with a variety of instruments, such as a hand bearing compass or a depth sounder.

## POSITION LINES

If you are alongside a charted mark, you know exactly where you are and can confidently plot a fix on the chart. At other times, a navigator must obtain a fix by producing a minimum of two position lines. To do this, you need to measure either the bearing or the distance of a known object and then plot the resulting line on the chart. Measuring the bearing of an object produces a straight position line, whereas measuring the distance of an object produces a curved one (p.256).

There are several ways in which a navigator can obtain position lines. These include using a hand bearing compass, identifying a transit (pp.244–45), watching a light just clearing the horizon, using the depth sounder (p.256), or using a GPS or radar set (p.257).

## SINGLE POSITION LINES

A single position line will not be sufficient to give you an accurate fix. You need to cross it with a second, and preferably a third, as an error check. However, a single line does tell you that the boat is situated somewhere along the line. If the position line is at right angles to the track, it will confirm how far along the track you are. Single position lines formed by a transit are useful when entering harbors, or as a clearing line (p.244).

## CHOOSING MARKS

Before you can plot a visual fix, you must identify two or three sea- or landmarks on the chart that are within sight. It is preferable to use three marks, as any error is then much more obvious. If you are using only two objects, try to pick marks that are about 90° apart, as this will give the most accurate result. If you are using three marks, it is best if they are about 60° apart. Choosing marks that are quite close to the boat will increase your accuracy: if you are a long way from the mark, a typical error of just 3° in the bearing will produce a significant positional error. If you are close to the mark, however, the error will be much less. It is vital that you identify the correct marks on the chart, or your fix will be worthless.

## COMPASS BEARINGS

Take bearings using the hand bearing compass from a point on the boat that is known to be free of deviation (p.237). Brace yourself securely and take three bearings on each mark; it is helpful if someone else writes down the bearings as you take them. Before you can plot the position lines, you must use the three readings to calculate the average bearing of each

### SINGLE POSITION LINE ▷

*A single position line can tell you only that the boat is located somewhere along the bearing drawn on the chart from the mark.*

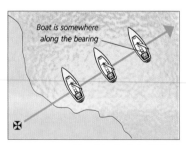

### THREE-POINT FIX ▷

*Three visible objects that are also marked on the chart can be used to give you an accurate fix. If possible, choose objects that are about 60° apart, take their bearings, and plot the position lines from them on the chart. The size of the triangle (cocked hat) that they form is a good guide to the accuracy of the fix.*

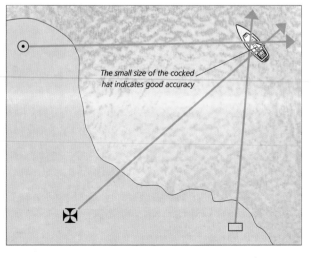

mark. If you plot in °T on the chart, you must correct the compass bearing by applying variation (*p.236*). Plot the position line on the chart by drawing a line through the object on the correct bearing. Remember that the bearing from the object to the yacht is the reciprocal of the bearing you measured. Add or subtract 180° from a bearing to calculate the reciprocal.

## COCKED HAT

When you take bearings of three marks, it is very unlikely that the three position lines will meet at one point. Instead, they will probably form a triangle. This is known as a "cocked hat." The size of the cocked hat is a

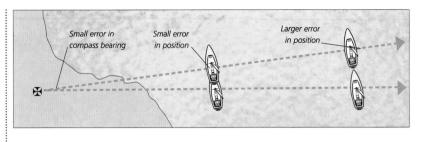

Small error in compass bearing

Small error in position

Larger error in position

good guide to accuracy – the smaller it is, the better. Draw a circle around the triangle and label it with the time and log reading. For added safety, you should assume that your position is at the corner of the triangle that lies closest to any hazard along the proposed track. You should therefore shape the next course from that point.

## △ BEARING ERRORS

*When you take a compass bearing of an object, there is always the possibility of errors because of the difficulty in holding a compass steady on a moving deck. Small bearing errors are inevitable, and will result in larger positional errors when the object is far away. Take bearings on closer objects, when possible, to minimize errors.*

# TRANSFERRED POSITION LINES

There are occasions, such as when you are sailing along a coastline, when there is only one identifiable sea- or landmark in sight. In such cases, it is possible to obtain a useful fix using two position lines taken at different times on the same mark. This is known as a running fix or a transferred position line.

### PLOTTING AND ACCURACY

This type of fix will be as good as your plotting skills and the accuracy that course, speed, and tidal information allow. It relies also on the helmsman steering a steady course between the two bearings. Take the first bearing as you approach the mark, and the second one when you have passed it and its bearing has changed by up to 90°. You must note the time and the log reading when you take each bearing. The use of GPS to fix position has reduced the need for this type of fix, but it is still a useful way of practicing essential skills.

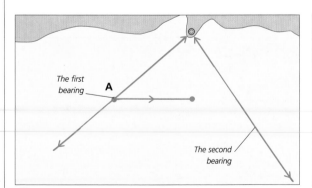

*The first bearing*   **A**

*The second bearing*

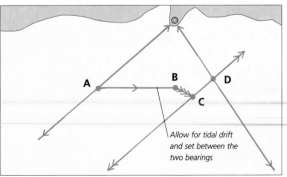

**A**   **B**   **D**

**C**

*Allow for tidal drift and set between the two bearings*

**1** Take the first bearing and note the time and log reading. When the bearing has changed by 60–90°, take the second bearing and note the time and log reading. Plot both bearings on the chart. From any point along the first bearing (A), plot the boat's water track allowing for leeway.

**2** Measure the distance sailed along the track. From that point (B), lay off any tidal set and drift experienced between taking the two bearings (B–C). Now transfer the first position line to point C. The boat's position at the time of taking the second fix is where the first line intersects the second one (D).

## DISTANCE OFF

When you know the distance of the boat from a mark, you can use it to plot a position line. Whereas a bearing on a mark produces a straight line of position, a distance off a mark gives a curved line of position. Curved position lines can be combined with other curved or straight position lines, obtained by any means, to give a fix.

Distance off can be obtained from a radar range or by using a visual rangefinder or a sextant. At night, you can obtain distance off by observing the light from a lighthouse when it first appears or disappears over the horizon as you sail toward or away from it (below). Once you have obtained a distance off an object, set your compasses to the distance. With one point on the object on the chart, draw the curved position line.

## LIGHTS RISING OR DIPPING

*A light rising or dipping on the horizon can be used at night to obtain a position line or a fix. If you are approaching a charted lighthouse, note the time the light (not its loom) first appears above the horizon. When you first see the light, note the time and take a bearing on it with the hand bearing compass. You will need to know your height of eye above the water.*

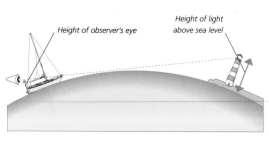

Height of observer's eye

Height of light above sea level

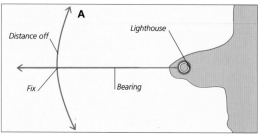

A

Lighthouse

Distance off

Fix

Bearing

## LANDMARK HEIGHT

On charts, the heights of lighthouses and other landmarks are given as height above mean high water spring tide (MHWS; *p.247*). On most occasions when you wish to know the height of a landmark, the tide will be lower than the MHWS level.

To work out the object's actual height above sea level at any time, you must calculate the height of tide at that time. Using the almanac's tidal curve for the closest standard port to your position, work out the height of tide (*p.247*). Deduct the height from the height of MHWS as shown in the almanac. Add the result to the charted height of the lighthouse or other object. If the height of tide is higher than the MHWS level, subtract the difference from the charted height of the landmark.

**(1)** Note the charted height of the light and allow for the height of tide to get the actual height. Now, with your height of eye, and the light's height, use the almanac's distance off tables to find your distance off the lighthouse.

**(2)** Plot the bearing of the lighthouse on the chart and, with the dividers set to the distance off the lighthouse, scribe an arc (A) to cut the bearing. This is the boat's position at the time the light first rose above the horizon.

## USING DEPTH SOUNDINGS

A depth sounder is a useful but often forgotten device for checking on a fix deduced from other sources. On occasions, it can also be used to obtain a position line. Using a depth finder in this way is easiest if it is set to show the water's depth from the surface. Check that yours is not set to measure the depth from the bottom of the keel or the transducer level.

## CHECKING FIXES WITH SOUNDINGS

Before using the depth sounder for checking fixes, you need to be able to convert the depth observed to a sounding at chart datum (*p.247*). This is known as a reduction to soundings. To do this, use the tidal curves (*p.248*) for the nearest standard port to find out the current height of tide above chart datum. Subtract the current height of the tide from the observed depth to get the figure at chart datum. Now compare this with the sounding marked on the chart at your fix position. If they agree, you have a useful confirmation of your fix. If they are different, you should check your calculations and confirm the position using another information source.

## CREATING FIXES WITH SOUNDINGS

Depth soundings can also be used to create a fix. Although this type of fix is not very accurate, it is valuable in fog or when other fixing aids are not available. This method works best when you are sailing into shallower or deeper water across the depth contours as marked on the chart.

Note the time, course, and log reading, and take a depth sounding. Now hold a steady course and take a depth sounding at regular intervals, noting the time and log reading on each occasion. Once you have a series

| Time | Log | Distance between soundings | Soundings in meters |
|------|-----|---------------------------|---------------------|
| 0640 | 55.1 | – | 46m |
| 0650 | 56.0 | 0.9 | 38m |
| 0700 | 56.9 | 0.9 | 25m |
| 0710 | 58.0 | 1.1 | 17m |
| 0720 | 59.1 | 1.1 | 10m |

### △ ▷ FIX BY SOUNDINGS
*On tracing paper, plot the water track and the tidal set and drift to obtain the ground track. Mark the log readings on the water track. Then draw lines parallel to the tide vector to cut the ground track. Note the depth soundings at these points. Finally, match the line of soundings to the chart to find your EP.*

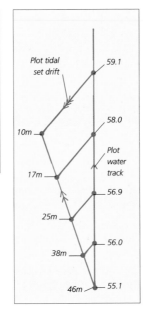

of depths, reduce them to soundings as for checking fixes. Use the results to plot your position.

## PLOTTING SOUNDINGS
The easiest way to plot soundings is to lay a piece of tracing paper on the chart, aligning its edges with lines of latitude and longitude. Plot the boat's water track (pp.250–51) on the tracing paper between the first and last soundings. Then plot the ground track by applying tidal set and drift. Mark the log readings along the water track. From these points, draw lines running parallel to the tidal vector and cutting the ground track. At the points on the ground track, write the depth readings reduced to soundings. Now slide the tracing paper over the chart until the first depth sounding is at the EP when the first depth sounding was taken. Make sure the tracing paper is still aligned with the lines of latitude and longitude. The depth soundings should now agree with the depths on the chart. If they do not, move the tracing paper around until you find a

good match. If there is no other good match nearby, the last depth reading indicates the position of the boat at the time of the reading.

## USING GPS
A GPS set offers potentially the most exact fix available, with an accuracy of approximately 330ft (100m) for 95 percent of the time for a standard GPS set, or about 33ft (10m) with a DGPS unit (pp.240–41). A GPS set measures its precise position from at least four satellites and calculates the intersection of the curved position lines obtained. A DGPS set offers increased accuracy by using radio signals from a base station to refine the satellite signals and reduce built-in errors.

A GPS fix is nearly always available, so it can tempt the navigator to rely exclusively on the system. This must be avoided, especially when close to hazards, as there is always a risk of a set failure or even that the system will be unavailable for some reason. A prudent navigator welcomes the simplicity and accuracy of GPS, but

always double-checks the information against an EP or a fix obtained from another source.

A GPS set displays the boat's position in degrees, minutes, and tenths of a minute of latitude and longitude. However, this is not usually the best means of presentation for the small-boat navigator. Plotting a latitude and longitude position on the chart can be awkward and lead to errors. A better way is to find a suitable sea- or landmark near the track, and program its latitude and longitude into the GPS as a waypoint. The GPS can then be set to display the boat's position as a bearing and distance from the waypoint, which is much easier to plot on the chart. Once you have plotted the fix by GPS, mark it with the time and log reading, note the depth as a rough check of position and compare the fix with the EP. If there is a significant discrepancy, try to double-check by using another source of information.

## USING RADAR
A radar set enables the navigator to measure bearings and distances of features that are displayed on the radar screen and can be identified on the chart. Using radar effectively requires its own skills and experience (p.241). Radar reflections from coastlines can be confusing, making accurate identification of objects on screen difficult. Reflections from buoys can be hard to separate from "clutter" created by a rough sea.

Radar bearings are not as accurate as radar ranges, so the best sort of radar fix uses the distance off two, or preferably three, objects. These are then plotted as curved position lines using a pair of compasses. The boat's position is fixed where the position lines intersect. The size of the cocked hat signals the accuracy of the fix.

# PASSAGE SKILLS

*O*nce you have learned the individual navigational skills
of pilotage, shaping and plotting a course, and fixing a
position, you will be ready to navigate on an extended offshore
passage. The navigator's job begins well before the cruise itself:
you need to plan the trip carefully and make sure that you have
all the relevant charts, pilot books, and other references that
you may need on passage. You must also prepare contingency
plans to cope with rough weather or fog.

### A COMPLETE PASSAGE

Navigation from one harbor to
another starts with pilotage out of
the first harbor to a position called
the departure point that can be
fixed on the chart. From there,
the navigator shapes the course
required to reach the destination.
He periodically works up an
estimated position (EP, *p.253*),
obtains a fix (*p.254*), and evaluates
any errors found, to check that the
boat is staying close to the required
track. Once the boat reaches its
destination, the navigator reverts to
pilotage to guide it to a safe berth.

### PLANNING A PASSAGE

Plan the passage using a small-scale
chart that shows both the departure
point and the destination. Pencil the
required tracks on the chart and
identify the position of any point
at which you will make a course
alteration. If you have a GPS unit
(*p.240*), program these points into it
as waypoints. Make sure that they are
clear of hazards, and double-check
their latitude and longitude. It is best
to try to avoid using waypoints that
are published in pilot books or the
almanac because of the possibility
of printer's errors in the latitude and
longitude figures. Also, navigators of
other small boats are likely to use

published positions too, which means
that several yachts may all be heading
for the same position guided by their
GPS units and autopilots.

### ENSURING A SAFE PASSAGE

Carefully check along your track to
make sure that it is clear of dangers.
Adjust the track as necessary to keep

away from any charted hazards such
as overfalls (waves breaking sharply
over shallows or where currents
meet) or tide races. Note any traffic
schemes, and if you have to cross
one, plan to do so with the boat's
heading at right angles to the lane.

### MAKING PASSAGE NOTES

Once you are satisfied with the track,
transfer your notes to a notebook so
that you can refer to them later.
Calculate the total distance of the
passage and the distance between
turning points or waypoints. Note all
track bearings between turning points
and details of navigation marks that
you expect to see along the way. List
the times and heights of low and high
water for the days you will be sailing.
Then mark up the tidal atlas with the
correct times on each page, starting at
the page for high water. Finally, make

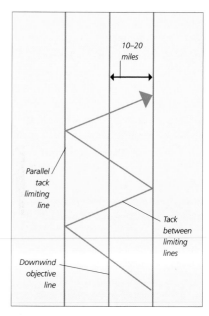

Diverging tack limiting line — 5–10° angle

Downwind objective line

Tack between limiting lines

10–20 miles

Parallel tack limiting line

Tack between limiting lines

Downwind objective line

△ **DIVERGING TACK LIMITERS**
*For short distances, draw a line on the
chart downwind from the objective, then
draw two lines on either side, diverging by
5–10° from the center line. Tack each time
your EP reaches a tack limiting line.*

△ **PARALLEL TACK LIMITERS**
*For longer distances, draw a line on the
chart downwind from the objective, then
draw two parallel lines on either side,
about 10–20 miles apart. Tack each time
your EP reaches a limiting line.*

notes about your destination harbor from the pilot book. You should aim to be familiar with all aspects of the passage before you start.

## NAVIGATING TO WINDWARD

If your destination lies to windward, it will be impossible for the navigator to shape a course to steer. The boat will have to beat to windward. This means that the heading will be determined by the course that the helmsman can steer close-hauled, and it will change every time the boat tacks. In this situation, the navigator concentrates on recording the course steered, and periodically plots an estimated position.

When you beat to windward, there is always a chance that the wind will shift to one side or the other of its initial direction. If you get too far to one side of the direct course you may lose ground because of wind shifts. To minimize this risk and fully exploit gains from wind shifts, draw tack limiting lines (*left*) on the chart and stay within them.

## ROUGH-WEATHER PASSAGES

In rough weather, the navigator has to work down below while the boat is pitching and heeling. Experience and a resistance to seasickness are great advantages in this situation. You should also try to limit the time you spend at the chart table by doing as much passage planning as possible before setting off. Rough weather can quickly lead to tiredness, which increases the risk of mistakes. Always double-check all information and remember to allow for steering errors and log errors, which tend to be more significant in difficult conditions. When you plan a passage, you should always identify safe harbors and have an alternative plan in case weather conditions deteriorate.

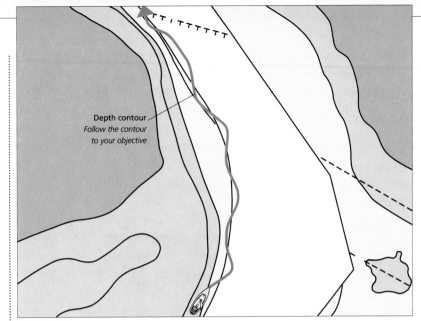

Depth contour
*Follow the contour
to your objective*

## NAVIGATING IN FOG

The onset of fog immediately removes the possibility of obtaining visual fixes to determine position. If possible, the skipper will want to get into shallow water to minimize the risk of collision with large ships, so the navigator must be prepared to navigate to a safe anchorage or harbor. A GPS set will continue to deliver position-fixing information. However, you must check this data against another source, and never rely on it alone to guide you to a harbor or other hazardous area. Probably the best electronic aid to have in these conditions is radar, as it will provide both position-fixing and collision-avoidance information. A GPS set together with a radar enable you to cross-check all information. Be as accurate as possible when working up your dead reckoning (DR, *p.252*) and EP positions and compare them with all available information from a depth sounder and electronic aids.

## FOG AND DEPTH SOUNDINGS

The depth sounder can provide valuable information when you are navigating through fog. By reducing the observed depth to soundings

## △ USING DEPTH SOUNDINGS

*Aim to cross the chosen depth contour to one side of your objective. When you cross the contour line, turn towards the objective and follow the line by zig-zagging back and forth across it using the depth sounder.*

(*p.256*), a depth reading can confirm an EP or fix. Alternatively, a line of soundings can be used to fix a position (*pp.256–57*).

Depth soundings can also be used to follow a contour line on the chart. If you are trying to find a buoy at the entrance to a harbor, for instance, it may lie near a depth contour. Choose a suitable contour, making sure that there are no charted hazards along it. Calculate the height of tide to add to the depth at chart datum to get the actual depth of water at that time. Then you should plot your approach. You should try to cross the depth contour well to one side of the mark you are aiming for before turning toward it. Then steer a zigzag course that crosses and re-crosses the contour, keeping an eye on the depth sounder all the time. This course will lead you to your objective.

# WEATHER

THE MOST AWESOME natural phenomenon on earth is the weather. From light breezes to hurricanes, from spring showers to monsoon rains, it affects everything we do, yet we have no control over it. No one is more reliant on the weather than the sailor – without wind there could be no sailing, yet too much of it makes sailing hazardous. Understanding weather systems, their causes and effects, forms an essential part of every sailor's skills.

*Spectacular forked lightning strikes a harbor entrance. Thunderstorms are relatively infrequent far out to sea, but quite common close to land.*

# CAUSES OF WEATHER

*Weather occurs in a relatively narrow band of the atmosphere, called the troposphere. This extends about 10 miles (16km) above the earth's surface at the equator, diminishing to half that thickness at the poles. As the sun warms the earth's surface, some of the heat is transferred to the air above. This effect is greatest at the equator and least at the poles. Warm air tends to rise, and cold air to sink, causing vertical movements of air and creating changes in air pressure. These movements and pressure changes take excess heat from the equator toward the poles, stabilizing global temperatures and preventing the equator from becoming progressively hotter and the poles from becoming progressively colder.*

## ATMOSPHERIC PRESSURE

Air exerts a downward force under the influence of gravity. This force, known as atmospheric pressure, is measured in millibars (mb). At all times, we experience atmospheric pressure that is equal to the weight of the column of air above us. The average pressure at sea level is about 1013mb, but pressure on the earth's surface varies widely from this mean figure because of differences in air temperature. Cold air is dense and heavy and tends to sink, resulting in high atmospheric pressure. Warm air is less dense and lighter and tends to rise, resulting in low pressure. Vast circulation systems develop around the planet as warm air rises and cold air moves in to replace it.

Changes in atmospheric pressure are a significant indicator of changes in weather conditions. This makes a barometer or barograph (a barometer that provides a continuous record) an important forecasting aid aboard a yacht. If the pressure is rising, good weather may be on the way. If it is falling, stronger winds and poor weather may be imminent.

## ISOBARS

Pressure is shown on weather maps by lines called isobars, which join areas of equal pressure in a similar way to contour lines on a chart. In some places, isobars completely enclose areas of relatively high or low pressure, known as anticyclones and depressions respectively (*pp.264–67*). The spacing between isobars on weather maps represents the pressure gradient between high and low in the same way that contours on a map indicate a shallow rise or a steep hillside. The closer the isobars, the steeper the pressure gradient and the stronger the wind in that area.

## DEW POINT

Air contains water vapor, which it collects as water evaporates from the earth's surface. Air can hold large amounts of water, but it eventually becomes saturated. Warm air is capable of carrying far more water vapor than cold air, but it will become saturated if it cools down. When warm air cools, the excess water vapor condenses into droplets and forms clouds, mist, or fog. The

temperature at which this occurs is known as the dew point. If air is cooled by its proximity to a colder surface, such as the sea, fog forms when the air reaches the dew point.

## CLOUDS

There are three main ways in which clouds form: air is heated by radiation from a warmer area of land or sea and rises through convection currents; air is forced to rise when it meets obstacles such as mountains; or air rises over a mass of colder, denser air. As the air rises it cools. When it reaches its dew point, clouds form.

Clouds occupy three main layers: high cloud is usually above 20,000ft (6,000m); medium-level clouds are at 7,000–20,000ft (2,100–6,000m); and low cloud lies up to about 7,000ft (2,100m). Different types and shapes of clouds form (*pp.268–69*) within these bands. Clouds are an invaluable guide to the dominant weather system, and provide the best visual forecasting aid for assessing likely change.

## RAIN, HAIL, AND SNOW

Water vapor can combine into droplets and fall as rain, hail, or snow. Droplets that form at higher altitudes in tall clouds freeze into snowflakes or hailstones. They will reach the earth's surface in that form if the air is cold at low levels. The capacity of a cloud to produce precipitation depends on its height and size. Expect heavy rain from large, tall clouds but little, if any, from a thin layer of low cloud.

## AIR MASSES

An air mass is an enormous volume of air with particular characteristics. Its type depends on whether it is warm or cold, wet or dry. When an air mass starts moving because of global pressure differences, it is known as an airstream. An airstream from a polar region is cold. If it has traveled over water to reach its present position, it will be relatively wet, but if it has traveled over land, it will be relatively dry. These differences lead to an airstream being classified as Polar, or Arctic, Maritime (cold and wet), Polar Continental (cold and dry), Tropical Maritime (warm and wet), and Tropical Continental (warm and dry).

## HOT OR COLD AIRSTREAMS

When a cold airstream travels over warmer sea or land, it picks up heat in its lower levels. This forms convection currents that rise as air columns. If a column stays warmer than the surrounding air, it continues upward, creating unstable conditions that generally produce heaped clouds and good visibility. Wind is likely to be gusty as stronger, higher-altitude winds are drawn down to the earth's surface. The amount of cloud and rain depends on whether the air is wet or dry.

The opposite occurs when a warm airstream travels over colder land or sea. The air near the earth's surface cools, and any rising pockets of warmer air quickly cool and stop rising. This is a stable airstream and features layer cloud, steadier winds, and reduced visibility.

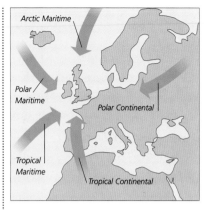

△ EUROPEAN AIRSTREAMS
*Different types of airstreams converge on Europe, including cold, wet Polar Maritime airstreams, and warm, dry Tropical Continental airstreams.*

---

# WORLD WEATHER

The temperature differences that exist between the poles and the equator, together with the spinning of the earth, result in pressure being generally distributed in bands around the planet. These bands of relatively low pressure or high pressure create fairly stable wind systems over the oceans.

### PRESSURE DISTRIBUTION

Lower-pressure bands are found at the equator and the mid-latitudes, and bands of higher pressure at the poles and the sub-tropics. The arrangement is disturbed by temperature changes caused by land masses, but over the sea, the bands of pressure result in semi-permanent wind systems.

### WIND DIRECTION

Air tries to move directly from an area of high pressure to an area of low pressure; this flow is felt as wind. The spinning of the earth makes the winds in the northern hemisphere bend to the right, whereas those in the southern hemisphere bend to the left.

WINDS AND PRESSURES ▷
*The spin of the earth deflects wind to the right in the northern hemisphere and to the left in the southern hemisphere.*

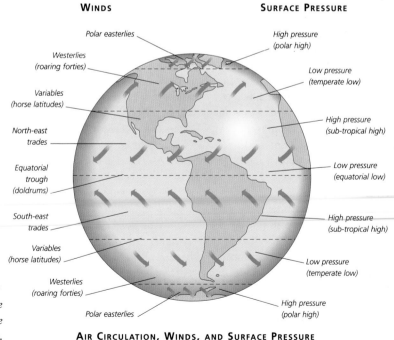

**WINDS**

Polar easterlies
Westerlies (roaring forties)
Variables (horse latitudes)
North-east trades
Equatorial trough (doldrums)
South-east trades
Variables (horse latitudes)
Westerlies (roaring forties)
Polar easterlies

**SURFACE PRESSURE**

High pressure (polar high)
Low pressure (temperate low)
High pressure (sub-tropical high)
Low pressure (equatorial low)
High pressure (sub-tropical high)
Low pressure (temperate low)
High pressure (polar high)

**AIR CIRCULATION, WINDS, AND SURFACE PRESSURE**

# WEATHER SYSTEMS

*The local weather conditions that we experience are part of larger weather systems – the patterns of weather distributed over the whole planet. Most pleasure-sailing takes place in the tropical and temperate zones. The tropics are dominated by the trade winds. The weather is usually fair, but with localized thunderstorms. Westerly winds predominate in temperate zones, although the weather is changeable because of the passage of depressions and anticyclones, and the influence of polar fronts.*

## ANTICYCLONES

Anticyclones are high-pressure areas. They are shown on synoptic charts by pressure readings higher than the surrounding areas and by fairly widely spaced isobars (*p.262*).

Winds blow clockwise around an anticyclone in the northern hemisphere and counterclockwise in the southern hemisphere. The strongest winds blow around the outer edge; winds toward the center are lighter. Anticyclones can cover very large areas and usually move quite slowly. Sometimes they remain static for days or even weeks.

Anticyclones typically bring good weather, with light to moderate winds and clear skies. Thin layers of cloud may persist, but the clouds usually disperse. A temperature inversion (*p.269*) may form in anticyclonic conditions, and cause hazy weather or fog. A well-established and large anticyclone will interact with passing depressions, and may force them off course around its perimeter. Winds will increase between the anticyclone and the depression, where tightly packed isobars, squeezed between the two weather systems, indicate a steep pressure gradient. In this situation, strong winds under cloudless skies may be encountered.

## DEPRESSIONS

Depressions are areas of relatively low pressure. They are shown on synoptic charts by pressure readings that are lower than the surrounding areas and by isobars that are closer together toward the center of the low-pressure area.

Winds blow clockwise around a depression in the southern hemisphere and counterclockwise in the northern hemisphere. The strongest winds are found near the center of the depression, and lighter winds around the outer edge. Depressions vary considerably in size, speed, and intensity, but they typically travel from west to east.

Depressions typically bring unsettled weather, strong winds, and heavy rainfall, with the worst weather near the center of the low pressure. Most depressions originate from activity at a polar front (*right*), although they can form in other circumstances, including very thunderous conditions.

## WIND AND PRESSURE SYSTEMS

Air will attempt to move directly from high- to low-pressure areas, but it can do this only at the equator. Elsewhere, the rotation of the earth causes the wind to be deflected – to the right in the northern hemisphere and to the left in the southern hemisphere (*left*). This deflection causes the wind to blow in a circular pattern around the pressure systems.

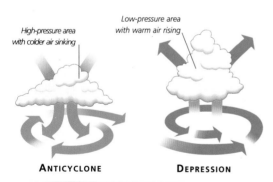

High-pressure area with colder air sinking

Low-pressure area with warm air rising

**ANTICYCLONE**

**DEPRESSION**

Wind blows counterclockwise

Wind blows clockwise

**ANTICYCLONE**

**DEPRESSION**

◁ **NORTHERN HEMISPHERE**
*In the northern hemisphere, the wind blows clockwise around anticyclones and counterclockwise around depressions. This is because of the spin of the earth, which causes the wind to be deflected to the right.*

◁ **SOUTHERN HEMISPHERE**
*In the southern hemisphere, the wind blows counterclockwise around anticyclones and clockwise around depressions. This occurs because the spin of the earth deflects the wind to the left.*

## WIND DIRECTION

The direction of the wind is always expressed in compass points (north or north-east, for example), which describe the direction from which the wind is blowing.

In the northern hemisphere, wind revolves clockwise around anticyclones and counterclockwise around depressions, with the isobars forming closed, concentric circles around both weather systems.

To find the approximate direction of a low-pressure system's center in the northern hemisphere, stand with your back to the wind; the low will be on your left. In the southern hemisphere, it will be on your right. The opposite applies to a high-pressure system.

Above about 2000ft (600m), the wind, known as the gradient wind, is more or less parallel to the isobars. At the earth's surface, however, friction will slow wind down and deflect it – in towards a depression, and outwards away from an anticyclone. Over the ocean, friction causes a deflection of 10–15°; it can be double this over land. In unstable airstreams, wind brought down from higher altitudes can cause gusts, making the wind closer in speed and direction to the gradient wind.

The spacing of isobars indicates the gradient between high and low pressure, and hence the wind speed. This can be predicted by measuring the isobar spacing on a synoptic chart. Remember, however, that the wind speed is greater for a given isobar spacing when the isobars are curved around an anticyclone than when they are curved around a depression. Scales are given on synoptic charts to calculate wind speed from the isobars.

## POLAR FRONTS

A polar front is a demarcation line between two powerful and different airstreams – a warm airstream originating from a subtropical high, and a cold, polar one. When the airstreams meet, the cold, dense air pushes the warm air upwards, forming a wedge under it. Activity at the front is the cause of depressions (p.266). Polar fronts twist their way around the earth moving between about 35° and 60° north and south, depending on the season.

## ▽ SATELLITE PHOTOGRAPHY

*Satellite photographs of weather systems can be received by satellite communications equipment or via the internet. Such images are a useful way of forecasting weather conditions. Here, a forced-color image reveals cloud moving along a cold front.*

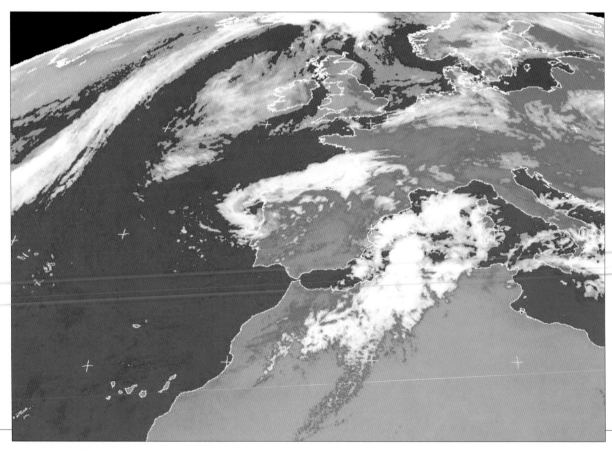

# PASSAGE OF FRONTS

*Understanding the passage of a frontal depression and the associated changes in conditions is important for the offshore sailor. Depressions are often forecast in advance, but their speed and direction of movement can be unpredictable. It is an advantage if you can make your own judgments, based on observation. The type of weather you experience depends on where you are in relation to the center of the low. Here, an observer in the northern hemisphere is situated to the south of the low's center as it passes.*

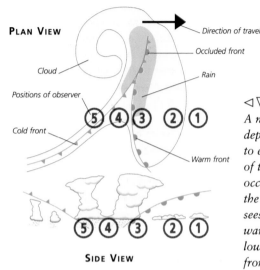

PLAN VIEW

Direction of travel

Occluded front

Cloud

Rain

Positions of observer

⑤ ④ ③ ② ①

Cold front

Warm front

⑤ ④ ③ ② ①

SIDE VIEW

◁▽ **PASSING DEPRESSION**
*A northern hemisphere depression passes from west to east, with its center north of the observer. There is an occluded front (p.267) near the center, but the observer sees the warm front, the warm sector (a trough of low pressure), and the cold front pass in turn.*

# FRONTAL DEPRESSIONS

Along a polar front, a warm, westerly airstream meets a cold, easterly one. The warm airstream is lifted above the cold one, which slides underneath, creating unstable conditions that can lead to depressions.

Depressions are born along the polar front when a pocket of warm air encroaches on the neighboring cold airstream. This pocket creates a small wave in the front, with its crest on the polar side. In the middle of the wave, the air is warmer and rises faster, thus creating an area of low pressure and allowing cold air from the polar side to push in from behind to take its place. As the low-pressure area deepens at the crest of the wave, clearly defined fronts appear ahead of and behind the central trough of low pressure, curving out from the center of the low. These fronts form the demarcation line between the adjacent areas of warm and cold air.

① The presence of thin, high cirrus clouds, which are composed of ice crystals, indicates an approaching depression about 12–24 hours away. The speed and extent of the cirrus clouds are guides to the depth of the depression. The other clear indication of an imminent depression is the barometer reading, which will start to fall.

② Closer to the warm front, the cirrus cloud thickens into cirrostratus (high-layer cloud). A halo may appear around the sun or moon, caused by moisture in the upper atmosphere. The barometer will continue to record falling pressure. The wind will back (swing counterclockwise), often from westerly or south-westerly to southerly or south-easterly.

③ On the approach of the warm front, the cloud thickens into altostratus and then nimbostratus with a lowering cloud base. The wind strength increases and often backs further, and the barometer drops more quickly as the center of low pressure moves closer. Visibility is reduced under the low cloud base, and rain begins to fall as the front moves closer.

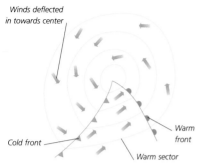

Winds deflected in towards center

Cold front

Warm front

Warm sector

**NORTHERN HEMISPHERE**

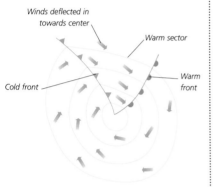

Winds deflected in towards center

Warm sector

Cold front

Warm front

**SOUTHERN HEMISPHERE**

④ As the warm front passes over the observer, the wind veers, often to the south-west or west, and the barometer stops falling. The rain eases or stops, but visibility is poor with low cloud or mist. If the center of the low is some distance away to the north, the cloud layer is likely to be thinner, and breaks in the cloud cover may appear occasionally.

⑤ The cold front is often marked by cumulus or cumulonimbus (huge heaped clouds). The pressure may drop again because of a trough of lower pressure ahead of the front. There may be heavy rain, fierce gusts and squalls, and sometimes thunderstorms. As the front passes, the wind usually veers sharply north-west and the pressure starts to rise.

◁ **FRONTAL DEPRESSION**

*Depressions typically form when a pocket of warm air encroaches into the neighboring band of cold air along the polar front. The front curls around the pocket, forming a wave with a warm, leading front and a cold, trailing one.*

## WARM AND COLD FRONTS

The leading front is called the warm front because it has warm air behind it, pushing over cooler air ahead. The trailing front is known as the cold front, and has cold air behind it. The cold front pushes under the warm air in the warm sector ahead. The cold front moves faster than the warm one.

## OCCLUDED FRONT

As the cold front catches up with the warm front, the cold front pushes the warm-sector air off the surface, and the two fronts form an occluded front. Depending on whether the air behind the occluded front is colder or warmer than the air in front, it will be a cold-front type or a warm-front type. A cold occluded front is more active than a warm one, bringing heavier rainfall and higher gusts on the passage of the front.

## LIFESPAN OF DEPRESSIONS

Because cold fronts move more quickly and catch up with warm fronts, depressions have a limited lifespan. Secondary depressions can, however, form along the cold front of a dying depression. These are often smaller, develop faster, and can be more intense than the parent.

Depressions vary greatly in size, duration, and severity, but all continually change as they grow, interact with other weather systems, and eventually die. They can move at 50 knots or more, but those that cover a very large area tend to be much slower-moving.

## DIRECTION OF DEPRESSIONS

Frontal depressions in temperate latitudes, in both hemispheres, tend to move from west to east, with the center of the depression towards the cold airstream on the polar side.

In the early life of a frontal depression, the low-pressure system tends to move in the same direction as the upper airstreams. This is approximately the same as the direction of the isobars in the warm sector (the area between the fronts). As the depression matures, it reaches higher into the high-altitude jet-stream winds and begins to move in their direction.

Towards the end of its life, the depression system will generally slow down. It may also change direction – usually to the north in the northern hemisphere, and to the south in the southern hemisphere.

# DAILY CHANGES

*If you are sailing near the coast in settled conditions, the weather you experience will change throughout the day. This effect is known as the diurnal weather variation. It is caused by the sun heating the land and, to a far lesser extent, the ocean. Understanding diurnal effects enables you to predict wind speed and direction change during the day, and adjust your sailing plans accordingly. When sailing at night, you will understand when an inversion may form and bring light winds.*

### MORNING TO AFTERNOON

As the land heats up with the rising of the sun, it warms the air above it. The warmed air rises through convection currents. As it goes higher into the troposphere, it gradually cools and sinks again. The convection currents are marked by cumulus clouds that form as water vapor carried in the cooling air condenses into droplets. As the convection currents grow in strength, they reach an altitude where the winds are stronger than they are at the earth's surface. The sinking currents then bring down parcels of upper air, causing an increase in wind strength and a possible change in wind direction at the surface.

Convection currents reach their peak activity in the mid- to late afternoon, when clouds are at their highest and winds at their strongest. If the convection currents are particularly active, they may produce showers from rain-bearing clouds and thunderstorms may occur.

### EVENING TO NIGHT

As the land cools in the late afternoon and evening, the convection currents stop and the wind drops in strength. On clear nights, an inversion effect may form (*right*). This is an indication of settled weather.

### TIPS FOR SAILORS

Study the weather forecast before you go on the water. If conditions seem stable and are being influenced by a nearby high-pressure system, check the clouds when you reach your sailing area. They will provide the clues to identify local heating of the land. If small cumulus clouds are evident in the morning, expect to see diurnal effects bringing stronger winds in the mid- to late afternoon.

### THROUGH THE DAY

*By studying the types of clouds that appear through the day, you can make many deductions about the sort of weather and the wind conditions to expect. Practice observing clouds and making predictions to improve your skills.*

△ CUMULUS

*Early convection currents produce small cumulus clouds and variable winds. Deep clouds indicate that the good weather may not continue through the day.*

△ ENLARGING CUMULUS

*Cumulus may increase in size. Large clouds with high tops may produce rain showers. Stronger gusts with wind shifts are found near the clouds.*

△ MIXED CUMULUS

*Larger cumulonimbus sometimes develop among smaller cumulus. These are very active areas and can produce heavy showers and even hailstones.*

# UNDERSTANDING INVERSIONS

It is normal for the temperature of the air to cool as it rises. However, in settled weather, an inversion of this usual state of affairs may arise. Inversions occur when colder air becomes trapped under warmer air. This often happens in the evening or at night, when the land cools down quickly under clear skies, making the air near the earth's surface cool more rapidly than air at a higher altitude.

### THE INVERSION EFFECT

When an inversion has formed, it separates low-level wind from wind at a higher altitude, preventing the two from mixing. This stops the usual effect of high-altitude wind speeding up low-altitude wind. The wind at surface level then slows down because of friction. The lightest winds occur around dawn, and fog patches may form when the air temperature reaches its lowest level.

### INVERSION BREAKING

When the sun rises, it heats the land and forms convection currents. These columns of warm air penetrate through the inversion layer, causing the surface winds and high-altitude winds to mix again.

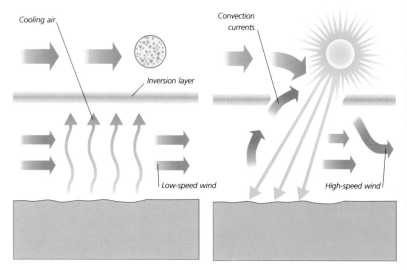

**AN INVERSION FORMING**

Cooling air

Inversion layer

Low-speed wind

**AN INVERSION BREAKING**

Convection currents

High-speed wind

### △ THUNDERSTORMS

*A rising air mass under a large cumulus or cumulonimbus cloud may produce a thunderstorm. Heavy gusts and big wind shifts occur at the base of the storm.*

### △ CLEAR SKIES

*As the land cools, convection currents die and clouds disappear. With nightfall, the land cools quickly as there are no clouds to trap the heat. An inversion may form.*

### △ DAWN MIST

*At dawn, winds will be very light or calm and fog may develop. Near to land, the fog is likely to evaporate as the sun rises and warms the ground.*

# THE EFFECTS OF THE LAND

Understanding global weather patterns, depressions, and anticyclones is a great help when predicting changes in the weather, but the coastal or inland sailor also needs to understand how weather patterns can be influenced by the land. When you are sailing well offshore, you will experience wind conditions that are dictated by the nearest pressure systems; nearer to land, local effects can interfere with the established pattern and cause localized changes in the weather.

## LAND AND THE WEATHER

Land influences the wind and weather in a number of ways. Diurnal changes (pp.268–69), ocean breezes, and land breezes all result from convection currents that are formed over the land. The effects are greatest in summer, when clear skies allow the earth's surface to heat and cool quickly.

## LAND AND HEAT

Air is not warmed by the sun, but rather by the ocean or land over which it travels. Land heats and cools far more rapidly than the ocean, and different surfaces heat and cool at different rates. The topography and nature of the land determine how much heat it can absorb and radiate.

Flat beaches and fields close to the coast heat up quickly in the morning, and large convection currents form above them. Steep hillsides and valleys stay cooler, whereas large urban areas can absorb considerable heat.

## LAND AND WIND

Land can alter the direction and strength of the wind. Wind blowing at a shallow angle onto a steep, high coastline will tend to be deflected parallel to the coast. River valleys also tend to deflect the wind up or down the valley. If the wind blows more directly onto or off any coastline, however, it will be bent to blow at right angles to the shoreline. When wind blows over land, the increased

surface friction slows it down. An onshore wind may be strong at the coast, but a few miles further inland its speed will be much reduced. An offshore wind will pick up speed as it leaves the coast and blows over the smoother ocean. This is important if you are planning a trip and estimating the strength of the wind at sea.

## WIND SHADOWS

When you are sailing close to land, be aware of the effects of wind shadows (areas of reduced wind speed). An offshore sailor will notice the large wind shadows often found in the lee of large islands, and the coastal sailor will be affected by smaller features in harbors and rivers. Trees, buildings, ships, and high ground can all disrupt the passage of the wind and cause lulls, gusts, and wind shifts. Sailors who race on inland water need to be particularly aware of wind shadows and microclimate disturbances caused by very localized heating and small convection currents.

## OCEAN BREEZES

One of the most obvious examples of winds caused by localized heating is the coastal ocean breeze, common in stable weather conditions during the summer. When coastal land is heated by the morning sun, large convection currents build up. As the air over the

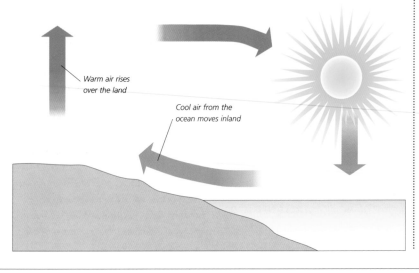

Warm air rises over the land

Cool air from the ocean moves inland

◁ **OCEAN BREEZE**
*During the day, warm air rising from the land creates an area of low pressure that is filled by cold air coming off the ocean, resulting in an ocean breeze. The tops of the convection currents above the land are marked by cumulus clouds. Ocean breezes die down when the land starts to cool.*

**KATABATIC WIND ▷**

*In areas where there are steep cliffs or mountains on the coast, katabatic winds may occur. This often occurs on cloudless nights, when the land cools rapidly. Air moving over the cold ground becomes cooler and flows quickly downhill, pulled by gravity. When a land breeze effect combines with a katabatic wind, the resulting wind can be quite strong.*

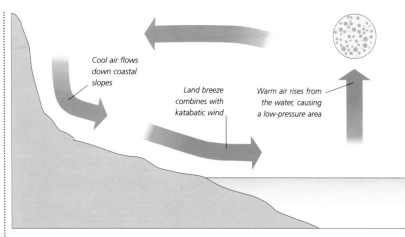

Cool air flows down coastal slopes

Land breeze combines with katabatic wind

Warm air rises from the water, causing a low-pressure area

land heats up, it rises and the pressure drops. Over the ocean, the air remains relatively cool and moves towards the low-pressure area to replace the rising air. A circulation system, driven by the convection currents, quickly develops and an ocean breeze is born.

## OCEAN BREEZES AND GRADIENT WINDS

An ocean breeze typically blows directly onto the coastline, but will be modified by any gradient wind (the wind caused by pressure systems). If the gradient wind is blowing onto the coast, the ocean breeze will add to it, causing stronger winds in the middle of the day. If the gradient wind is offshore, the two may cancel out each other, and light winds or calm may result near the coast. A well-established ocean breeze may be felt 5–10 miles offshore and some miles inland, but, in the early stages of its

development, it may extend only a few hundred yards from the shoreline. The presence of cumulus cloud along the coastline is a sure indication of a developing ocean breeze. Even if the day dawns cloudless and windless, an ocean breeze may bring a stiff onshore wind by midday. Ocean breezes drop off as the land cools later in the day.

## LAND BREEZES

A land breeze is the direct opposite of an ocean breeze. At night, under clear skies, the land cools quickly while the ocean retains its heat. Air over the land cools and sinks, thus raising the pressure; air over the ocean stays relatively warm and continues to rise. Once again, convection currents are set up, but this time the wind blows off the land. Land breezes are

usually lighter than sea breezes, but their effects may be felt several miles out to sea. They are typically stronger in autumn when the ocean is warmer than it is in spring or summer.

## KATABATIC WINDS

Sinking currents of air from mountains are known as katabatic winds. They may be experienced near mountainous coastlines where cool air, drawn down the slopes by gravity, causes a wind to blow down the slopes and out to sea.

Katabatic winds usually occur at night and may blow for several miles out to sea. A land breeze combined with a katabatic wind off a steep headland can bring strong gusts.

## ZEPHYR WINDS

Zephyrs are gentle winds that occur when air over land is warmed and rises, allowing cooler air over the water to drift off the lake or river.

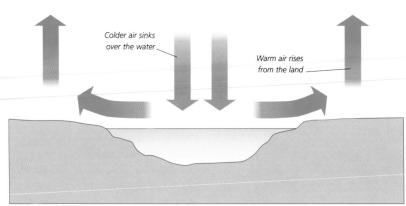

Colder air sinks over the water

Warm air rises from the land

◁ **ZEPHYR WIND**

*In otherwise calm conditions, warm air rising from the banks of a river or edges of a lake creates an area of low pressure, into which cold air flows from the river or lake. This results in a zephyr wind, a gentle wind that can be exploited by inland dinghy sailors.*

# STORMS

*B*ad weather is caused by low-pressure systems and their ascending currents of air. When a large volume of humid air is forced rapidly upwards, intense activity takes place and a revolving circulation of air is created. Frontal depressions (p.266) can cover very large areas and produce fairly strong winds, but smaller, yet more intense low-pressure systems, such as thunderstorms, tropical revolving storms, and tornadoes, are responsible for even more severe weather.

### THUNDERSTORMS

A thunderstorm is created by a very intense but localized area of low pressure that can produce very strong winds and heavy rain or hail. Thunder and lightning add to the drama. In tropical regions, thunderstorms are fairly common, often occurring at night. They are less frequent in temperate latitudes where they occur more often over large land masses such as North America. At sea, thunderstorms usually form along the line of a cold front.

### THUNDER CLOUDS

A thunderstorm starts when a huge volume of air is forced upwards by localized heating or by being pushed upwards by cold air at a front. The large convection currents form huge banks of cumulus cloud that push upward and grow larger – a sign that a thunderstorm may develop. If the system becomes sufficiently active, cumulonimbus clouds form. These towering, dark and forbidding clouds reach great heights and have characteristic anvil-shaped tops that point in the direction the storm is traveling. The higher the cloud top, the more intense the storm. Ice crystals form in the anvil top. They collide within the cloud and create static electricity, which discharges to earth as lightning. Low rolls of cloud, created by violent internal air currents, form along the base of a storm, resulting in heavy rain or hail. This is also where the strongest winds and wind shifts are found. Behind the thunderstorm, the wind and temperature drop.

### SAFETY AT SEA

If you are at sea when a thunderstorm approaches, the best course of action is to get out of its path. However, if the storm is going to pass over you, it is advisable to turn into it to get through it as quickly as possible. If you are heading in the same direction as a storm and are overtaken by it, you will spend longer within the storm.

### REVOLVING STORMS

Tropical revolving storms are known by different names in different parts of the world: in the Atlantic they are hurricanes, in the western Pacific they are typhoons, and in the Indian Ocean they are cyclones. They are born in low latitudes and are marked by enormous banks of cloud that reach to the limit of the atmosphere, indicating a very intense depression. The depression covers a much smaller area than a frontal depression but the pressure gradient is much steeper, causing winds in excess of Force 12, and very heavy and steep oceans.

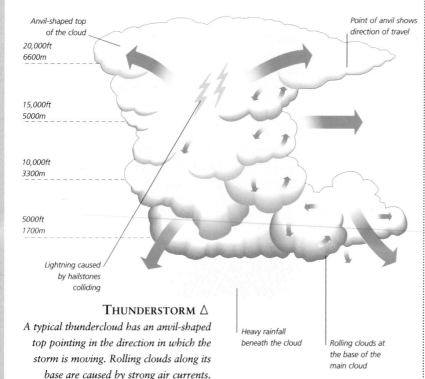

Anvil-shaped top of the cloud

20,000ft 6600m

Point of anvil shows direction of travel

15,000ft 5000m

10,000ft 3300m

5000ft 1700m

Lightning caused by hailstones colliding

#### THUNDERSTORM △

*A typical thundercloud has an anvil-shaped top pointing in the direction in which the storm is moving. Rolling clouds along its base are caused by strong air currents.*

Heavy rainfall beneath the cloud

Rolling clouds at the base of the main cloud

## WIND CHARACTERISTICS

During a revolving storm, the winds spiral inwards towards the center of the depression at all heights through the storm, instead of blowing along the isobars at higher levels, as they do in a normal depression. The winds revolve counterclockwise in the northern hemisphere and clockwise in the southern hemisphere. At the center of the storm there is an "eye" in which the wind is temporarily calm, but the seas are rough and confused without the controlling influence of the wind. The clouds may clear for a short time but the respite will be brief as the opposite wall of cloud approaches, containing more violent winds. The wind is at its strongest close to the eye and visibility is seriously reduced, often to zero, as the air is filled with flying foam and spray.

## STORM ORIGINS

Tropical storms usually develop on the eastern side of oceans, and mature as they travel westward or north-westward in the northern hemisphere, or west or south-westward in the south. In their early stages, they usually move slowly at 10–15 knots, later increasing in speed to 25 knots or more. As they near the western side of the ocean, they may curve north or north-easterly in the northern hemisphere, or south or south-easterly in the southern hemisphere.

## FORECASTING STORMS

Most tropical storms occur in fairly predictable seasons, such as July to September in the Atlantic, but they can develop at other times, too. The birth, growth, and development of tropical storms are monitored by forecasters using weather satellites, and sailors may receive warnings issued by radio. When sailing in tropical latitudes, a drop in barometric

pressure of 5mb or more is a warning of an approaching storm. Other signs may include a large ocean swell, significant changes in wind speed and direction, and cloud building from high cirrus through altostratus to heaped cumulus.

## SAFE REFUGES

Sailors who think they are in the path of a tropical storm should try to avoid being caught in the most dangerous semi-circle, which is to the north of the center in the northern hemisphere, and to the south of the center in the southern hemisphere. A tropical storm is extremely dangerous to all craft but especially to small yachts. Safe refuges, known as hurricane holes, can be found in areas liable to these storms, but most harbors present as many dangers as being at sea.

## TORNADOES

A tornado is the most violent small-scale disturbance and is far more common over land than at sea, occurring most frequently on the eastern plains of North America. Forming in hot, humid, thunderous conditions, tornadoes are created by severe convection currents that occur in large cumulonimbus clouds. A tornado's diameter is usually only a few hundred yards, and it will rarely travel more than a few miles. In that distance, however, it can cause more destruction than almost any other natural phenomenon. Winds at the center may reach 200 knots, and the exceptionally low pressure can rip houses apart and throw cars in the air.

## WATERSPOUTS

A waterspout is a type of tornado that is found at sea. It forms under heavy cumulonimbus clouds that contain strong convection currents. As a waterspout forms, a funnel-shaped

△ **WATERSPOUT**
*Strong convection currents produce a funnel-shaped extension at the base of cumulonimbus clouds. The powerful revolving motion of the wind in this cloud draws water off the surface of the ocean, creating a spinning mass of spray.*

cloud extends from the base of the cumulonimbus cloud towards the ocean. Its revolving motion causes a spinning mass of spray to rise from the ocean. If the waterspout continues to develop, the end of the funnel meets the spray cloud and forms a spinning column between cloud base and ocean. The top and bottom of the column travel at different speeds so it quickly takes up a slanting position and eventually breaks up. A waterspout is a localized and short-term event but can present a serious danger to small craft. A waterspout is less severe than a tornado, typically lasts less than 30 minutes, and covers an area 100ft (30m) in diameter. Waterspouts move slowly, but can be erratic, and are more common in tropical than temperate latitudes.

# FOG

When you sail in a small boat, your safety and enjoyment depend on your ability to see all around you and avoid any potential hazards or collisions. Fog, therefore, can be a significant problem at sea. Although there are four main types of fog, all are basically cloud that has formed at the earth's surface. Three types of fog are caused by air being cooled to the point where it can no longer hold its moisture in vapor form, so some condenses into water droplets. The fourth type is caused by air that remains at the same temperature but picks up more water until it reaches saturation point, when some of the water condenses. It is helpful to know the types and causes of fog in order to predict its duration and extent.

## RADIATION FOG

Often called land fog, radiation fog forms over land at night in clear conditions. During the night, the land cools rapidly by radiating its heat upwards. As there are no clouds to trap the heat, the air in contact with the land cools. When the temperature at the earth's surface falls below the dew point of the adjacent air, it becomes saturated and water vapor condenses to produce fog.

Radiation fog will only form when land cools rapidly under a warm, moist airstream that will probably have come off the ocean. This type of fog requires low wind speeds, otherwise vertical mixing warms the air at the surface. It commonly forms under high-pressure systems that bring settled weather and clear skies.

Radiation fog forms first as mist in low valleys, gradually thickening and deepening as more air is cooled.

During the early hours of the morning, it may extend several miles out to sea, but will disperse if the water temperature is higher than that of the land. In general, radiation fog poses little hazard to sailors, apart from in rivers and estuaries, where it may persist for some hours. Radiation fog quickly disperses when the sun rises – the land heats up, warming the air, raising its dew point, and lifting the fog. However, if overcast conditions come in at dawn, the land takes longer to heat up and the fog may persist.

## ADVECTION FOG

Also called sea fog, advection fog is the type that is normally found at sea. It is caused by a warm, moist airstream blowing over cooler water. It is most common during winter and spring, but may also occur in summer. Localized areas of ocean turbulence that bring cold water currents to the surface may also produce advection fog.

A warm, moist airstream moving from temperate to polar latitudes will form large banks of sea fog along a wide front as it is gradually cooled by moving over cold water. An example

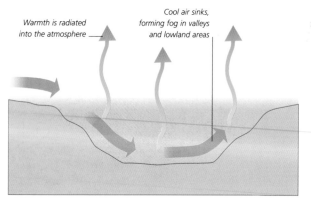

## △ RADIATION FOG

Radiation fog is formed at night during clear conditions, when rapidly cooling land cools the air above and makes water vapor condense into droplets. The fog forms first as mist in low valleys, and spreads and thickens as the air continues to cool.

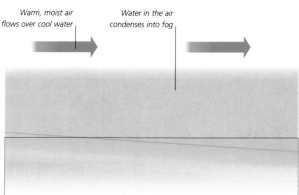

## △ ADVECTION FOG

When warm, moisture-laden air passes over cold water, it cools down to its dew point, the water vapor in the air condenses, and advection fog forms. Also known as sea fog, advection fog can be persistent, requiring a dry wind to disperse it.

**FOG FORMING** ▷
*A bank of advection fog forms where a warm and moist airstream flows over cold water. As the air cools, the moisture it contains is condensed to form fog.*

is the Grand Banks of Newfoundland, where a warm airstream that has picked up moisture from the warm Gulf Stream meets the cold waters of the Labrador Current.

Advection fog poses the greatest potential hazard to sailors. It can be very thick and persistent, even when there is a strong wind. Sea fog will disperse only when a change of wind brings drier air. In this situation, it is very important to determine the boat's position as accurately as possible.

## FRONTAL FOG

As its name implies, frontal fog occurs along the warm front of a depression. Warm air rises over cold air (*p.264*) and then cools rapidly to below its dew point to form a long, narrow strip of fog along the front. Frontal fog is often seen as low cloud, which can fall to sea level. It can also develop as high-level fog above otherwise clear conditions, obscuring high land and headlands from view. Frontal fog is not particularly persistent, but it can cause problems with piloting (*pp.244–45*) if the navigator wants to use landmarks such as transits or lighthouses.

## SEA SMOKE

Sea smoke is usually found in arctic and polar regions. Unlike other forms of fog – which form when warm, moist air cools – sea smoke occurs when cold air absorbs moisture as it passes over a warmer ocean. The excess moisture cannot be absorbed by the cold air, so it immediately condenses into fog. At the same time, however, the air is being warmed by the ocean so its dew point rises and the fog next to the ocean disperses. The warmer air then rises to be cooled again by the air higher up, so the fog reappears. This type of fog produces an effect that resembles smoke, as it quickly forms, disperses, and reforms. Sea smoke is not a particular problem for sailors. It lasts only a short time, until the air is warmed by the ocean sufficiently to eliminate the effect.

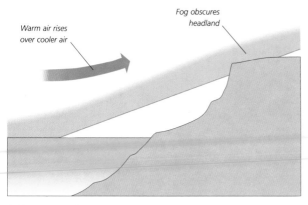

Warm air rises over cooler air

Fog obscures headland

### △ FRONTAL FOG
*Frontal fog develops when warm, moist air at the front of a depression rises over colder air. This causes the temperature of the warm air to fall below its dew point. Frontal fog causes most problems for sailors when it obscures landmarks.*

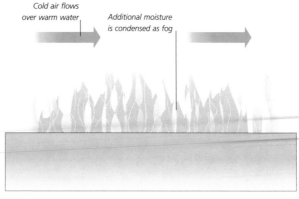

Cold air flows over warm water

Additional moisture is condensed as fog

### △ SEA SMOKE
*Cold air flowing over a warmer ocean absorbs and immediately condenses any water evaporating off the ocean, forming fog. The water warms the air, raising the dew point and dispersing the fog. Higher up, the air cools again and the fog reforms.*

# FORECASTING

*W*eather forecasting is a very complex subject. Although you can learn how to make general assessments of conditions and reasonably good predictions of what to expect in the near future, you will also need to take advantage of any suitable published forecasts that are available to you. You can then compare these forecasts with your own observations to produce an overall picture that you can use when planning a sailing trip or during an offshore passage.

## WEATHER FORECASTS

You can obtain weather forecasts from a variety of sources. Television, radio, newspapers, and the internet are good sources of information. They provide simple, generalized forecasts that cover land areas. Some of these sources also offer more detailed synoptic charts showing pressure systems, isobars, fronts, and wind strengths. Specialized maritime forecasts are broadcast by public radio stations in many countries. These may include details such as storm and gale warnings. Specialist forecasts can also be obtained from coastguard services and coastal radio stations.

Weatherfax provides weather forecasts specifically for mariners. To obtain these forecasts, you need to have dedicated receivers or software that can be used on a PC that is connected to a radio. In addition to weather data, other receivers provide a range of navigational and safety data. Some receivers display the information on screen, but most have a built-in printer.

## WEATHER MAPS

A weather map is the most useful means of obtaining information about weather systems, their speed and direction of movement, and the winds associated with them. If you can obtain a professionally produced weather map, you have a good starting point for predicting approaching weather and modifying your predictions through observation.

You can obtain weather maps and satellite weather pictures from many sources, including specialist sites on the internet. Alternatively, you can draw your own weather map using radio weather forecasts. These usually include a general synopsis and predictions for particular sea areas and recent, recorded readings at weather stations of wind strength and direction, pressure, precipitation, and visibility. By plotting this information on a chart, you can construct the pattern of isobars and the direction and speed of movement of areas of high and low pressure. This sounds complicated, but is within the capability of any reasonably experienced cruising sailor.

*SYNOPTIC CHART ▷*

*Synoptic charts used in weather forecasting feature information such as the movement of fronts, pressure systems, and wind strengths and directions.*

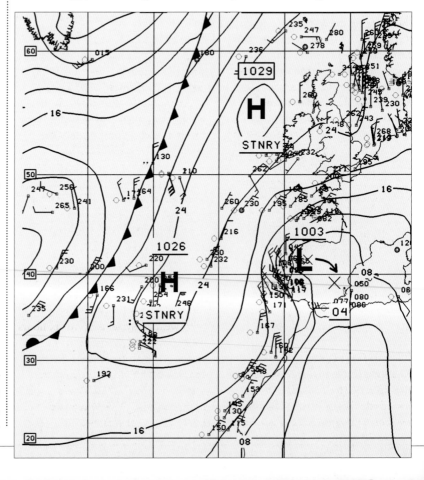

## BAROMETERS

The most useful forecasting tool aboard a small yacht is a good-quality barometer. This can be calibrated by calling the local coastguard to obtain the present correct reading and adjusting as necessary. The actual pressure reading is less important, however, than its direction and rate of change – rising or falling pressure and the speed of change is an indicator of imminent weather changes. Pressure readings should be taken every hour and recorded in the logbook.

A recording barometer, called a barograph, makes a continuous reading of pressure on a paper graph, providing a ready reference when it is required. Traditional barographs can be susceptible to the motion of a small boat but electronic versions, which do not have this problem, are available.

## ANEMOMETERS

It is useful to be able to measure wind speed and direction. This can be done by an electronic instrument with a masthead vane and anemometer, or by a hand-held cup anemometer and a hand bearing compass.

If you use hand-held instruments, take readings on the windward side of the boat. Remember, too, that these instruments only provide apparent wind direction and strength, so you must record boat speed and heading and calculate the true wind speed and direction. Alternatively, integrated instruments can provide true wind speed and direction if they are connected to an electronic compass. Record the true wind information in the logbook on an hourly basis.

## PSYCHROMETERS

Many electronic logs are made with a temperature sensor built into the transducer. This allows the user to note sea temperature, which is a good guide

to the risk of fog. However, sea temperature information is more helpful when it is used in conjunction with readings from a psychrometer. This piece of equipment has a dry bulb thermometer for measuring temperature and a wet bulb thermometer for measuring humidity. It is used in conjunction with tables that enable you to predict the dew point temperature of the air. By comparing dew point information and the sea temperature, you can make a much more accurate assessment of fog risk (pp.274–75).

## USING OBSERVATION

If you are unable to receive useful forecasts at sea, you will be reliant on your own observations to monitor the weather. Once you become used to the passage of weather, you will be able to predict the speed and severity of approaching fronts.

If you are in tropical latitudes, you should monitor the barometer and expect to see gradual diurnal changes. If the pressure starts to drop significantly and you see cloud increasing at high altitudes and a building ocean swell, expect an approaching storm. The center of the storm will be in the direction from which the sea swell is coming. In temperate latitudes, approaching depressions are signaled by falling pressure and a wind that backs initially under building high cloud.

Wherever you are in the world, you can use clouds to forecast weather. High clouds are associated with weather systems up to six hours away. If they are wispy and white, fine weather is imminent. Clouds that are lifting and dispersing are also indicative that good weather is approaching. Clouds at a lower level relate to current weather. If they are

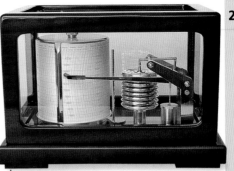

△ BAROGRAPH
*A barograph is a recording barometer that traces a line on graph paper to provide a continuous record of pressure. Electronic versions are also available, which display pressure changes over time on a graphical display.*

dark, heavy, and lowering, poor conditions and rainfall are likely to be on their way. Another way of forecasting rain is to observe whether there is a halo around the sun or moon. This haze is caused by the refraction of light by ice crystals carried in moisture-laden clouds.

## BEAUFORT SCALE

Before the introduction of measuring instruments, wind strengths were expressed on the Beaufort Scale. This was devised by Admiral Francis Beaufort in 1805 to describe the effects of wind. At first, the Beaufort Scale (pp.278–79) related the wind strength to the amount of sail a tall ship could carry. This was later modified to include the effects of wind observed on land and at sea. The Beaufort Scale is still used to define wind strengths at sea, and the Beaufort Forces are now defined as speed in knots. The descriptions are just as useful now as they were originally, allowing an observer to judge wind speed on land or at sea without the use of instruments.

# BEAUFORT SCALE

| Force | Mean Speed | Description | On the Shore | Dinghy Sailing |
|-------|-----------|-------------|--------------|----------------|
| 0 | Less than 1 knot | Calm | Smoke rises vertically and flags hang limp. | Drifting conditions. Heel the boat to maximize sail efficiency. Make gentle movements. |
| 1 | 1–3 knots | Light air | Smoke drifts slightly, indicating wind direction. | Gentle forward movement. Flatten sails and balance boat bow down and heeled. |
| 2 | 4–6 knots | Light breeze | Light flags and wind vanes move slightly. | Steady speed is possible. Sail upright with full sails for maximum power. |
| 3 | 7–10 knots | Gentle breeze | Light flags extend outward. | Hull speed possible. High-performance dinghies may plane. Ideal for learners. |
| 4 | 11–16 knots | Moderate breeze | Paper lifted off the ground. Small branches move. | Planing on most points of sailing. Crew fully extended. Beginners should head for shore. |
| 5 | 17–21 knots | Fresh breeze | Small trees sway visibly and tops of trees move. | Ideal conditions for experienced crews, otherwise capsizes are common. |
| 6 | 22–27 knots | Strong breeze | Large trees sway and wind whistles in telephone lines. | A dinghy sailor's gale. Only experienced crews with good safety cover should race. |
| 7 | 28–33 knots | Near gale | Whole trees are in motion. It is difficult to walk against the wind. | Most sailing dinghies remain on the shore. If they are taken on the water, they are likely to be overpowered and damaged. |
| 8 | 34–40 knots | Gale | Twigs are broken off trees. Progress on foot very much impeded. | Dinghy sailing not possible. Dinghies should be securely tied down on shore. |
| 9 | 41–47 knots | Severe gale | Chimney tiles and slates blown off roofs. Fences blown down. | Dinghy sailing not possible. |
| 10 to 12 | 48+ knots | Storm to hurricane | Trees uprooted and considerable structural damage likely. Extremely rare inland. | Dinghy sailing not possible. |

| CRUISER SAILING | WAVE HEIGHT | SEA STATE IN OPEN WATER |
|---|---|---|
| Becalmed. Use engine. | 0ft (0m) | Mirror-like water. |
| Very slow sailing upwind. Downwind spinnaker hard to keep filled. | Less than ¼ft (0.1m) | Ripples form on the water. |
| Slow sailing upwind with little heel. Spinnaker fills downwind. | Up to 1ft (0.3m) | Small wavelets with smooth crests. |
| Pleasant sailing. Spinnaker fills and sets well downwind. | Up to 3ft (0.9m) | Large wavelets with crests starting to break. |
| Hull speed achieved by most yachts. Some small cruisers start to reef. | Up to 5ft (1.5m) | Small waves and frequent white horses. |
| Medium-sized cruisers start to reef. Crew wear and clip on safety harnesses. | Up to 8ft (2.5m) | Moderate waves and many white horses. |
| Most cruisers reefed. Wear and clip on harness. Seek shelter if inexperienced. | Up to 12ft (4m) | Large waves, white foamy crests. Spray likely. |
| Seek shelter or sail away from land to ride out any forecast storms. Family crews may have problems coping. Most cruisers deep-reefed. | Up to 20ft (6m) | The sea heaps up and waves break. Much spray. |
| Use a deep-reefed mainsail and small headsail. Close and secure hatches and companionways against water. Only essential crew should be on deck. | Up to 25ft (8m) | Moderately high waves of greater length that frequently break. |
| Danger of knockdown. Some crews may continue to sail; others heave-to or run before. Depending on the ocean state, a trysail could be set. | Up to 30ft (10m) | High waves with breaking crests and flying spray. |
| Stay well away from coastlines. Survival conditions. Danger of 90° knockdowns and full capsizes. | 30–52ft (10–16m) | Very high waves. Ocean becoming heaped up and white. Visibility affected. |

# PRACTICAL BOAT CARE

THE LEVEL OF MAINTENANCE a boat requires
depends on its age, size, type, and complexity,
and the amount of care an owner wishes to
lavish on his pride and joy. Whereas the owner
of a general-purpose dinghy need only give his
boat an occasional wash and check over, the
owner of a cruiser should be able to service
and maintain a variety of onboard systems.

*Boats stored on the shore require the correct
support to avoid damage and prevent them falling
over in high winds. A custom-built cradle is ideal.*

# THE HULL

*The amount and type of maintenance that a hull requires depends on the material used in its construction. Fiberglass offers strength, low maintenance, and easy replication of mold-built boats. Wood in the form of plywood, veneers, or strip planking combined with epoxy resins makes strong, light, molded hulls that are aesthetically pleasing, but traditionally built wooden hulls require considerable regular maintenance. Steel or aluminum hulls are strong and resilient.*

### GENERAL MAINTENANCE

Always check underwater surfaces every time you dry out or lift the boat, and repair any damage immediately. Check the topsides regularly, and repair even minor damage as soon as possible. All boats that are kept afloat need a coat of antifouling paint at least once a year to combat underwater fouling from weed and barnacles. Check with other boat owners to see what is recommended in the area in which you plan to sail, because there are various formulations designed to be most effective in specific locations.

### FIBERGLASS HULLS

Production-built fiberglass boats are finished with a smooth gel coat that protects the underlying laminate and produces a shiny surface. The gel coat is quite easily damaged by impact, and repairs must be made quickly to stop water from penetrating the laminate. This is not usually a difficult job, but it can be tricky to match the color and blend the repair with the existing gel coat. Maintenance is a matter of cleaning and polishing the gel coat to restore the shine. Polishing gradually reduces the thickness of the gel coat, which will also age from exposure to ultraviolet light. Eventually, the time will come when a coat of paint is needed for cosmetic purposes.

### STEEL AND WOODEN HULLS

Both steel and wooden hulls are protected by a paint layer. Minor collisions usually result in nothing more than damage to the paint layer, which is easily repaired. If a steel hull weeps rust, it indicates that the paint system has broken down, allowing moisture and air to attack the steel. This may require sandblasting to remove the old paint and surface rust. Modern paints make it much easier to

get a lasting finish on steel, but it is vital that the surface is thoroughly prepared and that the paint supplier's instructions are closely followed. Two-pack polyurethane paints are much harder and longer-lasting than the single-pack types, but require more work if small areas need to be touched up. They are not, however, suitable for traditionally constructed wooden hulls, which require the greater flexibility of single-pack types. A quality two-pack polyurethane paint that is applied properly should last about five years, with an annual polish; a conventional single-pack polyurethane is likely to need renewing every year or two.

### ALUMINUM HULLS

Aluminum is strong and lighter than steel, and hulls made of this material need paint only for cosmetic reasons. For low maintenance it makes sense to leave an aluminum hull bare, as its surface will form an oxidized layer that turns matte grey. If painted, the surface must be carefully prepared according to the paint supplier's instructions and a hard, two-pack polyurethane should be used.

### THROUGH-HULL FITTINGS

Many modern yachts have a large number of through-hull fittings for engine-cooling water, toilet intake and discharge, and galley and shower sump pumps. All of these holes in the hull are potential causes of sinking, so the fittings must be checked regularly. Damage to metal through-hull fittings is often caused by a process called

◁ **ANTIFOULING PAINT**
*Applying antifouling is one of the least popular maintenance chores, but it is essential to prevent underwater fouling, which will slow the boat considerably.*

electrolysis (*see below*). Check metal through-hull fittings by withdrawing a fastener. Consider removing and checking the entire fitting if there is any sign of corrosion on the fastener. Grease all seacocks at least once a season, and open and close them regularly to ensure they do not seize. If you are planning a new boat, minimize the number of through-hull fittings by using standpipes to which all inlets and outlets are connected.

## REPAIRING DAMAGE

If you sail a fiberglass boat, always carry some epoxy filler and gel coat of the appropriate color aboard to repair minor chips and grazes. Clean out the damaged area, de-grease and dry it thoroughly. If the damage is quite deep, fill with epoxy filler to just below the surface, allow it to cure

then apply gel coat, leaving the surface slightly raised. For shallow grazes use only gel coat. Cover the area with plastic film taped into place and wait for the gel coat to cure. Once hard, it can be rubbed back using fine sandpaper and a rubbing paste to finish the job and polish the surface. More serious damage can be repaired by a skilled owner using a glass cloth or mat, but it is usually better to employ professional help.

If your boat has a painted hull, carry some topside paint on board to touch up minor damage. Fill deep scratches with an epoxy filler before painting. Hard, two-pack paints can be polished like gel coat.

Minor dents to aluminum and steel hulls can also be filled and painted, but more serious damage will probably require expert skills.

## KEEL AND HULL FITTINGS

Keel construction varies depending on the design of the boat. Many fiberglass production cruisers have their keels encased in the fiberglass molding, using lead or iron in the keel cavity to provide the necessary weight. Other craft have fin or bilge keels bolted onto the hull structure, and these bolts occasionally need to be checked for corrosion. The rudder and propeller-shaft bearings should be checked for wear once a season, and the propeller checked for damage.

### KEEL

If your cruiser has a keel that is bolted onto the hull, withdraw one or two bolts every few years to check for corrosion. If leaks occur at the junction of keel and hull, the keel should be removed and re-bedded on new sealant. A skilled amateur with the right tools can do this job; otherwise get expert help.

### RUDDER BEARINGS

Rudder bearings should be checked annually. This is done by grasping the bottom of the rudder and trying to move it fore and aft and from side to side. Movement indicates that there is wear in the bearings. Worn bearings should be replaced as soon as possible.

### PROP-SHAFT BEARINGS

Check the propeller-shaft bearings by vigorously pushing the propeller from side to side. If there is any significant movement, the bearings or the shaft may need to be replaced. Check the propeller itself for any corrosion or impact damage. If a blade is damaged, replace or repair it immediately. An unbalanced propeller can cause increased vibration, which may lead to failure of the bearings.

---

## PREVENTING ELECTROLYSIS

Electrolysis occurs because different metals, when in close proximity and immersed in sea water, tend to form an electric cell. A current flows, and the baser of the two metals is eaten away. Metals are ranked by their position in the galvanic series.

### ZINC ANODES

Many boats have fittings made of several different metals on the underwater part of the hull. To protect these from electrolysis, you should fit one or more sacrificial anodes. Zinc is a base metal in the galvanic series that determines the vulnerability of different metals. It will be attacked by electrolysis before any of the other metals and will protect them from corrosion. Zinc anodes must not be painted and should be replaced when half their bulk has been eaten away. Ask a supplier to help you decide on the best size and position of anodes. Any leak of current from the boat's electrical system will add to

the problem of electrolysis, so if your anodes are being quickly eaten away have your electrical system checked and repaired by an expert.

*Anode with strap for bolting to a hull*

### △ SACRIFICIAL ANODE

These are fittings made of zinc in various shapes and sizes. They are fastened near skin fittings, the rudder, and the propeller shaft to protect these important fittings from corrosion.

# DECK AND RIG

*Whatever the size of your craft, the condition of its deck and rig fittings is critical for handling efficiency and safety. Most of the equipment should require little in the way of maintenance, but it must be checked regularly for wear and the appearance of small cracks that indicate stress damage. All deck and rig hardware must be securely fastened, usually with bolts, and deck gear should have substantial backing plates to spread the load through the structure.*

## DECK HARDWARE

Deck hardware is all the equipment fixed to the deck. Most good-quality marine gear will give many years of reliable service as long as it is the correct size for the loads involved. The weak point is often where the gear is attached to the deck. Aluminum craft can have much of their gear welded directly to the deck; on other types of boat it is through-bolted and bedded down on a marine sealant to eliminate leaks. Over time, fittings may loosen and sealant will harden and crack. Check deck fittings for movement, and tighten fastenings if necessary. At the first sign of any deck leaks, remove the fitting and re-bed it on fresh sealant. Inspect the fitting and its fasteners for signs of corrosion.

## STAINLESS-STEEL FITTINGS

Many fittings and fasteners are made of stainless steel, which is resistant to rust because of a protective layer that forms on its surface in the presence of oxygen. If a stainless-steel fastener is sealed from the air, corrosion can occur in small crevices. High-quality marine fittings are polished after welding to remove surface irregularities. If they begin to rust, they can be buffed up to remove the surface damage at the source of the corrosion. Salt water speeds up deterioration.

## WIRE RUNNING RIGGING

Halyards are often made of wire with a rope tail. Alternatively, low-stretch ropes, such as Spectra and Vectran, can be used. They are more expensive, but are lighter and easier to handle.

Wire halyards can be made of flexible galvanized or stainless steel. Stainless wire is more common as it is less prone to rust. Damage in wire halyards usually occurs where they pass over sheaves (pulley wheels) in the mast that are too small in diameter. Watch out for broken wire strands, which indicate likely failure, and check the rope-to-wire splices.

## ROPE RUNNING RIGGING

Rope halyards, sheets and control lines should be checked regularly for chafe. Most damage occurs when a highly loaded rope rubs slightly against another rope, shroud, or lifeline. Make sure that all sheets and halyards have a fairlead and cannot rub on anything when under load. If damage occurs at the end of a rope, it can be cut off and the rope shortened; if it occurs in the middle, the best you can hope for is two much shorter ropes. Periodically end-for-ending the rope (reversing it) can lengthen its life. Make sure rope ends are sealed or whipped. Wash all your ropes in warm, soapy water from time to time to remove dirt and salt.

## STANDING RIGGING

Shrouds, forestays, and backstays are usually made of stainless or galvanized wire, although solid stainless rod rigging is also used on larger cruisers and racing boats. Standing rigging needs little maintenance other than periodic checks for broken strands. If you find any, replace the wire because any weakness compromises the strength of the entire rig. Occasionally wiping down the rigging will also remove dirt and salt crystals that can accelerate crevice corrosion, especially where wire enters the end terminals. All rigging screws should have toggles between them and the chainplates so that they are free to move in any direction without bending. Inspect them carefully for any signs of hairline cracks, which indicate stress damage. If your standing rigging is over ten years old, consider replacing it, even if there are no obvious signs of defects.

## SPARS

Most boats today have aluminum spars, although wooden masts and booms are still common and the use of carbon fiber is increasing.

Aluminum spars have anodized surfaces that are eventually roughened by salt crystals and contaminants in the air. Wash them off and finish the surface with a wax polish. They should be checked annually for corrosion around fittings (especially if stainless fasteners have been used) and for any hairline cracks. Pay special attention to the mast-step area, spreader roots, and rigging attachment points. Wooden masts require varnishing, oiling, or painting at least annually and possibly even more often in the tropics. Check for splits in the wood and signs of rot. Carbon masts are usually painted with a hard two-pack polyurethane and should be checked and cleaned like aluminum.

## SAILS

Keep an eye on your sails for damage to stitching, especially along seams, batten pockets, and around high-load areas such as the corners. Scan these areas every time you hoist or lower a sail, and when you are sailing, walk around the deck to see if the sails can rub on any part of the mast, standing rigging, or lifelines.

The stitching is where most damage occurs. It is usually caused by chafe, often against the shrouds and spreaders. If the source of the chafe cannot be moved or the sail re-trimmed, fitting anti-chafe patches at strategic points can help. A small rip in a panel can quickly develop into a large tear in a sudden gust. Early action with a needle and thread can prevent damage spreading rapidly. Large areas of damage can be repaired temporarily using sticky-backed cloth and stitching, but should be dealt with by a sailmaker as soon as possible.

Sails should be washed thoroughly in fresh water as often as is practical to remove salt crystals and dirt that abrade the cloth. Always cover sails when not in use, as long exposure to sunlight will weaken the cloth.

## SAIL DAMAGE AT SEA

If a sail rips when it is in use, you must get it down as soon as possible, otherwise the damage will quickly get worse. If it is a headsail, replace it with another and stow the damaged sail. If it is the mainsail, lower it completely, unless it is possible to reef the sail so that the damaged area is not exposed. If conditions allow, take the mainsail off the mast and boom and repair it down below. Your repair at sea need only be sufficiently well done to allow you to return to port. Once on the shore, however, the damage should always be assessed by a sailmaker as soon as possible and professionally repaired.

---

## PATCHING A SAIL

You should be able to undertake minor sail repairs at sea. This usually involves either replacing seam stitching or patching rips in a sail panel.

### SEWING KIT
A sailmaker's palm (a leather thong with a metal insert), a set of needles, waxed thread, and sail material.

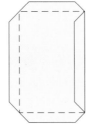 **1** Cut a patch to cover the tear. Trim the corners, and turn the edges under.

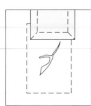 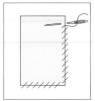  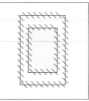

 **2** Place the patch centrally so that it covers the tear on all sides.

**3** Oversew neatly around the turned-under edges of the patch.

**4** Turn the sail over, and then trim the torn area to make a rectangle.

**5** To finish the repair, oversew around the edges of the rectangle.

---

## CARING FOR WOOD

Woodwork requires a good deal of care, especially if it is above deck where it is exposed to the elements. The best way to reduce your workload is to get rid of all woodwork on deck, but for many sailors its esthetic attraction justifies the long hours of maintenance it needs.

### VARNISHING WOOD
Varnishing is necessary at least annually in temperate climes and as often as every few weeks in the tropics. Single-pack polyurethane varnishes are appropriate for traditional wooden construction, but a harder, two-pack varnish is better on stable, molded wood surfaces. To get an excellent finish, the wood must be dry and sanded to a very smooth finish. At least ten coats of varnish must be applied, starting with one or two thinned coats. The surface must be lightly sanded between each coat for maximum adhesion and gloss. Only apply varnish in warm, dry and calm weather conditions.

### COATING WOOD
An alternative to varnish is to use a wood oil or polymer coating, which can very effectively seal the wood and give an acceptable finish while requiring little maintenance.

**BARE TEAK DECKS**

# THE INTERIOR

*M*any different materials are used in the interior of a yacht. These range from the wood and soft furnishings that make a cabin into a comfortable living area, through to the electrical and mechanical gear used for operating the boat. These items are fitted into an environment that is often poorly ventilated and exposed to a wide range of temperatures and humidity conditions. They need to be looked after carefully and checked regularly or they will quickly deteriorate.

## WOODEN SURFACES

Wood is the traditional material for boat interiors. It is popular because it is easy to work with and looks warm and natural; even boats with fiberglass or metal hulls often have plenty of wood below deck.

It is also traditional for most interior wood to be varnished. A varnished finish looks very attractive if the wood is good quality and has been fashioned by an expert shipwright. However, varnish must be well applied in a sufficient number of coats to produce a deep gloss. On stable wooden surfaces, such as plywood or laminates made up with veneers, a two-pack polyurethane varnish gives the hardest and most durable finish, which should last for at least five years. Wood in older boats will probably have been finished with tung oil or single-pack polyurethane varnishes. These require annual re-varnishing to stay in top condition. If the quality of the wood or existing varnish is not perfect, consider using a matte or eggshell varnish; this will hide far more flaws than a high-gloss finish, which exaggerates defects.

## VARNISH CARE

Re-varnishing is best done during the spring or fall, when conditions are warm and dry but not too hot. Cold, humid conditions produce a much poorer finish. During the sailing season, wipe down varnished surfaces occasionally, and touch up any small scratches when they occur to prevent moisture from penetrating the wood.

## PAINTED AND FIBERGLASS SURFACES

Although painted surfaces are easier to maintain than varnished ones, they are not as common aboard yachts. As with varnishes, conventional and single-pack polyurethane paints need more regular re-painting than two-pack finishes and are softer and more vulnerable to scratching. However, they are cheaper and easier to use, especially when you need to touch up an area of minor damage. Painting is best done in warm, dry weather.

Many fiberglass craft have a molded interior, designed to give smooth surfaces that are easy to clean and do not require painting. Although these can look cold, they are practical, particularly in the heads where easy-to-clean surfaces are essential.

◁ **DIFFERENT MATERIALS**
*Cruiser interiors use several different materials in their construction and furnishings. Here, a galley has wooden lockers, a hard-wearing laminate for worktops, and stainless-steel sinks.*

## SOFT FURNISHINGS

Bunk cushions on boats are usually a compromise because most bunks have to double as seating during the day. Bunk cushions that are comfortable to sleep on are often too soft for good seating, and good seats are usually too narrow to be used as bunks. Many production cruisers are built within a stringent budget, and savings are sometimes made in soft furnishings. When the time comes to upgrade or re-fit an older boat, improvements can often be made in this area.

Open-cell foam is generally used for bunk cushions while closed-cell foam (which does not absorb moisture but is much harder) is more common for cockpit cushions that may get wet. A wide range of fabrics can be used for covering cushions. Vinyl is sometimes used as it is water-resistant, but it is uncomfortable to sit on, especially in hot weather. In small yachts, where there is greater risk of water finding its way below, vinyl can be used on the underside of cushions with fabric on the top. Turn the cushions over if there is a danger of them getting splashed, but use them right way up at other times. If bunk cushions do get wet, both the foam and the cover will need to be cleaned thoroughly to remove the salt, otherwise the cushion will never dry out completely.

Many owners brighten up their yacht's interior with curtains, carpets, and scatter cushions. Take these off the boat when laying up for winter otherwise they will get damp and may develop mold. Carpets can be pleasant in port, but should be taken up at sea if there is any likelihood of water getting below. Waterproof carpet is highly effective and, although it is expensive, only a little is needed to cover the cabin sole of a small yacht. Have somewhere dry and out of the way to stow loose furnishings when you go to sea, or they will end up in a soggy mess on the cabin sole.

## DECKHEADS AND HULL SIDES

Many deckheads and hull sides are lined with plywood panels covered in foam-backed fabric to provide extra insulation and hide constructional features. Because they usually need to be removable to allow access to fasteners, wiring, or plumbing, the panels are often fastened in place with small amounts of Velcro. After a few years it is not uncommon for these panels to sag or become detached. They can be replaced quite easily, or re-covered and re-fastened with more substantial amounts of Velcro or positive-push fasteners.

**SLEEPING CABINS ▷**
*Medium-sized and larger cruising yachts often have separate sleeping cabins, usually up forward and aft, beside or behind the cockpit. Some have upper and lower bunks, as does this aft cabin.*

## VENTILATION

Adequate ventilation is essential for comfort aboard a boat in all conditions. It can be provided through hatches, opening ports, or dedicated ventilators. Boats without enough ventilation will stay damp inside, encouraging deterioration and mold.

### HATCHES
Hatches can bring a welcome flow of air in hot conditions, but, in most cases, they need to be closed at sea.

### OPENING PORTS
Opening ports can be useful, especially if they open from a stern cabin into the cockpit where they will be protected. Those fitted in the hull or cabin sides should be shut when under way.

### VENTILATORS
The best ventilators are of the Dorade type, which allow air in but divert any water back to the deck. These can be left open most of the time but should be closed off in very severe conditions.

### CUT-OUTS AND LOUVERS
Louvered doors and cut-outs in furniture can be used to encourage air to circulate around lockers.

# ELECTRONICS

*Most cruising yachts rely heavily on their electrical system. Electricity is used to run navigation and communications equipment, lighting, entertainment systems, and refrigeration. Consequently, there is a need to generate and store sufficient power to operate the gear. Although modern boats tend to be reasonably dry down below in most conditions, electrical equipment must be of good marine quality and should be well installed and maintained, otherwise it can deteriorate very quickly. If you sail a small boat, you should not rely totally on its electrical supply. There should always be a back up system that will allow the boat to be sailed and navigated, and the crew to be kept comfortable, in the event of a power failure.*

## DC SYSTEMS

Yachts typically use 12- or 24-volt DC (direct current) systems, with the power supplied by a bank of batteries. These are often stored in the bilges to keep their considerable weight as low as possible. Batteries are designed for specific purposes; the automotive type, often seen aboard small boats, is not designed for marine use.

An automotive battery delivers a short burst of high current to a car's starter motor. Once the engine is running, an alternator meets the needs of the car's electrical system. Aboard a boat, batteries start the engine, but must also deliver power to electrical gear when the engine is not running.

## BATTERIES

The best batteries for marine use are deep-discharge or traction batteries. Both these heavy-duty types are designed to be "deep-cycled." This means that they can be discharged to a low percentage of their capacity and subsequently recharged when the engine is running. A good marine battery will be able to handle many hundreds of charge-discharge cycles,

which would quickly destroy an automotive battery. It is good practice to have one battery for engine-starting and another for the domestic loads. If your batteries are stowed low in the bilge, consider having a smaller one higher up to run the radio equipment in an emergency, such as if the main batteries were flooded.

## BATTERY CARE

Most batteries require occasional topping up with distilled water to replace battery fluid, which evaporates when the battery is charged. They give off hydrogen gas when they are being charged, so the battery compartment should be well ventilated.

Gel batteries, in which the electrolyte is a gel rather than a liquid, require no maintenance and cannot

> ### SELECTING EQUIPMENT
> It is extremely important to use the best-quality electrical gear that has been designed specifically for use in boats. No other equipment will be as reliable or as safe in marine conditions.

spill battery fluid. They are totally sealed and do not give off hydrogen gas. They are more expensive than conventional batteries, but have obvious advantages for use on boats.

All batteries should be fastened down securely so they cannot come loose in the event of a knockdown, and conventional batteries should be mounted in a drip-tray to catch any spills of electrolyte. The state of charge of a conventional battery can be checked with a hydrometer, which measures the specific gravity of the electrolyte. If you are leaving the boat unattended for some time, ensure that the batteries are fully charged. Do not leave them heavily discharged for long, as this will shorten their life.

## CHARGING SYSTEMS

The most common charging system aboard small boats uses an alternator belted to the engine. Whenever the engine is run, the alternator supplies power to the batteries with the amount of power delivered being controlled by a regulator.

In recent years, so-called "smart" regulators have been developed, which are far more efficient than the simple type built into most alternators. They sense the condition of the battery, its temperature, state of charge, and the voltage delivered by the alternator, and they automatically deliver the best charge to the batteries. Using a smart regulator significantly improves the performance of your batteries and reduces recharging times.

## WIRING

Only marine wiring should be used aboard a boat. The best type of wiring has good-quality insulation surrounding multiple strands that have been tinned by drawing them through a solder bath. Untinned copper wire in a marine environment quickly develops a green coating that extends inside the insulation, increasing the wire's resistance to the flow of electricity and making it more brittle. All wiring should be well secured and is best run in plastic conduit and hidden behind headliners or hull paneling.

The wiring must be able to handle the maximum current drawn by the equipment with as small a voltage drop as possible between the battery and the equipment. Wires that carry high loads, such as those between the batteries and the starter motor, should be of an adequate size and as short as possible to minimize voltage drop.

If you are buying a boat that is more than five years old, look carefully at the electrical system. If the best materials were not used initially, they may need replacing. It is also likely that extra equipment has been added to the existing system, which could cause problems in the future.

## AC SYSTEMS

Some larger yachts employ an AC (alternating current) generator to run onboard domestic electrical systems in the same way as they would be run on the shore. However, the majority of small and medium-sized cruisers have little need for AC power generation.

The most common AC system is an arrangement that can be plugged in to a shore-based supply when the boat is in a marina. This is often used to run a battery charger when alongside and to provide power for running domestic equipment.

An AC system must be kept totally separate from the onboard DC system and must be installed and maintained properly to avoid potentially fatal electric shocks. If AC power is needed to run small appliances when the boat is not plugged into a shore power source, an inverter can be fitted to convert the supply from DC to AC.

## EXTENDING THE SYSTEM

Unless you have a thorough understanding of your boat's electrical system, you should consult an expert before making modifications or adding new gear. Most problems with electronics on boats arise because the system was badly installed, the materials are poor quality, or additional equipment was fitted without considering the extra loads placed on the system.

### INSTALLATION

Always turn off the batteries before working on the distribution panel or adding or removing equipment. If you are installing gear that draws a high current, consider whether you need to increase the capacity of your battery bank or your charging system. Also, you must ensure that wiring and terminals of a suitable size are used and that there are appropriately sized contact breakers in the new circuit. All equipment should be connected to the positive and negative bus bars at the boat's distribution panel with a fuse or, preferably, a contact breaker for each item. Wiring runs should be well secured, and preferably run through a conduit. Maintenance and replacement will be made much easier if you have a wiring diagram of your boat's systems.

**ELECTRIC DISTRIBUTION PANEL**

## ALTERNATIVE ENERGY

Some cruising boats make use of alternative forms of energy production. Wind generators, solar panels, and water generators are all popular means of delivering charge to the batteries without running the engine. All have their benefits and shortcomings and their use depends on where you sail and how you use your boat.

### WIND POWER

Many cruisers use a wind generator to provide electrical power to help keep batteries fully charged without needing to run the engine. Wind generators vary in their size and efficiency. Small ones put out little power in most wind strengths but are useful for maintaining batteries when the boat is unattended.

### WIND GENERATOR ▷

*A wind generator is usually mounted on a pole at the stern, clear of rigging and high enough to prevent injury.*

# PLUMBING

O n boats, plumbing can be quite complex and must be constructed with gear designed for marine use. It must be properly installed and regularly serviced. Freshwater systems store water for sinks in the galley and heads, and for the shower. They often include a hot-water supply. Separate systems are used for bilge pumping, engine cooling, and flushing the heads. You should understand how each system works and the maintenance it requires, and carry spare parts on board.

## FRESHWATER SYSTEMS

Water tanks may be fiberglass, stainless steel, or polyethylene. They should be mounted to keep their weight as low as possible. In metal-hulled boats they can be welded in, thereby creating a double bottom and using space efficiently. If space cannot be found for rigid tanks, flexible ones can be used in small spaces, but must be protected from chafe. All tanks and piping must be properly supported and secured against movement of any kind. Tanks should have inspection covers for access and cleaning. They must also have vents to allow air to escape as they are filled. If possible, take the vent up under the deck in a

high loop before leading the end into the bilge. This will prevent water from overflowing when the tank is full.

## HOSES AND MANUAL PUMPS

Various types of plumbing hose are available. Avoid clear plastic, as algae will grow inside the pipe where light penetrates. Rigid plastic piping is ideal and offers a range of valves, couplings, and junctions that makes the plumbing system easy to install and maintain. If hot water is used in the system, make sure that the piping you select can handle the heat.

The simplest freshwater system uses a manual pump at the galley and heads sinks. These require no power,

are very reliable, and discourage high water consumption. If sited properly, they are easy to maintain and repair.

## PRESSURE PUMPS

Increasingly, even quite small yachts have a pressurized hot and cold water system. Although convenient, these increase water consumption, as well as running costs and maintenance. For reliability, choose a quality pump that is suitable for the job, and include an accumulator tank in the system.

Pressure pumps work by sensing the pressure drop when a tap is opened. If an accumulator tank is fitted in the system, its pressure reservoir smooths the operation of the system and frees the pump from having to repeatedly switch on and off to maintain pressure. This extends the pump's life and makes the system quieter. A manual pump should be fitted in case the pressure system or electronics fail.

## BILGE PUMPS

A yacht should have at least two bilge pumps, one of which must be manually operated and should be sited within reach of the helmsman. If your boat is holed below water, bilge pumps can gain you vital seconds while you

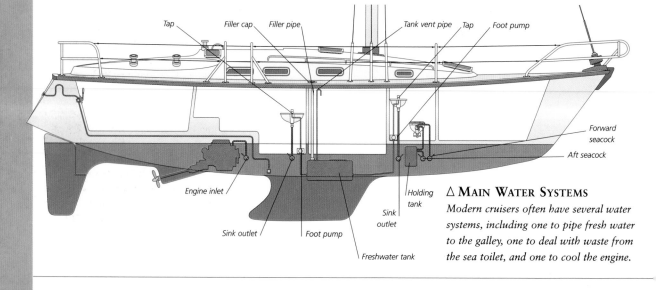

Tap    Filler cap   Filler pipe      Tank vent pipe   Tap   Foot pump

Forward seacock

Aft seacock

Engine inlet

Holding tank

Sink outlet

Sink outlet    Foot pump

Freshwater tank

## △ MAIN WATER SYSTEMS

*Modern cruisers often have several water systems, including one to pipe fresh water to the galley, one to deal with waste from the sea toilet, and one to cool the engine.*

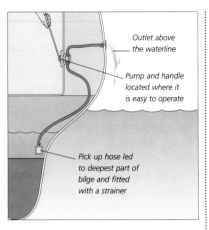

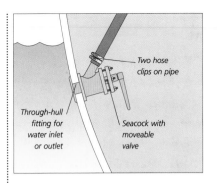

△ **SEACOCK**
*A seacock is a valve that can be shut to close the through-hull fitting.*

## △ BILGE PUMP
*The bilge pump can be vital in a flooding emergency, so it must be well maintained and the hose fitted with a strainer to prevent it becoming blocked by debris.*

that it is not designed to handle. Most sea toilets are operated by hand, with a pump drawing in sea water to flush the bowl and pump out waste. Use reinforced hose for the pump's inlet and outlet, both of which must be fitted with seacocks. Some countries prohibit the discharge of sewage from yachts. In this case, you will require a holding tank into which all waste is pumped. When the holding tank is full, it is emptied at a marina pumping station or by the toilet's own pump when you are well offshore.

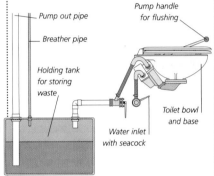

△ **SEA TOILET**
*The sea toilet is an important piece of equipment and must be kept well maintained if it is to be reliable.*

## SEACOCKS
Although it is best to have as few through-hull fittings as possible, some are unavoidable and must be fitted with good-quality seacocks. Seacocks may have a tapered plug valve, a gate valve, or a ball valve. All types should be opened and closed regularly to stop them from seizing in position. They should also be cleaned and greased on a regular basis. All hoses attached to through-hull inlets or outlets should be fitted with two stainless-steel hose-clips for safety.

make emergency repairs. Most of the time, however, they are used to remove water that accumulates in the bilge. The pick up hose should lead to the deepest part of the bilge and should have a strainer fitted to prevent debris blocking the pump. Shallow bilges may require two pick up hoses – one to port and one to starboard – so that the pump can operate with the boat heeled. Any separate watertight compartments must have their own pumps or be plumbed to the main one.

Electric bilge pumps can be used to supplement the manual unit and can be fitted with float switches that automatically activate the pump when the bilge water rises. Offshore cruisers often have a damage-control pump, which can remove large amounts of water in the event of a holing. Strip and clean all pumps regularly so that they are always ready for use.

## SEA TOILETS
Make sure that every member of the crew understands how the sea toilet works and never put anything into it

---

## GAS SYSTEMS

Bottled gas is the most popular fuel for onboard cookers and is sometimes used for heaters. The gas system must be made from the best-quality materials and be checked and serviced regularly. When not in use, the bottle must be turned off to prevent leakages.

### GAS SAFETY PRECAUTIONS
Store gas bottles in a sealed locker that drains overboard so any leaks cannot accumulate in the bilge. Use good-quality marine gas piping or flexible hose and ensure there is no risk of chafe. If you have a gimballed cooker, make sure there is some slack in the hose to allow it to swing freely.

Consider fitting a remote-controlled solenoid valve near the bottle, with the control switch by the cooker, so that the gas can be turned off at the bottle when not in use. Check all the joints for leaks using soapy water. A gas detector is a sensible precaution. It should be fitted with its sensor in the bilge but clear of any bilge water.

# ENGINES

*The majority of cruisers are fitted with an auxiliary engine that provides a charging facility for the boat's electrical system in addition to motoring capability. Today's marine engines are light and comparatively reliable. As well as using them for motoring or motor-sailing when the wind is not fair, many sailors use engines in preference to sails for entering harbor and berthing. The drawback with this approach is that some sailors fail to become adept at handling a boat in close quarters under sail and get into trouble when the engine fails. Sailors who rely on their engine for boat handling and for running a complex electrical system must fully understand their engine installation and be able to maintain it in good condition.*

## DIESEL ENGINES

The most common type of marine engine is an inboard diesel that drives the boat via a gearbox and propeller shaft. Diesels ignite their fuel by the heat of air compressed in the cylinder. An injector pump and fuel injectors deliver measured amounts of diesel to the combustion chamber at high pressure, and at exactly the right time in the compression cycle. Very high compression ratios are required to achieve the temperature needed to ignite the fuel, so a diesel has to be tougher than a gasoline engine (and is therefore heavier). Diesel engines are more expensive to buy than gasoline units, but they are cheaper to run.

## CARING FOR DIESEL ENGINES

When they are well maintained, diesel engines are very reliable, but it is vital that they receive clean fuel. There

### INBOARD DIESEL ENGINE ▷
*Most small yachts have an inboard diesel engine, which is often located under the companionway steps. The steps are removable to allow access to the engine.*

should be at least two filters in the fuel line, one of which must be able to separate off water. Water accumulates in fuel tanks through condensation and encourages diesel bacteria, which ruins the fuel pump and injectors. Keep the tank topped off to reduce condensation, clean and change the filters regularly, and use antibacterial and water-absorbing additives to keep the fuel as clean as possible.

## GASOLINE ENGINES

Marine gasoline engines are similar to car engines and are common on high-speed power boats. They need an electrical circuit to provide a spark to ignite the fuel, which can be a problem because electric ignition systems are vulnerable to moisture. Gasoline engines operate at lower compression ratios and are lighter than diesel engines. Gasoline is an explosive fuel. However, as long as the engine is properly installed and operated, the risk of explosion should be low.

## OPERATING GASOLINE ENGINES

If a gasoline engine is fitted, the fuel tank must have a shut-off valve that is closed when the engine is not in use. An extractor fan, ducted to the lowest

part of the engine compartment, is needed to extract fumes. It should be run for five minutes before the engine is started and all the time it is running.

## COOLING SYSTEMS

Most inboard engines (gasoline or diesel) are cooled by water. In the simplest systems, raw salt water is pumped around the engine and used to cool and quieten the exhaust system. This eventually leads to corrosion in the engine's water channels. Larger engines typically use fresh water with a header tank to feed it around the engine. A heat exchanger inside the header tank contains salt water that is pumped through the system to cool the fresh water before being expelled via the exhaust.

An impeller pump is used to circulate the water. If a blockage occurs, the water flow is reduced or stopped and the engine will overheat. The impeller pump is also likely to be damaged. Ensure that there is a good flow of water through the cooling system by checking the exhaust and cleaning the seacock's weed trap on a regular basis. Carry a spare impeller and learn how to change it.

## CHECKING LUBRICATION

Always check the oil level before using the engine, and every 3–4 hours while it is running. The engine manual will tell you which type of oil to use and how often to change it. If you do not use the engine much, change the oil more regularly than is recommended. Install oversized oil filters to keep the oil clean. This helps prolong the life of diesel engines, which do not react well to short periods of use at low loads followed by long periods of idleness.

The gearbox requires a special oil that will be specified in the manual. Include the gearbox oil level in your pre-start engine checks.

## OUTBOARDS

Most outboards are gasoline two-stroke units, but four-strokes are available. Diesel outboards are also available, but are comparatively heavy. Outboards are sometimes used on small cruisers, but they are most likely to be carried for use on the tender. They are ideal for the latter as they are light, portable, and self-contained, and can be lifted up when in shallow water. Their main disadvantages are that they are relatively expensive to run and are vulnerable to theft. When buying an outboard, pick one that is the right size for the tender. One that is too large will be heavy and will consume more fuel; one that is too small will not have the power to push the tender at a reasonable speed.

## CARING FOR OUTBOARDS

Although they are often clamped to a block on the pushpit when not in use, outboards are better stored away from the elements, preferably in a cockpit locker that is sealed from the interior.

Two-stroke outboard motors need an oil-and-gasoline mix. It is vital that the correct oil is used and is mixed in the ratio specified in the manual. Most outboards are water-cooled. You should check that the cooling water is flowing freely, otherwise the engine will overheat and may be damaged.

## LAYING UP AN ENGINE

If you keep your boat on the shore in the winter, you should take measures to protect the engine from deterioration while it is not being used.

### WINTERIZING AN ENGINE

- Change the engine and gearbox oil (run the engine for a few minutes beforehand to heat and thin the old oil; this makes it easier to pump out).
- Change the oil filters.
- Clean out the fuel line's water-separation filter.
- Top off the fuel tanks to reduce the chance of condensation forming in the tank.
- Remove the diesel injectors (if you have a diesel engine) or spark plugs (if you have a gasoline engine) and inject oil in the bores while turning the engine over by hand.
- Thoroughly clean the outside surfaces of the engine, starter motor, and alternator.
- Grease all moving parts lightly or spray them with a water repellant such as WD40.
- Drain the cooling water system and flush through with an antifreeze mixture.
- Remove the impeller from the water pump, place it in a plastic bag, and tie it to the pump so that you do not lose it.
- Disconnect the battery and grease the terminals.
- Store the battery somewhere warm and dry, charging it occasionally during the winter.
- Tie a note to the engine to remind yourself what needs to be done before the engine can be started.
- During the winter, turn the engine over by hand occasionally, and oil the bores.
- After winterizing your outboard, store it in a warm, dry place to protect it until you need to use it again.

# RUNNING REPAIRS

*Every cruising yacht should have sufficient tools and spare parts on board to enable basic repairs to be carried out at sea so that the boat can get back to harbor. The selection of spare parts that you need to carry depends on the type of boat that you own and the distances you sail. It is all too common for an emergency to develop from a small initial failure, so it is imperative that the skipper is capable of carrying out running repairs as and when they are required.*

## SPARE PARTS

You will not require many spares if you tend to daysail close to your home port. However, if you are long-distance cruising you should carry sufficient spares to keep all essential systems operable. Some items are not possible to repair at sea, such as an electronic autopilot. If the failure of such an item would have a significant impact on the voyage, it is advisable to carry full replacement units.

## ESSENTIAL SPARES

Opinions as to what spare parts are essential will vary according to the experience of the skipper and the crew. A novice skipper may consider the engine to be a vital piece of equipment, whereas someone who is very confident in his own skills and the boat's performance under sail will be less concerned about loss of engine power. This is especially true if the boat has an alternative system for charging the batteries, or if there are oil lamps and other simple facilities that will allow the cruise to continue without the need for electrical power.

Every skipper should make sure he knows exactly what items of equipment are essential for the safety of his crew and his boat, and he should be able to identify items that will significantly affect its ability to complete a passage. He should also know which items are useful but that could be dispensed with if necessary.

## TOOLS

You should carry a selection of tools to repair all essential equipment, together with the instruction manuals where available. Go through your boat and examine every piece of equipment and how it is secured. If you might need to remove it at some stage, check the size and type of fasteners and ensure you have the right screwdriver, wrench, or socket for the job. Check the engine manufacturer's recommendations for the engine toolkit and again ensure that you are carrying all the necessary wrenches, sockets, and allen wrenches to work on the engine. Also, make sure that you have wrenches and other tools to service seacocks, and check that there is enough room around each seacock in which to use them.

## STORING TOOLS

The best way to store tools is to use custom-built plastic toolboxes. These have compartments of various sizes to keep everything neat, and are easy to secure. A comprehensive tool kit could be split among several boxes, according to the type of tool and how frequently it is required. This will make it quicker to find the tool that you need, and makes arranging

## CONTENTS OF A BASIC TOOL KIT

Tools for use aboard your boat should be of the best possible quality, otherwise they will quickly deteriorate in the damp conditions prevalent at sea.

They should be kept lightly oiled and stored securely. The following list is an example of the contents of a tool kit that would be useful for making basic repairs.

- Screwdrivers – all head types and sizes, including electrical screwdrivers
- Wrenches – an assortment, including an adjustable wrench
- Socket set
- Mole wrench
- Electrical wire crimper

- Wire cutter
- Hacksaw and spare blades
- Wood saw
- Power drill (12V), drill bits and screwdriver bits
- Hand drill and bits
- Brace and bits

- Pliers and electrical pliers
- Hammers and a mallet
- Set of chisels
- Files
- Torch
- Mirror (to see into confined spaces)
- Bolt cutters

storage easier. It is a good idea to obtain boxes that have individual compartments for small items. These can be useful for frequently used spares such as tape or split rings, shackles, or fasteners.

## REPAIRS AT SEA

Repairs are much simpler to carry out in harbor, but it is sometimes necessary to do them at sea. In this case the job will be much easier if you have somewhere to work where you can spread out your tools and hold the item you are working on securely. Some long-distance cruising boats incorporate a small workbench. This is an ideal solution, but most yachts do not have the space. A useful alternative is to have a strong piece of wood that is cut to fit across the cockpit, between the seats, and to which you can fasten a small portable vice to hold the work securely.

---

# USEFUL SPARES

Some of the vital and most useful spares and kits are listed below. You should also consider carrying replacement units for items that are essential to the running of your boat but are not repairable.

## ENGINE SPARES

Sparkplugs and coil (gasoline engine)
Injectors (diesel engine)
Repair kits for fuel and water pumps with seals and impellers
Set of hoses
Oil filters
Fuel filters
Sets of gaskets, seals, and O-rings
Fuel
Oil and grease
Fuel antibacterial additives (diesel)
Spare ignition key

## ELECTRICAL SPARES

Fuses – all types used on board
Bulbs – including navigation lights
Terminal fittings
Connecting blocks
Soldering iron and solder
Wire – assorted sizes
Tape – insulating and self-amalgamating
Batteries (for flashlights and so on)
Distilled water (for topping up batteries)
Hydrometer (for checking batteries)

## ASSORTED SPARES

Sail repair kit (*p.285*)
Sticky-backed sail repair tape
Piston hanks
Whipping twine
Mainsail slider
Rope – spare lengths of various sizes
Shackles – assorted
Bottlescrew
Clevis pins
Split pins
Split rings

Bulldog clamps
Rigging wire – a length equal to longest used on board
Marine sealant
Underwater epoxy
Waterproof grease
Petroleum jelly
Paint and varnish (minor repairs)
Epoxy glue and fillers
Fiberglass tape and cloth
Nails, screws, and bolts – assorted
Wood – assorted pieces

---

# MAINTENANCE PLANNING

Use a notebook to record all items and equipment that need repairs or regular maintenance. This makes it quick and easy to identify the most important work and to plan time and materials for the job.

## SCHEDULING REPAIRS

Maintenance jobs are much easier and more pleasant to carry out when the weather is good. Try to schedule regular maintenance sessions and keep your list of repairs as short as possible during the sailing season.

## MAKING A LIST

Make time to take the occasional tour through your boat checking all possible sources of problems and making a list of repairs as you go. Once you have checked structural fixtures above deck, work your way through the interior. Run all electrical and mechanical systems to ensure that they work and have not been affected by moisture.

## WHAT TO LOOK FOR

• Check structural items to ensure that their fastenings have not loosened. Sailing to windward in large waves can put a considerable load on the forward parts of the boat and the main bulkhead. Take a look down below when the boat is sailing hard to see if there is any movement of the hull or bulkheads.
• Check the area where chainplates come through the deck and look for signs of water that would indicate a leak around these fittings.
• Look for any leaks around fittings, windows, or hatches.
• Check along the hull-to-deck joint for signs of water leakage.
• If water regularly appears in the bilge of a fiberglass or metal boat, track its source and seal the leak.
• In fiberglass boats, check the decks for crazing caused by stress.

# STAYING SAFE

SAILING IS GENERALLY SAFE despite the potentially hostile environment in which it takes place. If safety is to be maintained, however, it is crucial that participants understand the risks, accept responsibility for their own well-being, and sail within the bounds of their experience. Staying safe depends as much on attitude, seamanship, and common sense as on equipment.

*Flares are a primary means of signaling distress when in sight of land or other vessels. Here, a crew member attracts attention with a red hand-held flare.*

# EMERGENCY REPAIRS

A cruising yacht's crew must be prepared to deal with all eventualities once they cast off and head out to sea. Although most passages will be enjoyable and uneventful, the crew will occasionally be presented with an unwelcome challenge, such as a hole in the boat, dismasting, loss of steering, a fouled propeller (which renders the engine useless), or even a fire. All skippers must plan for such contingencies, carry the right spares and equipment, and drill the crew in emergency procedures.

## HOLING AND LEAKS

If the boat is holed above the waterline, perhaps in a collision, you have some time to assess the situation and take action. If the damage is below the waterline, however, immediate action is required to prevent the boat from sinking. Your priorities must be to eliminate or minimize the inrush of water, and to commence pumping to keep the boat afloat.

First, turn on all electric bilge pumps, and the damage control pump if fitted, and have a crew member work the manual pump. If you have spare crew members and the water is already over the cabin sole, instruct them to use buckets in order to scoop water through the companionway into the cockpit. You may be able to add to the pumping capacity by removing the engine-cooling water inlet hose from its skin fitting and putting the end in the bilge.

Sometimes the source of the water is not obvious, in which case, suspect a broken engine-cooling water hose or toilet hose, or a failed seacock or through-hull fitting. If the leak is from a hose, turn off the seacock. All seacocks should have a wooden plug tied to them so that if a seacock fails, you can quickly use the tapered plug to block the hole. If the inrush of water is from a hole in the hull skin,

it should be easy to locate unless it is behind paneling, in which case you may have to rip interior furniture away to expose the source of the leak.

Your objective is to block the hole as effectively as possible by whatever means available. Bunk cushions, sail bags, or any other soft material can be pushed into the hole and held in position with a brace, such as the fender board or other suitable length of wood. You can purchase an umbrella-like piece of equipment that is pushed through the

hole and opened on the outside. Water pressure then seals it against the hull and stops the leak. Whatever material you use, you need to be innovative and act quickly to block the hole before the inrush of water overwhelms your pumps. Once the hole is blocked from the inside, you may be able to lower a sail over the hole on the outside using lines led under the hull to hold it down. Fasten the lines at suitable strong points on deck, such as handrails.

The size of the hole and how deep it is below the waterline determine the amount of water coming in. Water pressure increases rapidly with depth, so a hole low down will create a high-pressure jet of water that will be difficult to stop. If the hole is near the waterline, you may be able to heel the boat to raise the hole out of the water or at least reduce the pressure.

If you cannot stem the inflow, and if your boat does not have watertight

### BLOCKING A HOLE ▷

*It is important to block the hole, particularly below the water line, by whatever means you can. Push bunk cushions, sail bags, or any other soft material (folded as many times as possible) into the hole, and hold in position with a brace such as the fender board.*

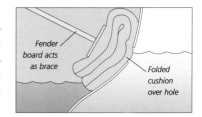

Fender board acts as brace

Folded cushion over hole

**USING A BUNK CUSHION**

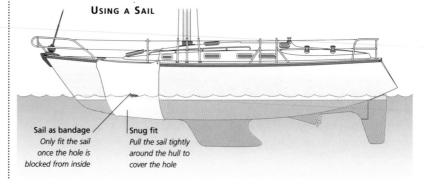

**USING A SAIL**

Sail as bandage
*Only fit the sail once the hole is blocked from inside*

Snug fit
*Pull the sail tightly around the hull to cover the hole*

**DISMASTED YACHT ▷**

*The priority is to get the broken pieces on board or cut away so that they cannot damage the hull. The boat's motion will be jerky without the mast, so there is an increased risk of falling overboard.*

compartments, your best hope lies in the ability of your pumps to keep up with the flooding. Assess the situation quickly, and if it is clear that you will not be able to keep the yacht afloat, you must commence the procedure for abandoning ship (*pp.304–05*). If your boat is near shallow water and the tide is falling, another option may be to deliberately ground the vessel. This will allow you to patch the damage before the tide rises again.

## DISMASTING

Dismasting usually occurs when a piece of rigging or a terminal fitting gives way. This usually happens in rough conditions, but can occur in calm weather if the fitting has been weakened earlier and suddenly gives way. The mast will fall roughly downwind as the sails pull it over the side. As soon as this happens, the motion of the boat will change dramatically as it loses the inertia of the rig high above the hull. The motion will be quick and jerky and it will become difficult to stand and work on deck. The immediate priority is to prevent the broken pieces of mast, still attached to the boat by rigging, halyards, and control lines, from damaging the hull or decks. Ideally, try to recover as much of the broken mast as possible for use in constructing a jury rig (a makeshift rig to get you to safety). Recovery is often impossible in rough weather; you will usually have to cut away the rig to prevent it from holing the hull. You will need a large pair of bolt cutters to

cut standing rigging; the alternative – disconnecting the standing rigging at the chainplates – is a difficult task in rough conditions.

Assess the situation once you have cut away or recovered the gear. You may be able to reach port under power if you have sufficient fuel, but do not start the engine until you have checked and re-checked that there are no ropes in the water that may foul the propeller. If motoring is not an option, then attempt to improvise a jury rig – perhaps using the spinnaker pole and a storm jib – that will allow you to sail downwind, albeit slowly.

## STEERING FAILURE

Steering failure occurs most frequently aboard wheel-steered boats as a result of a steering-cable failure, which can often be prevented by regular checks and maintenance. Tiller-steered boats have simpler systems with less to go wrong, but it is wise to carry a spare tiller for use in the event of a breakage.

Rudder hangings or bearings rarely fail – if a problem does occur, it is generally in the rudder-control system. An emergency tiller must be available in a wheel-steered boat, and you should practice using one before it is needed. Deck layout may necessitate the use of relieving tackles to control the makeshift tiller. Undertake a dummy run to try these out to make sure you know how to rig and use such a system if necessary.

If the rudder or its fittings fail, you will have to find another way of steering the boat. An emergency sweep can sometimes be constructed by bolting the spinnaker pole to a floorboard and lashing it to the pushpit or stern rail. Alternatively, you may be able to tow two small drogues off each quarter and adjust these to steer the boat. How well the boat balances under sail will determine whether it is possible to steer in this way, but you will have to reduce sail to keep the boat under control.

## FOULED PROPELLER

Fouled propellers are quite a common occurrence, especially in busy sailing areas with many moorings, fishing nets, and lobster-pot lines to snag the unwary. Propellers are usually fouled by a rope caught and wrapped around the propeller shaft. Synthetic materials often melt and fuse because of the heat generated by friction. This creates a solid mass around the propeller and shaft, which stops the engine.

Prevention is far better than cure. Be alert to ropes in the water, and check that your own ropes do not fall over the side: there is little worse than being immobilized by your own warp.

Another effective preventative measure is to fit a shaft cutter. These are mounted ahead of the propeller. They have a serrated edge with sharp teeth that catch and cut any rope or plastic that comes near the propeller.

If, despite all your precautions, a rope does foul the propeller, you are likely to have a difficult task freeing it.

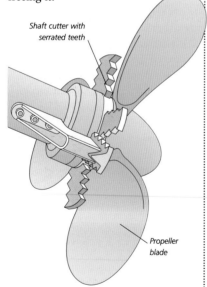

*Shaft cutter with serrated teeth*

*Propeller blade*

### △ SHAFT CUTTER

*Fitting a shaft cutter to the propeller shaft ahead of the propeller is a good way to minimize the risk of fouling.*

If the engine was turning at low speed and you can still reach an end of the rope, you may be able to free it by turning the engine slowly, by hand if possible, in the opposite direction to that in which the propeller was turning, while pulling on the rope.

It is more likely, however, that the only remedy is to cut the tangled or fused material away. This may require someone going over the side with a sharp knife, something that is both difficult and hazardous to do at sea. This should be attempted only in calm weather by someone wearing a wet suit and with a safety line tied around them. In harbor, you may be able to dry out alongside or heel the boat, or trim it down by the bow sufficiently to reach the prop from the dinghy. Always ensure the engine is stopped if anyone is working near the propeller.

## FIRE FIGHTING

Fire on board is most typically the result of a cooking accident, an electrical fault, or an explosion in the gas or fuel supply. There is little to be done in the event of an explosion, as it is likely to destroy the boat. Prevent such an eventuality by fitting and maintaining the gas and fuel supply properly, and install a gas detector with a loud warning bell. Avoid bringing naked flames near to gas appliances, and do not run the engine or other machinery when re-fuelling or when working on the engine.

Fire must be combated as soon as it starts if it is to be brought under control with the minimum of damage. Ensure that there are fire extinguishers of appropriate types in all the key areas, and test them regularly to make sure that they work.

---

## WHICH FIRE EXTINGUISHER?

Mount a foam or dry powder extinguisher close by the galley and engine compartment and others in the forecabin and a cockpit locker. Fit enclosed engine compartments with a remote carbon-dioxide ($CO_2$) extinguisher, which can be operated either manually or automatically.

Pressure test all extinguishers now and again and invert dry powder extinguishers monthly to prevent the powder inside from compacting in the bottom. Know how and when to use each of the different extinguishers and brief the crew thoroughly in their use.

| TYPE OF FIRE | METHOD OF EXTINGUISHING FIRE |
|---|---|
| Combustible materials | Foam or dry powder extinguisher. Aim extinguisher at the base of the fire. |
| Engine fire | $CO_2$, foam, or dry powder extinguisher. Turn off fuel supply at tank. |
| Electrical fault | $CO_2$ or dry powder extinguisher. Turn off battery system at isolating switch. |
| Cooking fire | Foam or dry powder extinguisher, or fire blanket. Use the blanket to smother flames. |

# BEING TOWED

If your boat has been disabled and you have been able to summon assistance, you may have to accept a tow from another vessel. Towing at sea is difficult and must be handled correctly if the tow is to be successful and not result in further damage to your boat. Be aware that taking a tow may make you liable for a salvage claim by the towing vessel. Try to negotiate and agree a fee before accepting a tow, and supply your own tow rope. If possible, agree a destination and speed of tow with the other vessel's skipper.

## TOWING A SAILING DINGHY

Sailing dinghies sometimes take a tow in light winds or before or after a race. When you are being towed, lower the mainsail and pull the centerboard almost fully up. Leave the rudder in place and steer to follow the wake of the towing boat. A dinghy can be towed alongside or astern. Several dinghies can be towed together in line astern or herringbone fashion.

## TOWING A CRUISER

Towing a cruiser places high loads on both the towed and towing vessels, but the towed yacht is especially vulnerable if it is being towed by a much larger vessel. Ships often cannot travel at a slow speed without losing steerage way, and their minimum speed will often impose very high strains on the yacht being towed. Avoid taking a tow from a much larger vessel unless there is no alternative. If the tow is to take place in rough seas, or if you have to be towed for some distance, rig a towing bridle made up of one or more heavy warps, attached to the strongest parts of the yacht to distribute the loads throughout the structure. Use a long, springy nylon warp, or the anchor chain, to form the tow rope. Ensure that it is long enough to reduce snatching loads on the warp, otherwise it may break.

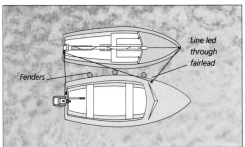

### △ TOWING A DINGHY ALONGSIDE
*If a single dinghy is being towed in calm conditions, it can be fastened alongside the towing boat as above. Otherwise, tow astern to avoid damage – tie a painter around the mast and lead it through a fairlead at the bow.*

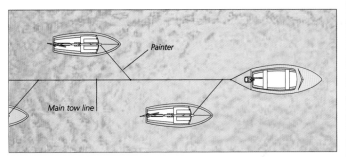

### △ TOWING HERRINGBONE FASHION
*If several dinghies are being towed they will either be arranged one behind the other or in a herringbone arrangement as shown. In the latter, each boat uses its rudder to steer, and the painter is led directly from the mast to the main tow line, not through the bow fitting, and fastened with a rolling hitch (p.167).*

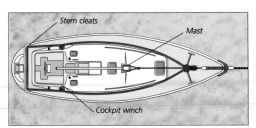

### △ TOWING BRIDLE
*Rig your mooring warps to form a towing loop at the bow with the warps leading from the bow cleats back to the cockpit winches, stern cleats, and mast. Attach the towing warp or chain to the towing loop and use plenty of chafe protection on the towing warp at the fairlead.*

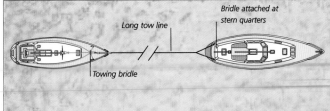

### △ TOWING A CRUISER
*A long tow rope in a rough sea will reduce shock loading and reduce the danger of the towed yacht over-running the warp if it surfs down seas from astern. If this is still a danger, the yacht under tow should trail a warp astern to help stop it surfing on waves. Steer the yacht carefully in the wake of the towing boat to stop it sheering to one side, which dramatically increases the towing loads.*

## SIGNALING FOR HELP

If you are in sight of help and have no other signals, the easiest international distress signal for a small-boat sailor to use is to slowly raise and lower his outstretched arms.

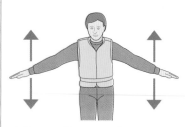

△ **SIMPLE DISTRESS SIGNAL**
*Stand facing in the direction of potential assistance and slowly raise and lower your outstretched arms from down by your sides to above the shoulders. Keep repeating the signal until you receive an acknowledgment. You can combine this signal with others, such as sounding SOS on a foghorn, to attract attention.*

# DISTRESS SIGNALS

*If an emergency on board has developed beyond the ability of the crew to deal with it, the time has come to ask for help. Distress signals are only ever used when a boat or crew member is in grave and imminent danger and immediate assistance is required. If you see or hear a distress signal, you are legally obliged to render speedily all possible assistance. The small-boat and cruising sailor is most likely to use radio, EPIRB (emergency-position-indicating radio beacon), or flares to signal for help.*

## RADIO

Sending a distress call by radio is often the most practical way of seeking help when the electricity supply is working. Most yachts carry a VHF (very high frequency) radio and some also use MF (medium frequency) radio. VHF radio is limited to line-of-sight operation between the transmitting and receiving aerials. In practice, this means reception of about 40 miles (65km) from a coastal radio station with a high aerial or 10 miles (15km) between two yachts at sea. An MF set has a longer range of about 200 miles (320km) but is much more expensive and requires more power. A ship's license is required to install a radio and the user needs an operator's license. Modern VHF sets that conform to the GMDSS (Global Maritime Distress and Safety System) and are fitted with Digital Selective Calling can be triggered to send an automatic distress signal that identifies the vessel in distress and transmits its position if connected to a GPS set.

For older sets, distress, urgency, and safety signals are transmitted by international agreement on VHF Channel 16 or 2182kHz on an MF transmitter. The recognized radiotelephony distress signal is the word MAYDAY and indicates that a vessel is in grave and immediate danger. Use of the distress signal imposes general radio silence, which must be maintained until the emergency is over and the distress signal is canceled by the authority controlling the emergency response.

To send a distress signal, check that the VHF (or MF) set is turned on and has power. Switch to high power to transmit. The form the message takes is vital (*see MAYDAY box, left*). Listen for a reply which, in coastal waters, should come at once. If no reply is heard, check that the set is transmitting and try again. Once you have made contact, it is important to repeat your position.

Urgency signals are used to send an urgent message concerning the safety of the boat or a crew member, but when you are not yet in grave and imminent danger. It may be that a crew member has been injured and requires medical assistance or your boat has been rendered helpless and is drifting, but is not in danger of sinking. In such cases the PAN PAN signal is used, repeated three times. The PAN PAN message is usually broadcast initially on Channel 16 or 2181kHz, but if the message is long you should switch to a working channel once contact has been made. The PAN PAN signal takes priority over all but a MAYDAY message.

The safety signal, which consists of the word SÉCURITÉ spoken three times in succession, indicates that the transmitting station is about to send an important safety, navigational, or weather warning.

## EPIRB

Another radio aid common aboard yachts that sail offshore is an EPIRB (emergency-position-indicating radio beacon). This transmits a distress signal to satellites that are part of the GMDSS, which locate the EPIRB's position and relay the information to a rescue coordination center.

On purchasing an EPIRB, it is registered with the name and details of the vessel to which it belongs so that search and rescue services have this information in the event of the EPIRB being activated. EPIRBs can be manually or automatically activated.

## OTHER SIGNALS

Although radio, flares, and EPIRBs are the main ways of signaling distress or urgent situations, code flags, shapes, and sound signals are sometimes used when in sight of another vessel or the shore.

◁ **CODE FLAGS N OVER C**
*This combination of flags indicates "I am in distress and require assistance."*

◁ **CODE FLAG V**
*This code flag signals "I require assistance."*

◁ **CODE FLAG W**
*Hoisting this flag signals "I require medical assistance."*

◁ **BLACK SQUARE OVER BLACK BALL**
*This signals distress. You can hoist any black spherical object – a buoy, for example – to form the ball.*

**SOS SIGNAL – SIGNALS DISTRESS**

## TYPES OF FLARES

All boats that sail on the sea should carry some flares. The type and number carried depends on the distance you sail from shore. A dinghy may carry a couple of hand-held red flares, whereas a cruiser sailing offshore will need a more comprehensive selection. Keep them dry and replace them before their renewal date.

| PARACHUTE FLARE | BUOYANT SMOKE | MINI-FLARES |
|---|---|---|
| **RED FLARE**<br>Fires a bright red flare up to 1,000ft (300m) that burns for about 40 seconds. Use when some distance from help. Not good in low cloud, when they are better fired downwind under the cloud. | **ORANGE SMOKE FLARE**<br>Once ignited is dropped into water to leeward of boat and emits dense orange smoke. Used for signaling position to searching aircraft. Burns for about two minutes. | **RED FLARE**<br>For personal use and kept in jacket pocket. Useful in man-overboard situations. Can be hand-held or rocket type. Helps boat locate person in the water. |

### HAND-HELD FLARES

| WHITE FLARE | RED FLARE | ORANGE SMOKE FLARE |
|---|---|---|
| Not a distress signal but a way of warning other vessels of your presence. Always stow one within easy reach of the helmsman. | Burns with a bright red light for about a minute with a range of about 3 miles (5km). Use to indicate your exact position when within sight of assistance. | Emits bright orange smoke and burns for about 40 seconds. It is used in daylight and good visibility, and is best in light winds. |

**303**

DISTRESS SIGNALS

# ABANDONING SHIP

*I*f an emergency situation develops to the point where you *may* have to abandon ship, the decision to do so must be carefully considered. Unless the yacht is in imminent danger of sinking, you will be safer staying aboard than taking to a life raft. Whether the skipper accepts an offer of rescue from a helicopter or another vessel, the decision ultimately to abandon ship will depend on his confidence in the yacht, his crew, and his own ability to get the yacht to port.

### ABANDON SHIP PREPARATION

Speed is vital if you have to abandon a sinking yacht and your life raft is the only option open to you. First, prepare the life raft for launching and ensure that the crew dress in their warmest clothing, with full oilskins, harnesses, and life jackets. If time allows, the crew should gather together items that may be useful in the life raft. Fill sealable containers with extra drinking water, and collect cans of food and a can opener in case you are in the raft for a long time. A chart, compass, and plotting tools will also be useful, as will a hand-held GPS, a portable VHF radio, extra red flares, a signaling torch and a knife. An offshore yacht should have a panic bag containing these items ready for just such an emergency. This bag should be kept close to the companionway.

Once everything is prepared, do not rush to launch the raft, but do everything possible to save the yacht.

### THE LIFE RAFT

The term "life raft" suggests that it is a guaranteed lifesaver. In reality, rafts often do not fulfill these expectations.

A life raft should be of a style approved by your national authority for the type of sailing you intend to do, and should be large enough to hold every member of the crew. Try to take a short course in using the raft to familiarize yourself with the inflation mechanism, the difficulty of boarding from the water, and how to right the raft if it flips. Life rafts are packed in a solid container or in a flexible valise and should contain emergency equipment to help you survive in the raft. However, this equipment is the minimum required; check what yours contains and prepare your panic bag accordingly. If possible, supplement with equipment salvaged from the yacht before you abandon ship.

If you are obliged to use a life raft, always stream the drogue as soon as you have boarded. Trailing this mini-underwater parachute beneath the raft will slow down its drift and help to prevent a capsize.

It is important that life rafts are serviced regularly in accordance with the manufacturer's instructions.

## LAUNCHING THE LIFE RAFT

*When you are ready to launch the raft, cut or untie its lashings but leave its painter tied to a strong point on the vessel as this is needed to inflate the raft.*

Be careful not to lose your footing

**①** Launch the raft by throwing its container over the leeward side. A sharp tug on the painter will inflate it.

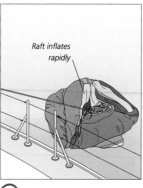

Raft inflates rapidly

**②** The raft will take about 30 seconds to inflate. If the raft inflates upside down you must right it before boarding.

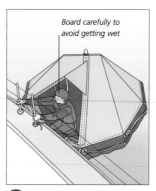

Board carefully to avoid getting wet

**③** As soon as the raft is inflated, the first crew member boards. Rig an additional mooring line in rough seas.

Help any crew in the water into the raft

**④** Once all the crew are aboard, release or cut both painters. Bail out water and shut canopy openings.

HELICOPTER RESCUE ▷

*Using the trail-line technique, the helicopter first lowers a nylon line across the yacht before moving to hover to one side. The line pulls in the winchman.*

## HELICOPTER RESCUE

When the boat is within flying range of the coast, helicopters are frequently used for search and rescue operations. The helicopter's crew decides how to rescue the yacht's crew, and if possible will communicate directly using marine VHF. Always follow their orders exactly and help them complete the rescue as quickly as possible; the time they are able to spend hovering at the scene will be limited. Where possible, position the boat head-to-wind (or nearly so), with all its sails lowered, and ensure that all crew are wearing life jackets. If you can, motor slowly into the wind or, if you are drifting, slow the rate of drift by streaming a drogue from the bow or lowering the anchor and chain.

The helicopter will not hover directly over the yacht because of the danger of becoming entangled in the rig. Depending on the circumstances, the rescue may take place in one of the following three ways: from a dinghy towed behind the yacht, from the water, or by using a trail-line technique. If it is to be a dinghy rescue, connect it to the yacht with a long warp of about 100ft (30m) and put only one person in it at a time. The helicopter will lower a lifting strap or send a winchman down to assist the survivors.

If no dinghy is available, or the conditions are too rough, you may have to be picked up from the water. Each crew member in turn is tied to a long warp and enters the water to drift astern of the yacht where he is then retrieved by the helicopter.

Alternatively, the helicopter may use a trail-line method. A long nylon line, carrying a weight on the lower end with its the upper end attached to the helicopter's recovery hook, is lowered across the yacht so that the crew can grab it. Once the yacht's crew have the line, the helicopter moves off to one side of the yacht. The line must not be made fast on board but should be pulled in as the helicopter lowers the winchman or lifting strap. The line is attached to the lifting hook by a weak link designed to break if the line snags. Pull in the line until the winchman or lifting strap is within reach, and flake it down so that it cannot snag and is free to run. Be careful not to touch the winch wire until its end has been earthed by the sea or winchman, because static electricity can give an unpleasant shock. Once the winchman is on board, follow his instructions. When the winchman and the first survivor are being lifted off the yacht, the nylon line is fed out. Keep hold of the end if further casualties are to be lifted and the procedure repeated.

## SHIP RESCUE

If a ship or life boat comes to your assistance you should follow her skipper's instructions as to how he intends to recover your crew. In rough seas it is extremely hazardous to come alongside another vessel, especially if your rescuer is a large ship. A life boat will normally come directly alongside, and your crew should be ready to board it quickly under instruction from the life boat crew.

A large ship may lower a boat if the size of the seas permit, but in very rough seas it will probably stop to windward of the yacht to create a smoother area in the ship's lee. This is hazardous as the ship will drift downwind rapidly, and the yacht and her crew will be vulnerable to a hard collision. The ship's crew will lower a ladder or scrambling net over the side, which the yacht's crew must climb. If you have to jump for a ladder or net, wait until the yacht is on the top of a wave to lessen the danger of being crushed between ship and yacht, and climb up as quickly as possible.

# FIRST AID

*The crew's welfare afloat is the responsibility of the skipper. He should be aware of any existing medical conditions among his crew, and if specific medicines or treatment are required. Each crew member must inform the skipper of any condition that may affect his performance and ability to contribute to the sailing of the yacht. The skipper should ensure that a suitable first-aid kit and good first-aid manual are aboard. At least one crew member should have some first-aid training.*

## BE PREPARED

Fortunately, sailing is a healthy and relatively safe sport and serious injuries are rare. Most commonly, sailing accidents result in simple cuts and bruises. However, you must be prepared to deal with more serious accidents if you are to be truly responsible for the welfare of your crew. First-aid kits are commercially available to suit all types of sailing.

When planning long voyages, consult your doctor, who can arrange for you to carry prescription drugs such as strong painkillers and antibiotics.

## BLEEDING

Small cuts and abrasions are the most common form of injuries afloat. Their treatment is aimed at stopping the bleeding and preventing infection. Raise the injured part and rinse the wound under fresh running water to remove dirt. Use sterile gauze swabs to clean the wound and dry the area gently. If the wound is a small cut or scrape, apply an adhesive bandage, taking care not to touch the sterile part. For larger wounds, use a sterile dressing held in place with a bandage.

## SPRAINS, DISLOCATIONS, AND FRACTURES

A sprain occurs when the ligaments of a joint are stretched or torn. It is very painful and may be mistaken for a broken bone.

A strain occurs when the tendons and muscles are torn. The damaged area will swell. Pain and tenderness are made worse by movement, or the victim may be unable to move the joint, which will develop a bruise. Strains and sprains should both be treated by resting the joint and applying a cold compress to reduce the pain and swelling. Apply gentle pressure with a pad and bandage and elevate the limb to reduce bruising.

A dislocation is usually caused by a twisting strain on a joint that causes displacement of the bones at the joint. The victim may feel a sickening pain and be unable to move the joint. The area will look deformed and will swell. Support the injured limb, prevent movement, and seek medical assistance. Use pillows or rolled towels or blankets to support the limb, and use a sling if an arm has been injured.

A suspected fracture should be treated by immobilizing the limb and obtaining medical assistance. The movement of a small boat can make immobilization difficult. Use a splint, either the inflatable type designed for the purpose, or one improvised from something suitable on the boat. Use padding to protect the limb and make sure that the splint is long enough to reach well above and below the

## CUTS

*Deep cuts and severe bleeding require prompt action to stem the blood loss. Pressure must be applied to the wound using a sterile dressing if possible.*

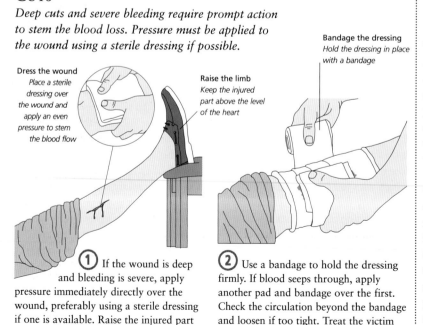

**Dress the wound**
*Place a sterile dressing over the wound and apply an even pressure to stem the blood flow*

**Raise the limb**
*Keep the injured part above the level of the heart*

**Bandage the dressing**
*Hold the dressing in place with a bandage*

(1) If the wound is deep and bleeding is severe, apply pressure immediately directly over the wound, preferably using a sterile dressing if one is available. Raise the injured part above the level of the heart.

(2) Use a bandage to hold the dressing firmly. If blood seeps through, apply another pad and bandage over the first. Check the circulation beyond the bandage and loosen if too tight. Treat the victim for shock (*p.308*) and seek medical help.

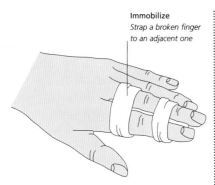

Immobilize
*Strap a broken finger
to an adjacent one*

△ **Fracture**
*A broken finger can be held immobile
by using an adhesive bandage to strap
it to an adjacent finger.*

fracture. If the broken bone has
pierced the skin, there is an increased
risk of infection: be sure to dress the
wound before attaching a splint.

## Burns
Burns are a hazard on a small boat,
especially in the galley and around the
engine. A burn victim will experience
pain, and if the burn is extensive,
shock and dehydration. Treat burns
with plenty of cold water immediately
and continue cooling the area for at

least ten minutes. Give the patient
frequent fluids to replace those lost
by dehydration and cover the burn
with a nonadhesive dressing, without
applying pressure. Anything more
severe than a mild, first-degree burn
should receive medical attention as
soon as possible.

## Head Injury
A blow to the head is always a
potential danger, and usually occurs
when a person is struck by the boom.
The victim may suffer a cut to the
scalp, which should be treated as a
wound. He may also suffer concussion
or a skull injury. While there may
be no obvious damage apart from
swelling, you should keep the person
under observation. Watch carefully
for signs of concussion. These include
drowsiness, nausea, vomiting, and
dilated or uneven pupils. You should
avoid letting the person sleep after
a heavy impact until you are quite
certain that he is not suffering from
concussion. If the person was knocked
unconscious or shows signs of
concussion, try to seek medical
assistance as soon as possible.

## FIRST-AID KIT
If you daysail in coastal waters
and are close to medical help
in the event of an emergency,
a simple first-aid kit will
suffice. For long passages away
from immediate help, keep
a more comprehensive kit to
allow you to treat victims of
accidents and injuries. Below
are the suggested contents for
a basic first-aid kit.

**Essential Supplies**
A basic first-aid kit should contain:
- Assorted sterile dressings
- Sterile gauze pads
- Assorted adhesive bandages
- Crepe and conforming bandages
- Triangular bandages
- Bandage clips, tape and safety pins
- Scissors and tweezers
- Sterile wipes for wound cleaning
- Plastic disposable gloves
- Face mask
- Painkillers
- Antiseptic cream
- Eye bath and lotion
- Thermometer
- Good first-aid manual

# SEASICKNESS

Few sailors can honestly claim never to have suffered
from seasickness. Always carry antiseasickness
treatments and ensure that sufferers use a preventative
treatment before sailing or the onset of rough weather.
Some drugs can cause drowsiness, so regular sailors
should experiment to find out which suits them best.

**Minimizing Sickness**
Seasickness, like all motion sickness, is
caused by disturbance to the balance
mechanism in the inner ear. You can
do several things to help prevent its
onset. Preventative treatments take
time to work and will not be effective
once seasickness has begun: take them
several hours before sailing. Have
plenty of rest before you sail and avoid
rich food and alcohol. If you start to feel
sick, sit where you can get a good supply
of fresh air and keep your eyes on the
horizon – this helps the sense of balance.
Take your mind off your feelings of
sickness through involvement in sailing
the boat. Avoid working at the chart
table or galley if possible, as the motion
down below often makes the feelings
worse. Avoid becoming cold or damp
and eat dry food to settle the stomach.
If you go below, lie down if possible
until you feel better. Most people suffer
only mild seasickness, which soon
passes. If a crew member is suffering
badly, they can become weak and
immobilized. In this case, the skipper
should return to harbor as speedily as
possible. Once in calm waters, the
problem will usually disappear quickly.

## SHOCK

Shock can follow any serious injury. Watch the victim closely for signs following an incident and treat accordingly.

### DEALING WITH SHOCK

Shock can be detected by a rapid pulse, a gray-blue skin, especially the lips, and sweating or a cold, clammy skin. These symptoms may develop to include weakness or giddiness, nausea or thirst, shallow and rapid breathing, and a weak but rapid pulse. If the victim's condition deteriorates further, he may become restless, gasp for air, and eventually even lapse into unconsciousness.

Keep the victim warm. Raise his legs and loosen any tight clothing at neck, chest, and waist. If possible, treat any injury and monitor the victim's pulse and breathing. Do not leave him alone or allow him any food or liquid. If he is thirsty, moisten his lips with water. Get medical help as soon as possible or seek advice by radio.

### SUNBURN

Prevention is better than cure, so always use sunblock and wear a hat and long-sleeved shirt. If you do get sunburned, cool the area with fresh water, cover the skin with light clothing, and move into the shade. Take frequent sips of fresh water to avoid dehydration. If the sunburn is mild, apply aloe vera or calamine lotion to soothe your skin.

### HEATSTROKE

This can occur after prolonged exposure to high heat and humidity or heavy exercise in hot weather. Signs include restlessness, headache, dizziness, flushed and hot skin, and a fast, strong pulse. Body temperature will be raised and could reach 104°F (40°C) or more. In severe cases, the patient may lose consciousness. You need to lower the victim's temperature quickly. Lay him down in a cool place and remove his clothes. Cover him with a wet sheet, and keep wetting it at intervals. Fan the patient until his temperature falls below 100°F

(37.5°C). At this point, replace the sheet with a dry one and seek professional medical assistance.

### HEAT EXHAUSTION

This is caused by extreme loss of salt and water through prolonged sweating. The symptoms include headaches or cramps, pale and moist skin, a fast, weak pulse, and a slightly elevated temperature. If these symptoms occur, cool the patient and replace lost fluid and salt. Lay the victim down, elevate his legs and give him plenty of water to drink, preferably lightly salted.

### HYPOTHERMIA

Hypothermia occurs when the body's temperature drops below 95°F (35°C), and is common after immersion in water below 68°F (20°C). The first signs are intense shivering that becomes uncontrollable, and difficulty in speaking. As the body temperature drops to about 90–86°F/32–30°C, shivering decreases and the patient becomes clumsy, irritable, and slurs

## RECOVERY POSITION

If a victim is unconscious but still breathing, he should be put in the recovery position so that he is supported in a stable position and cannot choke on his tongue or vomit. You may be able to do this on a bunk or on the cabin sole, or in the cockpit if the victim's injuries make it unwise to move him below.

### MOVING PATIENT INTO POSITION

With the victim on his back, open the airway and straighten his legs. Place his arm closest to you alongside his body. Bring his other arm across his body and hold the back of his hand against his cheek. With your other hand, pull up his far leg, holding it just above the knee. Roll him toward you until he is lying on his side by pulling on his leg, while keeping his hand pressed against his cheek. Check that the airway is still open. Bend his upper leg at the knee so that it is at right angles to his body. Monitor the casualty's breathing and pulse every few minutes until you can obtain medical assistance.

*Head faces arm at right angles to his body*

△ **RECOVERY POSITION**
*The victim is placed on his side in a stable position with his airway open.*

his speech. Further heat loss leads to inability to reason, loss of muscle control, and slowed pulse and respiration. By the time temperature has dropped to about 80°F (27°C), the victim loses consciousness and his heartbeat becomes erratic. Any further drop in temperature results in death.

The first step in the treatment of hypothermia is to prevent further heat loss and start to warm the victim. Remove wet clothes and replace with dry ones, if possible. Wrap the sufferer in a space blanket, exposure bag, or sleeping bag, and keep his head warm as well. Feed the victim warm drinks and high-energy food. Obtain medical assistance as soon as possible.

## DROWNING

If you recover someone who is unconscious from the water you must first check for a pulse and signs of breathing. If the person is not breathing, begin resuscitation; if no pulse is felt, start CPR (*see right*). A yacht's sidedeck is often too narrow to work on the victim, so move him into the cockpit as quickly as possible and lie him flat on a cockpit seat or on the cockpit sole.

If you succeed with resuscitation, put the victim in the recovery position (*see left, below*) to let any swallowed water drain from his mouth. If he has been in the water long, or if it is cold, he is likely also to be suffering from hypothermia, so you must try to warm him up. Check for other injuries. If he can be moved, get him below, out of the wind, and strip his wet clothes before covering him with several warm layers.

Once the casualty regains consciousness, he may be suffering from shock. Look for the signs and treat accordingly (*see left, above*). Use the radio to call assistance and get the patient medical help.

## RESUSCITATION

*If the casualty has stopped breathing, you must immediately attempt resuscitation. If no pulse is felt you must also start cardiopulmonary resuscitation (CPR). Time is of the essence and the victim's recovery depends on quick and effective action.*

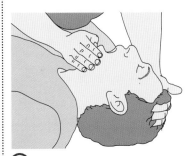

**①** Place the victim on his back. Ensure the airway is open by placing one hand under his chin, one hand on his forehead, and tilting his head back gently. Check for any obvious obstructions in his mouth and remove using one finger.

**②** Pinch his nostrils. Take a deep breath, place your lips over his and form a good seal. Blow into his mouth for about two seconds and watch to see that his chest rises. Remove your mouth and allow his chest to fall. Repeat, and check his pulse.

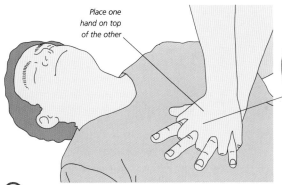

Place one hand on top of the other

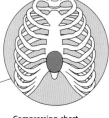

**Compressing chest**
*Find the spot where the bottom rib meets the breastbone*

**③** If no pulse is felt after the second breath, you should start the process of CPR. To do this, you should first kneel at the casualty's side. Place your middle finger on the point where the lowest rib meets the breastbone and put your index finger above it. Then place the heel of your other hand above this point. This is the area of the chest to which pressure should be applied. Interlock your fingers with one hand on top of the other, ready to compress the chest.

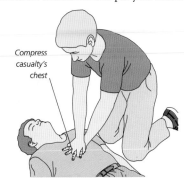

Compress casualty's chest

**④** Kneel with your shoulders above the victim's chest and, with arms straight, compress about 1½–2in (4.5cm). Release the pressure but keep your hands in place. Repeat 15 times at a rate of about 15 compressions in ten seconds. Then give two breaths of mouth-to-mouth resuscitation and check breathing and pulse. Continue this cycle until you detect a pulse and he starts to breathe for himself. Put him in the recovery position. Get medical aid as soon as possible.

# GLOSSARY

## A

**ABAFT** Behind, at, or toward the stern of a boat.

**ABEAM** At right angles to the fore-and-aft line of the boat.

**AFT** Toward, at, or near the stern.

**ANCHOR** A heavy device attached to a boat by a cable (the warp) and dropped overboard to secure a boat to the riverbed or seabed, with the help of its flukes. To drop anchor is to release the anchor into the water; to weigh anchor is to raise it.

**ANCHORAGE** A sheltered area away from strong winds and tides, or where it is safe to drop anchor into good holding ground (or a combination of both). It can also mean the ground into which the anchor is dropped.

**ANCHOR WINDLASS** The crank- or motor-driven mechanism used on some cruisers to raise the anchor by winding the rope or chain around a drum or barrel.

**ANCHOR CABLE** The chain used to attach an anchor to the boat. See *Warp*.

**ANEMOMETER** An instrument that measures apparent wind speed.

**ANODES** Sacrificial zinc fittings that are fastened near skin fittings, the rudder, and the propeller shaft, to protect them from corrosion through electrolysis. The anodes corrode first.

**ANTICYCLONE** High-pressure area of weather.

**ANTIFOULING PAINT** Special paint applied to the hull to prevent underwater fouling from weed and barnacles, which would slow the boat.

**APPARENT WIND** The combination of true wind (that which we feel when stationary) plus the wind produced by motion.

**ASTERN** Backward, outside, and abaft the stern.

**ATHWARTSHIPS** From side to side, toward the beams, acrossways.

## B

**BACKING THE JIB** To sheet the jib to windward; used when sailing away from a head-to-wind position and sometimes when tacking.

**BACKSTAY** The wire leading from the masthead to the stern on a cruiser. Prevents the mast from falling forward and is used to tension the forestay.

**BACKWIND** When a mainsail is let out beyond its best trim, it backwinds or flaps in its front half and spills wind. Used to reduce heeling in strong winds.

**BALANCE** A boat is balanced when it is upright both fore-and-aft and athwartships. See *Balanced helm* and *Trim*.

**BALANCED HELM** When a boat has a balanced helm it will have little tendency to turn. If you let go of the tiller, it will continue on a straight course. See *Weather helm* and *Lee helm*.

**BAROGRAPH** A recording barometer, which makes a continuous reading of air pressure on a paper graph.

**BATTEN** A light wooden, fiberglass, or plastic strip that slots into a pocket sewn into the aft edge (leech) of a sail to support the roach.

**BEAM REACH** Sailing with the wind blowing directly over the side of the boat; potentially the fastest point of sailing.

**BEARING** The direction of an object from your boat, or between two objects. Both are measured in degrees relative to north. See *Heading*.

**BEARING AWAY** Turning the boat away from the wind; the opposite of luffing.

**BEATING** To sail to windward, close-hauled, and zigzagging, to reach an objective to windward.

**BEAUFORT SCALE** A descriptive scale used for measuring wind strengths.

**BENDING ON** The traditional term used to describe fitting the mainsail onto the boom.

**BERMUDAN MAINSAIL** A mainsail with three sides.

**BERMUDAN SLOOP** A rig with a triangular mainsail and a single headsail.

**BILGE** The rounded parts of the hull where the sides curve inward to form the bottom.

**BILGE KEEL** A twin keel, used on boats designed to be able to dry out sitting upright. Sometimes used in conjunction with a shallow central keel.

**BILGE PUMP** Pump to remove water that accumulates in the bilge.

**BLOCK** A pulley through which a rope is passed.

**BOLTROPE** A reinforcing rope along the edge of a sail.

**BOOM** A horizontal spar or pole, used to extend the foot of a sail and to help control the sail's position in relation to the wind.

**BOOM VANG (OR KICKING STRAP)** A line that prevents the boom from rising when the mainsail is set.

**BOTTLESCREW** A fitting to adjust the tension in the shrouds and forestay.

**BOW** The forward end of a boat. Opposite of stern.

**BOW-FITTING** Fitting to which the forestay, and jib are attached.

**BOWER ANCHOR** The main anchor on a boat.

**BOWLINE** (pronounced "bo-lynn") Knot used to make a loop in the end of a rope or to tie to a ring or post.

**BOW LINE** Also known as the head rope, the bow line is a mooring warp that runs from the bow to a point on shore ahead of the boat. Opposite of stern line.

**BOWSPRIT** A spar projecting from the bow of some boats, allowing headsails to be secured further forward, thus extending the sail plan.

**BREAST ROPE OR LINE** A mooring rope for cruisers, sometimes used in addition to the four main warps to hold the boat alongside.

**BRIDGE DECK** A raised area that separates the cockpit from the cabin.

**BROACH** A broach may occur when a boat is sailing in moderate to strong winds, and the sails are not properly balanced; the boat will inadvertently turn broadside to the waves.

**BROAD REACH** Sailing with the wind coming over the port or starboard quarter of the boat.

**BUOYAGE** A system of navigation marks used to identify hazards and safe channels.

**BUOYANCY TANKS** Sealed compartments within the hull of sailing dinghies that provide added buoyancy so that the boat will float if capsized or swamped.

**BURGEE** A small triangular flag flown from the top of a mast, serving as an indicator of apparent wind.

## C

**CABIN** The living quarters below deck.

**CABIN SOLE** The floor of the cabin.

**CAP SHROUDS** See *Shrouds*.

**CAPSIZE** When a boat tips over to 90° or 180°.

**CARDINAL MARKS** Forms of buoyage, used to indicate large or individual hazards in the water.

**CATAMARAN** A twin-hulled boat consisting of two narrow hulls connected by two beams and a trampoline or rigid deck.

**CENTER OF EFFORT** All the forces acting on a sail's surface can be thought of as one force acting on a single point, which is known as the center of effort. See *Driving force* and *Sideways force*.

**CENTERBOARD** A plate that pivots inside a centerboard case, and is lowered below the hull of a sailing boat to resist leeway. See *Daggerboard*.

**CENTERLINE** The center of a boat, on the fore-and-aft line.

**CHAINPLATES** Metal fittings on each side of the boat, and at the bow and stern, to which the shrouds, forestay and backstay are attached.

**CHART DATUM** Datum of charts, from which soundings and drying heights are measured.

**CLASS** A group of boats of the same design.

**CLEARING LINES** Used in navigation to keep the boat clear of potential hazards by defining the boundaries of a safe zone. See *Safe track*.

**CLEAT** A wooden or metal fastening with two small horns pointing in opposite directions, around which ropes are made fast.

**CLEW** The lower aft corner of a fore-and-aft sail.

**CLOSE REACH** Turning away from a close-hauled course by about 20° brings the boat onto a close reach.

**CLOSE-HAULED** Sailing as close to the wind as possible, with the sails pulled in tight.

**CLOVE HITCH** A knot used for short-term mooring to a ring or post, or for hitching fenders to a rail.

**COACHROOF** The raised cabin trunk in the middle of the boat.

**COCKPIT** The working area, usually towards the stern of a boat, from which the boat is steered.

**Col Regs** "Rules of the road", or International Regulations for Preventing Collisions at Sea.

**Communication systems** Radio and/or satellite systems on board most yachts for communication with shore stations and other boats.

**Companionway** A ladder or steps leading down from the cockpit to the cabin (below deck).

**Compass deviation** Compass alignment may differ from magnetic north, due to onboard magnetic fields. Compass deviation varies with the course, and is measured in degrees, east or west of magnetic north.

**Compass north** The direction in which a compass points. If there is no local magnetic interference, it will point to magnetic north.

**Crew** Can mean either all the people on board, or everyone else except the helmsman. On a dinghy, the crew is often only one person, with separate tasks from those of the helmsman. To crew means both to work as a member of the crew (including the helmsman) or to work alongside a helmsman with your own distinct tasks.

**Cringles** An eye in a sail. See *Reef points*.

**Cruising chute** See *Gennaker*.

**Crutches** See *Rowlocks*.

**Cunningham control** A rope for adjusting tension in the luff of a mainsail or jib.

**Cutter** A single-masted yacht with two headsails, a staysail (inner headsail), and a jib (outer headsail).

## D

**Daggerboard** A plate that is lowered vertically through a daggerboard case and is used to resist leeway. See *Centerboard*.

**Danbuoy** A weighted, floating marker pole that attaches to a lifebuoy to improve visibility.

**Davit** A cranelike device fitted with a tackle for suspending or lowering equipment.

**Dead run** See *Running*.

**Depression** Low-pressure area of weather.

**Dew point** The temperature at which water vapor held in the air condenses into droplets and forms clouds, mist, or fog.

**DGPS** Differential GPS units (an enhanced global positioning system) receive information from a network of satellites and a ground station. See *GPS*.

**Dinghy** A small boat, powered by sail, oars, or an outboard motor; usually designed to accommodate one or two people.

**Direction** Measured clockwise as an angle relative to north. See *Heading* and *Bearing*.

**Dismasting** When the mast breaks, usually because a piece of rigging or a terminal fitting has given away. See *Jury rig*.

**Distance** Measured in nautical miles.

**Dodgers** Weather cloths that can be laced along the lifelines for added protection in the cockpit.

**Downhaul** A rope for hauling down sails or for controlling a spar such as the spinnaker pole; opposite to uphaul.

**Downwind (or offwind)** All courses that are

further away from the wind than a beam reach are known as downwind, or offwind, courses; opposite of upwind.

**DR** Dead reckoning position. It is plotted on a chart by drawing the course steered from the last known position and measuring off the distance sailed according to the log. See also *EP*.

**Drift** The strength of a tidal stream; as opposed to tidal set.

**Driving force (or drive)** The force produced by the sails to drive the boat forwards. Maximum driving force depends on sails being trimmed correctly.

**Drogue** An object towed, usually over a boat's stern, in order to reduce speed.

## E, F

**EP** Estimated position. EPs are plotted at regular intervals on a chart and compared with a fix to help with any errors in plotting.

**EPIRB** Emergency-position-indication radio beacon. A radio aid that transmits a distress signal to satellites that are part of the GMDSS.

**Fairlead** Any bolt, ring, loop, eye, or pulley that guides a rope in the direction required.

**Fiddles** Used below deck, fiddles edge all horizontal surfaces such as tables, to stop objects falling off them when the boat heels.

**Figure eight** A stopper knot, used to prevent a rope end from running out through a block or fairlead.

**Fin keel** A single, central, ballasted keel.

**Flukes** The barbs of an anchor.

**Fluxgate compass** A compass that uses an electronic circuit to sense the lines of magnetic force.

**Foils** The underwater parts of a boat, such as the centerboard (or daggerboard) and rudder.

**Foot** The bottom edge of a sail.

**Fore** At, near, or towards the bow.

**Fore and aft** In line from bow to stern; also on, or parallel to, the centerline.

**Foredeck** The deck nearest the bow.

**Foreguy** On large boats, the downhaul for the spinnaker pole is known as the foreguy.

**Forestay** A stay to stop the mast falling backward. It leads from the masthead to the bow-fitting. A headsail may be attached to the forestay.

**Freeboard** A boat's freeboard is the height of the topsides out of the water.

**Freer** A wind shift; when the wind moves aft you are freed. Opposite of a header.

## G

**Galley** A boat's kitchen.

**Gennaker** A sail that is a cross between a genoa and a spinnaker. Sometimes called a cruising chute.

**Genoa** A large headsail that overlaps the mast and usually sweeps the deck with its foot. See *Jib*.

**Gimbals** The fittings that allow an object (such as a galley stove) to swing so as to remain upright when the boat heels.

**GMDSS** Global Maritime Distress and Safety System; a standard to which modern VHF radio sets, satellite communication systems, and EPIRBs conform. It allows an automated distress signal to be sent that identifies the vessel in distress and transmits its position if connected to a GPS set.

**Gooseneck** The universal joint fitting fixed to a mast, which attaches the boom to the mast.

**Grapnel** A light anchor for small boats; also a device with a multiple hook at one end and attached to a rope, which is thrown or hooked over a firm mooring.

**GPS** Global Positioning System. GPS receivers on board calculate position using information from a network of satellites. See *DGPS*.

**Ground track** The course followed, relative to the seabed. See *Water track*.

**GRP** Glass-reinforced plastic, from which many boat hulls are made.

**Gunwale** (pronounced "gunnel") The top edge of the side of the hull.

**Guy** A rope that controls the spinnaker on the side toward the wind. It runs through the end of the spinnaker pole.

## H

**Halyard** A rope or wire that is used to hoist a sail (or to hoist a flag or other signal).

**Hand bearing compass** A portable compass that allows bearings to be taken all around the boat.

**Hanks** The clip rings by which a sail is attached to a forestay.

**Head** The top corner of a triangular sail, or the top edge of a four-sided sail.

**Header** A wind shift; when the wind moves forward you are "headed". Opposite of a freer.

**Heading** The direction in which you are steering the boat. See *Bearing*.

**Heads** Often used to mean only the sea toilet, but can also mean the compartment containing the toilet, washbasin, and shower.

**Headboard** The reinforced top corner of a mainsail, to which the halyard is attached.

**Headsail** A sail set in front of the mast.

**Heaving-to** Bringing a boat to a halt by sheeting the headsail to windward. After the event, a boat is described as "hove-to".

**Heel** When a boat tilts to one side at an angle as it sails, it heels. The heel of the mast is its bottom end.

**Heeling force** A force created by the vertical separation between the sideways force and the resistance from the keel, causing the boat to tilt to one side. See *Heel*.

**Helmsman** The person who steers the boat.

**Hounds** The position at which the shrouds and forestay attach to the mast.

# I–K

**IALA** International Association of Lighthouse Authorities, which organizes buoyage.

**IMPELLER PUMP** A pump that uses a small propeller-like rotator (the impeller) to pump water. Often used in an engine water pump.

**INBOARD ENGINE** A motor or engine situated in the hull, as opposed to an outboard engine.

**ISOBARS** Lines shown on weather maps to indicate pressure. They join areas of equal pressure in a similar way to contour lines on a chart.

**JACKSTAYS** Lengths of webbing or wire that run along the length of both sidedecks, to which the crew attach their harness lifelines when working on deck.

**JIB** A triangular headsail (a sail in front of the mainsail).

**JIBING** Turning the stern of the boat through the wind. See *Tacking*.

**JIB SHEETS** Ropes used to trim (or "sheet") the jib.

**JURY RIG** A makeshift rig that you construct to get you to safety following a dismasting.

**KEDGE ANCHOR** A lighter anchor than the main, or bower, anchor.

**KEEL** The lowest part of a sailing boat, fixed to the hull for stability and to resist sideways drift (leeway).

**KETCH** A two-masted yacht with the aft mast (mizzen mast) smaller than the main mast and stepped ahead of the rudder post.

**KICKING STRAP** See *Boom vang*.

**KNOT** The unit of speed at sea, defined as one nautical mile per hour.

# L

**LATITUDE** The grid lines on a map or chart running east to west, and parallel to the equator.

**LAZYJACKS** Restraining lines rigged from the mast to the boom to retain the mainsail when it is lowered and stowed on the boom.

**LAZY GUY** A leeward guy left slack when using a spinnaker.

**LEAD LINE** A line with a weight attached used to measure the depth of water.

**LEECH** The aft edge of a sail.

**LEEBOARDS** Wooden boards fitted along the inboard edge of a sea berth, to prevent the occupant from falling out of the berth in rough conditions. See *Leecloths*.

**LEECLOTHS** Canvas cloths stretched along the inboard edge of a sea berth, to prevent the occupant from being thrown out in rough weather. See *Leeboards*.

**LEE HELM** If the boat turns to leeward when you let go of the tiller, it has lee helm. See *Weather helm* and *Balanced helm*.

**LEE SHORE** When the wind blows onto the land, the shore is called a lee shore. See *Onshore wind*.

**LEEWARD** (pronounced loo'ard) The direction in which the wind blows (downwind); opposite of windward.

**LEEWAY** The difference between the course steered and the course actually sailed (because of sideways force).

**LIFELINES** Safety rails or wires fitted around the deck edge, supported by stanchions.

**LOGBOOK** A record of position, course, distance run, and other crucial information, kept when cruising.

**LONGITUDE** The grid lines on a map or chart running north to south, between the North and South Poles.

**LONG KEEL** The traditional type of keel, running for half to three-quarters the length of the vessel.

**LUFF** The forward edge of a sail. To luff (or to luff up) is to bring the boat's head closer to the wind. Opposite of bearing away.

# M

**MAGNETIC NORTH** The direction of the magnetic North Pole.

**MAGNETIC VARIATION** The angular difference between magnetic north and true north, which alters year by year as the magnetic Poles move.

**MAINSAIL** (pronounced mains'l) The principal fore-and-aft sail on a boat.

**MAINSHEET** The rope attached to the boom and used to trim (or adjust) the mainsail.

**MAINSHEET TACKLE** A system of blocks through which the mainsheet is run, to make it easier for the helmsman to hold and adjust the sheet.

**MAST** A vertical pole to which sails are attached.

**MAST GATE** The point where the mast passes through the foredeck of a dinghy.

**MAST SPANNER** A device on catamarans, used to control the angle of a rotating mast.

**MAST STEP** A recessed wooden block or metal frame, which receives the heel of the mast.

**MASTHEAD** The top of a mast.

**MAYDAY** The internationally recognized radio distress signal (repeated three times in succession) for use when you are in grave and imminent danger. It takes priority over any other kind of message. See *PAN PAN*.

**MOORING** A permanently laid arrangement of anchors and cables, to which a boat can be secured.

# N, O

**NAUTICAL ALMANAC** A yearly calendar giving statistical information, such as tidal data, for a wide area.

**NAUTICAL MILE** The unit of distance at sea, defined as one minute (1') of latitude. It is standardized to 6076ft (1852m), slightly longer than a land mile.

**NEAP TIDES** These tides have the smallest range between high and low water. Opposite of spring tides.

**NO-SAIL ZONE** Since boats cannot sail directly into the wind, there is a no-sail zone on either side of the direction of true wind. The closest that most boats can achieve is an angle of 45° on either side.

**OARLOCKS** U-shaped fittings used to support the oars and act as a pivot when rowing. Fitted into sockets in each gunwale.

**OFFSHORE WIND** A wind that blows off the land.

**OFFWIND** See *Downwind*.

**ONSHORE WIND** A wind that blows onto the land.

**OUTBOARD ENGINE** An engine mounted externally.

**OUTHAUL** A rope used to haul out something, such as the mainsail outhaul, which hauls out the clew of the mainsail.

# P, Q

**PAINTER** A rope attached to the bow of a dinghy or small boat that is used to moor the vessel.

**PAN PAN** An internationally recognized distress signal that takes priority over all except a MAYDAY message.

**PIGGING LINE** A small block with a light line attached to it, used instead of reaching hooks when flying a spinnaker.

**PILE MOORINGS** Moorings made of large wooden or metal stakes (piles) driven into the seabed, with fittings to which mooring warps are tied.

**PILOTAGE** Navigation by eye, compass, and chart, when in sight of land.

**PINCHING** Sailing too close to the wind inside the no-sail zone.

**PLANING** The motion of a dinghy when it skims across the water like a speedboat.

**PLOTTER** A device for plotting a course, used in conjunction with the grid of latitude and longitude lines marked on a chart.

**POINTS OF SAILING** The direction in which a boat is being sailed, described in relation to its angle to the wind. Collectively, these angles are known as the points of sailing. See *Beam reach*, *Broad reach*, *Close-hauled*, *Close reach*, *Head-to-wind*, *No-sail zone*, *Running*, and *Training run*.

**PORT** The left-hand side of a boat, when looking forward.

**PORT TACK** The course of a boat when the wind is blowing over a boat's port side.

**POSITION LINE** A navigational aid to help plot a fix on a chart. Usually a minimum of two position lines are needed.

**PRE-BEND** The amount of bend set in a mast before sailing.

**PROP WALK** The paddlewheel effect of a turning propeller. Prop walk pushes the stern of the boat sideways in the same direction in which the propeller rotates.

**PSYCHROMETER** A piece of equipment for forecasting weather, particularly fog.

**PULPIT** An elevated and rigid metal rail around the bow of a boat.

**PUSHPIT** An elevated and rigid metal rail around the stern of a boat.

# R

**RAKE** The amount that a mast leans aft from upright.

**RAM'S HORNS** Inverted hooks onto which a sail's luff cringles are sometimes fixed.

**RATCHET BLOCK** A type of pulley, containing a ratchet, sometimes used for an aft-mainsheet system, to reduce the load the helmsman has to hold. See *Mainsheet tackle.*

**REACHING** Sailing with the wind approximately abeam; see *Beam reach* and *Broad reach.*

**REACHING HOOK** On a dinghy, a hook fitted just aft of the shrouds, on each side of the turning blocks (for spinnaker sheets).

**REEF** To reduce a boat's sail area when the wind becomes too strong to sail comfortably under full sail.

**REEF KNOT** A knot that is used for tying the ends of rope of equal diameter, usually a sail's reef lines when putting in a reef.

**REEF POINTS** Light lines sewn to the sail to tie up the loose fold in a sail when it is reefed.

**RIG** The arrangement of the sails, spars, and masts on a boat. To rig the boat is to step the mast and bend on the sails. See *Rigging.*

**RIGGING** The system of wires and ropes used to keep the mast in place and work the sails.

**RIGGING LINK** A piece of equipment used to attach the shrouds and stays to the chainplates.

**ROACH** The curved area on the leech of a sail, outside a straight line from head to clew.

**RUDDER** A movable underwater blade that helps to steer the boat, controlled by a tiller or wheel.

**RUNNING** Sailing directly downwind (i.e, with the wind right behind you, or nearly so) on either a port or starboard tack. A dead, or true, run is slightly different from a training run.

**RUNNING FIX (OR TRANSFERRED POSITION LINE)** A useful fix, using two position lines taken at different times on the same mark (e.g, when sailing along a coastline and there is only one identifiable sea- or landmark in sight).

## S

**SAFE TRACK** The course you follow through constricted water. See *Clearing lines.*

**SCULLING** A way of propelling a dinghy by manipulating a single oar over the stern in a figure-eight pattern.

**SEACOCK** A valve that can be shut to close a through-hull fitting.

**SÉCURITÉ** A safety signal, indicating that a transmitting station is about to send a safety, navigational, or weather warning.

**SETTING SAILS** The process of bending-on and hoisting sails ready for sea. Trimming a sail correctly. See *Trim.*

**SHACKLE** A U-shaped link with a screw pin, used to connect ropes and fittings. A shackle key unscrews shackle pins.

**SHEET** The rope attached to the clew of a sail, or to a boom, which can be tightened or eased to trim (adjust) the sail.

**SHEET BEND** A knot used to join two ropes.

**SHEAVES** The pulley wheels in blocks.

**SHROUDS** The wire ropes on either side of the mast, which support it.

**SIDEWAYS FORCE** Part of the force generated by the sails pushes a boat sideways. The effect is resisted by the centerboard or keel.

**SKEG** A projecting part of the hull that supports the rudder.

**SLIP LINE** A doubled line with both ends made fast on board so that it can be released from on board.

**SLIPWAY** A launching ramp.

**SLOOP** A single-masted boat with only one headsail set at any one time.

**SPARS** Any piece of nautical gear that resembles a pole.

**SPINNAKER** A large, light, downwind sail set from a spinnaker pole.

**SPINNAKER POLE** A pole used to extend the spinnaker clew away from the boat and allow the sail to set properly.

**SPRINGS** Mooring warps to help prevent the boat from moving ahead or astern when moored.

**SPRING TIDES** Tides that have the largest range between high and low tides.

**STANCHION** An upright post used to support the lifelines.

**STARBOARD** The right-hand side of a boat, when looking forward.

**STARBOARD TACK** The course of a boat when the wind is blowing over a boat's starboard side.

**STAY** A wire running fore or aft (forestay or backstay) to support the mast.

**STEM** The main upright timber or structure at the bow.

**STEP** A wooden block or metal frame, forming a recess in the deck or keel, which receives the heel of the mast.

**STERN** The rear or after part of a vessel. Opposite of bow.

**STERN LINE** A mooring warp that is run from the stern of the boat to a point on shore astern of the boat. See *Bow line.*

**STERN QUARTERS** The aft corners of a boat.

## T

**TACK** The forward lower corner of a fore-and-aft sail. Also, under sail, a boat is either on a starboard tack or port tack. See *Tacking.*

**TACKING** Turning the bow of the boat through the wind. See *Jibing.*

**TAIL** To pull on the free end (the tail) of a sheet or halyard when winching.

**TELL-TALES** Light strips of fabric, sewn or glued onto sails to indicate the best trim for the sail.

**TENDER** A small boat used to ferry people and provisions to and from a bigger boat.

**THWART** A seat fixed across a dinghy or a tender.

**TIDAL DRIFT** The strength of a tidal stream at any time.

**TIDAL SET** The direction of a tidal stream at any time.

**TIDAL STREAM** A horizontal flow of water caused by the rise and fall of the tide.

**TIDE TABLES** A record of the times and heights of high and low water for every day of the year.

**TILLER** Rod by which the rudder is controlled, for steering.

**TILLER BAR** A rod that connects the two tillers on a catamaran.

**TOE RAILS** Straps of webbing under which a dinghy crew hooks their feet when sitting out, to help keep them in the boat.

**TOPPING LIFT** A rope running from the masthead to the boom end used to support the boom when the mainsail is not hoisted.

**TOPSIDES** The sides of the hull between the water line and the deck edge.

**TRAINING RUN** Sailing downwind, but 5–10° off a true run.

**TRANSOM** A surface forming the stern of a boat.

**TRANSOM FLAPS** Flaps in the transom through which unwanted water can escape.

**TRAPEZE** A wire used in high-performance dinghies, to enable the crew to place their weight further outside the boat than they would if just sitting out.

**TRAVELER** A slide that travels along a track, used for altering sheet angles.

**TRIM** Sail trimming is the constant adjusting of the sails to create (or maintain) the force to drive a boat forward, and to keep it at the correct angle.

**TRUE NORTH** The direction of the True North Pole. See also *Magnetic north* and *Compass north.*

**TRUE WIND** The wind that we feel when we are stationary.

**TWIST** In a sail, the twist is the difference between the angle of the sail it its foot and its head.

# U–Z

**UPHAUL** A rope for adjusting the height of the spinnaker pole; opposite to downhaul.

**UPWIND** All courses that are closer to the wind (heading more directly into it) than a beam reach are called upwind courses; opposite of offwind or downwind.

**WARP** Any rope used to secure or move a boat.

**WATER TRACK** The course you want to steer through the water to achieve a ground track after allowing for the effects of any tidal stream.

**WEATHER HELM** If the boat, under sail, turns to windward when you let go of the tiller, it has weather helm. See *Lee helm* and *Balanced helm.*

**WEATHER SHORE** When the wind blows off the land, the shore is called a weather shore. See *Offshore wind.*

**WINCH** Devices for pulling in sheets and halyards.

**WINDWARD** Toward the wind; opposite of leeward.

**WING-AND-WINGING** Sailing directly downwind (running) with the mainsail set on one side and the foresail set on the other.

# INDEX

# ACKNOWLEDGMENTS

**THE AUTHOR** would like to thank Gary Pearson, Mark Elson, Will Upchurch, and Ben Willows of UKSA (United Kingdom Sailing Academy), Cowes, Isle of Wight, for assistance with dinghy sailing reference photography. Thanks are also due to Rival Bowman Yachts Ltd for the use of a Starlight 35, and to Julian Fawcett from Rival Bowman for his sailing assistance. Grateful thanks to all those who gave valuable assistance to the project, including Douglas Peterson for use of his RIB and for making the Alamo an ideal retreat for editorial lunches; Jeff Morgan for driving the RIB; Chris Woodbridge for casting a professional sailing and instructional eye over the content material; and Tanya, Wibbs, and Jo for their understanding.

Warmest thanks go to all at Studio Cactus who triumphed despite the odds, and in particular to Sharon Moore who was the rock on which the project's foundations were secured.

**DORLING KINDERSLEY** would like to thank the following:
**Editorial:** Adele Hayward for start-up project management
**Design:** Tracy Hambleton-Miles and Tassy King for start-up project management
**Administration:** Christopher Gordon

**STUDIO CACTUS** would like to thank Nicola Hodgson, Jane Baldock, Victoria Harwood, Simon Adams, and Jane Laing for additional editorial assistance; Alison Shackleton for design assistance; Laura Harper for proofreading; Hilary Bird for compiling the index; and Amanda Hess for general assistance.

Thanks to Martin Pass at Audi UK, Milton Keynes, for organizing and providing the cars for the photoshoot, and to Performance Sail Craft Ltd for providing the Laser and the location. Clothing throughout the cruiser section provided by MUSTO Ltd. MUSTO is a registered trademark of MUSTO Ltd.

We would also like to thank the following people for the use of their photographs and reference material:
**Audi:** 42-43
**Kelvin Hughes Ltd, Southampton**
**Damien Moore:** 24, 26, 27bl, 164br, 238r, 277, 283
**Musto Limited:** 54b, 55bl, 55r, 55tl, 164bc
**Raytheon Marine Company:** 237cl, 240br
**Simpson Lawrence:** 237tl, 244bl
**Starlight 35**
**Steve Sleight:** 165cl, 195tr, 226tr, 289bc
**United Kingdom Hydrographic Office**
**Westerly:** 151cr

**PICTURE CREDITS** Dorling Kindersley would like to thank the following for their kind permission to reproduce their photographs: (Abbreviations key: t=top, b=bottom, r=right, l=left, c=center)
**Photography by Steve Gorton except:**
**Geoffrey Hilton Barber:** 17tr
**Jim Baerselman:** 148bl, 186bl
**Beken of Cowes Ltd:** 12tl, 13br, 45br, 111br, 151bl, 151br, 190br, 200bl Bridgeman Art Library, London/New York: Alan Jacobs Gallery, London 10tl
**Christel Clear Marine Photography:** 16bl, 46bl, 53crb, 70bl, 90b, 112bc, 133tc, 140tl, 144bl, 151tr, 165br, 185tl
**Julie Dunbar:** 53crt
**Dundee Satellite Receiving Station, University of Dundee:** 265b
**Geoscience Features:** 269bc
**Kos Pictures:** 6, 53clb, 146-47, 179tr, 229tl; David Williams 216bl;

F Salle 131br
**Frank Lane Picture Agency:** 268bc; B & D Hosking 275tr; Brian Cosgrove 266bc; Chris Demetrion 269br; Francois Merlet 266br; H Binz 260-61; H Hoflinger 273tr; Larry West 268bl; Martin Smith 226bl; Maurice Nimmo 269bl; R Thompson 266bl; S McCutcheon 267bc, 267bl, 268br
**Ocean Images:** 120bl
**Pickthall Picture Library:** PPL Ltd 11; Alastair Black 112crb, 123tl, 305tr; Barry Pickthall 56b, 86br, 105t, 299tr; Bob Fisher 133tr; Gary John Norman 162bl, 285br, 287tr; Gilles Martin-Raget 134bl; Ingrid Abery 119tl, 142bl, 143tl; Jamie Lawson-Johnston 151tl; Jon Nash 152tr, 296-297; Jono Knight 2, 106-07, 129br, 130, 145br; Mark Pepper 280-281; Onne van der Wal 286bl; Peter Bentley 111tr, 113tl, 124br, 133tl, 282bc; Peter Danby 89bl, 117br; Skip Novak 15tr
**Patrick Roach:** 20bl, 49br, 65cb
**William Payne Photography:** 160br, 160bl, 161tl, 289br, 292br
**Rick Tomlinson:** 8-9, 14bl, 18-19, 62tr, 106-107, 182b, 187tr
**Turtle Photography:** 4tr, 50, 53cra, 53tl, 53cla, 53bl, 53br, 53tr, 64bl, 65b, 69br, 71ca, 71tl, 109tr, 109tl, 109clb, 109cla, 109br, 109bl, 109crb, 109cra, 145tl, 228b
**US National Weather Service:** 276br

**Jacket photography:** Christel Clear Marine Photography; Kos Pictures; Anthony Blake; Musto Limited; Plastimo/B.Y. Leglatin; Patrick Roach
**Author photograph:** Tanya Sleight
**Endpapers:** Patrick Roach

**Illustrations by Peter Bull Art Studio.** Additional illustrations by David Ashby, Martin Woodward, Quo Kong Chen, Robert Campbell, Claire Pegrum, Steve Cluett